D1617378

Women and the Republican Party,
1854–1924

WOMEN IN AMERICAN HISTORY

Series Editors
Anne Firor Scott
Nancy A. Hewitt
Stephanie Shaw

*A list of books in the series appears at
the end of this book.*

Women and the Republican Party,

1854–1924

MELANIE SUSAN GUSTAFSON

University of Illinois Press

URBANA AND CHICAGO

© 2001 by the Board of Trustees
of the University of Illinois
All rights reserved
Manufactured in the United States of America
C 5 4 3 2 1

∞ This book is printed on acid-free paper.

Library of Congress Cataloging-in-Publication Data
Gustafson, Melanie Susan
Women and the republican party, 1854–1924 / Melanie Susan
Gustafson.
p.   cm. — (Women in American history)
Includes bibliographical references and index.
ISBN 0-252-02688-8 (cloth : alk. paper)
1. Women in politics—United States—History.
2. Women political activists—United States—History.
3. Women's rights—United States—History.
4. Republican Party (U.S. : 1854–   ) I. Title. II. Series.
HQ1236.5.U6G87   2001
306.2'6'0820973—dc21   2001001658

Contents

Acknowledgments

IT GIVES ME great pleasure upon completing this book to acknowledge the many colleagues and friends who provided help and support. I begin with Mary Rothschild, Katherine Jensen, and Kathryn Kish Sklar. I first met Mary and Kitty when they visited the University of Wyoming, where I was an undergraduate studying with Kath. Mary came to help Kath initiate an oral history project, called "Lives of Wyoming Women," and they hired me as one of the interviewers. This experience turned me into an aspiring historian and grounded me in the public humanities. About the same time, Kitty came to Wyoming to give a talk about teaching women's history, and my recollection is of her facing a mostly hostile audience who doubted the field's importance or significance; her responses to their questions made me proud to be a women's historian and a woman. To this day, Kath, Mary, and Kitty continue to help me intellectually and professionally, and, as they well know, this book would not have been published without their active support.

I am grateful to Harriet Alonso, William Chafe, Blanche Wiesen Cook, Noralee Frankel, Janice Harris, Nancy Hewitt, Alice Kessler-Harris, Lola Van Wagenen, Stephen Wrinn, and Susan Yohn for listening to my ideas, sharing their work with me, and providing continual encouragement over the years. Many more colleagues, friends, and family members took an interest in my work and provided many kinds of help. I am especially grateful to colleagues who provided comments at conference sessions, shared works in progress and unpublished papers, and answered my queries for information, including Kathryn Anderson, Paula Baker, Mark Brady, Jackie Braitman, Clark Davis, Ellen DuBois, Rebecca Edwards, Maureen Flanagan, Anna Harvey, Gerda

Lerner, Karen Madden, Donna Schuele, and Linda Van Ingen. To all of them I am appreciative.

The Friday Faculty Forum in the Department of History at the University of Vermont has allowed me to try out original ideas; I especially thank Denise Youngblood, Sam Hand, and my former colleague Doris Bergen for help and insights. I am also thankful to the individuals within the American Historical Association and the Society for Historians of the Gilded Age and Progressive Era who have worked hard to ensure that women and men historians talk and listen to each other.

The University of Vermont provided institutional help with numerous grants that enabled me to travel to archival collections and academic conferences and to take time from teaching for research and writing. A fellowship from the Huntington Library allowed me the opportunity to move deeper into nineteenth-century sources. The Huntington also provided me with a summer of collegial conversation, and I would like to especially thank Bill Deverell for helping guide me to California.

While working on this book I took on another project, an anthology on partisan women, co-edited with Kristie Miller and Elisabeth Perry. These two historians have taught me much about collaborative work and the world of their grandmothers, and I am grateful to them for their help and friendship.

My greatest debts are to Susan Ware and David Scrase, whose commitment and involvement touch every page of this book. As my Ph.D. advisor at New York University, Susan always read my work with a keen eye, provided me with a sounding board for my ideas, and encouraged me to make a place for myself in the profession. I am honored that she has chosen to continue to work with me and thank her for her always wise advice. David brought his considerable linguistic skills to numerous readings of this manuscript, and I thank him for his help with the complexities of writing and revision.

Nancy Hewitt, Harriet Alonso, and Anne Scott read the entire manuscript carefully, and I profited immensely from their comments and encouragements. Marjorie Spruill Wheeler also read this manuscript—twice—and I cannot begin to express my gratitude to her. Her thoroughness, careful comments, and generosity were crucial in shaping the final book.

Karen Hewitt took me on as one of her authors at the University of Illinois Press, and I will be always grateful that she could see that something good could come out of the unwieldy manuscript that I first presented to her. Michele May picked up where Karen left off, and I am appreciative to her and her colleagues, Theresa L. Sears and Matt Mitchell, for their work on my book.

Finally, this book could not have been written without the help of many archivists and librarians around the country, and I thank the staffs at the

American Heritage Center, Bancroft Library, Bailey-Howe Library at the University of Vermont, Boston Public Library, Carl Albert Center Congressional Archives, Chebeague Island Library, Chicago Historical Society, Columbia University Library, Houghton Library, Huntington Library, Library of Congress, Mabel Smith Douglass Library at Rutgers University, Massachusetts Historical Society, Moorland-Spingarn Research Center at Howard University, New York Public Library, Schlesinger Library, Sophia Smith Collection, State Historical Society of Iowa, Harriet Beecher Stowe Center, and Swarthmore College Peace Collection for all their assistance.

* * *

An earlier version of portions of chapter 3 appeared as "Partisan and Nonpartisan: The Political Career of Judith Ellen Foster," in *We Have Come to Stay: American Women and Political Parties, 1880–1960,* ed. Melanie Gustafson, Kristie Miller, and Elisabeth Perry (Albuquerque: University of New Mexico Press, 1999), 3–12. Used by permission of the University of New Mexico Press.

An earlier version of a portion of chapter 4 appeared in "Partisan Women in the Progressive Era: The Struggle for Inclusion in American Political Parties," *Journal of Women's History* 9.2 (1997): 8–30. Used by permission of the *Journal of Women's History.*

An earlier version of a portion of chapter 6 appeared in "Florence Collins Porter and the Concept of the Principled Partisan Woman," *Frontiers: A Journal of Women's Studies* 18.1 (1997): 62–79. Used by permission of Frontiers Editorial Collective.

Abbreviations Used in the Text

AASS	American Anti-Slavery Society
AERA	American Equal Rights Association
AWSA	American Woman Suffrage Association
DNC	Democratic National Committee
LWV	League of Women Voters
NACW	National Association of Colored Women
NAWSA	National American Woman Suffrage Association
NFAAW	National Federation of Afro-American Women
NFRW	National Federation of Republican Women
NLWV	National League of Women Voters
NPWCTU	Nonpartisan Woman's Christian Temperance Union
NWP	National Woman's Party
NWSA	National Woman Suffrage Association
RNC	Republican National Committee
RNEC	Republican National Executive Committee
RWNEC	Republican Women's National Executive Committee
WCTU	Woman's Christian Temperance Union
WLNL	Women's Loyal National League
WNRA	Woman's National Republican Association

Introduction

BY EARLY 1854, people across the Midwest had come to the conclusion that it was time to create a new political party to protest the extension of slavery. In March, in a schoolhouse in Ripon, Wisconsin, fifty-four citizens adopted the name "Republican" for their new political organization to protest the Kansas-Nebraska Act. The name was the only logical one to counter the charm of "Democracy," wrote Alvan Bovay, one of the conveners of the Ripon meeting.[1] In July, another group of politicians utilized the name Republican when they convened in a formal convention in Jackson, Michigan, and adopted a platform censuring slavery as "a great moral, social, and political evil."[2]

As the Republican movement spread throughout the Midwest and East, Horace Greeley, the editor of the *New York Tribune,* encouraged its adherents to use the name "'Republican, no prefix! no suffix; but plain Republican.'"[3] These Republicans were on their way to creating a permanent partisan place on the political landscape by the end of 1854, when the entire ticket of Michigan Republicans was elected to office. Six years later the Republican party captured the White House with the election of Abraham Lincoln. It would dominate national politics for most of the next seventy-two years.

There were three women at the founding meeting of the Republican party in Ripon, Wisconsin, and women have been attending local, state, and national Republican gatherings ever since.[4] To demonstrate their loyalties, Republican women wrote partisan literature and created other campaign materials, gave speeches, worked to influence voters, and, when they had the right, voted the party ticket. Sometimes Republican women acted in concert with men; other times they operated through separate women's clubs and associations. This study is an examination of their efforts and contributions to the creation of the political life of the late nineteenth and early twentieth centuries. It begins in the years just before the party's founding and concludes just after the passage of the Nineteenth Amendment in 1920. A primary aim of this study is to demonstrate that the history of women's partisan activism extends longer and deeper than has generally been recognized.

Another aim of this study is to reexamine the impact of women's disfranchisement. This study contests the accepted notion that widespread disfranchisement prevented women from being organized into parties before 1920; the Republican party was supported by voting and nonvoting women. Women's disfranchisement is a crucial factor in understanding the course of women's political history, because it informed women's political opportunities and choices in significant ways, advanced the idea that women were a separate political group, and was an influential factor in the gendering of politics. Disfranchisement did not, however, prevent women from participating in partisan politics. In contrast to voting, a right formally extended by governments, the parameters of nonpartisan and partisan activism were not bound by laws. In the nineteenth century, communities of people with shared values determined the practices of party politics. Parties were political representations of public cultures. Laws creating new restrictions on parties were written in the late nineteenth century, and these reshaped the partisan landscape, but partisanship continued to be a political identity that people could take on whether or not they voted. However, the lack of formal voting rights meant that women's experiences in party politics were different than men's experiences. By examining women's partisan history as part of the larger history of women's political culture, especially the struggle to change voting laws, this study provides a new perspective on how women fashioned their political strategies and identities before and after 1920.

The passage of the Nineteenth Amendment is an important political moment, but as recent scholarship shows, it is not a "great divide" in women's politics.[5] There are important continuities between women's politics before 1920 and after: women acted in partisan ways, and parties organized women; men were reluctant to relinquish political power to women, and they practiced this reluctance by passing suffrage laws and party rules that instituted inequalities of representation; and nonpartisanship was an important aspect of women's political culture. As the political scientist Anna Harvey has argued, the history of women's disfranchisement cast a "long shadow" over women's politics in the twentieth century.[6] By looking deeply into the history of women and the Republican party before 1920 and in the four years after, I hope to provide new ways to evaluate the meaning of the Nineteenth Amendment.

The distinct roles women played in the Republican party were influenced by the needs of the party and party leaders and by the strategies and ideologies of women's separate political reform movements—what historians have come to call women's political culture.[7] The relationships between the party and women's political culture are explored throughout this study. Neither was a static entity, and as their parameters shifted so too did the relationships between them. At the heart of the women's political culture that I discuss here is the woman suffrage movement. In 1848, six years before the founding of the Republican party, the first women's rights meeting was held in Seneca Falls, New York, and by the time the party had reached the White House the movement had spread across the country; after the Civil War, woman suffrage became a central focus of the larger women's rights movement. As the dominant political party and as the party born out of the antislavery agitation, the Republican party became the focal point of women leaders seeking allies for their causes.

Chapter 1 traces women's demonstrations of Republican loyalty before and during the Civil War and shows how antislavery politics served as a connecting link between women and the Republican party. After the Civil War that link was weakened, when activists split over the Fourteenth and Fifteenth Amendments. Chapter 2 explores the tensions between women's rights leaders and Republicans that emerged after the Civil War and the development of nonpartisanship as a strategy for some woman suffragists. The acknowledgment of women in the national party platforms in the 1870s and the creation of a Republican women's auxiliary in the late 1880s kept women in the Republican fold even as nonpartisanship became a crucial component of women's political culture. These factors are discussed in chapter 3. Chapters 4 and 5 examine debates about women's partisanship and nonpartisanship in the important election of 1912, when the Republican party split and the new Progressive party provided women with greater access to partisan structures. Chapter 6 explores the legacy of 1912 for the campaign strategies of Republican women in 1916 and the reemergence of an old question, the appropriateness of women holding political office. The final chapter highlights how women were welcomed into the Republican party in 1920 and 1924 when the Nineteenth Amendment was passed and more women had the opportunity to enroll in parties and vote in the national election.[8]

One of the most remarkable things I encountered in my research was the consistent difficulty people had, and still seem to have, with women taking on political roles. In the early 1920s, the prominent Republican leader Harriet Taylor Upton wrote, "It's the strangest thing how men understand their wives, their daughters, their mothers, their cooks, their stenographers and the rest of the woman contingent, but when she appears in the role of voter it's all different. No matter how well I know a man in business or society he discovers some new and altogether strange things in me when I talk with him about politics."[9] Substitute the word "partisan" for "voter" and Upton could have been talking about people's reactions to women in Republican party politics before the 1920s. People had great difficulty adjusting to women acting in political ways before and after 1920, whether they were enfranchised or disfranchised.

This difficulty is rooted in deeply held ideas about womanhood and manhood. Associating women and men with specific definitions of womanhood and manhood has been, and continues to be, a stabilizing influence in society. In politics this works by providing people with a quick way to read others' political interests. These gendered definitions have allowed for and justified political inclusions and exclusions that generate additional political boundaries based on sex, normalizing roles not only in the political realm but in all of the areas where politics reaches, which means everywhere. As a result, people who sought to increase women's political presence and power generated public debates not only about the proprietary boundaries of women's politics but also the very meanings of public womanhood.

This study follows those debates through 1924, but they continued in different variations for the rest of the twentieth century. How much changed over the course of the twentieth century is not the subject of this book, but the words of the former governor of Vermont, Madeleine Kunin, give some indication of the continuing trouble people have in associating "woman" with "political." In her 1994 autobiography, Kunin writes that the "female politician is unexpected; her presence provokes a brief digression during which the public wanders off into internal musing about how this woman is like a man and yet not like a man."[10]

I am convinced that it is not simply the low number of women in prominent political positions that accounts for people's inability to respond to or deal with women in politics. It is a lack of history. This lack of history has meant that the public continually observes the political woman as an awkward, illegitimate, or misbegotten phenomenon. A lack of history has been especially damaging for women seeking political influence, because it has meant that at the same time women have been forced to answer questions about the legitimacy of their presence, they have also had to reinvent the traditions and records on which they should have been able to build. This has been an ideological and a practical struggle, and it has helped to keep women on the peripheries of partisan politics.[11] The absence of history, of a social memory, has meant that women have had to repeatedly establish and prove, to themselves and to others, that they have the ability to make political contributions and the right to pursue their individual political paths.

This study is one attempt to reclaim and reexamine the history of partisan women. My focus is on national politics, and I emphasize the efforts of leading Republicans and women's rights activists. Some of these leaders, like Elizabeth Cady Stanton, Susan B. Anthony, Jane Addams, and Mary Church Terrell, may be familiar. Other women who emerged as important figures in this history, including Anna Dickinson, Judith Ellen Foster, and Mary Ann Shadd Cary, are probably less familiar. Together, their stories help demonstrate that women have been active in the Republican party since its founding days and show that many women saw partisan politics as both an obligation and an opportunity. Through a focus on the interactions of women and men in Republican party politics and the relationship between the party and women's political culture, this study also stresses the complicated tensions of this history. These tensions had important consequences for the woman suffrage movement as well as for women's other reform efforts, including the temperance movement and the African-American women's club movement. In the end, women's engagement of the Republican party testifies to the incredible resiliency of party politics in shaping the landscape and culture of American politics.

1. Loyal Republican Women, 1854–65

ON SEPTEMBER 10, 1860, Elizabeth Cady Stanton and a group of women from Seneca Falls, New York, presented a banner to the town's Wide-Awake Republicans, a marching club of young men who urged the party to keep "wide-awake" on the slavery question. The Wide-Awakes "caught the spirit of the campaign for freedom" and swept the country like an "electric current" as they marched and rode through towns and cities like tireless regiments, waving torches that symbolized their intelligence and truth. Their uniforms were oilcloth capes made by the "free, fair fingers" of Republican women. Together, these men and women of the Republican party were "the most brilliant and attractive in the history of political organization," and their visible partisan displays were a challenge to a politics dominated by "old settlers, whose political ideas are in a state of paralysis," reported the *New York Tribune*.[1]

Republicans had chosen Abraham Lincoln of Illinois and Hannibal Hamlin of Maine as their presidential and vice-presidential candidates at the May national convention in Chicago, and a platform had been agreed upon. Nevertheless, only two months before the election the party was tense with friction. Factions vied to promote their issues, and the party was being dragged in different directions. The most divisive issue was slavery.[2]

The Seneca Falls lawyer John B. Murray touched on this dissension in Republican ranks in his thank-you speech to the women of the town. Seeking to encourage demonstrations of their overall party loyalty, Murray called on the women who assembled in this small town in upstate New York to support the Republican party, even "though it may fall short of what you and perhaps many others may feel to be the correct position" on the issues.[3] In these last months of the campaign, the time had come to promote unity and close ranks around the party's candidate for president. This election was critical for the Republican party. Supporters believed that if they did not win this, their second attempt for the White House, the party would surely die. In addition to a platform that would satisfy or appease voters, a dynamic campaign using eye-catching tactics was needed to draw the party's diverse supporters to rallies and the polls. The Wide-Awake clubs were one such strategy. Asking women to lend their influence on the party's behalf was another.

The next evening, the Wide-Awakes marched to the Stanton home to continue the ceremony to honor the women who honored them. Holding aloft lighted torches and playing martial music, they were greeted by the women's rights leaders Elizabeth Cady Stanton and Susan B. Anthony, Stanton's husband, Henry, and friends of the family. Three cheers for all present and short speeches by those being honored were followed by a longer serenade of music, as Elizabeth Stanton and the others "Waltzed and Polkaed on the piazza" of the Stanton home. It was a grand affair, according to Anthony.[4]

Banner presentations, torchlight parades, and flag raisings were common campaign rituals in the mid-nineteenth century. Political contests were community affairs acted out in the streets, as women and men rallied together to ensure their party's electoral success.[5] In the 1850s and 1860s, Republicans held rallies in regions where there was strong Republican support, like upstate New York, and even in localities where Republican support was minimal, such as Virginia, where only 1 percent of the population was Republican. Just nine days before the Seneca Falls ceremony, thirty-three young women of Martinsville, Virginia, demonstrated their partisan loyalties by presenting a flag to the local Lincoln Club. The women's attire symbolized a nation divided over the issue of slavery; sixteen of the women wore white, another sixteen wore black, and one wore red to represent Bleeding Kansas.[6]

It is hard to estimate how many women supported the Republican party in its early years. Historians have no votes to count where women are concerned, so a statistical analysis of election results is not possible, but newspaper reports, private correspondence, and official records make it clear that women have been active and vigorous Republican supporters since the party's founding in 1854. Drawn to the party for a variety of reasons, women showed a diversity of backgrounds and positions on issues that were as various as men's. Strong beliefs about unfolding political events, loyalties to individual candidates, family or community traditions, and a desire to affect public policy influenced women's partisan loyalties in a world where politics was understood as party politics. As one African-American woman wrote in the weekly *Anglo-African,* "The colored women are as interested in politics as the colored men of the Republican party."[7]

In newspaper reports, women's presence at Republican party events was reported as routine and unremarkable; many stories are almost perfunctory and simply illustrate women's partisan visibility. Women's attendance at the weekly meetings of the New York City Young Men's Republican Union and at the Republican Central Campaign Club's regular meetings were described as common occurrences. They were noted to be among the visitors who called on Lincoln at his home during the campaign of 1860. In New York City, women occupied the front, reserved seats at the grand mass meetings of the Republicans of Brooklyn, joined in the grand rally of the German Republicans at Cooper Institute, and "crowded" the Palace Gardens to hear candidates speak.[8]

The "ubiquitous fair sex" was well represented at the "grand Wide-Awake carnival" in Paterson, New Jersey, in October 1860, a *New York Tribune* reporter wrote; the women were "encouraging by their presence the champions of Freedom." Their voices, however, seemed striking. When the women "attempted a feminine cheer on occasion," this reporter wrote, it was not "a failure; but it sounded, to use a mild term, peculiar, and was eminently touching."[9] That the sound of partisan women's voices sounded peculiar (to some) had less to do with numbers or frequency than with people's understandings of the gendered parameters of politics.

In 1860 no American women could vote in national elections, although some had what was called "partial" or "limited" suffrage, granting them the right to vote in specific local elections. Disfranchisement, as well as property laws and interpretations of citizenship, erased women's independent legal and political status, but it did not prevent them from participating in partisan politics.[10] Women's presence was encouraged by a set of deeply rooted ideas about women as mothers, wives, and daughters who could have influence in the civic world by representing virtue, principles, and civility. As John B. Murray told the women of Seneca Falls, "there are no mothers, no wives, no daughters throughout the land who have not at least some feeling as to the result of this canvass [campaign]," and it is "proper" for them to publicly express their sentiments "in behalf of our candidates . . . of Freedom."[11]

The emergence of the Republican party marks a new chapter in the political history of the United States. The efforts of abolitionists and women's rights leaders—the labor as well as a language essential for political operations—benefited the party immensely. Abolitionists and women's rights leaders, two groups that often overlapped, helped the Republican party evolve from a fusion effort into the dominant party of the nation. As a result, new dynamics were introduced into partisan politics. But the political conditions of partisan politics in the antebellum and Civil War years that encouraged women's partisan activism existed within larger social and political contexts that placed unique limitations on that participation. Again and again, as the history of Republican women for the next seventy years would demonstrate, rewards did not necessarily follow displays of partisan loyalty.

The Creation of the Virtuous Political Woman

Women have been active in partisan politics since parties were first created in the United States. Both Federalists and Democrats, but mainly the Federalists, welcomed women at party events because women were associated with private virtues that were seen as necessary for the survival of the republic.[12] The political culture of late-eighteenth-century republicanism, specifically what historians call Republican motherhood, regarded women as embodiments of virtue with an obligation to use their status as wives and mothers to help a new generation of virtuous citizens flourish. People believed that women's influence should be focused not only on their own families but also on their communities and the nation.[13] With the encouragement of men, women demonstrated their virtue through party loyalty.

The appearance of women at party meetings was greeted with cheers and praise because women served the needs of parties and partisan men. Politics in the early national period was infused with antiparty sentiment, and party leaders needed to create ways to suggest that their party was better and nobler than the opposition.[14] Women's presence allowed partisan men to present themselves, as well as party politics itself, as proper for the political order; partisan men sought the positive reflection of women's virtuous representation.[15] By opening up politics to virtuous women, partisanship became legitimate, and party loyalty, the essence of partisanship, became a responsible political act.

By the mid-nineteenth century, the growing cultural emphasis on the importance of motherhood melded with the expanding sentimentalization of American culture and strengthened the notion that women "personalized the nation" through their actions. Viewed and admired as "the emotive center of the nation," women linked the private and public spheres of life with their political presence and virtuous and principled actions.[16] A primary duty of a virtuous and moral woman was to lend her influence for the good of the country, demonstrate the best of American values, and support the best men. Rendering this influence over one's own family and lending one's influence for a larger cause became key tenets outlining the proprietary boundaries around women's public actions. Where men were seen as driven into the passionate factionalism of politics by personal ambitions and steered by their willingness to use coercion to enhance their own position, women's natural inducement to influence was seen as flowing from a disinterested compassion and guided by a desire to create social harmony. As the political culture of the nineteenth century became concerned with corruption of all sorts, women's moral and housekeeping qualities became even more valuable in politics. If men could not purify politics, then maybe women's presence could.[17]

By the time political parties became the essential structure or system for defining and organizing politics in the 1830s, "principles" had replaced "virtue" as the key word justifying political engagement, and women took on the representative role of not only instilling virtue but also sustaining principles. By then, as one historian has observed, more Americans had come to embrace parties and to "develop partisan commitments and loyalties of tremendous strength, intensity, and vitality because parties expressed their deepest values, beliefs, and preferences. Parties became communities of loyalists with shared values, emotive memories, symbols, and commitments."[18] The parties that people joined in the nineteenth century were private associations unregulated by the state, loose coalitions of like-minded people interested in common goals that were most important at the local or state levels. Membership was not determined by enrollment but by participation in the rituals of the party and demonstrations of party loyalty. The Whigs followed the Federalists' lead and systematically encouraged women to demonstrate their partisan loyalties at rallies, parades, and other public celebrations. The Whigs went one step further by also supporting women who established political clubs.[19]

By the mid-nineteenth century, most Americans saw politics as party politics; to be political was to be partisan. While not all people were necessarily involved in politics, political parties were seen as an inevitable feature of the workings of governance and were often the political lifeblood of communities.[20] Loyalty to a political party, or partisanship, had become by the end of the century the "common language of public life" and a "lens through which to view the world."[21] Antiparty sentiment still held power in some pockets of public life and appeared with regularity even in party circles as a means of reproach or promotion, but, overall, parties became more central to politics as the electorate was enlarged with changing suffrage laws and presidential contests became more vigorous.[22]

At the same time that women engaged in partisan activities, they also created a network of benevolent and charity organizations to provide services and help to individuals and communities challenged, confused, or harmed by the rapid changes brought about by the Industrial Revolution. The evangelical religious associations and voluntary reform associations that sprang up during the era of the Second Great Awakening allowed women to participate in civic life and contributed to a stronger identification of women as moral-standard bearers for their families, communities, and the nation, even as that definition expanded with the increase in women's public activities. By the mid-nineteenth century, as one historian has written, women "strode in and out of legislative halls—places where, in theory, females were not welcome. There they lobbied for new laws, sought appropriations for their organizations, and argued for changes in status—in short, they worked hard to influence the leadership of local, state and national governments."[23]

Lobbying was a political skill Emma Willard learned when she moved from Middlebury, Vermont, to Troy, New York, to found one of the nation's first women's academies. Willard wrote that she was determined "'to inform myself, and to increase my personal influence and fame as a teacher, calculating that, in this way I might be sought for in other places, where influential men would carry my project before some Legislature, for the sake of obtaining a good school.'"[24] The governor, DeWitt Clinton, and the New York legislature did not fund her school, but four thousand dollars raised by the Troy Common Council allowed her to open her doors to women students in 1821. With these early women's academies, Republican motherhood entered a new stage, as women teachers provided another example of women's "devotion and service to others, selflessness, sacrifice."[25] Over time, education also became an avenue to political influence in local communities, as women were appointed or elected to school boards and positions as superintendents.

While pursuing individual agendas, women often emphasized that their public roles complemented men's, and they sought to cooperate with men in ways that further advanced their own opportunities and expanded their expectations. The cooperation between women and men, as well as women's challenges to men over the distribution of community resources and power, worked differently for white women than it did for African-American women. Free black women spoke and wrote about political issues throughout the nineteenth century, but they did so from a conditional freedom, and their efforts were primarily directed inward toward their communities. Racial discrimination, a lack of access to state resources, and their exclusion from almost all formal partisan and electoral politics contributed to a worldview that emphasized community commitments. Black women's partisan activism was grounded in an ideal of mutuality rather than a belief in women's virtuous nature or moral superiority. This difference, complicated by regional distinctions, would lead white and black women on separate political trajectories. What they shared was a willingness and desire to pursue their goals through the framework of partisan politics.[26]

Whether women acted as the icon of Liberty in a parade organized by a party club or wrote campaign literature for a third party that attacked established parties as corrupt, women's partisan activism was legitimate and necessary. Local, regional, and national political structures and ideas determined the extent of that legitimacy, but women had their place. Even if the outcome of the partisan rallies, conventions, and parades was voting in an election, and thus formally excluded women, partisan politics itself did not. Like the partisanship and partisan activism of propertyless men before the 1840s, women's partisanship before 1920 did not require the right of the vote.[27] Disfranchisement shaped the formal parameters of women's participation in electoral politics, but it did not determine their providence in partisan politics.

Women's disfranchisement, however, was important in that it coexisted with women's early partisan activism, and thus women's political experiences were shaped differently than men's. For men, the culmination of the campaign season was voting. For women, it was watching men vote. For some women, this state of relations prompted a better understanding of voting as a male privilege that influenced not only the activities of election day but also public activism before and after the campaign season. Women's recognition that disfranchisement could relegate them to the periphery of politics and make their stands on issues less important to the candidates, voters, or policy makers contributed to the growth of a woman suffrage movement that emphasized equal rights in addition to a cooperation based on gender difference.[28] Thus the dual nature of being included in and excluded from party rituals encouraged women to fight for formal political recognition. Women's partisanship, as much as women's work in benevolent and reform organizations, contributed to the development of the women's rights movement.

The Abolitionist Prelude

Whigs and Democrats dominated the political culture of the 1840s and early 1850s, but they were challenged by numerous third parties that developed because the two national parties were unable to deal with or resolve the most controversial issue of the day, the growing sectional crisis over slavery.[29] Among the most influential third parties of the mid-nineteenth century were those created by antislavery advocates: the Liberty party, founded in 1839; the Free Soil party, formed in 1848; and the Republican party, established in 1854.[30] Together, these parties created a dynamic political culture in which every issue was seen as "a struggle in which the very existence of the republic was at stake."[31] These third parties were broad entities that fused the civic world of benevolent and reform organizations with the electoral world of voting and legislating. As such, they provided women with a new path into partisan politics, as antislavery activism moved from moral suasion to practical politics.

Women had been active in the antislavery movement since its first appearance, and by the beginning of the 1830s they had established their own organizations. By the end of the decade, the movement was struggling with the question of women's proper roles, specifically whether women should have equal membership and be hired as agents and lecturers. The American Anti-Slavery Society (AASS), founded in 1833, championed women's equal participation and their right to speak in public before what were then called "promiscuous" audiences, which meant audiences of women and men.[32] Led by William Lloyd Garrison, the AASS saw antislavery and women's rights as part of a worldwide effort for human rights and embraced immediatism, the idea that people must immediately act against corrupting influences and structures.[33]

While Garrison supported women's rights, he believed that partisan and electoral politics had no place in a reform strategy because they were at best ineffective in changing people's ideas and behavior and at worst corrupting influences. Women should be enfranchised, the argument went, so they could reject the vote. Charged with a millennial spirit, these reformers believed moral suasion would bring about a spiritual transformation of social and political culture. The state or political parties could not forward the abolitionist cause, Garrison argued, because participation in electoral or partisan politics involved moral compromise. As the abolitionist Angelina Grimke wrote to Catharine Beecher, partisanship meant "'sacrificing principles to power or interest,'" and she objected to the idea of women *or* men acting partisan.[34] The abolitionist Lydia Maria Child also argued against partisan political activism, stating that "public sentiment *must* act through politics," but it "cannot be made *by* political machinery."[35] To these reformers, partisanship was linked to the corrupting influences of electoral politics rather than the moral influences of benevolent and reform work.

Other antislavery advocates disagreed with the Garrisonian assessment about how to eradicate slavery. They believed the time had come to transform moral questions into public policy issues that would be legislated and regulated because "the tactics of moral suasion . . . had failed to produce tangible results."[36] These reformers created the antislavery parties, arguing that government could enhance liberty, freedom, and equality. If the public world was corrupt, they would purify it, and they would do so without being morally compromised. They consistently framed questions "in terms of electoral means and goals" and placed "their faith in legislative change."[37] Their activism increased the number of voices from antislavery activists at national party conventions, helped make political parties more central to American political life, and pulled women into electoral politics through the door of partisanship.

One event that moved women from moral suasion to direct politics was the massive abolitionist petition campaigns in the 1830s and 1840s. Petitioning, a traditional right of women "inherited through the common law of England and long used in securing redress of individual grievances," had become a favorite instrument of antislavery women in the 1830s.[38] They followed the example set in 1829 by Catharine Beecher and Lydia Sigourney, who organized the first national women's petition campaign to protest the removal of Native Americans from the Southeast. In their "Ladies' Circular," Beecher and Sigourney argued that women were "protected from the blinding influence of party spirit" and urged women readers to use their influence on behalf of Georgia Indians.[39] So numerous were the antislavery petitions sent to Washington by women asserting their influence that Congress enacted a gag rule, allowing it to ignore these petitions and other protests against slavery. But the petitioning continued, and so did attempts to present them to Congress.[40] The next year, the AASS sent antislavery petitions with four hundred thousand names to Congress; 70 percent of the signatures were women's. In 1840, petitions with more than two million signatures were sent, and Congress reenacted the gag rule.[41]

The unwillingness of legislators to read and act upon these petitions shattered some abolitionist women's beliefs about how change could be achieved and stimulated their engagement of partisan politics as it fostered the development of the women's rights movement. Petitioning was seen as a duty, a principled act, and was understood as a crucial tool if women's voices were to be heard in political arenas. As an 1839 circular sent to antislavery women calling on them to prepare another petition campaign stated: "'It is our only means of direct political action. It is not ours to fill the offices of government, or to assist in the election of those who shall fill them. We do not enact or enforce the laws of the land. The only direct influence which we can exert upon our Legislatures, is by protests and petitions.'"[42] The gag rule taught women that even the right to petition their government was a contested issue and that new means of achieving political influence were needed.[43]

The changing political culture of the 1830s and 1840s fueled the fire for the first women's rights conferences, where women "addressed forcefully the ways in which women had not been fully absorbed into the republican political order, although they were citizens."[44] Women's rights advocates worked on many issues in the early 1850s, but their most controversial demand was for all women to have the right to vote. They battled against legal and political inequities, transformed the temperance crusade into a movement that emphasized rights as well as morals, and campaigned for equal opportunities in education, employment, and public life. They sought the same rights and responsibilities given to men and demanded that a woman's political or civic identity be independent of any family relationship.[45] To reach these goals, a leading group of women's rights activists created a central committee that organized annual conventions to define their agenda and strategies. These activists saw conventions of all types "as perhaps the best stage for fashioning women into political actors."[46] Before and after convention times, women were advised to work within their communities as individuals rather than as a group guided by the machinery of an organization and to rely on alliances with supporters in various partisan and nonpartisan organizations.[47]

Among this small group of women's rights leaders was Elizabeth Cady Stanton, who closely watched the development of antislavery parties. She was allied with the Garrisonians, but like many other reformers she was losing faith in moral suasion.[48] In the formation of the Liberty party she saw a new political advantage for women. As she wrote to a friend in England, "I am of this party" because it can serve as "a connecting link" between antislavery advocates scattered in different organizations but united by the idea that institutional and legal reforms to eradicate slavery were as important as changing people's ideas.[49]

The women's rights activist Antoinette Brown Blackwell, who became the first American woman ordained minister in 1853, also saw the Liberty party as a chance for the antislavery forces of women and men to have a new political impact. She wrote to her friend and future sister-in-law Lucy Stone in 1851 that she had attended the Liberty party convention in Buffalo, New York. The Liberty party was a skeleton at that time, as most prominent antislavery advocates had moved on to the Free Soil party, but she supported it because of its emphasis on righteousness in government. She told Stone that the definition of a "Liberty party man" given by the party's founder, Gerrit Smith, a cousin of Elizabeth Cady Stanton, was "any man or woman" who immediately and fully demands a "righteous civil government, whether he is a voter or not, and whether, he votes with their party or not."[50] Like many of their colleagues in the abolitionist and women's rights movements, Stanton and

Blackwell believed that participating in partisan politics was a necessary step for reformers. These women and men who embraced electoral solutions to societal problems created a vital connection between their reform movements and political parties.[51]

Jane Grey Swisshelm also saw promise in the Liberty party. She was a journalist who penned articles advocating women's rights, protesting slavery, and opposing the war with Mexico for a newspaper in her hometown of Pittsburgh. Born in 1815, she was raised in a Calvinist home and became an antislavery advocate at an early age. In 1832 she broke with the Garrisonians over the question of political action, and by the early 1840s she was a supporter of the Liberty party, even though party leaders, as she wrote in her autobiography, "had given formal notice that no women need apply for a place among them."[52]

The leaders of the Liberty party might not have wanted to offer women a formal place in the party, but Swisshelm found a way to support it by becoming a partisan journalist and writing articles championing the party.[53] She was careful with her advocacy and signed her articles with her initials for "fear of embarrassing the Liberty party with the sex question."[54] In 1847 she established her own newspaper, the *Pittsburgh Saturday Visiter* (her spelling), as a Liberty party organ. The next year she moved on to the Free Soil party, attended the national conventions, went to Washington, D.C., where she became the first woman to sit in the reporters' gallery of the Senate, and wrote about the campaign in the form of letters to the *New York Tribune.* The lack of formal recognition from the antislavery parties did not deter her. In 1856 she attended the first national convention of the Republican party in Philadelphia. Bringing with her lessons learned in previous attempts to take a partisan role, Swisshelm recognized that "it might injure rather than aid the party to have a woman take a prominent place in it," so she chose to work on behalf of the party through the acceptable female channel of writing. Her newspaper, the *Visiter,* she noted, was "thoroughly Republican."[55]

Susan B. Anthony also attended Republican meetings in the 1850s. Her first was in 1855, and afterward she wrote that, "had the accident of birth given me a place among the aristocracy of sex, I doubt not I should be an active, zealous advocate of Republicanism."[56] Participating in partisan politics heightened Anthony's awareness of her disfranchisement, and, like Swisshelm, who was also a women's rights advocate, she could fuse her women's rights activism and her partisanship. The difference was that Swisshelm was ready to present, or cloak, her partisan activism in the proper ways. She used her initials when signing her articles; she attended conventions as a journalist and supporter but did not make demands for official recognition, fearing these might injure a party. Such caution was a feature of the partisan politics Anthony mildly tolerated before and during the Civil War. Her tolerance diminished after the war, as influential Republicans rejected efforts to include women's rights on the national political agenda.

Political Wives and the First Republican Campaigns

Moral proclamations, sectional animosities, and bitter partisan debates permeated the Republican party's first national campaigns in 1856 and 1860.[57] The party's dominant ideology was the ideal of free labor, a belief that opportunity and social mobility should be shared by all. After the Panic of 1857, the calls for free labor intensified, and, in spite of great organizational problems, the party was able to unite its diverse group of supporters around the summons to "save the first principles of American liberty—free speech, a free press, free soil, free Kansas."[58] Calls for free labor were heard throughout the North and Midwest and were especially strong in places like the "Burnt Over District" of New York, where the evangelical fervor of the Second Great Awakening and abolitionist sentiment infused politics with a strong moral tone and women made up almost half of those attending Republican meetings in the 1850s.[59] Lydia Maria Child stated that "politics" had not "bitten" her before this election, but with such "mighty issues" at stake, she wrote a friend from her home in Wayland, Massachusetts, "I cannot be indifferent."[60]

The first national Republican party nominating convention was held in June 1856 in Philadelphia. According to Jane Grey Swisshelm, the success of the convention was due in part to the wife of one of the delegates, Samuel Purviance.[61] The Purviances were from Swisshelm's home town of Butler, Pennsylvania. He was elected to Congress in the 1850s, first as a Whig and then as a Republican, and in the mid-1860s he was a member of the National Executive Committee of the Republican party. By the time Swisshelm wrote this comment in her 1880 autobiography, Purviance had been retired for four years; he would die two years later.

Swisshelm's assertion about Purviance's wife raises the question of her definition of "success" as well as her motivation for making such an assessment. She may have believed it to be true; it may have been an attempt to win a courtesy or favor from one of them; it may have been a tribute to a long friendship. Or she might have invoked a woman's presence to demonstrate that the party was sound and proper from its beginnings because women were there. Whether her claim is true is not the question here; there is no evidence to support it. But it is an insight into what some people saw as a new focus in politics in the 1850s. Political wives were taking center stage as representatives of party virtue.

The most prominent woman of the 1856 campaign was Jessie Benton Frémont. The wife of the Republican presidential candidate John C. Frémont
and the daughter of the Democratic senator Thomas Hart Benton of Missouri, she was known for her independence and intelligence.[62] Her independence was demonstrated by her elopement in 1841, at age seventeen, with John
Charles Frémont, whose fame as an explorer and leadership in the 1846 Bear
Flag uprising against Mexican rule in California made him a valuable political candidate for the new party. It was also demonstrated by her turning away
from the party of her family, the Democrats, to the Republicans. Her intelligence became evident during John Frémont's candidacy.

The campaign of 1856 was as ugly as any in the nineteenth century. Violence in Kansas and in the Senate chamber made slavery the prominent question of the campaign. The new Republican party's platform called for the
prohibition of "those twin relics of barbarism, polygamy and slavery," in the
territories and stated its opposition to "legislation impairing liberty of conscience and equality of rights of citizens."[63] In an era of intense nativism,
Democratic newspapers attempted to smear the Frémonts and taint the Republican party with Catholicism, while removing the contamination from
themselves, by publishing stories claiming that John Frémont had "carved a
cross on the Rock Independent when making his first western expedition"
and that the Frémonts were married by a Catholic priest.[64] As the *Democratic
Review* put it in 1865, John Frémont represented " 'aristocracy, prescription,
sumptuary laws, a meddling priesthood, and all that [had] so often proved
itself at war with the principles of individualism and the true progress of
mankind.' "[65]

In counter-stories the Republican party promoted the romantic nature of
the Frémonts' elopement and placed the couple at the center of campaign
propaganda. Jessie Frémont's appeal was more than sentimental, however; it
was moral. Republican women, their hatred of slavery already fueled by nov-
els such as Harriet Beecher Stowe's *Uncle Tom's Cabin* and *Dred,* were inspired
by her abolitionist views, and they crowded campaign rallies carrying ribbons
and banners promoting "Frémont and Our Jessie," "Jessie's Choice," and
"Jessie for the White House."[66] Abolitionist women had found in Jessie Frémont another reason to enter the partisan fray of politics. Lydia Maria Child
wrote of Jessie Frémont to a friend, "bless her noble soul! Isn't it pleasant to
have a *woman* spontaneously recognized as a moral influence in public affairs? There's *meaning* in that fact."[67] The association of antislavery with
womanhood also gave partisan men another reason for encouraging wom-
en's support.

Jessie Frémont was a crucial link in the party's campaign strategy in 1856
not only because she served as a positive symbol of romantic, enlightened,

or principled womanhood. Republican strategists were so afraid that John Frémont would say the wrong thing during the campaign that they made Jessie Frémont a key member of a committee "entrusted with the task of preventing any gaffes" by the candidate.[68] John Frémont had been chosen as the Republican standard-bearer because "he seemed to be a clean-cut young man without political scars, a rare specimen in a period of intense antislavery agitation."[69] But as the Republican backer Horace Greeley noted, the fact that he was "the merest baby in politics" was a cause for concern.[70] He needed all the help he could get.

Republicans lost the campaign for the White House, but the party leader Salmon Chase concluded that the party was "stronger than anything except victory could make us."[71] That strength resulted from significant Republican victories, including the election of Chase as governor of Ohio and the Massachusetts congressman Nathaniel Banks as speaker of the United States House of Representatives, as well as the growing northern opposition to the South and "Slave Power."[72] Republicans attacked the South throughout the campaign and after their loss continued to proclaim that all slaveholders and their supporters "were engaged in a conspiracy to destroy liberty and republicanism."[73]

Party leaders downplayed Frémont's loss to the Democrat James Buchanan by concentrating on what they had done right, including relying on the contributions of women. Reports indicate that Jessie Frémont's Republican associates held her in the highest regard for her "undeniable political ability," and one Ohio Republican even wrote that she "would have been the better candidate."[74] Jessie Frémont represented the party's best efforts to harness the emotional power of antislavery sentiment.[75] Women's contributions to the party were more than symbolic, however, and party leaders understood this. They witnessed women's active participation at campaign meetings and rallies. They hired women as speakers, including the well-known temperance and women's rights reformer Clarina Howard Nichols, who gave speeches about the situation in explosive Kansas. Lydia Maria Child, who had moved from a position of moral suasion into the political abolitionist camp with her support of the Republican party, wrote campaign literature.[76]

If Jessie Frémont is an example of how family ties allowed women to participate in campaign politics, Elizabeth Cady Stanton's situation shows how these could also create restrictions. The difference between Frémont and Stanton also demonstrates how difficult it was for some party leaders to envision broader roles for women in the party. In 1855, when she began attending Republican meetings, Stanton was forty years old and the mother of five children; her last two children would be born in 1856 and 1859. At the same time that she dedicated her energies to building the women's rights movement, she also worked to support the political party she saw as the best hope for the promotion of human rights and liberalism, the abolition of slavery, and women's collective advancement. She had, she wrote Susan B. Anthony in 1855, "attended all the Republican meetings."[77]

Stanton usually attended Republican rallies and meetings in the company of her husband, Henry Stanton, who became the head of the speaker's bureau for the Republican party in 1856.[78] During the campaign the party desperately needed stump speakers, especially in the free states of Illinois and Indiana, where Republican leaders were complaining that they were being ignored while New York and Pennsylvania were getting all the attention. Henry Stanton was unable to fulfill all the pleas for speakers, and the campaign suffered as a result.[79]

If he had looked to the person at his side, he would have found a perfect Republican speaker. Elizabeth Stanton had already proven her written and oratorical political skills as president of the New York Woman's Temperance Society and in her speeches before the annual women's rights conventions and the New York legislature, where she discussed extending the married women's property law. Henry Stanton, along with Elizabeth's father, wanted her to limit rather than expand her public commitments.[80] Elizabeth Stanton wrote Anthony: "To think that all in me of which my father would have felt a proper pride had I been a man, is deeply mortifying to him because I am a woman."[81] Women speakers were simply not a part of Henry Stanton's organizing strategy for the new party.

Elizabeth Stanton's family obligations further curtailed her political work. While her husband traveled widely for his political and legal careers, her domestic duties meant that she had to choose carefully the political meetings that she attended, especially those outside of Seneca Falls. As she wrote Anthony, she wanted to do more for women's rights: "My whole soul is in the work, but my hands belong to my family."[82] By 1859, after her last child was born and her father's death had left her financially secure, she was freed somewhat from family obligations. She found her freedom to participate in political affairs further enhanced two years later, when the family moved to New York City, where Henry Stanton took a patronage position as deputy collector at the Customs House, a reward for his work on behalf of the Republican party.[83] That Elizabeth Stanton chose to attend Republican meetings throughout these years despite her family situation indicates the importance she placed on participating in partisan activities.

Partisanship was part of Stanton's political identity, and the limitations placed on her ability to participate in politics on the same plane with men caused her to reflect. She wrote a letter to Anthony in 1859 that echoed Anthony's 1855 statement about her womanhood preventing her from becoming a zealous Republican. The political events of the day, Stanton wrote, "all conspire to make me regret more than ever my dwarfed and perverted womanhood. In times like these, everyone should do the work of a full-grown man. When I pass the gate of the celestials and good Peter asks me where I wish to sit, I will say, 'Anywhere so that I am neither a negro nor a woman. Confer on me, great angel, the glory of White manhood, so that henceforth I may feel unlimited freedom.'"[84] Her despair, however, was probably mixed with a new hope. In 1860 the Republican party won the White House with the election of Abraham Lincoln.

The Supreme Court's *Dred Scott* decision, the question of popular sovereignty, and the trial and execution of John Brown set the stage for the campaign of 1860. Slavery and sectionalism were the central issues; the tariff was also hotly debated. Republican delegates assembled in convention in Chicago to nominate their party's candidates and write the party's platform. By the end of the convention, the party had also chosen members of its Republican National Committee (RNC) to serve for the next four years, and an Executive Committee, with Edwin D. Morgan of New York as chair and George G. Fogg of New Hampshire as secretary, had been selected.[85] The events of the convention were covered by hundreds of reporters. Mary Livermore, who edited a Universalist newspaper with her husband in Chicago, was the only woman reporter.[86]

The nomination of Abraham Lincoln of Illinois did not satisfy all supporters of the party. Some, including Susan B. Anthony, believed that Lincoln and the party's stand on slavery was "shamefully weak and trembling."[87] These abolitionists made plans for a protest "Political Anti-Slavery Convention," and Anthony encouraged Stanton to accept the invitation sent to her by political abolitionists to attend a convention scheduled for Syracuse.[88] Stanton attended the convention, which nominated her cousin Gerrit Smith for president, but in the end she and Henry Stanton stayed in the Republican camp and campaigned for Lincoln.

Republicans in the campaign of 1860 invoked living memories of the crisis of Bleeding Kansas and the caning of Charles Sumner and combined them with striking images of its popular candidate. The key to the party's ideology, and contributing to its extensive support, was "its multifaceted nature."[89] This meant a broad platform advocating the nonextension of slavery, a moderate tariff plan, a homestead act, rivers and harbor legislation, a Pacific railroad, and legislation prohibiting discrimination against naturalized citizens.[90] Even more, it meant the ability to provide the moral consensus necessary to mobilize people politically. That mobilization gave the Republican party its national electoral victory in 1860 and helped hold the party together through the crisis of the Civil War.

During the campaign and when she accompanied her husband to the White House, Mary Todd Lincoln did not win the hearts of Republican supporters as had Jessie Benton Frémont. She did, however, support her husband's efforts to win the presidency. Her interest in politics developed when she was young, and she actively worked in her husband's earlier campaigns.[91] When Abraham Lincoln ran for Illinois's seat in the U.S. Senate, Mary Lincoln "joined him in filling several tiny notebooks with the name and partisan allegiance of each legislator."[92] Her position as political advisor and partner was so clear to Abraham Lincoln that when he learned he had won the presidential election, he ran home and cried, "'Mary, Mary, we are elected.'"[93]

Daughters joined wives in promoting family members in partisan politics in the 1860s. Overshadowing even the first lady was Catherine Chase Sprague, one of the most prominent women in the exceptional and rarified world of Washington partisan politics. The daughter of the well-known abolitionist and Republican leader Salmon P. Chase, she moved to Washington, D.C., with her widowed father in 1860 when he was elected to the U.S. Senate. After serving only two days in the Senate, Chase was appointed to be secretary of the treasury in Lincoln's administration, a position he held until June 1864, when he sought his party's presidential nomination for the second time. Kate Chase was an ardent supporter of her father's political career, and in late 1863, after she married one of the richest men in America, William Sprague, a senator from Rhode Island and a cotton manufacturer who was previously governor of his state, she dedicated not only her energies but also much of her husband's fortune to helping her father attain the presidency. She was, newspaper accounts stated, "one of the most remarkable women ever known to Washington Society."[94]

Kate Chase Sprague's partisan activism was guided by her father's desire to become president of the United States. Her mother's death allowed her to become a surrogate helpmate to her father, who was known for his abolitionist legal and political work, especially his efforts defending fugitive slaves and in founding the antislavery parties. In 1860, when she was nineteen years old, Sprague worked behind the scenes to help her father win the Republican nomination. Like Mary Lincoln, she wrote to supporters and kept records of their responses.[95]

By the 1860s women across the country were demonstrating their partisan loyalties. These women joined the wives and daughters of Republican party candidates and leaders to campaign for the party. Jane Grey Swisshelm, who had moved to Minnesota three years earlier, became known as "the mother of the Republican party" in the state for her editorials condemning slavery in her newly established paper, the *St. Cloud Visiter,* and especially for those opposing the James Buchanan administration. These editorials provoked local Democratic party loyalists to destroy her newspaper office, and she was forced to suspend publication. She fought back by establishing another paper, the *St. Cloud Democrat,* and taking to the lecture circuit to promote the Republican party.[96] Her stock speech, "Women and Politics," began with "an account of the wrongs heaped upon women by slavery, as a reason why women were then called upon for special activity" in politics. She then moved on to explain that men who were politicians needed to "lift their politics to the height of a man, and make them a habitation for men, not reptiles." Once the laughter died down, she concluded by denouncing the Buchanan administration.[97]

The Republican Star: Anna Dickinson

In 1860 the Republican party captured the White House and would hold on to power for almost twenty-five years, as the country divided, was shattered by warfare, and finally reunited to face new political, social, and economic challenges. The woman who took center stage in the early part of this era of Republican dominance was Anna Dickinson.[98] "Like a meteor," wrote the editors of the *History of Woman Suffrage,* Dickinson appeared on the political frontier, "as if born for the eventful times in which she lived, and inspired by the dangers that threatened the life of the republic."[99] Her fall from the Republican pedestal in 1888 demonstrates how important it was for partisan women to follow political currents. By the turn of the twentieth century, her partisan accomplishments were all but forgotten, and she died in 1932 in Goshen, New York, broken and penniless.

Dickinson spoke publicly for the first time at a meeting of the Quaker "Friends of Progress" at Clarkson Hall in Philadelphia in January 1860.[100] She was seventeen years old. The subject of the meeting was "The Rights and Wrongs of Women," and from the audience she directed challenging words to the night's speaker.[101] Her short but eloquent and bold questions led to speaking invitations from people interested in hearing what this young woman had to say about the political questions of the day.

Dickinson's debut at the podium occurred at a Pennsylvania Anti-Slavery Society meeting in Kennett Square, thirty miles from Philadelphia, just after Lincoln's election. In her speech, she praised the Republican party but was also critical of its stand on slavery. "'What did the Republican party of Lincoln maintain?'" she asked. "'Only that it opposed the extension into the territories of the evils of slavery.'"[102] This was not enough, she argued. Her careful choice of words and her willingness to criticize the party for not being bolder made her a welcome ally of prominent abolitionists and the radical wing of the Republican party.

Dickinson was born into a family of Quakers and abolitionists in 1842. Her father died when she was two; she claimed he died after giving a passionate antislavery speech. John Dickinson had worked as a dry-goods merchant but had never been able to bring his family of five children out of poverty. With the help of a local philanthropy, Anna was able to go to the Friends' Select School and then the Westtown Boarding School, run by the Philadelphia Yearly Meeting of Friends.[103] After about five years of formal schooling, pressure to help support the family led her into the world of employment, and at the age of fifteen she became a copyist at a publishing house and then at a law firm in Philadelphia. By the next year she was a schoolteacher traveling to nearby small county schools.[104]

Dickinson began giving public expression to her politics in 1856, when she submitted a letter to William Lloyd Garrison's *Liberator* condemning the violence against antislavery advocates in Ohio and calling on northerners to resist such tyrannies.[105] It brought her to the attention of a wider circle of abolitionists who became her early political mentors. Many of these abolitionists, like Dickinson herself, were Quakers. Among the most prominent were Dr. Hannah Longshore, Philadelphia's first woman medical doctor and a lecturer on women's health, and Lucretia Mott, active in Garrisonian abolitionism and an organizer with Elizabeth Cady Stanton of the 1848 Seneca Falls women's rights convention.[106] These friends arranged for Dickinson to give her first major speech at Concert Hall in Philadelphia in February 1861. She took as her subject the topic that had first brought her to the public's attention, "The Rights and Wrongs of Women." Eight hundred people listened to her two-hour speech.[107] Within weeks she was giving more political speeches to small and large gatherings, participating in the "heated discussions" of antislavery meetings, and developing "a clear comprehension of the province of laws and constitutions; of the fundamental principles of governments, and the rights of man."[108]

Dickinson's new friends helped her in other ways as well. They arranged for her to leave her position as a schoolteacher in Bucks County to take a position as an adjuster at the U.S. Mint in Philadelphia. The drain on male labor during the Civil War resulted in a shortage of men to work in government offices; young women filled these jobs. The position at the mint paid more than a schoolteacher's and helped Dickinson support her sister and mother, a financial obligation she would meet for many years.

While working at the mint, Dickinson continued to give political speeches. Her boldest speech was given in September 1861, a few days after the defeat of Union forces at the battle of Ball's Bluff. She denounced Gen. George McClellan, the commander of the Army of the Potomac, whose competence was already being questioned by some politicians and the public, as a traitor.[109] A month later she was fired from her job by the director of the mint, the former governor of Pennsylvania, James Pollock, for her criticism of McClellan. Dickinson wrote William Lloyd Garrison that her dismissal was due not to her comments about McClellan directly but to her "grave offense, being a woman" who expressed those comments in public.[110]

At the end of 1861, Dickinson found herself without a steady income but still obligated to care for her family. With encouragement from her circle of abolitionist friends, she now sought to make a living from the podium. The abolitionist and woman suffrage leader Elizabeth Buffum Chace of Rhode Island became her new mentor. Along with Garrison, Chace helped arrange a series of speaking engagements for Dickinson at antislavery and women's rights meetings in the Northeast during the early part of 1862. She spoke in the Fraternity Course in Boston's Music Hall on "The National Crisis."[111] In their short biography of Dickinson in *A Woman of the Century* (1893), Frances Willard and Mary Livermore wrote that, "Miss Dickinson in her younger days was a woman of singular powers of sarcasm, of judgment, of dissection of theories and motives, and of eloquence that can be understood only by those who have heard her on the platform."[112]

Dickinson became a political speaker just as women's rights advocates agreed to put their agenda on hold for the duration of the war. There would be no national conventions, and suffragists instead dedicated themselves to "infus[ing] into the politics of the nation a purer morality and religion."[113] The move was spearheaded by Elizabeth Cady Stanton and, more reluctantly, Susan B. Anthony and aided by prominent women like Jessie Benton Frémont. They founded the Women's Loyal National League (WLNL) to keep women organized, and they made it clear that "as women, we might not presume to teach men statesmanship and diplomacy." They explained that they "felt it our duty to call the nation back to the a, b, c of human rights."[114] The final resolution adopted at the May 1863 meeting read: "Resolved, 7. That the women of the Revolution were not wanting in heroism and self-sacrifice, and we, their daughters, are ready in this war to pledge our time, our means, our talents, and our lives, if need be, to secure the final and complete consecration of America to freedom."[115]

Women, Anthony declared, should "no longer be the mere reflector, the echo of the worldly pride and ambition of the other half of the race." According to the record of the WLNL's meeting, her statement was followed by applause, showing that there was apparent agreement that women would do more than serve as cultural or political symbols.[116] They also emphasized that they were cooperating with the men of the Republican party, whom they described in their list of resolutions as the "men of a nation, in a political party," dedicated to freedom, peace, and a republic founded on the principles of justice, and who had "lifted politics into the sphere of morals and religion, where it is the duty of women to be co-workers with them in giving immortal life to the NEW nation."[117]

Giving "their time and thought wholly to the vital issues of the hour," the WLNL embarked on a mammoth petition campaign aimed at a constitutional antislavery amendment.[118] Working in service with and for the Republicans and with the backing of prominent women and men, including Jessie Benton Frémont, Frederick Douglass, and Robert Dale Owen, they collected four hundred thousand signatures, two-thirds from women, which were sent to Congress. These petitions contributed to the passage of the Thirteenth Amendment that prohibited slavery in the United States.[119] Like the antislavery petitioning campaigns of the 1830s, this campaign increased women's focus on the federal government as a location for political change. At the end of the war, these women called for a new constitution for the nation, "in which the guarantee of liberty and equality to every human being shall be so plainly and clearly written as never again to be called in question."[120]

While Wendell Phillips praised Anna Dickinson at the first anniversary meeting of the WLNL, the moratorium on women's rights agitation opened up new political prospects for her.[121] Without her friends from the women's rights movement making demands on her, she could dedicate herself to speeches on the national crisis. The timing was perfect. Already notable for her antislavery speeches and her dynamic presence on stage, she was the ideal speaker for the Republican party, which needed to counter the public's feelings that the war was dragging on too long. Awareness of Dickinson's criticisms of McClellan only helped her reputation. McClellan was a Democrat.

In early 1863, Dickinson was invited by New Hampshire Republican leaders to stump the state for the coming campaign. The Republican party needed all the help it could get. The end of 1862 "carried gloom and discouragement and despair to every Northern home."[122] Public depression fed partisan disputes. New Hampshire Republicans were involved in a bitter gubernatorial contest, and the party needed every supporter it could draw on to gain momentum against the rising popularity of Peace Democrats (or Copperheads).[123] Dickinson was seen as the perfect person to represent the party's moral consensus. Only twenty years old, she, like other early women partisan speakers, represented the virtuous moral woman. She was the daughter, or sister, who visited soldiers in Union hospitals. Her speeches about "Hospital Life" encouraged the women who supported the men who fought.[124]

The secretary of the New Hampshire Republican State Committee, Benjamin Franklin Prescott, asked Dickinson to direct her appeals to women who had sons in the war.[125] Republican women in New Hampshire were ready to hear how they could give aid to their party and the nation.[126] Dickinson followed Prescott's advice and brought her audiences to tears with her graphic descriptions of the effects of war, but she also chose to discuss the controversial Emancipation Proclamation issued by Lincoln on January 1, 1863. Moving her speech from the drama of the wounded to the politics of emancipation, she defended Lincoln and the course of the war. She repeated her points in twenty speeches across the state. The Republican victory in New Hampshire established her as a "political power."[127]

Dickinson's fame in Republican circles grew quickly, and Republican leaders asked her to speak in the Maine and Connecticut campaigns. Again her job was to counteract the growing popular dissatisfaction with the war. If the Emancipation Proclamation had increased Republican popularity among some people, the first National Conscription Act of March 3, 1863, had driven other supporters away. With two weeks remaining in the Connecticut gubernatorial campaign, Dickinson entered a state rife with hostility about the war. She spoke daily, her carefully constructed speeches a blend of her own material and information given to her by Republican leaders. Tailoring her talks to her audiences, she spoke of the hospitals she had visited, the need to demonstrate national loyalties for the benefit of soldiers in the field, and the protective tariff. Her closing speech in Hartford on the eve of the election was delivered to a packed house.[128]

Dickinson's political star rose, as her stump speeches were followed by Republican victories.[129] J. G. Battenson, the chair of the Connecticut Republican State Central Committee, thanked her for her "valuable service" and the political enthusiasm she inspired by her "many evidences of conviction to faith and good works." As previously arranged, he enclosed a check with his thank-you letter.[130] Praise for her campaigning also came from women friends. Lillie Chace, the daughter of Elizabeth Buffum Chace, wrote Dickinson that she was happy for her success because "I am a *woman*" and thanked her "for the great work thee is doing for us, while laboring for the country."[131]

Elizabeth Cady Stanton saw a different side of the Connecticut campaign. During Dickinson's two weeks of lectures in Connecticut, according to Stanton, Republicans were asked to stay away from the packed houses to give Democrats room to hear Dickinson speak. The aim was to win over their votes. Stanton said that all women were "*shut out*" of the meetings because they could not vote.[132] Evidently, Connecticut Republican leaders saw no need to follow New Hampshire's strategy of appealing to women to support the party.

Stanton had experienced the exclusion of women from Republican rallies before, during the last month of the 1855 campaign, when the prominent Free Soil/Republican leader and senator John Hale came to Seneca Falls to lecture. On the day of his speech, she met a Republican editor on the street and stated, "'I suppose we are to hear Hale tonight,'" to which the editor replied: "'*We*, we do not wish to spare any room for ladies; we mean to cram the hall with voters.'" Stanton responded that it was not her fault that she was an "unavailable" person, and she had done her best to be a voter. She went to the meeting, she told Anthony, and "found a dozen women already there."[133]

From Connecticut, Dickinson traveled to New York City to give a speech at the Great Hall of Cooper Union to an estimated audience of five thousand. Sitting on the platform were influential Republican men whom Dickinson would interact with for years to come: Horace Greeley, Theodore Tilton, and Henry Wilson. Introduced by Henry Ward Beecher, the most prominent clergyman of the day, she spoke for two hours about slavery, war, and the tragedy of Union military defeats because of timid generals. This war between the North and the South, she claimed, was a "'people's war for free government.'" She called on the audience to join the quest to extend the liberties protected by the Union and declared that "'the freedom of the world is at stake.'"[134] At the conclusion of her speech there were cries for a speech by Beecher, but he responded: "'Let no man open his lips here to-night; music is the only fitting accompaniment to the eloquent utterances we have heard.'"[135] In addition to increasing her fame, the payment of one thousand dollars for her speech increased her personal fortune.[136]

Then she finally returned home to Philadelphia, where later that summer she made a speech at the National Hall, sharing the platform with the abolitionist leader Frederick Douglass and the congressman William D. Kelley in the successful effort to raise three black regiments.[137] Kelley, the father of Florence Kelley, who would become one of the leading women reformers of the early twentieth century, began a lengthy correspondence with Dickinson, calling her "my dear daughter" and promoting her to other influential Republicans.[138]

Dickinson's growing reputation and circle of political friends brought more invitations to speak from the stump during the fall 1863 campaigns. Pennsylvania and Ohio Republican leaders approached her for speeches. Encouraged by Kelley, but also by the promise of a thousand dollars a day for twelve days of speeches, she chose to campaign in Pennsylvania. The high pay compensated for the party's request that she travel to the mining districts, where opposition to the conscription act had already led to outbreaks of violence that targeted Republicans. Dickinson worked hard for the Republicans in Pennsylvania and contributed to their victory in the gubernatorial election. But neither the state nor national Republican committees paid her the promised twelve thousand dollars for her speeches. Without a written contract or someone to hold accountable, she had no recourse. It was an experience she would not forget.

After the Pennsylvania campaign, Dickinson took to the lecture circuit, earning a hundred dollars for her talks to various audiences. Then she traveled to Chicago for the Northwestern Sanitary Fair, arranged by the Republican Mary Livermore of the United States Sanitary Commission. It was, Livermore wrote Dickinson, to be a "great moral demonstration, rebuking disloyalty and upholding freedom." Dickinson agreed to give two lectures at the fair, but only after Livermore agreed to pay her five hundred dollars for the first evening and a hundred dollars for the second.[139] Clearly, Dickinson knew that she could command high fees, and she demanded ones that equaled those given to male lecturers. Mixing partisan stump speaking with lyceum speeches, Dickinson earned over twenty thousand dollars a year during the height of her career.[140]

Then came a major triumph for a woman in the political arena. At the invitation of one hundred senators and congressmen, Dickinson became the first woman to speak at the Hall of the House of Representatives on January 16, 1864. Always one to use drama to demonstrate her politics, she had planned to denounce Lincoln's reconstruction plan because it granted amnesty to all Confederates except those who held high political office. She showed her Republican colors, however, by calling for Lincoln's reelection when the president entered the hall soon after she began speaking.

Dickinson's speech, by all accounts, was dramatic and successful. The proceeds from ticket sales to the event supported the Freedman's Bureau, established the next year by an act of Congress. Within a few months, however, she grew alienated from the Republican leadership. She had never been paid for her speeches in Pennsylvania, and she was increasingly discouraged by Lincoln's planned policy of reconstruction, seeing it as too moderate and too compromising. The war was dragging on, and people were looking for new solutions, new leaders, and new systems of support. Some looked for change to come from leaders within their political parties; others looked for new leadership from outside.

Anna Dickinson joined in the discussion about who might replace Lincoln as the Republican party's presidential candidate and help the Republican party live up to its promises. Lillie Chace of Rhode Island wrote Dickinson that she "must do what seems to thee best but it seems to me as if after thee had tried nobly to lift the Republican party up to thy level and failing thee was going down to theirs. This is the evil of our politics."[141] Susan B. Anthony told Dickinson that with a choice between "'the two evils'" of the Republicans and Democrats, she should "'choose neither.'"[142] Anthony had long opposed Lincoln because he believed in the enforcement of the Fugitive Slave Law, and she argued that Republicans had always had, yet failed to take, the opportunity to place a greater stress on individual rights and human liberty.[143]

Also involved in the campaigning of 1864 was Kate Chase Sprague, since her father was again looking to the presidency. Salmon Chase maneuvered to unseat Lincoln as the party's nominee and had formed a committee headed by Samuel C. Pomeroy, a senator from Kansas, to promote his candidacy. The committee issued numerous public statements, including one that attacked Lincoln and his administration as "a swarm of official leeches" and touted Chase's "clean and unimpeachable" record.[144] Sprague used her husband's money to finance the publications of these statements, but the reaction was not what they expected.[145] There was an enormous outcry by Republican politicians, including denunciations from the floor of Congress, which harmed Chase's chances for winning support away from Lincoln. He withdrew from the race, and Sprague would have to wait four more years to again promote her father's prospects for the presidency, and then it would be within the Democratic camp. Becoming "the first woman ever to play an active role at a party nominating convention," she set up offices for her father in a hotel near the new Tammany Hall building in New York City.[146] Chase did not win the Democratic nomination in 1868. He left the convention with "tears in his eyes," and the ambitions of Kate Chase Sprague "to be First Lady were shattered." If "she had been a delegate," one historian has speculated, "the result might have been different."[147]

Like Dickinson and Anthony, Elizabeth Cady Stanton engaged in the discussion about the future of the Republican party and its best presidential candidate in 1864. Unlike Dickinson, she had no financial reasons to find a middle ground between radicals and moderates; and unlike Sprague, she did not have family considerations guiding her. Her position on the Lincoln administration was made clear in a letter she wrote to Caroline Healey Dall: "I want the women of the nation to give some expression of their desire in favor of a complete overthrow of the present dynasty."[148] In the spring of 1864, she signed a call by the Central Frémont Club of the City of New York announcing that there would be a Radical Republican Convention in Cleveland, Ohio, to nominate John C. Frémont, the party's 1856 candidate, for president.[149] Frémont continued to be the favorite of abolitionists who believed that the Republican party was straying from its antislavery principles. In choosing to work for Frémont, Stanton made it clear that she considered the Republican party still to be the surest site for political power.

Stanton, joined by Anthony, used the New York City offices of the WLNL to champion Frémont.[150] When criticized by Dall for turning the league from a moral organization of women supporting the war effort into "an electioneering caucus," Stanton shot back that women had long demonstrated their partisan loyalties with positive results. Abby Kelly Foster understood the importance of the slavery issue to the "exciting campaign of 'Tippecanoe and Tyler too'" better than almost anyone, Stanton wrote Dall, and she asked, "What man did more than Anna Dickinson to save the election in Connecticut and Pennsylvania?"[151] Partisan differences strained the WLNL, and they would create problems in other women's organizations after the Civil War.

Wendell Phillips supported Stanton's efforts to win the nomination for Frémont but wrote her that he did not want to give a nominating speech for Frémont. Nor did he want the American Anti-Slavery Society to be committed as a party vehicle for Frémont. "We shall confine the American Anniversary to individual expressions of opinion but let the society keep uncommitted if we can so far direct its actions," Phillips wrote Stanton. "My judgement would be for your league to do the same."[152]

When Lincoln won the party's nomination at the Republican convention in Baltimore during the second week of June, Frémont ran on a separate ticket but failed to win the backing of prominent Republicans.[153] Eventually, lack of support and negotiations with Republican leaders resulted in Frémont's withdrawal from the presidential race and helped Lincoln's chances for winning the election. General Sherman's capture of Atlanta, Georgia, in September provided a further guarantee.

In spite of Lincoln's nomination, tensions in the Republican party continued. When Lincoln vetoed the Wade-Davis bill, which called for a harsher reconstruction plan for southern states, some radicals began saying they might support the Democrats. Among them was Anna Dickinson, but she, like many others, backed away from the Democratic party when it nominated George McClellan as its candidate. These Republicans continued to criticize Lincoln even after his nomination but were careful to express support for what they called "their" party. Dickinson wrote in a letter to Stanton that she considered Lincoln a "scoundrel" and would rather lose her reputation than vote for him.[154] She knew her words made her seem a renegade to some in the party who saw her, she wrote, as having "deserted a good cause, for refusing to work with 'my party' to swell its triumphs." She stated that she would support "the party represented by Abraham Lincoln," but in the end she had "no 'party' save that which strives with sword and pen . . . to save this country."[155] During the last months of the campaign, Dickinson campaigned for the party in Pennsylvania.

Despite the ongoing tension in the party, Frémont's withdrawal from the race and McClellan's nomination on the Democratic ticket brought moderate and radical Republicans in line. Unlike the spectacular campaigns of earlier years, the campaign of 1864 took place in a more somber atmosphere.[156] The country was in no mood for boisterous celebrations. In the end, Lincoln carried all the loyal states except three—Kentucky, Delaware, and New Jersey.

As the war came to a close, and in his final days in office, Lincoln continued to face criticism. Radicals in the Republican party saw his plan for reconstructing the Union as too moderate, and conservatives felt it was too harsh. Debate over Lincoln's plan came to an end with his assassination in April 1865. The tension was now between Andrew Johnson and the Radical Republicans in Congress, who organized a Republican Congressional Committee to keep their forces together as a voice against Johnson's more moderate plan for reconstruction. At the center of that tension was a proposal for a Fourteenth Amendment to the U.S. Constitution that would answer the question of the citizenship status of newly freed slaves. As blueprints for the amendment began to circulate around the country, it immediately became clear to women's rights activists that the rights of citizens, including the right to vote, were to be limited to the "male citizen," not women, regardless of race, and were to be defined at the national as well as state levels. The Fourteenth Amendment increased the political distance between Congress and the president, resulting in the House of Representatives voting for Johnson's impeachment. It also created a new debate about citizenship rights among Republican activists outside Congress, especially those who had worked through the organizational channels of the abolitionist and women's rights movements before and during the Civil War. At the center of this debate were loyal Republican women.

2. The Entering Wedge: Republicans and Women's Rights, 1866–84

NORTHERN WOMEN earned praise for their wartime efforts in the Sanitary Commission and the WLNL.[1] Their endeavors also taught them important lessons, including "that they had an equal interest with man in the administration of Government, enjoying or suffering alike its blessings or its miseries."[2] To translate praise into rights, league women became advocates for a new national constitution that included a "clearly written" affirmation of "liberty and equality to every human being" that was "never again to be called into question."[3] When the issue of political rights was "up for discussion," argued women's rights advocates, "there could not be a better time to get all the agitation possible in regard to woman's claims."[4]

The public discussion of women's rights after the Civil War was part of a larger political conversation about citizenship rights as human rights. It was an important historical moment, and at its end, when women's hopes for concrete rewards in the form of suffrage laws were crushed by the course of reconstruction politics, a group of women's rights advocates turned away from a broad focus on human rights to a narrower conception of women's rights.[5] Seen from a distance, this can be regarded as the beginnings of "an autonomous feminist movement."[6] For the loyal Republican women of the time it was also the beginning of an era of tensions, and "the woman suffrage movement became the toy of the Republican party," wrote the editors of the *History of Woman Suffrage* in 1881, as women and their struggle for rights were "trifled with . . . like the cat with the mouse in the fable."[7]

These tensions were rooted in debates over the Fourteenth and Fifteenth Amendments, cultivated by the reality and rhetoric of partial suffrage for women at the state and local levels of politics and enhanced by the appearance of new dynamic third parties. Some easing of tensions came during the election years of 1872 and 1876, when the Republican party acknowledged women in the national platforms. These affirmations kept many women in the Republican fold, but other forces created more tensions and contributed to increased expressions by women of their political independence from the Republican party. For some women this meant new affiliations with other political parties. For others it meant creating political paths outside of partisan politics, and by the 1880s nonpartisanship would become a pragmatic cloak worn by virtuous political women.

The Fight for Equal Rights

In 1865, Elizabeth Cady Stanton and Susan B. Anthony were ready to engage a new strategy to raise public awareness about women's rights. Before the war they had employed a strategy of annual women's rights conventions organized by a central committee. Now they wanted a more permanent organizational home for their movement and sought to merge the WLNL with the AASS so the two organizations could work together for equal rights regardless of sex and race. As Anthony would put it, "the time for Negro or Woman specialties is passed," and an organization to promote human rights was needed.[8] Members of the AASS agreed with Stanton and Anthony's assessment, and the result was the establishment of the American Equal Rights Association (AERA) in May 1866. The preamble to the new organization's constitution stated that "in the reconstruction of our government we again stand face to face with the broad question of natural rights, [and] all associations based on special claims for special classes are too narrow and partial for the hour."[9]

In response to questions of whether the AERA would work for women's rights as well as the rights of African Americans, the president of the association, Wendell Phillips, stated: "One question at a time. This hour belongs to the Negro."[10] Women's rights activists like Stanton and Anthony, who had supported the AASS before and during the war and who had taken its cause in a broad direction through the WLNL, were outraged by Phillips's statement and their realization that the organization was going to work actively for a Fourteenth Amendment that excluded women; it was compounded later by the Fifteenth Amendment.[11] Stanton wrote to the editor of the *National Anti-Slavery Standard*, "It is all very well for the privileged order to look down complacently and tell us, 'This is the negro's hour; do not clog his way; do not embarrass the Republican party with any new issue; be generous and magnanimous; the negro once safe, the woman comes next.' . . . If our rulers have the justice to give the black man suffrage, woman should avail herself of that new-born virtue to secure her rights; if not, she should begin with renewed earnestness to educate the people into the idea of universal suffrage."[12]

To challenge people's limited perceptions of women's place in politics and to move from rhetoric to action, Stanton ran in June 1866 as an independent candidate for the Congress of the United States in the Eighth Congressional District of New York. In her appeal to voters, she wrote that she had "no political antecedents to recommend me to your support," but she made her partisan leanings clear by declaring that her "creed is *free speech, free press, free men* and *free trade*—the cardinal points of democracy."[13] Her aim was to test the legal right of a woman to run for office, and if she won, she stated, she would "demand *universal suffrage*." Her candidacy was also an attempt to focus attention on the Republican party. It would be, she stated, "a rebuke to the dominant party for its retrogressive legislation in so amending the National Constitution, as to make invidious distinctions on the ground of sex." Concluding her appeal by invoking racial and nativist arguments, she pointed out that the newly freed slaves as well as the "millions of foreigners now crowding our Western shores" represent not "property, education or civilization" but "incoming pauperism, ignorance and degradation." Only the suffrage of "wealth, education, and refinement of the women of the republic" would ensure the nation's "justice or safety."[14] Stanton received twenty-four votes to the Democratic winner's 13,816 and the second-place Republican's 8,210.[15]

Stanton's candidacy did not result in a legal challenge over women running for public office, but it represented a small population willing to embrace a broad definition of human rights that included voting rights for women and their right to hold office. At the May 1866 meeting of the AERA, Henry Ward Beecher proposed that the rights of women should be championed by the organization and went so far as to connect women's office holding to women's war work. A woman, Beecher stated, "makes as good a postmistress as a man does a postmaster," and he saw nothing wrong with the prospect of women voting and voting themselves into office. Sounding like a radical supporter of Republican motherhood, Beecher concluded that "a woman that can bring up a family of strong-brained children, and make good citizens of them, can be President without any difficulty."[16] For most people, however, the idea of women holding political or public office was still anathema, and women would move cautiously on this issue.

Not all suffragists spoke out against the AERA and the Republican party for their lack of support for women's rights. Anna Dickinson shared the feelings of Frederick Douglass that the Republicans were the best hope for the nation during Reconstruction and needed to be supported. They stressed that because the South was still unrepentant, those who spoke on behalf of black rights in the South did so "under national bayonets."[17] Dickinson, sources suggest, was among the first to suggest that black men would need constitutional protections for voting rights, and while she and others were forward-looking in their recognition of the need for constitutional protections, they could not predict the ways that southern state governments would circumvent those rights.[18]

Republican leaders' ability to ignore women's rights at the national level as they rewrote the Constitution to protect the rights of African-American men led some women suffragists to attempt to generate support for their cause at the state level. In June 1867 this meant agitation at the New York State Constitutional Convention.[19] Later that year it meant activism in Kansas, where a new state constitution was being voted on. While their suffrage ally, Lucy Stone, stayed behind in New York to run the offices of the AERA, Stanton and Anthony traveled to Kansas and stumped the state on behalf of proposals to strike the words "white" and "male" from the state's list of voter qualifications.

When Republican leaders in Kansas chose to campaign for black suffrage only, Anthony and Stanton announced that women would defect to the Democratic party, arguing that its minority position for the last ten years made it ripe to take up woman suffrage both for principled and practical reasons.[20] Support came not from the state Democratic party but from George Train, a Democrat who supported woman suffrage but opposed black suffrage. Anthony and Train toured the state together and used racist arguments to challenge Republicans.[21] The defeat of both black and woman suffrage in Kansas had enormous ramifications. The Kansas campaign taught Republican party leaders a lesson; they "blamed the 'side issue' of woman suffrage for the failure of black suffrage, sounding the alarm for any future attempts to combine both measures at the polls."[22] For women suffragists, feeling even more "politically isolated and betrayed," it meant the time had come to create yet another new organization to fight for their rights.[23]

At the May 1868 meeting of the AERA, when it was suggested that a new organization be created as a symbolic turn against the Republican party, the convention erupted into intense debate. Lillie Chace, who attended the convention with her mother, wrote Anna Dickinson that the suffragists had a "jolly fight! Lucy Stone was mildly indignant. Fred Douglass scowled like a thunder cloud on friend and foe alike." Susan B. Anthony, whom Chace described as the incarnation of wrath and defiance, received the most criticism for her "mismanagement and extravagance and Trainism," a reference to her association with George Train during the Kansas campaign. The attacks, Chace wrote, led Anthony to declare herself the "Napoleon of the Woman's Rights Movement."[24]

The AERA debates of 1868 occurred within the context of an election year that saw Republican party politics full of tension and arguments, as the party looked for a candidate to replace the discredited Andrew Johnson. Suffragists debated not only electoral politics but the party's unwillingness to move on the issue of women's rights. The Universalist minister Olympia Brown stated bluntly that most suffragists wanted to continue to support the Republican party, but it had sacrificed its principles. Lucy Stone echoed her accusation.[25] Anthony made her stand on the party clear; she "stood outside of any party which threw itself across the path of complete suffrage for women, and therefore she stood outside of the Republican party, where all her male relatives and friends were to be found."[26] No women, she declared, "should belong at present to either party; they should simply stand for female suffrage."[27] According to Stanton, the Republican party was responsible for establishing "an aristocracy of sex on this continent" when it sacrificed its principles by expanding citizenship and voting rights for African-American men before, and without, women. As the editors of the *History of Woman Suffrage* would later put it, women had "well learned the lesson taught in the early days of anti-slavery and the Republican party, that all compromises with principle are dangerous."[28]

To some, however, ignoring the demands of a small group of women who claimed their right to vote as a right of citizenship might not have been a compromise at all. "Abstract rights were never understood to be abstract enough to include women," writes the historian Nancy Isenberg, because "the polity—the fictive people—were embodied, or engendered, as male."[29]

Despite the constitutional revisions, many women were pulled to the Republican party. This was especially true for black women in the South who saw political participation as an expression of freedom and autonomy. Black women attended state constitutional conventions as well as state and local Republican party conventions and actively campaigned for Ulysses S. Grant and the Republican party in 1868.[30] These women would probably have agreed with the estimation of the poet and writer Frances Ellen Watkins Harper, who believed that race was a major determinant of how people lived their public lives and therefore any strategy for political change needed to take this into account.[31]

When the AERA met in New York City in 1869, the issue of race versus sex came to a head. Those who wanted to support the Republican party and those who felt they should not or could not do so found that they could no longer work together. The loyal Republicans, led by Henry Blackwell and Lucy Stone, formed the American Woman Suffrage Association (AWSA). They disseminated their ideas through their newspaper, the *Woman's Journal*. In the first issue, Henry Blackwell wrote an editorial, "Political Organization," in which he argued that to win the "'universal support which is essential to political success, Woman Suffrage must cease to be treated as a symbol of social innovations. It must be urged as a purely political question upon its own merits.'"[32]

The Republican critics, headed by Anthony and Stanton, formed the National Woman Suffrage Association (NWSA) and attempted to turn their back on the Republican party. They were joined by Anna Dickinson, Harriet Forten Purvis, and Mary Ann Shadd Cary, among others. Those who found it difficult to choose one organization over the other, such as Frederick Douglass and Sojourner Truth, "attended meetings of both groups."[33]

Women's Rights

At the founding meeting of the NWSA, Anna Dickinson delivered what was called one of her greatest speeches, "Nothing Unreasonable," a history of women's enslavement to men. The NWSA newspaper, the *Revolution,* with its motto "Principle, Not Policy—Justice, Not Favors—Men Their Rights and Nothing More—Women Their Rights and Nothing Less," became a symbol and vehicle of their independence from the Republican party.[34] Instead of seeing themselves in the position of having to prove themselves to the Republican party, or any party, NWSA suffragists demanded that it was time for a party to prove itself to women.[35]

NWSA leaders emphasized a political rhetoric of sexual difference and claimed their right to vote not only as individual citizens but also as members of a sex.[36] Arguing that sex consciousness was central to social organization, the founders of the NWSA stressed not their similarity to men as citizens of the nation, not human rights, but their differences from men. Women must have the vote, they reasoned, because, as Stanton put it, "'what we need to-day in government, in the world of morals and thought, is the recognition of the feminine element, as it is this alone that can hold the masculine in check.'"[37]

Suffragists brought this message to every political function that they could. Susan B. Anthony wrote to Elizabeth Harbert that women "should be present in person if possible—by memorial, petition, and resolution, any way, in every political gathering" during campaign seasons. Enemies of women's rights, she added, are "delighted so long as women are busied with repairing their damages all about them, but alarmed when they propose to take a hand in preventing the damages."[38] Congress became the location of consistent suffrage agitation. In January 1869, the Republican senator James Harlan of Iowa had granted Anthony and others their first congressional hearing to present the question of woman suffrage. The next year, Republicans granted Victoria Woodhull the privilege of presenting a memorial advocating woman suffrage to the U.S. House Judiciary Committee, propelling this flamboyant woman into the national political limelight.[39] The NWSA suffragists made it clear that they were attending these meetings not as partisans but as independent political actors.[40]

In January 1872, as the country geared up for another long campaign season, women were again granted an appearance before the U.S. Senate Judiciary Committee. Of the three presenters, Susan B. Anthony, Elizabeth Cady Stanton, and Isabella Beecher Hooker, Anthony's words were the most direct and challenging. Pointing out women's long history of petitioning for their rights, she informed the committee members that she had made a new promise to herself: she would no longer beg for rights. Instead, she "would come up to Congress each year and demand the recognition of them under the guarantees of the National Constitution."[41] At the heart of her argument were two points. Recognizing that the Republican party was concerned about its continued dominance of national politics, she stated that the party would harm itself if it did not move on the question of woman suffrage. Another party would stake that claim and win women's allegiance. Therefore, it was logical for the Republican party to court women's loyalties; it would build party strength. "What we ask of the Republican party, is simply to take down its own bars," she demanded, because women "can wait no longer."[42]

Susan B. Anthony believed that the Republican party would be eternally harmed for not supporting women's pursuit of rights. The party, she claimed, was "trembling lest it should fall into the minority," and she predicted that only their defeat at the polls would move the suffrage movement forward.[43] Other women echoed the threat, stating that if neither the Republicans nor Democrats take "up our cause, then the best men from both will form a new party" that "serves principles, and secures great National needs."[44]

Anthony's speech echoed comments suffragists had been making privately and publicly since the end of the Civil War; the route to suffrage might well be outside the Republican party, and the party would be harmed by its unwillingness to move on women's rights. On a visit to Chicago in 1869, Elizabeth Cady Stanton wrote to the *Revolution*: "While politicians are trying to patch up the Republican party now near its last gasp, the people in the West are getting ready for a new national party." She predicted that the new party would "combine the best elements of both the old ones, soon to be buried forever out of sight."[45] A new political party, the Prohibition party, was formed in Chicago in 1869. It would play a major role in women's partisan history, but it did not capture Stanton's loyalties. Still, her favorable mention of the new party is an indication of her frustration with the Republicans as well as her understanding of the importance of third parties in pushing political items onto the national agenda.

After presenting the suffrage memorial to the Senate in January 1872, Anthony also traveled West to give suffrage speeches and hopefully build support for the cause at the grassroots level. If her cynical or bleak outlook came from her long history in the Republican party and its continued silence on the question of woman suffrage, her optimism and willingness to work so hard stemmed from recent suffrage victories in the West.

Partial Suffrage

By the 1870s, partial suffrage for women existed in specific localities across the country as territories, states, and municipalities granted women the right to vote in certain elections. In 1838 Kentucky gave widows with school-age children the right to vote on school issues in their county districts. The next state to do the same was Kansas, twenty-three years later; Michigan and Minnesota followed in 1875, and Colorado in 1876. By 1890, nineteen states allowed women to vote on school questions, and three others allowed women to vote on tax and bond issues. In 1887 Kansas gave women municipal suffrage and inaugurated three decades of struggle over this suffrage right.[46]

The first victory for full woman suffrage came in the Wyoming territory in December 1869, when an all-Democratic legislature and a Republican governor, John A. Campbell, passed a bill introduced by William Bright to allow women to vote in all territorial elections.[47] Bright argued that women should have suffrage before blacks, and since blacks had suffrage, so should women. When the territory applied for statehood in 1890, and it became known that many members of Congress would not approve the application because women could vote, Wyoming's political leaders declared, "we will remain out of the Union a hundred years rather than come in without the women."[48]

Wyoming's suffrage victory was followed by the Utah territory victory of 1870. With a female population forty times that of Wyoming's, the majority of whom were Mormon, the victory in Utah was more controversial than that in Wyoming. Granted by a Mormon-dominated legislature, woman suffrage in Utah was complicated by the issue of polygamy. For orthodox Mormon women, enfranchisement meant maintaining "political solidarity with the brethren, thus ensuring social and religious solidarity; church membership was the same as partisan politics or loyalty to any special interest group."[49] As such, even though Utah women participated as delegates at the 1872 state constitutional convention, which voted to include woman suffrage in the new state constitution, national suffrage leaders shied away from promoting Utah as the advance guard of suffrage. Still, they denounced efforts in 1872 by some members of Congress to repeal Utah's woman suffrage law as a way to attack polygamy.[50] In 1887 the continuing controversy led to Utah's woman suffrage act finally being revoked by the Edmund-Tucker Act; woman suffrage was reinstated in 1896. Colorado in 1893 and Idaho in 1896 completed the early victories for full woman suffrage. The next wave of suffrage victories also happened in the West: Washington in 1910, California in 1911, and Oregon, Kansas, and Arizona in 1912.[51] Population pressures, frontier and territorial mentalities, race relations, revisions of constitutions and codes of laws, the influence of traveling suffrage organizers, as well as the motivations of individual party and community leaders are all believed to have been varying influences on these woman suffrage successes.

The suffrage victories provided for three things: the example of women as voters; an attempt to use women's partisanship as a leverage, or threat, against party leaders for a greater recognition of women's right to vote; and, as women divided over party loyalties, new challenges for suffragists who were attempting to build a political movement outside of party structures. The results were both immediate and long-term. People reacted immediately to the reality of women voting, as they attempted to give it meaning, but it took more than a decade for the impact of women's partial suffrage to present a challenge to politics as usual. In that time, the growing volatility of national party politics and a broadening of women's public activism had as much of an impact on ideas about women in politics as had women's actual voting practices.

In newspapers, women's magazines, suffrage papers, and the *Congressional Record*, Americans learned from stories and testimonies how woman suffrage had brought decorum to voting places. These stories and testimonies downplayed the issues voters faced on election day and the question of women's right to vote. Instead, they emphasized political style. As Laramie's Baptist minister wrote in a letter to a local newspaper in 1870, during the first election in which the women of Wyoming could vote: "I saw the rough mountaineers maintaining the most respectful decorum whenever the women approached the polls, and heard the timely warning of one of the leading canvassers as he silenced an incipient quarrel with uplifted finger, saying 'Hist!

Be Quiet! A woman is coming!' And I was compelled to allow that in this new country . . . I had witnessed a more quiet election than it had been my fortune to see in the quiet towns of Vermont."[52] Wyoming, both as a territory and after it became a state in 1890, and then Colorado, after woman suffrage was passed by a referendum vote in 1893, would become the most important testimonials to the evolution and (it was hoped) the culmination of women's activism in politics.

That testimony had two important elements. First, women's interest in politics was touted by suffragists as helpful to the course of political activity as well as the issues before the state; women's presence "cleaned up" polling places and brought into them a tangible morality through a concentration on social issues. Second, women's participation in electoral activity was deemed legitimate but not overly intrusive; women voted, but, even when and where they were eligible, few women sought elective office. The woman suffrage movement, in turn, gained legitimacy from the example and notice of women as proper voters.[53]

Comments about the positive aspects of women's presence in politics were as common in the 1870s as they had been in the early republic. Women who were demanding greater formal inclusion in politics had a reason to encourage the promotion of the idea that they improved the "tone and manner" of political proceedings even if improving decorum was not their aim.[54] In emphasizing that they were cooperating with men in ridding politics of corrupting influences (rather than competing for jobs), they hoped to win greater recognition for their cause. The polish woman suffragists put on political proceedings was a way to smooth their acceptance at a time when their allies were dwindling and their opposition was increasingly impervious to their demands.

Almost all of the approximately one thousand women who were eligible to go to the polls in Wyoming territory to cast their first votes in September 1870 actually voted. Newspaper reports disagreed on their partisan impact. Balloting was not secret, but voting decisions were not recorded by gender. James H. Hayford of the Republican *Laramie Sentinel,* who claimed that he had scrutinized the voting process, stated that most women selected Republican ballots. Other reporters also claimed women voted mostly Republican, but the *Cheyenne Leader,* also a Republican paper, maintained that women's votes were divided between the Republican and Democratic parties.[55] In the end, the conclusion of most reporters was that women's voting was unremarkable.

After women in Utah won the vote, Anthony wrote to one new voter there that the women should "'not so much try to get women elected to the offices as to get the best persons, whether men or women. . . . I do hope your women therefore will set a good example of proving it is not the spoils of office they are after.'" It would harm the woman suffrage movement, she argued, "'if the vast majority of your women should prove themselves mere partisans.'"[56] This message from suffragists to women voters to prove that they transcended partisanship grew stronger as the century came to a close.

"Full suffrage" before the Nineteenth Amendment did not mean women had the right to run for or hold political office, and Western woman suffrage opened up this old question for new evaluation. Nationally, women held various political appointments in the 1860s, but they were mostly accepted in jobs such as running post offices or sitting on school boards. During his first term in office, Grant appointed the first "women postmasters."[57] Utah women won the right to vote and the right to run for local offices in 1870 but were "ineligible for nomination to state legislative and executive offices." They won the right to hold all political offices in the 1895 Constitution, a move pushed for by the Democratic party, and immediately ran for and won state offices.[58] In 1873 the California legislature passed a law making women eligible for all school offices.

Wyoming women moved more slowly. Women began to sit on grand and petit juries in 1870, and their presence made male jurors drop the practice of drinking, gambling, and smoking and chewing tobacco during breaks while on duty. By 1871, judges had "stopped the use of women on juries on grounds that jury service was not an adjunct of suffrage," and women did not serve on juries again until 1950.[59] In 1870 as well, women held their first offices as justices of the peace when Caroline Neil, of Point of Rocks, and Esther Morris and Francis Gallagher, of South Pass City, were appointed by the secretary, Edward M. Lee. Little evidence of Neil and Gallagher's service exists, and after eight months, a partial term, Morris was not renominated for service.[60] Mary Davis was elected justice of the peace in Tie Siding, Wyoming, in 1876, and Susan Johnson was appointed postmistress in Cheyenne in 1880, but only two other women ran for office between 1871 and 1891; "one received eight votes, the other five, when at least five hundred votes were needed for election."[61] In 1894 the Republican Estelle Reel was the first woman elected to state office when she became Wyoming's second superintendent of public instruction.[62] These small numbers, however, were transformed into successes for woman suffrage. Suffrage leaders used testimonies from Wyoming and other places to describe the working of woman suffrage with broad, positive strokes. Women did not move too quickly, did not compete too strenuously, and did not upset the apple cart. Testimonies about decorum on election day and women's minimal move into public offices soothed people's worries that women would usurp political authority. Wyoming would remain an example of the successes of woman suffrage at the same time that it demonstrated the limitations of what voting rights meant for women's greater political activism.

The Republican Party Splits: Liberal Republicans

Following what was now tradition, Susan B. Anthony traveled to Cincinnati in May 1872 to attend the first of the season's presidential nominating conventions to win support for the woman suffrage cause. At the start of the year Republicans had split into two factions, the Liberal Republicans and the Regular Republicans, as its advisors grappled with the new political conditions of the Reconstruction era. The Liberals held the first nominating convention of the year. Anthony and Laura De Force Gordon, a leading woman suffrage organizer from California, attended the Cincinnati convention to present what Anthony called an unrestricted suffrage proposition for adoption in the platform.[63]

Before the convention, Anthony asked for help from Benjamin Gratz Brown, who had supported woman suffrage since he was elected to the Senate as a Republican in 1863 and who had won the governorship of Missouri as a Liberal Republican in 1870. Brown did not answer her letter, and she read his silence as being "driven by party necessity." Anthony also hoped for support from other Republicans who had shown their approval for woman suffrage, including George Washington Julian, a senator from Indiana, and Theodore Tilton, the editor of the *Independent*. As the Liberals moved through the steps of nominating Horace Greeley for president, Benjamin Gratz Brown for vice president, and writing their platform, the women found the convention delegates uninterested in their issue. It was all about "political exigency," Anthony argued.[64]

Dismayed at the silence of the Liberal Republicans, Anthony reasoned that the woman suffrage cause "is just where the anti-slavery cause was for a long time. It had plenty of friends and supporters three years out of four, but every fourth year, when a President was to be elected, it was lost sight of; then the nation was to be saved and the slave must be sacrificed. So it is with us women." She concluded that women were welcomed by politicians "to fill empty seats" at political gatherings and to "wave our handkerchiefs and clap our hands," but when women "ask to be allowed to help them in any substantial way, by assisting them to choose the best men for our law-makers and rulers, they push us aside and tell us not to bother them."[65]

After the Cincinnati convention, Anthony set off for New York City to deal with another partisan problem. She learned that her colleagues in the NWSA had chosen a new route for suffrage, the creation of a People's party. The catalyst for this new political party was Victoria Woodhull. Woodhull's fame had grown rapidly in reform, business, and political circles after she established with her sister the brokerage firm of Woodhull, Claflin, and Company. Propelled by spiritualism and then helped by Cornelius Vanderbilt, Woodhull moved from business onto the lecture circuit and into politics. Woodhull was determined to eclipse Anna Dickinson as the most celebrated woman lecturer in America.[66]

In 1870, in an attempt to demonstrate that women could move to the top in all areas of the public sphere, Woodhull announced her candidacy for president of the United States. The next year, using her connections with influential men, including the Republican congressman Benjamin Butler of Massachusetts, she presented her woman suffrage memorial to the U.S. House Judiciary Committee. Woodhull's memorial caught the attention of Stanton and Anthony, who sought to enlist her help in building the NWSA.

Elizabeth Cady Stanton, Isabella Beecher Hooker, and Matilda Joslyn Gage endorsed Woodhull's idea of a separate political effort that challenged the Republican dominance over politics and therefore over the question of woman suffrage. Stanton wrote Woodhull that "the Republican party is in its dotage, so weak in the knees it cannot bear its own weight, and so blind it cannot tell its own friends."[67] The call for the May 1872 meeting of the NWSA stated that the purpose of the meeting would be to work for a "People's Convention" to form a new political party. The call denounced the Democratic party and stated that the Republican party had "been false to its own definition of Republican Government" by "denying that 'citizen' means political equality."[68]

When Anthony learned of the call for the "People's Convention," she hurried back to New York City. Plans for the meeting were getting underway, and she immediately let it be known that she was strongly opposed to the formation of an oppositional party, calling such a move "folly" because "nominees without electors were incongruous," and she demanded that her name not be associated with the effort.[69] By her own force of will, and because the contract to hire the convention hall was in her name, Anthony was able to divide the efforts of the NWSA and the People's party convention. While supporters of Woodhull moved forward with their own plans, the women of the NWSA passed a resolution at their convention stating that they would call a nominating convention if Republicans or Democrats continued to ignore their cause. But for now, for Anthony, the case of a new party was closed.[70]

Woodhull changed the name of her party to the Equal Rights party, announced her candidacy for president, and selected Frederick Douglass as her vice-presidential candidate. Douglass neither accepted nor declined the nomination and did not actively participate in the party. By the time of the election, Woodhull was in jail, arrested with her sister under the newly passed Comstock Law, which prohibited the use of the U.S. mail for the distribution of obscene materials. They were arrested after the author of the law, Anthony Comstock, arranged the mailing of the November 2, 1872, issue of *Woodhull and Claflin's Weekly,* which detailed the scandal of the love affair of Henry Ward Beecher and Elizabeth Tilton. This scandal would dominate the lives of many reformers well into 1874.[71]

The Regular Republicans

In the end, it was the Regular Republicans and not the Liberal Republicans, the Democrats, or the Equal Rights party organizers who gained the support of most of the active suffragists. In June 1872 the Regular Republicans met in Philadelphia and nominated Ulysses S. Grant for a second term with Henry Wilson, a senator from Massachusetts, as their vice-presidential candidate. Patriotism, prosperity, and morality would become the most frequent themes of Republican politics after the Civil War, and they were already in evidence at the 1872 Regular Republican convention.[72] The proceedings opened with the abolitionist Gerrit Smith praising Grant for passing an anti–Ku Klux Klan law and working to "crush out Ku-Kluxism, and save the negro and the few white men who defend the negro from that bloody, fearful, and terrible vengeance threatened against them."[73] The emphasis of the convention was on how far the country had come under Republican leadership, and central to that point was the participation of African-American delegates. John R. Lynch of Mississippi stated that African Americans "look to the Republican party as our political parents. We are born of them. . . . we rejoice that the Republican party has made a sentiment, and gives expression to it in this great Union, that our Republic, like a rainbow, is not complete without its darkest color." According to the convention report, Lynch's speech was followed by laughter and applause.[74]

Many of the speakers at the Regular Republican convention addressed the idea that the mission of the Republican party had ended and its work was done. Not so, stated O. P. Morton, a senator from Indiana, who asserted that the party's work "will not be done until there is equal protection under the law extended to men of every race and color, and to all men of all political views in every part of the United States." The Republican party, Morton concluded, "has a great mission to perform, a mission that is no less than taking care of this country." To succeed in that mission, the party would "hold fast to principles rather than to men."[75]

Susan B. Anthony and Henry Blackwell were among the supporters of woman suffrage who attended the convention. With the help of Henry Wilson, a senator from Massachusetts, they were able to maneuver through the platform committee and assemble a plank that gave women their first official recognition by the party. By the time the Republican National Convention of June 1872 had ended, women's rights activists had cause for celebration. For the first time, the Republican party formally acknowledged women's place in political life with this fourteenth plank of the national platform: "The Republican party is mindful of its obligations to the loyal women of America for their noble devotion to the cause of freedom. Their admission to wider fields of usefulness is viewed with satisfaction, and the honest demand of any class of citizens for additional rights should be treated with respectful consideration."[76] "And this recognition of Woman's claim," declared Henry Blackwell, "will prove to be the thin edge of the entering wedge of a complete endorsement of woman suffrage."[77]

To suffragists, this was "the thin edge of the entering wedge which shall break women's slavery in pieces and make us at last a nation truly free—a nation in which the caste of sex shall fall down by the caste of color, and humanity alone shall be the criterion of all human progress."[78] But before disillusioned Republican women would fall back into the Republican nest, they wanted to see what the Democrats had to say. Anthony wrote Stanton that she "scarcely [has] a hope that Baltimore will step ahead of Philadelphia in her platform."[79] Stanton wrote Blackwell that she also doubted that the Democrats might give women a "whole plank" rather than a "splinter."[80] It was not a long wait for the Democrats' response to the women. The Democratic convention was held in Baltimore in early July, and the party remained silent on the woman question.

Henry Blackwell was convinced that the Republicans' 1872 promise to consider with respect the demands of any group of citizens for additional rights would bring forth a suffrage victory, and he encouraged Anthony and Stanton to embrace the party.[81] Stanton hesitated. She believed that what she called the "splinter" in the platform was simply another instance of men asking women to lend their influence for a party's success without promising a tangible reward for their work. It is "an invitation to us," she wrote, "to give our influence," but in return it gives only "an implied promise of eventual recognition."[82]

Stanton wrote Anthony that she did "'not feel jubilant over the situation'" and, in fact, had never felt "'so blue in my life. . . . I am under a cloud and see nothing.'"[83] Henry Blackwell tried to help her see the positive side and argued that the only way women would win the vote would be "by allying themselves to political movements of the country so as to become a *power* in politics. Parties are influenced quite as much by sympathy as by interest."[84] Stanton's cloud did lift, and although she had already issued a public endorsement of Greeley, she switched sides after being convinced by Anthony and Blackwell that this wedge would bring an end to women's disfranchisement.

Anthony's excitement contrasts with Stanton's hesitation. With this Republican plank, she stated, women "shall go rapidly onward."[85] Her enthusiasm about the Republican plank (and she could not help but note the irony of it being the fourteenth plank of the platform) is evident in her correspondence to other suffragists during the campaign. She saw the Republican plank as "the promise of things not seen," and she wrote to Blackwell that she would "clutch it as the drowning man the floating straw—and cling to it until something stronger and surer shall present itself."[86] She wrote Stanton that "'the Fort Sumter gun of our war is fired, and we will go on to victory almost without a repulse from this date.'"[87]

In response to the Republican recognition of women, Anthony and Matilda Joslyn Gage sent out a call to women to "lay aside our party preferences" and work for Grant and the Republican party.[88] Under the letterhead of the NWSA, the suffragists issued an appeal to the "Women of America," stating that "Philadelphia has spoken and woman is no longer ignored." Of the fourteenth plank of the platform, the appeal explained, "We recognize its meagerness; we see in it the timidity of politicians; but beyond and through it all, we farther see its promise of the future."[89] Women were "now fairly inside the political ring and can never again be snubbed out."[90]

The appeal to women to support the Republican party was a long one, and the Republican National Committee published thousands of copies for distribution. The party also asked Anthony to coordinate women's campaign work and offered her five hundred dollars for "moderate expenses of meetings of the women in the principal cities of the country."[91] The party's secretary noted that he wished the party had more funds to give to the women because he recognized the importance of their work. In fact, the party had strong-armed business leaders and patronage politicians for contributions and its war chest was full.

Anthony wrote Henry Blackwell and Lucy Stone that she felt the committee had given her "*substantial aid*" and that she was busy organizing women's meetings in New York and Massachusetts. She wanted only experienced speakers at the meetings, she wrote, because it was important that not one be a failure.[92] In addition to Anthony, Stanton, and Gage, the suffragists Olympia Brown, Isabella Beecher Hooker, Dr. Clemence S. Lozier, Helen Slocum, Mary Livermore, Mary Brown Hazlett, and Lillie Devereux Blake all campaigned for the party.[93] Blackwell encouraged Anthony to also contact Frances Ellen Watkins Harper, because "as a colored woman you would do well to have her come out and speak."[94] Helen Barnard helped with editing a paper called the *Woman's Campaign.*[95]

At the "mammoth rallies" of the 1872 campaign, Regular Republican women and men vied for space. When Brooklyn Republicans met at the Academy of Music, the "galleries and auditorium of the Academy were filled to their utmost capacity and even ladies who were unable to obtain seats were glad to find standing room in the aisles and sides."[96] A citywide "grand demonstration" of New York Republicans equaled "in magnitude and grandeur the great processions of 'Wide Awakes' in 1860," the *New York Times* reported. The marchers wore oilcloth capes and military caps similar to those worn by the young men of 1860, but these marchers were men who had served in the war.[97] These rallies "heralding the link of woman's cause to Republicanism briefly recalled the optimism of antislavery days."[98]

Divided Loyalties

Not all women's rights activists went into the Regular Republican camp in 1872. Antoinette Brown Blackwell supported her old friend Horace Greeley, as did Anna Dickinson. Dickinson was approached by both the Liberal and Regular Republicans for help in their campaigns. Henry Wilson, representing the Grant forces, promised her twenty thousand dollars for her work, an enormous sum for any stump speaker. She responded that Republican leaders in Pennsylvania had promised her twelve thousand dollars in 1868, but she never saw the money. She refused the offer.[99] The Greeley managers then approached her with the promise that she would be paid ten thousand dollars for her efforts.[100] Dickinson had already spoken out against Grant with speeches that focused on the corruption of his administration, and Greeley had been one of her backers for a long time; she was also a close friend of the editor of the *New York Tribune,* Whitelaw Reid. Yet Dickinson at first hesitated in accepting the Liberals' offer. For one thing, in 1869 Greeley's *Tribune* had turned away from its former support of women's rights and in so doing had ridiculed her along with others who gave women's rights speeches. Also, she was put off by the fact that the Greeley committee did not approach her until they saw the productive work being done by women for the Regular Republicans and realized that they needed to counter the impression that *all* women were for Grant.[101]

Dickinson finally relented, took up the Greeley offer, and agreed to give a speech on the last Friday in October at the Cooper Union in New York City. As plans for her speech moved quickly, work on a formal contract for her services seems to have been put aside. Her speech, "Is the War Ended?" was delivered to a packed audience and concentrated on the differences between Grant and Greeley. Grant and his administration were corrupt and dishonorable, she declared, while Greeley was forward-thinking and "stood for integrity, justice, and humanity."[102] The *Tribune* carried the entire text of her speech in its next edition.[103]

In the back of the audience at Cooper Union were Elizabeth Cady Stanton and Susan B. Anthony. Dickinson's speech for Greeley contributed to a growing rift between the NWSA leaders and Dickinson that never healed. Anthony was especially angered that she would choose to support the Liberals over the Regulars since the Grant faction had acknowledged women in the platform. The Regular Republicans may not have gone as far as endorsing woman suffrage, but their platform plank, Anthony believed, made them the more principled politicians in the contest.

Women Voters

At the end of the campaign season Anthony returned home to Rochester, New York. Acting on the conviction that she had the right to vote under the Fourteenth Amendment and following a political tactic that suffragists called the New Departure, she joined fourteen other women in her town to cast a ballot in the election. She proudly proclaimed that she had voted the straight Republican ticket.[104]

Between 1868 and 1872, hundreds of women across the country tried to register and vote.[105] Portia Gage made an unsuccessful attempt to vote in Vineland, New Jersey, in a local election in March 1868. In the fall election, 172 black and white women from Vineland made up their own ballots and cast them in ballot boxes also of their making; they continued to vote in this way in subsequent elections. The same month, Hannah Blackwell and Lucy Stone attempted to vote in the federal election in Roseville, New Jersey. From New Jersey to California, women's attempts to register and vote in federal and local elections continued in the early 1870s. The women voters in San Jose, California, were led by Sarah Knox-Goodrich; among them was the pioneering lawyer Clara Foltz.[106] Sojourner Truth attempted to vote in Battle Creek, Michigan. Abigail Scott Duniway and three other women, two white and one black, led the attempt in Oregon. Sixty-three women, including Belva Lockwood, Sara Andrews Spencer, and Mary Ann Shadd Cary, tried to register in Washington, D.C.[107]

Cary was among those who agreed with the argument that women had the right to vote because of the Fourteenth and Fifteenth Amendments. Cary had grown up in a community of abolitionists in Delaware, where her father was a leader in the Underground Railroad. After the passage of the Fugitive Slave Law in 1850, she and her family moved to Canada. She became a journalist, writing about the prospects for blacks in Canada, and eventually established her own newspaper. At the end of the Civil War, Cary, now widowed with two children, returned to the United States. She settled in Washington, D.C., and opened a school for black children and attended Howard University Law School.[108] Like Anthony, she argued that it was a "politically prudent strategy for the Republican party" to endorse the idea that women should be considered to have the right of the vote.[109] When the Republican party did not respond positively, she drifted away from the party, worked with the NWSA, and helped to found the Colored Women's Progressive Franchise Association.

Some women who voted were arrested, including five black women in South Carolina in October 1870. Susan B. Anthony became the most famous woman who voted, was arrested, and charged with illegal voting. She took to the lecture circuit to plead her case to the public. When the case finally reached the courtroom, the judge read a statement he had written before arguments had been made by both sides and instructed the jury to find her guilty. Fined one hundred dollars, Anthony declared: "I shall never pay a dollar of your unjust penalty. . . . And I shall earnestly and persistently continue to urge all women to the practical recognition of the old revolutionary maxim, that 'Resistance to tyranny is obedience to God.'"[110] In the end, she and her sister voters, as well as the election officials who had allowed them to vote, were pardoned by the Grant administration.

In relating the story of Anthony's trial, the editors of the *History of Woman Suffrage* placed it in a chapter called "Trials and Decisions," which connected it to women's efforts around the country to vote. The results of these efforts showed, they claimed, that the "design of the Government was evidently to crush at once, and arbitrarily, all efforts of women for equality of rights with men." More remarkable, they believed, was the fact that these decisions "were rendered in every instance by members of the Republican party."[111]

By 1875, with the Supreme Court ruling in *Minor v. Happersett,* the New Departure era came to a close, and suffragists again needed to create new ways to build their movement. The ruling held that the Constitution "did not automatically confer the right to vote on those who were citizens: suffrage was not 'coextensive' with citizenship."[112] The *Minor* ruling directed many suffragists back to focusing on a strategy of seeking a federal amendment for woman suffrage.

Grant won the election of 1872 and remained in the White House, but his administration became increasingly embroiled in scandals. These scandals resulted in new calls for civil service reforms and restrictions on the influence of capitalists and industrial leaders in politics. A new generation of politicians would carry forth these crusades through attempts to reform the Republican and Democratic parties and by establishing new third parties. They brought the country into a new period of intense party competition.

Horace Greeley was broken by public and personal losses in 1872. His wife died in late October, he was losing control over his newspaper, and he was defeated at the polls on November 5. One of the last people to visit him as he lay crippled by his losses was Anna Dickinson. He called her the "most generous woman alive" for giving up her lucrative lecture career to stump for his campaign.[113] Greeley, the man who helped name the fusion forces of 1854 "the Republican party," died on November 29.

Republican Recognition and Women's Responses

The campaign of 1876 signaled the beginning of new forms of party organization and activism. For the first time since before the Civil War, the two parties entered the campaign almost equal in strength, and both required a demanding focus on campaign organization. The new strength of the Democratic party came not only from its nearly complete hold over the "Solid South" but its gubernatorial and legislative victories in some northern and western states, including New York, New Jersey, and California. Years of battling Reconstruction policies and the continuing taint of corruption from the scandals of the Grant administration contributed to the formation of a limited Republican party agenda that focused on issues of currency and the tariff. Party leaders "settled into a comfortably limited agenda."[114]

When the Republican National Convention opened in Cincinnati in June 1876, woman suffragists were again ready to present their memorials. Convention leaders announced that one woman could speak before the convention, and Sara Andrews Spencer of the NWSA was chosen for the honor. Introduced to the convention by George F. Hoar, a senator from Massachusetts who had long been a supporter of votes for women, she read from a memorial prepared by Susan B. Anthony.[115] In 1872, Spencer stated, the Republican party had promised to treat "with respectful consideration" women's "honest demands," but it had not yet done so. The party had declared in the first and second planks of the 1872 platform that it had "established universal suffrage" and "justice, perfect liberty, and perfect equality for all" with the emancipation of four million slaves. If that was so, she asked, what about the ten million women citizens, "the wives and mothers and daughters of this republic?"[116] It was time to move forward and meet the promise of 1872.

Spencer was prominent in the small world of active woman suffrage workers by the time she attended the 1876 convention. Born in Savona, New York, in 1837, she moved with her mother and brother to St. Louis in 1850, after her mother had left her father. She attended school until age sixteen, leaving to take a job at the other side of the desk as a schoolteacher. By age nineteen, she was appointed principal of a grammar school for girls, becoming the youngest principal in St. Louis. When the Civil War broke out she moved to New York, and a letter of introduction resulted in a meeting with Horace Greeley and a job writing for the *Scientific American* and other publications. Near the end of the war, she married Henry C. Spencer and worked with him in his business, teaching a penmanship called Spencerian at their Spencerian Business College in Washington, D.C.[117]

Spencer became active in women's rights work in 1870 after hearing Victoria Woodhull argue that women had been enfranchised by the Fourteenth and Fifteenth Amendments. Her public fame in suffrage circles increased after she joined the women from the District of Columbia who attempted to vote in 1871. Spencer brought suit against the Board of Registration, which ruled in October 1871 that "'women are citizens, but have not the right to vote without local legislation.'"[118] By 1876 she was "the consummate suffragist-gadfly" for the NWSA and was instructed by Anthony to present the memorial to the Republican convention asking for the party's commitment to the enfranchisement of women.[119]

In spite of the *Minor v. Happersett* ruling that "the Constitution of the United States does not confer the right of suffrage upon any one," the memorial claimed that "the right to the use of the ballot inheres in the citizens of the United States." To back up this claim, Anthony presented a lengthy discussion of women's historical devotion to the republican ideals of liberty and freedom. She concluded, as she had often done before in speeches to partisan groups, with a hint of a threat. The "party that ceases to respect the vital principles of truth and justice is the party that dies," she stated, and "if you would have the party of the future be the Republican party, you must now take the broad noble ground of citizens' suffrage."[120]

After the suffrage memorial had been presented to the convention and sent to the Committee on Resolutions, the question of women's rights was essentially ignored, as the focus shifted to resolving contests between competing state delegations and discussing the question of Chinese immigration. Just when hope seemed to be lost, a platform plank was quickly introduced and endorsed. It read:

The Republican party recognizes with approval the substantial advance recently made toward the establishment of equal rights for women by the many important amendments effected by the Republican Legislatures, in the laws which concern the personal and property relations of wives, mothers and widows, and by the election and appointment of women to the superintendence of education, charities and other public trusts. The honest demands of this class of citizens for additional rights, privileges and immunities should be treated with respectful consideration.[121]

Would women come to the aid of the Republican party again, as they had in 1872 when the party first included a recognition of their concerns in the platform? Many did. During the campaign of 1876, in the centerpiece of banners waved by Republican supporters were illustrations of the candidate Rutherford B. Hayes and his wife Lucy. Like Jessie Benton Frémont in the campaign of 1856, Lucy Hayes was celebrated for her youth, beauty, and intelligence as well as her principles. The difference was that whereas Frémont represented abolitionism, Hayes represented the flourishing political issue of temperance.[122] Rutherford B. Hayes was a member of the Sons of Temperance but did not want this publicized during the campaign, fearing it would hurt him. Republican women saw no reason to ignore the fact that Lucy Hayes was a temperance supporter, and they cheered her during the campaign and applauded the announcement after Hayes's election that the president and new first lady would not serve alcohol in the White House.[123]

The temperance movement, and women's place in it, had grown enormously since the passage of the Maine Law in 1851. In describing one Republican gathering in 1884, the *New York Times* reported that "the proportion of ladies in the audience was unusually large for any mass meeting not held under the inspiration of the temperance cause."[124] The new party that Elizabeth Cady Stanton had witnessed being established in Chicago in 1869, the Prohibition party, also gained strength in the 1870s. Women were drawn to the party because it admitted them as full members and endorsed woman suffrage. Temperance women also organized separately from the Prohibition party. In 1873, out of the Woman's Crusade that began in Ohio and spread to neighboring states, the first women's temperance organizations were joined under the umbrella of the national Woman's Christian Temperance Union (WCTU). Among these organizations was the Woman's Temperance Society of Clinton, Iowa, formed by Judith Ellen Foster in 1873.

In spite of Lucy Hayes, the temperance issue, and the Republican platform plank, women and suffrage activists were divided in 1876. Sara Andrews Spencer and Henry Blackwell were delighted with the plank, but other suffragists were not so sure.[125] One commented that the Republicans had just "'thickened the old sop and re-served it.'"[126] After careful consideration, Stanton switched her partisan allegiances to endorse her friend Samuel Tilden as the Democratic party's presidential candidate, in part because as governor of New York he had appointed Josephine Shaw Lowell as the first woman member of the State Board of Charities.[127] The Republican party might praise women's political appointments, but it was the Democrats, Stanton believed, who had made the greatest leap.

Republican women participated in the campaign of 1876 that led to the disputed election of Rutherford B. Hayes but gained no rights or group rewards for their work. All the agitation and stump speaking for the Republican party, Harriet Robinson wrote, was good for the party but not for the woman suffrage movement, and women learned not to expect anything when Republicans were the party in power.[128] In 1880 Stanton declared that women had "'sat on a limb of the Republican tree singing "suffrage if you please" like so many insignificant humming-birds quite long enough.'"[129] Her feelings were echoed by Lucy Stone, who stated that "there is something pathetic in the way women hover on the outskirts of political life, striving for the success of the party they think right."[130]

Anthony's discouragement embraced not only loyal Republican women but women in all political parties. In the summer of 1880, she wrote the California suffragist Elizabeth Harbert that "what discourages me about women" is that they care more for "[their] political party . . . than for [their] own political rights." Sara Andrews Spencer, she was disheartened to learn, was giving support to the new Greenback party; Frances Willard, the president of the WCTU, was in the Prohibition party; others were in the Democratic camp. And, she wrote, "I dare say some of our women are fixing to go into the Republican caucus." Again she expressed disapproval of the Republican party, writing that she thought it should "die for its falseness of principle, but I do not see any better party struggling to take its place . . . all the parties are false to woman."[131]

Anthony and Ida Husted Harper would write in volume four of the *History of Women Suffrage,* published in 1902, that women "were wholly disregarded" in the platforms and shut out of the conventions from 1880 through 1892.[132] When suffragists asked the Republican National Committee for seventy-six tickets to the national convention in 1880, they were given only ten.[133] Anthony and Harper were wrong in their assessment that women were totally ignored by the Republican party from 1880 to 1892. Their calculation focused on their own efforts in the party in the 1880s and ignored other women who participated and created a new place for women in partisan politics.

The Party Appeal

After a deadlocked national convention went through thirty-six ballots, the Ohio Republican James Garfield won the presidential nomination in 1880, and as he prepared his campaign he had to make some serious choices about his allies. Garfield relied on his wife, Lucretia, for advice, and, according to one biographer, her "advice was moral as well as political."[134] She opposed the idea of allowing Roscoe Conkling, the powerful New York state senator and Republican party leader, into the inner circle. Instead, she championed James G. Blaine of Maine and his associate from New York, Whitelaw Reid. Lucretia Garfield had personal reasons for opposing Conkling's inclusion. She believed him to be of low morals; Conkling and Kate Chase Sprague were involved in a well-publicized extramarital affair. She also suspected that Sprague had a flirtation with her husband when she first arrived in Washington.[135]

Undeniably, many factors accounted for how politicians chose their political allies, but family connections, ideas of morality, and intimate feelings were often underlying if not overt factors in the decision. Whether or not James Garfield chose to side with Blaine instead of Conkling because of his wife's advice or because of other circumstances, the result of this decision was that his administration became saddled with an intense party factionalism that he could not overcome. Assassinated only months after his inauguration, Garfield left behind a divided Republican party. His successor, Chester Arthur, could not do much better to hold the party together, and the Republican party moved into the campaign of 1884 full of problems.

James G. Blaine, the secretary of state in the Garfield administration and one of the most charismatic men in the Republican party, possessed an ambition to become president that matched that of Kate Chase Sprague's father, Salmon Chase. In 1884 Blaine became the party's presidential candidate but was hampered by depictions of him as a corrupt politician in an era when political corruption had become so intolerable to many people that civil service reform bills were actually being enacted. In 1883, the Republican president Chester Arthur signed the Pendleton Act, which introduced merit into federal appointments and created the U.S. Civil Service Commission. Even the fact that Blaine was pitted against a Democrat who had been portrayed as an immoral man (Grover Cleveland had admitted to the "youthful indiscretion" of fathering the child of a woman he had not married) could not help him.

In a campaign that involved more mudslinging than discussion of issues, Republicans spurned the chance to wave the temperance flag by ignoring a memorial presented by the WCTU at the Republican nominating convention. Prohibition would make an appearance as a political issue in the campaign but not in the way that the Republicans had hoped. In spite of the trump card of Cleveland's character issue, Blaine's failure to denounce a Republican Presbyterian minister for associating Democrats with "Rum, Romanism, and Rebellion" in the last month of the campaign, as well as his continued association with industrial capitalists, harmed the party's efforts to build mass support. In the next campaign temperance women were welcomed and cheered as loyal Republican women.

Throughout the 1884 campaign, Republican women chose to present themselves as bearers of morality united with honorable men. In spite of their earlier denouncements of the party, Anthony and Stanton, along with Mary Livermore, issued a statement that called on women to "stand by the Republican party." These men, they declared, "are neither drunkards nor libertines and their relations with women are so noble that they will be accompanied to the national capital by wives and women friends of rare intelligence, high culture, and unquestioned moral worth."[136]

What kept women suffragists in the Republican fold, despite their view that the party had made the woman suffrage issue their "toy" and played with it "like the cat with the mouse in the fable"?[137] Why did they continue to believe that they needed to follow a partisan path, especially that forged by the Republican party? Individual loyalties and histories with the party that dominated national politics during the defining historical moment of the Civil War certainly played a part. The failure of political strategies such as the New Departure, where women attempted to use the Fourteenth Amendment as a political weapon, also forced women to retreat to party politics. Also important was their use of arguments for cooperation and complementary roles in politics. The political culture encouraged women to direct their arguments to the leaders and followers in political parties. Partisanship was imbedded in public life, "woven deeply and intricately" into society.[138] All these factors, plus the partial recognition given in the form of platform planks and the encouragement from party leaders to work in campaigns, led women into the partisan fray in the 1880s despite their disappointments.

There was another reason why women returned to support the Republican party. In her biography of Susan B. Anthony, Ida Husted Harper writes that Anthony and Stanton, "watching events from their secluded nook," were motivated to endorse the Republican party because of "the tendency of large numbers to rush to the support of the Prohibitionists, because of their suffrage plank; and they believed that if women were determined to work for some political party, the Republican at that time held out most hope."[139] At times, Anthony and other suffragists argued that they would support the party that supported woman suffrage; as Mary Ann Shadd Cary declared, African-American women suffragists "would support whatever party would allow them their rights, be it Republican or Democrat."[140] But with the appearance of third parties that attracted scores of women by supporting suffrage and giving women political visibility by electing them as delegates to conventions, which occurred not only in the Prohibition party but also in the Greenback and the Populist parties, Anthony and many other women retreated back to the Republican party. Anthony wrote Elizabeth Harbert that while suffragists should thank what she termed "minority reform parties" for their statements endorsing woman suffrage, she was suspicious of their next step. They "will cooperate with women just so long as women help them to fly their kite," she wrote, "but when the women ask the party to do something for them, then do they learn the fact that the party's purpose must hold precedence."[141] Anthony believed that issue-oriented parties like the Prohibition party would always put women's rights second.

And what of the new Equal Rights party, formed by Marietta Stow of California? In a newspaper she had established called the *Woman's Herald of Industry,* Stow asked, "Why not nominate women for important places? . . . Is not history full of precedents of women rulers?" The Republican party, she wrote, "has little else but insult for women," and so it was "quite time we had our own party; our own platform, and our own nominees. We shall never have equal rights until we take them, nor respect until we command it."[142] Long active in woman suffrage politics and more recently in the Greenback party, Stow announced in 1882 that she was running for governor of California as a candidate of the Woman's Independent Political party. By 1884 she was ready for national politics; she appropriated the name of Woodhull's Equal Rights party and decided to leave behind her platform of "anti-monopoly, anti-ring, and anti-Chinese" to concentrate solely on woman suffrage. She put forth the names of various women for president, and Belva Lockwood, a lawyer from Washington, D.C., accepted the honor.[143] Lockwood wrote in an autobiographical essay that she saw her candidacy as "the entering wedge, the first practical movement in the history of woman suffrage."[144]

Anthony had no use for any third party efforts, including those of the Equal Rights party. As she wrote a friend in Kansas, reflecting on the losing campaigns for woman suffrage there, the leading politicians of the "two parties, Peoples and Republican alike," must "make suffrage a party measure" through their conventions and newspapers. The lesson of defeat was that "when only one party puts a plank in the platform, it is used by the demagogues in the other party to make capital against woman suffrage."[145] Third parties might endorse women's rights and might have increased the vigor of partisan competition in the 1880s, but Anthony believed it best for women to steer away from them.

Party Clubs: Whose Idea?

The power of the third parties was seen in the election results of 1884. Divisions and coalitions led to the growth of the Democratic party and a loss for the Republicans. Grover Cleveland defeated James G. Blaine at the polls, and almost three decades of Republican dominance in national politics came to an end. The *New York Times* ran numerous articles after the election assessing what had happened and questioning what the Republican party would do now. The *Times* reported that Republican managers, especially those devoted to Blaine, were hard at work on a project that "deserves to rank as one of the brightest bits of far-sighted political work attempted in years." According to the paper, the project was a "woman's idea . . . and a shrewd one." Blaine did not take to it at first, but he soon came around. His wife's cousin, Mary Abigail Dodge, who wrote under the pen name Gail Hamilton, had "concocted the scheme" to which he was soon "converted."[146] The project was the formation of "permanent" Republican clubs.

Anthony had predicted in 1870 that when the Republicans "are out of power, they will betake themselves to the study of principles," and their loss of power would be "the only means by which conscience and courage can be injected into the heads and hearts of the Republicans, the only way to make them see the political necessity of enfranchising the women of the country and thereby securing their gratitude and through it their vote to place and hold that party in power."[147] Republicans did reflect on their loss of power in 1884, but their solution was not to give women equal rights. It was to give them auxiliary status.

3. Devotions and Disharmonies, 1881–1910

AT THE SAME time that Susan B. Anthony and other suffragists were exploring independent political paths outside the Republican party in the 1880s, other women were finding new ways to demonstrate their partisan loyalties and push for greater partisan rewards. Judith Ellen Foster, who founded the first woman's partisan organization formally recognized by the Republican party in 1888, was among those who challenged the retreat from the Republican party. The creation of the Woman's National Republican Association (WNRA) signaled a new phase for women in Republican party politics, and it contributed to a political debate among women about the consequences of partisanship and nonpartisanship. Unlike the debates and tensions of the late 1860s and 1870s, which were played out between Republican women and men, these new ones took place within women's reform organizations.

The association of women with nonpartisanship increased in the 1880s and 1890s despite the fact that women continued their partisan activism. This connection was based on an understanding of women as disinterested citizens upholding virtues and was manifested in the written and unwritten rules of women's reform organizations. Partisanship and nonpartisanship were not necessarily a contradiction for women at the end of the nineteenth century. But women's attempts to promote one path or the other, or hold both in balance, created new political tensions, shaped the development of the woman suffrage movement, and determined the development of the early years of the first national Republican women's auxiliary.

Judith Ellen Foster: Founder of the Woman's National Republican Association

In 1888 Judith Ellen Foster told women gathered in Washington for the first meeting of the International Council of Women that "Woman *is* in politics," but there was still the "unanswered question" of the form and meaning of women's relationship to politics. Drawing on observations from a recent trip to Europe, she questioned whether women's relationship to politics would be determined by the "mere accident of birth," as was Queen Victoria's. Maybe women would find their power through their use of "favor and caprice," as did the ladies of the imperial French court. Or they could act like the English Primrose Dames, who labored for the government without the vote. Turning to the United States, she said that women seeking government protections were in the "position of supplicants," like beggars, asking for help. Should American women, who "seek governmental protection for temperance, for education, for philanthropy, for industrial education," continue as beggars, pleading for favors and protections from their government?[1]

Her answer was a resounding no. American women needed all the political rights of men. The right to vote and hold public office would give them direct political power and enable them to enact their issues into legislation. Foster chose the last words of her speech before the International Council of Women with care, knowing they would be widely reprinted. She followed her call for gender equality with an emphasis on gender cooperation, stating, "Gentlemen, we do not threaten. No, no, no. We are of you and yours."[2]

Foster promoted a political strategy for women that recognized their historical exclusion from politics but also their aspirations to work with men in political parties.[3] She believed that women needed to engage in politics as nonpartisans and partisans. Her dedication to promoting both nonpartisanship and partisanship for women resulted in a political drama that played out in the WCTU and in the Republican party in the 1880s. It is a drama that underscores the diversity of women's political commitments, loyalties, and tactics at the end of the nineteenth century. It also highlights the passionate feelings that women invested in their politics and the powerful convictions that divided and united women.

Foster became the most famous woman in the Republican party at the end of the nineteenth century after she founded the WNRA in 1888 and built it into a organizing machine for the Republican party. Her interest in the Republican party was a result of her own individual political ideology, but it was also shaped by larger ideological and political currents. In the nineteenth century, faith in the millennial spirit decreased, women's reform politics increased with the establishment of single-issue organizations, and partial suffrage allowed women to place themselves as voters in the partisan world of politics. In this context, Foster's political career highlights women's partisan political choices. Her political differences with other women illustrate how important partisan identity was to women in the late nineteenth century.

Foster was born in Lowell, Massachusetts, in 1840 into a family whose ancestors fought in the American Revolution. Her father, Jotham Horton, was a Methodist minister who resigned from his church over the slavery issue; her mother was the daughter of a sea captain but was raised on a New England farm; and her brother "had been slain for speaking truth" about slavery. Her mother died when she was seven years old, and her father became her guide into the world, teaching her moral and political lessons, including the necessity of abolitionism as a moral choice and the "beauty of total abstinence" from liquor. According to one biographer, her background was religious, but the religion was "one of action. The future, while leaving her the notion of what woman is, might be expected radically to broaden her conception of what woman may do."[4]

By age fourteen, about the same time the Republican party was formed, Foster was an orphan, living first with her oldest married sister in Boston, where she attended the Charlestown Female Seminary, and later with another relative in Lima, New York, where she completed her schooling at the Genesee Wesleyan Seminary.[5] After graduating, she taught school until her first marriage to the Boston merchant Addison Avery in 1860, at the age of twenty. This marriage produced two children but ended in divorce after a few years. "'In the home of a brother,'" said a friend, "'she put on widow's weeds, sadder far than those that come at death.'"[6] Foster then moved to Chicago in 1868, lived with her brother, and supported her children by teaching music in a mission school. There she met and married Elijah C. Foster, a native of Canada and a recent graduate of the University of Michigan Law School. They moved to Clinton, Iowa, in 1869. Two more children completed the family.

Like a number of other women of her generation, Foster was introduced to her profession by her husband. He encouraged her to read law and supervised her education when she showed an interest in systematic study. She studied while raising her children and in 1872 became the first woman to be admitted to practice before the Iowa State Supreme Court. The Fosters established a law firm, Foster and Foster.[7]

Foster's partisan identity as a Republican came from her family's abolitionist background. She believed that the Republican party "is the party of action; its breath is progress; its speech is the language of the world; its dialect the rhetoric of the home and the farm and the shop." She also saw it as the leader on the important issues of the day, including temperance. "Its heroic constituencies are the thinking, moving, vital elements of American life. It holds within its ranks the armies of all reforms," she said.[8] Further contributing to Foster's partisan identity was an ability to focus on national as well as local issues and a willingness and desire to play a prominent part in national organizations for reform. Her professional identity as a lawyer may also have increased her confidence to act politically in male-dominated spheres.

The Fosters also worked side by side in the Iowa State Temperance Alliance.[9] Their legal work revolved around efforts to close down the saloons in their community. Whatever her personal motivation, whether it stemmed from her father's influence or her own political awareness, in 1873 Foster founded the Woman's Temperance Society of Clinton. In the same year, Eliza Stewart formed the Woman's League of Osborn, Ohio, and when the national WCTU was formed a year later at a conference in Cleveland, Ohio, this league became the first local chapter. The WCTU was an independent, nonpartisan organization of women that was born out of the crusades by midwestern women to close down saloons; its tactics were prayer vigils and friendly visits. These temperance activists saw the problem of drinking in moral and economic terms; families were harmed by the effects of alcohol when husbands and fathers spent paychecks in saloons.[10]

In 1879 Frances Willard became the president of the WCTU and built it into the largest women's reform organization of the late nineteenth century. While sentimental appeals would always be mixed in among the legal and economic analyses of the demon rum, and conventions would always be about songs, prayers, and presentations of bouquets, women's day-to-day organizing for temperance moved away from friendly visitors and moral suasion under Willard's leadership. Temperance workers generally believed that moral and legal suasion could coexist, but they emphasized the political sphere as the target for reform.[11]

Unlike Annie Wittenmyer, her predecessor who would withdraw from the organization with other antisuffragists in 1881, Willard strongly advocated woman suffrage, or the "home protection ballot." She believed that women had already gone through the stages of "petition work, local-option work, and constitutional-prohibition-amendment work" and that they had come to the stage where they needed to work for the ballot as a "home protection" weapon.[12] Willard called for direct action without ambiguity: Women must have the vote, they must let officials know they will not vote for them if they license saloons, and the result will be that *all* voters and *all* politicians will support prohibition.

Willard also believed that state and local unions should have a flexible relationship, except for dues, to the national organization, choosing their own programs and plans of action. To strengthen the connection between local unions and the national, and to fill the national's coffers, she established a system of selecting delegates to national conventions based on actual paid membership. After she was reelected in 1880, "political influence and power became one of her major concerns."[13]

What of women's immediate actions? What could they do until more women had the vote? Willard believed women could have the most influence by working to keep "politics from forming with the worst elements of society." She encouraged women to go to primary meetings in "the smaller and more reputable communities" to be "in at the birth" of bills and platforms. Waiting to attend a legislature, with the "enemy entrenched," is to be "in at the death." "Every effort," she argued, including attending primaries or registering opinions of temperance, "helps to obliterate party lines; or, more correctly, to mass the moral elements by which alone society coheres, against the disintegrating forces, which of themselves would drive us into chaos and old night."[14]

In 1880 Willard was invited to the national convention of the Prohibition party. According to contemporary reports, she was a sympathetic Republican and therefore declined the invitation, even though other prominent temperance women thought it an important political alliance.[15] She openly backed Garfield for president, but when he failed to endorse prohibition after he won she began working on an alliance between the WCTU and the Prohibition party. In the summer of 1881, Willard attended the National Temperance Society meeting in Saratoga, New York, and then the Prohibition party's Lake Bluff Convocation, outside Chicago. The strategy she finally implemented was well thought out and complemented the new WCTU "Do Everything" policy.[16]

Willard organized home protection clubs that were independent of the WCTU. They provided support within the union for Prohibition party affiliation as well as a constituency for WCTU-based influence at Prohibition party meetings. By the next year, her strategy had worked; the party was renamed the Prohibition Home Protection party, and Willard became a member of its central committee. She asked members of the WCTU who attended the 1881 national convention in Washington for pledges of allegiance to the new party, which would "unite North and South, help the work of constitutional prohibition and the enfranchisement of women."[17]

Willard's attempt to use the WCTU to promote and work with the Prohibition party prompted a major controversy within the movement. Her primary opponent in this matter was her good friend Judith Ellen Foster, who had become a major temperance player when the local Iowa women's temperance leagues affiliated with the national WCTU. She was elected to the office of superintendent of the Legislative Department (also known as the Office of Legislation and Petition), which she officially held until 1890, and she authored the organization's first constitution. According to Willard, the WCTU benefited from Foster's legal abilities, keen mind, and moral steadfastness. "Mrs. Foster's life, since the crusade of 1874, is part and parcel of the WCTU. She has never been absent from one of our national conventions, and her quick brain, ready and pointed utterance, and rare knowledge of parliamentary forms, have added incalculably to the success of these great meetings."[18] Foster noted, in return, her dedication to both Willard and the WCTU. "I loved her with a chivalrous devotion not common among women," she wrote in 1884. "My admiration was absolute and unquestioning. . . . I did not question her methods or exercise my judgment concerning them—I was only too happy to follow where she led."[19]

Partisanship and Nonpartisanship in the WCTU

Foster easily balanced her partisanship and nonpartisanship until the early 1880s, when she learned that Willard, as part of her "Do Everything" strategy, planned for WCTU women to move into partisan politics as the Home Protection party, merge with the Prohibition party, and create a new Prohibition Home Protection party.[20] As early as the Lake Bluff Convocation, Foster refused to allow the Iowa delegation to join the Prohibition Home Protection party. She advocated a formal policy of nonpartisanship for the WCTU.

Though a Republican, Foster did not argue from her partisan position. Instead, she argued that the WCTU should be nonpartisan because of the nature of the temperance question and the process of political change. She stated that temperance reforms "should be kept outside of *party* political action until the people through non-partisan agencies have secured so great popular support for these reforms that they may be safely championed by political parties." Different groups should educate and agitate, she asserted, and then legislation will be "secured through non-partisan measures. Then comes the machinery of the party and holds fast what has been secured through these other agencies." Nonpartisanship protected temperance legislation "from the varying fortunes of party politics," she concluded.[21] "What has the WCTU to do with tariffs or free trade, with hard or soft money, with railroads or mines?"[22]

As for the Republican party, she believed that neither women nor men had the right to ask it to insert a prohibition plank in its platform. She perceived temperance to be a moral and constitutional question. All parties, all voters, and all Americans should view temperance "on a moral plane, wholly apart from their views on tariff and soft money. . . . To marry the moral question and the political party would be quite too grotesque; it would mean the subjection of one and perhaps, in the end, the ruin of both." Foster believed that the Republican party, "seated in power for its strictly political doctrines, would from mere weight of moral excellence in its ranks, do more for temperance—as individuals—than any other party could."[23] She also believed that the Republican party could help other reform causes without creating official alliances. She was a suffragist and had seen what women's partisan differences were doing to that movement.

In an 1888 Republican party pamphlet, "The Republican Party and Temperance," Foster explored the historical and contemporary relationship between party and temperance ideology. To Foster, the 1888 race between Benjamin Harrison and Grover Cleveland was a "campaign of ideas," and the major issue was "the promotion of temperance and morality." Rather than focus on the moral side of the issue, Foster took a pragmatic view. She began by enumerating the states where Republican majorities had contributed to the passage of prohibition laws—in Maine, Vermont, Kansas, Iowa, and Rhode Island—and where the Democratic party had become the "open ally of the saloon." In what is a pointed criticism of the WCTU more than the Prohibition party, she stated that "as Republicans we deny the charges" made by the third party press and party platforms that the Republican party was less an advocate for "God, Home, and Native Land" than was the Prohibition party.[24]

Foster argued that in politics one must concentrate not on the individual but on the masses. Identifying herself as a woman and a temperance worker, she wrote that a voter should vote for men who advocate measures "most nearly approaching his ideal," but at the same time the "general welfare of the body politic should always be considered." This could only happen if one believed that their ideals were the correct ones for the survival of the nation. Foster believed in her ideals as such and saw the moral Republican party as the avenue of those ideals. The political party was the central place for action because the vote was the ultimate moral action in a democracy. Foster wrote: "With these solemn convictions and in these crucial times, political duties become sacred, even as religious vows: and the ballot-box a holy shrine."[25]

If temperance was not enough of an issue to convince voters to come into the Republican fold, Foster paraded the other issues that made the party more "humane," "progressive," and "moral" than the other choices before voters.

It stood for preservation of the union, the abolition of slavery, the work of reconstruction and internal improvements, and the promotion of labor and popular education. It was, in essence, a moral voice built on traditions in an increasingly nonmoral world, and Foster ignored the questions raised by others about the corrupting aspects of patronage and spoils.[26]

Ironically, it was through the language of nonpartisanship that Foster justified her partisan actions.[27] In an 1889 pamphlet, *The Saloon Must Go,* she explored in more depth the possibilities of a constitutional amendment for prohibition. But, as in her 1888 writing, the issue of partisanship is highlighted and pronounced: "Blind partisanship is inimical to patriotism; moral questions are likely to suffer when subject to the vicissitudes of party politics; but the temperance question when discussed on its own merits and before the whole people, secures popular approval by the cohesive power of truth." Thus she argued for constitutional prohibition, stating that "every legislator is sworn to defend the Constitution."[28]

Willard saw things differently. She stated that if women worked with the Prohibition party they would be "in at the birth" of bills and platforms, and they would help elect men who would forward their crusade.[29] "Moral suasion leads to legal suasion, and that involves in its national phases political suasion," she stated."[30] Ignored by the major parties, Willard believed that women's only place was in the Prohibition party.

Foster protested.[31] At every WCTU annual convention from 1882 until 1888, her resolutions that the WCTU enact a policy of nonpartisanship were debated and tabled. At the 1888 convention, in a move that everyone understood as demonstrating total support for the Prohibition party, the WCTU voted to back any party that endorsed prohibition and "home protection." Foster again sought to issue her protest but was refused a hearing.

Frances Willard's leadership in this transformation of policy is evident. In her annual presidential address of 1885 she used the imagery of being on the inside, at the beginning of things. She stated that "what we care for most is not tidings from the rear but 'news from the front.'" Calling her union an army, she immediately took on the question at hand: "the large majority, from a national outlook or an earnest conviction or both, were ready to declare that a party committed to the prohibition of the liquor traffic is the supreme need of the present time."[32]

What of the other parties? Willard argued that the "two great parties that are to millions of men the idols of the hour, do not enshrine our principles, and are but extinct volcanoes of past eruptions from the people's heart." She came down equally hard on both parties: "the Democratic party is the open party while the Republican is the secret ally of the liquor oligarchy in the realm of national politics. . . . We want the Democratic party to bite the dust, and will do our utmost to work its final overthrow."[33]

Refering to the defeat of Republicans in 1884, Willard stated that "a great party, long accustomed to the bewildering prerogatives of power, was hurled from its high place, and seeking for a scapegoat, turned in the fierceness of its baffled rage, and poured out its vials of wrath upon the devoted heads of women, who, up to that hour, had been accounted thoughtful, trustworthy, and patriotic."[34] Whether she had experienced or observed this rage against women from professional contacts or through public avenues such as the press, she turned the condemnation around. Republicans were no longer the natural allies for women reformers because they were guilty of blaming women for their loss of popularity.

If the reason for working against the Democrats and Republicans was that they were "the two sworn allies of the saloon," then what was the reason for pledging influence to any party, especially to a new party? The reason for Willard was clear. Nonpartisanship would keep women at the end of the army, outside positions of power. "Does not our nonpartisanship help the two old parties?" she asked. "Do we aid the new political movement that will tackle the liquor traffic and afterward shackle it, by remaining 'strictly non-partisan?' We are just far enough removed from the realm of 'practical politics' to see this new force on its ideal side. We are just enough developed on the faith side to carry it steadily in our prayers. We are just independent enough of obligations to capitalists and corporations, I mean just poor enough, to be able to say precisely what we think."[35]

Women, Willard believed, must be partisan. But what did she propose that the WCTU do? "I answer," she wrote, "we have simply let it be known to the whole world that we have discovered that the saloon is entrenched in politics even more firmly than in law, and that our sympathies, appreciation, and gratitude must necessarily go with the voters who carry this issue straight to the caucus, the convention, and the ballot-box. . . . We have, alas! no votes to give, but if we had, and when we get them, they shall count solidly for the [Prohibition] party."[36] Willard had countered the one stumbling block between male voters and female nonvoters. She found a way, in pledging the affiliation of her strong WCTU to the Prohibition party, to give and court favors, to have something to trade. She created bonds of loyalty and was leading women on the third party path that Susan B. Anthony was rejecting. Where Anthony had argued that a third party built on a single issue would ignore women's rights after they had used up women's energies, Willard saw herself as leading a crusade to transform public life and political culture for women and for men.[37]

Foster and her supporters attempted another avenue of protest. They refused to pay their dues to the national treasury, claiming that these were diverted to party political work. The WCTU responded by passing a resolution stating that anyone unfriendly to the Prohibition party "is hereby declared disloyal to our organization." With Foster leading the way, a group of women bolted the national organization. Foster and Ellen Phinney of Ohio established the Nonpartisan Woman's Christian Temperance Union (NPWCTU) as a rival to the national WCTU.

The differences between Foster and Willard throughout the 1880s highlight women's passionate feelings about their politics and show the convictions that divided and united women. Foster wrote Willard in 1884, "I thought you loved and trusted me. I thought I had proved my devotion." Foster declared to Willard that she loved her, "as I have never loved any other woman. Even in this I say to myself, 'she did not *intend* to hurt, she was so intent on accomplishing the plans which to her seemed just and good that she looked neither to the right or to the left.'" Then Foster finally got to the point: "But better than I love any human friend I love the interests of our WCTU work." That love led Foster to her protests, her defection, and her attempt to recreate what she believed to be the original intent of the WCTU in her new organization, the NPWCTU.[38]

Foster wrote an open letter to the WCTU women left behind, assailing them for personal attacks on her over the years as she promoted a nonpartisan policy for the WCTU while maintaining her Republican loyalties. Why, she asked, were other women allowed to exercise their freedom of political action without censure while Republican women were "subject to impeachment?"[39] Foster may have been disingenuous about her reasons for promoting nonpartisanship in the WCTU, as some women seemed to think. She may have wanted to protect the organization as a bastion for Republicans, who were fearful of losing women's support to the Prohibition party. Or she may have honestly believed that nonpartisanship was the only course for such a large national organization of women with different partisan loyalties. She may have also believed her own analysis that legislation on moral questions such as temperance was best pursued and protected outside partisan politics. Whatever her motivation and purpose, her action split the WCTU.

Foster's new NPWCTU proclaimed that it would "leave every individual member of our organization absolutely free to choose her party alliance and to follow her political convictions." Every woman, Foster wrote, should "respect the conscientious convictions of every other woman. . . . [and] any abridgment of this is a violation of the spirit of political liberty which underlies the Republic." Because they lacked the power of the ballot, women were encouraged to use their "influence" in the moral and political crusade for temperance and prohibition.[40] Foster hoped the NPWCTU would be a legitimate counterorganization to the WCTU, and she gathered around her a group of supportive women, including Florence Collins Porter of Maine, who became the recording secretary of the NPWCTU, and Ellen Phinney of Ohio, who became president of the organization in 1894.[41] Most early supporters of the NPWCTU came from Iowa, Pennsylvania, Massachusetts, and Ohio. A temperance woman ran the risk of being expelled from her local or state WCTU if she joined the NPWCTU. Marietta Bones, for example, had been president of the Webster, Nebraska, WCTU but was thrown out after attending the NPWCTU convention in Chicago in 1889 and accepting the position of secretary to that organization.[42]

The NPWCTU published the *Temperance Tribune* after consolidating three state WCTU papers: the *Iowa Messenger,* the *White Ribbon* of Pennsylvania, and the *Ohio State Paper.* Mrs. Joseph Weeks of Pittsburgh became the editor, and Mrs C. C. Alford of Bernardston, Massachusetts, was the publisher. In addition to the national *Temperance Tribune,* the NPWCTU published about sixteen general pamphlets. Fully half of the 1894 pamphlets concentrated on why the WCTU should be nonpartisan and why women should join the NPWCTU. Yet the contents of the other pamphlets and the divisions listing work within the *Tribune* show that much of their work continued to be "nonpolitical." Church meetings, "uplifting the poor," the education of children, and assistance to shut-ins were consistently reported as work undertaken by women across the country. Their departments included the Young Women's Work; Education; Evangelistic; Army, Navy, and Marine Corps; Literature; Industrial Training; Social Purity; and Mothers' Leaflets.[43]

The Woman's National Republican Association

The NPWCTU was only one avenue toward political power and influence that Foster followed after her official break with the WCTU. She attended meetings of the NWSA and became involved in the Woman's National Press Association.[44] She attended meetings of the National Council of Women of the United States and the Association for the Advancement of Women, where she stated that the "great service for woman is that in which woman forgets that she is woman and only remembers she is human."[45] For all her promotion of women's nonpartisanship, Foster was also a loyal Republican. So at the same time that she promoted women's nonpartisanship, she created a new space for women in partisan politics. In 1884 she campaigned for James Blaine, but her efforts began in earnest four years later.

In 1888 Foster attended meetings of "Anti-Saloon Republicans" in New York City and Chicago to support the call for a temperance plank in the Republican platform. In 1884 the party had ignored the temperance memorial presented by the WCTU, and some party leaders believed that any recognition of the temperance issue might have helped the party. As a result, at the June national convention the Republican party adopted a platform that included a weak resolution stating that the party "cordially sympathizes with all wise and well-directed efforts for the promotion of temperance and morality." It did not call for the abolition of the liquor trade. It was also silent on the question of equal suffrage.[46]

Foster ignored the party's silences and forged ahead. Her strategy was to establish a national organization of Republican women. In 1888 she used her connections to James Clarkson, the owner of a Des Moines, Iowa, Republican newspaper, a national Republican committeeman, and the founder of the National League of Republican Clubs, to gain entree into her favored Republican party.[47] Clarkson "more than any other man . . . revolutionized the political style of the Republican party in the late 'eighties and early 'nineties." He was a strong partisan who "would never lose his distaste for liberals," but who realized that a "middle course between traditional politics and reform" had to be steered.[48] At the same time that he recognized that independents had to be taken seriously within the party, he saw that the "spectacular appeals" to voters had lost their power. According to Clarkson, speaking before the Republican League of Clubs in 1893 about the campaign of 1884:

> All men who were active in that campaign will remember the surprise that came when the brass band, the red light, and the mass meeting seemed suddenly to have lost their power. That was the beginning of the change of political discussion from the open field, as in Lincoln's day, to the private home where each family began to examine and discuss for itself the policy of the parties to find which party promised the most for the elevation and comfort of that special home. It was an evolutionary result, arising from the demand of changing conditions from sentimental to economic issues—the evolution into education as the superior force in American politics.[49]

The way he chose to pursue this course, which has been called "educational politics," was to establish party clubs made up of the "best men in the community." For many, these clubs were a way to revive interest in the Republican party. For others, they were a means of municipal reform. For many women, they probably served these ends. They also gave women their first chance to organize and affiliate formally with the Republican party on a national level.

Politically, Clarkson and Foster were made for each other. They both had long histories in Iowa Republican politics; both disdained independent factions within the party that led to third parties; and both were dedicated to making the party stronger. For Clarkson that meant a centralized and efficient way to educate voters using the National League of Republican Clubs, established in 1887 as an arm of the Republican National Committee (RNC) to coordinate the efforts of the party clubs around the country. The RNC created the educational propaganda, and the league's clubs disseminated it.[50]

Alienated from the WCTU and having secured her nonpartisanship ideology in the cubbyhole of the NPWCTU, Foster went before the RNC in 1888 and proposed that the party recognize the establishment of the newly created WNRA.[51] When Benjamin Harrison of Indiana received the party's nomination for president, Foster wrote him that she was "busily engaged making plans for the organization of Women's Republican Clubs." She declared that she hoped "this new departure may be useful" and that she had received the "kind approval and assistance of the National Committee."[52] When the RNC officially recognized the WNRA, Foster became its first president and moved into offices that adjoined the RNC's in New York City.[53]

The WNRA was, in one sense, simply one of the hundreds of political clubs formed in the late nineteenth century.[54] Like other political clubs, it was revived during campaigns, lay dormant in between election years, and was guided by one or a few leaders who determined the influence and strength of the clubs. In their first campaign in 1888, Republican women across the country organized and campaigned for Harrison. The clubs they established looked similar to those created for early campaigns. They displayed banners of the candidates and their wives, gave speeches, and attended mass rallies.[55] They were determined to win back the White House, and they did.

The difference between the clubs that were formed before 1888 and those formed after was that the earlier ones were individual community efforts. With the establishment of the WNRA, women understood themselves as part of a national Republican women's effort. By 1892, fifteen state and numerous local clubs came under the banner of the WNRA, and maybe as many as one thousand existed in 1910.[56] Their object was to unite the community of women "in educational work and social influence for the maintenance of the principles of the Republican party in the home, in the state and in the nation." The clubs had three mandates. First, the women were to stimulate the study of government. This was carried on through an extension course in political education. The popular nonpartisan book series on history, civil government, and economics, "The Home and the Flag Reading Course," was recommended. These were to be followed by a series of papers and pamphlets that contained political news and arguments. Second, the women were to discuss and circulate party literature and pressure voters, especially first-time voters. Women were also directed to vote in all elections for which they qualified. Women were given sample ballots to learn the process in the comfort and safety of their own homes. Third, women, through the NRWA, were to work in all important local elections. Foster saw one of her major jobs to be advising "women to ignore the lures of total prohibition in general and the Prohibition party in particular."[57]

African-American women also organized on behalf of the Republican party in the 1880s, and sources indicate that they were welcomed under the WNRA umbrella. For example, a "Colored Harrison and Morton Campaign Club" was organized in the Nineteenth Assembly District in New York City in 1888. According to the *New York Herald,* the district was populated with "Virginia negroes" who were being "colonized" by Republicans.[58] Two white members of the WNRA, Mrs. F. T. Ovington of Clinton, Iowa, and Helen Boswell of New York City, helped organize about thirty black women into the Women's Republican Association of the Eleventh Assembly District of New York in 1892. Mary L. Hall was elected president and Alice Randolph secretary. The association, reported the *New York Tribune,* was "composed exclusively of colored women."[59]

A clipping reproduced in the WCTU papers, probably from a New York newspaper in 1892, includes information on this "Colored Ladies' Republican Club of the Eleventh Assembly District." It notes that the club was organized as an "auxiliary to Lawyer J. Ellen Foster's Woman's Republican Association." Reprinted next to this clipping is a newspaper cartoon titled "Campaign News from Republican Headquarters." It shows a mammy caricature of a black woman with bandanna, apron, kinky hair, large white lips, and bulging eyes addressing seven similarly drawn women from behind a wooden crate. On the wall are portraits representing Harrison and Reid. At the bottom of the drawing is the phrase, "The Thompson Street Influence Club is now fully organized." Black women and men participated in partisan politics within the political context of exclusionary policies and the social context of racism.[60]

Anna Dickinson and the Campaign of 1888

At the same time that Judith Ellen Foster and James Clarkson were working out a strategy for the WNRA, Clarkson approached another woman to work in the 1888 campaign. In the 1870s, Anna Dickinson maintained a place in the public eye by giving lectures, publishing books and plays, and appearing on the stage, but by the 1880s her fame had diminished, and she spent most of her time at home in West Pittston, Pennsylvania. Clarkson hired her to give twenty to thirty speeches at $100 to $125 each.[61] They even discussed the monies the Republicans owed her from earlier campaigns.[62]

Dickinson's new partisan career did not last long. Instead of concentrating on the political issue of the day, the tariff, she chose to "wave the bloody flag" and criticize Congress and the South for infringing on the rights of African Americans.[63] In the Midwest, she found that her speeches were not publicized or even organized. Returning east, she had even more trouble getting the party leaders to follow through on their commitments. They saw themselves as easing her off the stump; she felt that they had pushed her.[64] Clarkson would later say that the party had difficulty booking Dickinson because state committee chairmen had a "considerable hesitancy" about letting a woman be admitted into "the rush, noise, excitement, and cheer of political meetings," let alone allowing her to speak at them.[65] But Dickinson's gender was simply an excuse. The party did not like her message.

Benjamin Harrison defeated Grover Cleveland in 1888, and Dickinson's fury contrasted starkly with most Republicans' joy. In one of her last pieces of correspondence with Clarkson, she wrote to remind him that when she had agreed to work for the Republicans he had said, "the terms shall be as *we* propose them."[66] Her telegram was prompted by the fact that the party was refusing to pay her full fees. There was a dispute about the amount promised, and she was determined to be paid $4,250, the sum of $125 for thirty speeches plus a $500 bonus for Harrison's victory.[67] When party leaders called the amount excessive, Dickinson filed a suit against the RNC. She appealed to the president; he referred the matter back to the RNC.[68] The suit was dismissed on a technicality.

In 1895 and 1897 Dickinson again appeared in court, this time in suits against the doctors who, upon orders from her sister, committed her to the State Hospital for the Insane in Danville, Pennsylvania.[69] She won the suit for false and malicious confinement in 1897 and retreated to her home in Goshen, New York. She never received any monies from the Republican party, even though she tried in 1907 and 1908 to persuade former partisan allies and Republican leaders to take up her cause. They either refused or ignored her requests.[70] Anna Dickinson's death on October 22, 1932, at the age of eighty-nine, went unnoticed as Republicans engaged in the losing campaign that would keep them out of the White House until the election of Dwight D. Eisenhower twenty years later.

Political Campaigns and Partisan Rewards

The campaign of 1888 was a new experience for Judith Ellen Foster. Foster loved campaigns. In a speech delivered in Woodstock, Connecticut, in 1888, she said: "All hail election day! All hail the campaign which precedes it. Its pyrotechnics in music, in ornamentation, in human voices; its stirring of human passions and human activities; these for the time being are touched with heroic significance, and the ordinary citizen feels himself a part of the great mass of humanity, thrilled with its joys and touched by the sorrows of its universal heart."[71] She followed the party line and spoke for the protective tariff.[72] Temperance was not on the agenda of the Republican party's national leaders, but it was on Foster's. To speak for her cause, however, she had to be careful in how she addressed the issue. Her speeches were mainly attacks on the Prohibition party.

At the large Republican rally in Woodstock, Connecticut, Foster criticized the alliance of the Prohibition party and the WCTU. She stated: "It is boasted that the Third Party is the only political party which honors woman. Honors woman indeed! It appropriates her work and her influence to its own purposes and pays in fulsome flatteries; it gives to women seats in conventions and places their names on meaningless committees and tickets impossible of success. Flattery is cheap, full conventions are desirable, women's social and religious influence adds respectability to this propaganda."[73] She knew that women and men would understand her use of the word "influence"—it represented not only women's formal exclusion from electoral politics, because they were disfranchised, but also their identification as protectors of the weak.

While Foster criticized the Prohibition party for offering women only "flatteries," she was criticized herself for rewards of "sundry gifts of office, if not of money." The NPWCTU was seen as a front for the Republican party. Elijah Foster, the *New York Times* reported in 1891, was appointed general agent of the Department of Justice "at a salary of $3,600 a year." Rufus Tilton, the husband of Foster's "chief lieutenant," was a clerk in the Second Controller's office "at a fat salary," and "other able supporters of the 'Non-Partisan Woman's Christian Temperance Union,' have also comfortable berths at the public crib."[74]

Foster did seek and receive rewards, including the government appointment for her husband.[75] Working for the Republican party had certainly changed her life. The Fosters moved from Iowa to Washington, D.C. During campaign seasons, Judith Ellen Foster was either at the offices of the WNRA or was traveling the country as a speaker and organizer. She was never shy about promoting not only women in the party but also herself, her family, and her colleagues. She continually asked for and received various appointments from successive Republican presidents.[76] She was appointed to a committee to examine the impact of working conditions on wage-earning women in Massachusetts and Rhode Island. After a tour of factories in those states, she escorted sixteen working women to testify before the Finance Committee of the U.S. Senate as part of an effort to lobby for a protective tariff.[77]

Foster asked William McKinley for an appointment to the Industrial Commission.[78] He appointed her to inspect mobilization stations during the Spanish-American War. Theodore Roosevelt appointed her to investigate the status of women in the Philippines with the Taft Commission, as a U.S. representative to the International Red Cross Conference, and to study the working conditions of women and children in the United States.[79] William Howard Taft appointed her to inspect the prison system as a special agent of the Department of Justice.[80] In 1891, however, Foster did not perceive that she made enough money from her Republican connections, so she established herself as a circuit lecturer. "After all these years of public service," she wrote, "I am concluding that it is time I made money for myself."[81] Stump speaking for candidates often led to the lyceum and lecture circuit and offered speakers a way to make money between campaigns.

Foster's major partisan effort always was to increase women's presence and influence in the Republican party. It was an ongoing struggle, requiring constant reminders to the men of the party that women were able and willing volunteers. During the 1892 campaign the WNRA issued an appeal: "Republican Women: Please Take Action." It informed women that the WNRA was officially recognized by the RNC and had been invited by the Executive Committee of the National Republican League to attend its next convention. All Republican women were encouraged to attend, because "such opportunities are rare in the lives of women."[82] Republican women took action.

The 1892 Republican nominating convention in Minneapolis was a stunning convention for women. Women attended as official delegates for the first time, when the suffrage state of Wyoming sent Theresa A. Jenkins and Cora Carleton as alternate delegates.[83] Their presence was the result of Foster's efforts as well as an indication of the organizational work women were doing in suffrage states.[84] Jenkins had moved to Cheyenne, Wyoming, with her husband in 1877. She joined the WCTU in 1883 during a visit by Willard and helped organize the territorial WCTU. She was a celebrity in Wyoming politics and had been honored with the first speech at the official celebration for Wyoming's statehood in Cheyenne in 1890.[85] Invited to speak at the convention, she stated, "I am only here by the courtesy of the State." Her words echoed those of Foster, who told the assembled delegates, "We are here to help you. And we have come to stay."[86] Not one newspaper in the country "had a slur to cast" on the women at the 1892 convention.[87]

It is difficult to determine which women attended conventions in an "official" capacity in these years, and this is true for both black and white women. The difficulty is evident in a report about the Republican party leader Richard T. Greener's attempt in 1895 to gain recognition for African-American

women at a convention of Republicans meeting in Detroit, Michigan. Josephine St. Pierre Ruffin, Margaret Murray Washington, and Victoria Earle
Matthews, all representing the National Federation of Afro-American Wom-
en (NFAAW), were invited to the convention, and, according to one historian, Greener "succeeded in obtaining for the first time representation for Black
women at a Republican National Convention."[88] Whether these women were
there in service to the party or to lobby for their own cause is unclear.[89]

As they embarked on building a united national movement of black wom-
en, members of the NFAAW questioned their relationship to partisan politics. Like other women's groups, the NFAAW and its successor, the National
Association of Colored Women (NACW), also needed to discuss and resolve
organizational and individual members' relationships to partisan politics.
The NACW was founded in 1896 when the NFAAW merged with the National
League of Colored Women. The Republican loyalist Mary Church Terrell was
elected as the NACW's first president. Among those who led the new national
African-American women's club movement were the women at the 1892
convention. Margaret Murray Washington was a graduate of Fisk University, a principal at Tuskegee Institute, the wife of its president, Booker T. Washington, and the founder of the Tuskegee Woman's Club and the NFAAW.
Victoria Earle Matthews was a journalist who wrote for the leading black
newspapers of the day as well as for the *New York Times* and the *New York
Herald*. Through the *New York Age*, she championed Ida B. Wells's antilynch-
ing crusade. When the NFAAW was founded, she became a member of the
executive board and joined the editorial staff of its official journal. She would
go on to found a settlement house for women and girls, the White Rose
Mission in New York City, and become a lecturer.[90]

Josephine St. Pierre Ruffin worked for the United States Sanitary Commission during the Civil War and became active in women's clubs and reform
organizations during Reconstruction. From her home in Boston, Ruffin established the New Era Club in 1893, became its president, affiliated the club
with the Massachusetts State Federation of Women's Clubs, and edited the
first newspaper published by black women, the *Woman's Era*. She initiated
the call that resulted in the founding conference of the NFAAW; she sent out
the summons for women to meet after a southern white male journalist attacked the character of all black women. Her aim was to bring women together to discuss, demonstrate, and teach "an ignorant and suspicious world
that our aims and interests are identical with those of good aspiring wom-
en." Among the resolutions from the first NFAAW meeting was one that
"commended the Republican party for condemning lynching in its platform
and voiced regret that the Democrats did not."[91]

The NACW leader Fannie Williams argued that black women needed to pursue their "'political duties with no better and higher conceptions of our citizenship than shown by our men when they were first enfranchised,'" and this meant staying away from the "'spoilsmen and bigoted partisans.'"[92] Josephine Silon Yates agreed and argued that if the NACW went "after crosscuts and by-paths, it is doomed to the same death that has beset so many national bodies."[93] The nonpartisan argument held sway, and the NACW established itself as a nonpartisan organization. However, many African-American club women affiliated with the NACW were Republican loyalists, and so, at the same time that they built the club movement, they organized themselves into local Republican clubs, such as the Colored Women's Republican Club of Denver, Colorado, where black women mobilized to vote in a larger percentage than white women in the 1906 election.[94]

The route to national conventions might have been through organizations such as the NACW or the WNRA, but it was more often through local partisan clubs and through family connections. As a result of her work as the president of the Woman's Republican Club of Salt Lake City, Utah, Mrs. William H. Jones became one of two women alternate delegates to the 1900 Republican National Convention; the other was Susan West of Idaho. Four years later, West again attended the national convention as an alternate delegate and was joined this time by Eva Le Ferve and Emma C. Eldridge, alternates from Colorado, and Jennie B. Nelson, an alternate from Utah. Full delegate status came in 1908 to two Utah women, Lucy Clark and Susa Young Gates.[95]

Even though Republican women heeded Foster's call to action in 1892, the Democrats swept into office. Just before the campaign ended Foster wrote President Harrison: "In this campaign, as never before, the Republican party has recognized its women sympathizers. With solemn joy I feel the responsibilities of leadership. I am doing the best I can."[96] But behind this public mask of optimism and cooperation was frustration. Not only was the party again out of power, but its continued silence on the questions of temperance and woman suffrage disappointed Foster, who wrote to a friend that she was "at a loss to understand" the silence.[97]

Foster's fame as a Republican organizer grew during the campaigns of 1892, 1894, and 1896, as she successfully organized African-American and white women all over the Northeast and in the West.[98] In 1894 and 1896, the RNC sent her to Colorado and Wyoming to organize women voters. A long, hard-fought, but well-organized battle for woman suffrage in Colorado had been victorious in 1893 with the passage of a state referendum after Republicans recognized that the Populist party would hold on to its new power partly through the votes of women; the Populists supported woman suffrage. Foster stumped Colorado, and Republican women in Denver formed a "powerful organization," the East Capitol Hill Woman's Republican League.[99] The victory of the Republican party in Colorado, including the election of the Republicans Carrie Clyde Holly, Frances S. Klock, and Clara Cressingham, the first women state legislators elected in the country, not only increased Foster's fame in Republican circles. It also increased party leaders' understanding that voting women needed some attention paid to them.[100] Republicans rewarded Colorado women by instituting a system of male and female cochairs at the ward level in Denver and Boulder. They also began organizing the counties through gender-integrated teams.[101] This system, called "fifty-fifty," was an important precedent for organizing women into political parties, and as the passage of the Nineteenth Amendment became imminent, the suffrage leader and journalist Ellis Meredith helped bring the Colorado idea to national party politics.[102]

It would be a while before Republicans addressed the question of equality in party organizations, but the 1896 national Republican platform contains the following statement: "The Republican party is mindful of the rights and interests of women. Protection of American industries includes equal opportunities, equal pay for equal work, and protection to the home. We favor the admission of women to wider spheres of usefulness, and welcome their cooperation in rescuing the country from Democratic mismanagement and Populist misrule." It was enough to keep Foster hard at work. Assisting her in 1896 was Helen Varick Boswell, who had helped New York women, including Cornelia Stewart Robinson, establish a Republican woman's club in 1895, the West End Woman's Republican Club.[103] Boswell was born in Baltimore, Maryland, in 1869, attended the Friends Seminary there, and received her law degree from the Washington College of Law in Washington, D.C. Active in the women's club movement, Boswell was the chair of the Industry and Social Conditions Department of the General Federation of Women's Clubs and was selected by Taft to examine social conditions in Panama in 1907. There she organized the Canal Zone Federation of Women's Clubs. Like Foster, she was also active in the Daughters of the American Revolution.[104]

During the campaign of 1896 the Republican club women of New York "spread the gospel of the Gold Standard" to residents of the tenement houses, a strategy that "became one of the greatest assets in political work and was followed in due course in every city by Republican women, and, when women had the vote, by Democratic women."[105] Boswell recollected years later that women got to know each other during campaign season, and afterward "it seemed too bad to have the Republican women . . . separate."[106] When she took over the presidency of the WNRA after Foster's death, Boswell made a concerted effort to get local Republican women's clubs to function before and after campaign seasons. This had been Clarkson's stated purpose when he founded the National League of Republican Clubs in 1888. It took a while for her idea to come to fruition. Even though Republican women's clubs existed around the country in the late nineteenth century, most Republican women's organizations trace their origins to after 1920.[107]

Republicans won back the White House in 1896 with McKinley's election, and for the rest of her life Foster saw her party hold a prominent place in American politics. The year also serves as a hallmark of women's political evolution, as more women were being elected to political offices, and more woman suffrage laws were passed. In 1896 Idaho adopted a constitutional woman suffrage amendment on its first submission, and Utah women, whose suffrage had been stripped by Congress in 1887, regained the right to vote and were running for state office, encouraged there by the Democratic party. The Democrat Martha Hughes Cannon of Utah was the first woman state senator elected in the United States. The few Utah Republican women who ran either withdrew their names before the campaign ended or lost the election.[108] Democratic women did not have a national umbrella organization until 1912, but they were highly organized at the local levels by the end of the century.[109] Foster traveled the country to establish and nurture women's Republican clubs and to counter the work of local Democrats who were appealing to women's loyalties.

A Circle of Friends and Competitors

Partisan loyalty was not the only connection between Republican women. They often had attended the same women's seminaries or colleges; they joined the same women's clubs, and the club network linked them to other women with similar interests; a love of travel or a dedication to preserving history created connections; they read the same newspapers and magazines, and some women even owned, edited, or reported for them. The letterhead of the WNRA stationery in 1901 lists Judith Ellen Foster as president, Mary S. Lockwood as vice president, Emily S. Chace as general secretary, Helen Varick Boswell as organization secretary, Sarah E. Dean as press secretary, Mary Yost Wood as recording secretary, and Elizabeth F. Pierce as treasurer. These women shared more than party loyalty.

Mary Lockwood was a founder of the Daughters of the American Revolution in 1890; Foster and Boswell were active members. Lockwood organized the Washington Travel Club in 1880, and Dean attended its first meeting. For sixteen years, the club met every Monday night during the winter months. Members presented and discussed the history and culture of other countries; each year a different country was explored. The club also went on trips; the first was through Egypt.[110]

The women were also connected through the Woman's National Press Association. Foster was active; Mary Lockwood was its third president, and Belva Lockwood was its sixth.[111] Also a member was Clara B. Colby, whose Beatrice, Nebraska, *Woman's Tribune* was regarded as the official newspaper of the NWSA in the 1880s. It was her *Tribune* that covered the 1888 International Council of Women convention. She published 12,500 copies a day of the convention newspaper, and her success led her to move from Beatrice to Washington, D.C.[112] Reform politics, political conventions, and entertaining and educational clubs bridged differences and created bonds among women.

If clubs served to bring women together, partisan competition could divide them. Foster understood that most of the competition for women's loyalties happened at the local level. This made her travels necessary during campaign seasons. She also believed that emphasizing women's Republican visibility at the national level could win some women voters over to the party. This made women's presence at the national conventions especially important. In 1900 and 1904 Foster again opened WNRA headquarters and pushed for women's recognition at the national conventions. Boswell assisted her in Philadelphia in 1900 and from the Palmer House in Chicago in 1904. Mary Yost Wood, Foster's niece Elizabeth F. Pierce, and Mrs. George F. Lowell of Boston also took a hand in running the WNRA. Among the prominent women visitors to the Palmer House were Catherine Waugh McCullough and Jane Addams.[113] As Boswell later recollected, the women worked hard during the campaigns, but we "didn't have to stay in our home towns on election day to vote." In 1904 Boswell and Foster spent election eve at the theater in Washington, D.C.[114]

In 1908 the "'real fun'" was outside the convention hall, Alice Roosevelt Longworth observed, "'at the Headquarters of the national committee and of candidates, in the conferences that are peppered through the various hotels and are going on day and night.'"[115] The daughter of Theodore Roosevelt, Longworth shared the political excitement with Ruth Hanna McCormick, the daughter of the political boss Marcus Hanna. McCormick would later help lead Republican women through the transitional year of 1919.

Mary Garrett Hay also joined in the Republican excitement in 1908 by working at the New York headquarters under Boswell. She had been involved in Republican politics since she was a child in Indiana. Active in local temperance and woman suffrage politics, she moved to New York City in 1895 to join the national effort for woman suffrage. Hay's central place in woman suffrage politics and her work for the WNRA is another indication of the continual overlap of suffrage and Republican politics. In 1919 and 1920 the careers of Hay and McCormick would also be examples of the continued tensions between women's partisanship and nonpartisanship.

Women's Nonpartisanship

As women continued their labors in party structures at the national and local levels and won their first state offices, women's nonpartisan organizations continued to grow. Membership in the WCTU increased in these years, but the organization was no longer in the vanguard of the temperance campaign. Willard retreated from partisan politics and in 1896 was endorsing a strategy of nonpartisanship. The WCTU, after Willard's death in 1898, also retreated from active involvement in politics; nonpartisanship became its official policy after 1898.[116] No longer willing to endorse the Prohibition party, it emphasized censorship and regulation on behalf of social purity. Willard's "Do Everything" policy suddenly took on new meaning in this less political context.

Leading the fight against the consumption of alcohol was the Anti-Saloon League, a mixed-gender organization dominated by men that sought to "hold the balance of power" in elections, believing that to actively "enter the contest as a political party would have destroyed this possibility."[117] The expectation was that in holding a large block of votes, the Anti-Saloon League could force the parties to nominate candidates supportive of its aims. The league did not require its supporters to be temperate or dry but concentrated its attack on the saloon, a strategy that recalls the Woman's Crusade of the 1870s. Its name was chosen "to focus interest on the institution which was the fountain of the poisonous product" and allowed for an alliance between moderate drinkers and total abstainers without requiring support for total prohibition.[118] The league also determined support for candidates based on their willingness to support the league's aims and their voting records.

At the crux of the league's power in campaigns was its ability to mobilize its targeted voting block. It did this by building alliances with other organizations working for or supportive of its aims. But, more importantly, it did this by stirring men to vote and women and children to support them. Women and children became important to the league's success on election day and were viewed as workers who had determined parts to play. Most often their roles were to be moral voices in the increasingly secularized world. As nonvoters, women "paraded before the polling places wearing badges with these words: 'Vote Against Whiskey and For Me,' and 'Vote Against the Saloon—

I Can't Vote.'"[119] Women were also expected to work at home, convincing male members of their families of the worthiness of voting the dry ticket. Unlike the Woman's Crusade and the WCTU, women were playing auxiliary roles in the Anti-Saloon League.

Susan B. Anthony continued to be troubled by women's partisan activism, especially their advancement into elective offices. In 1890 the two wings of the woman suffrage movement—the NWSA and the AWSA—reunited under the name of the National American Woman Suffrage Association (NAWSA) and declared that they held a unanimous sentiment that the organization should keep "strictly aloof from all political alliances."[120]

Ten years later, Anthony and Anna Howard Shaw were refused an audience before the Committee on Resolutions at the 1900 Republican National Convention, "a courtesy which by this time was usually extended at all political conventions."[121] Finally, four women were granted a hearing before a subcommittee of the Platform Committee. Given ten minutes and a "chilly reception," they presented their arguments. The result was the following plank: "We congratulate the women of America upon their splendid record of public service in the Volunteer Aid Association, and as nurses in camp and hospital during the recent campaigns of our armies in the Eastern and Western Indies, and we appreciate their faithful co-operation in all works of education and industry." The plank as adopted did not contain the final clause written by its author, Judith Ellen Foster, which read: "We regard with satisfaction their unselfish interest in public affairs in the four states where they have already been enfranchised, and their growing interest in good government and Republican principles."[122] Republicans in places like Colorado might be moving forward in giving formal recognition to Republican women, but the national party was still hesitant. To suffragists like Anthony it was simply too much. She criticized the party as well as suffragists who worked in political campaigns, even though "none of the parties advocated giving them the right of suffrage," and, according to her biographer, she "pointed out the absurdity of hoping for 'good government' from any party until it was reinforced by the votes of women."[123]

For Anthony's generation, partisanship created divided loyalties, had proved a pointless strategy for gaining their rights, and was something to be exterminated from the suffrage movement. This view culminated in the NAWSA nonpartisan declaration. As the numbers of women supporting the suffrage movement and the numbers of women voters increased, however, partisanship was a reality to be dealt with. A new generation of suffragists leading the movement after 1900 would embrace new strategies to resolve the tension between partisanship and nonpartisanship.

Anthony controlled the NAWSA during its formative years, and she was helped by her "lieutenant," Carrie Chapman Catt. They created a unified plan of action and centralized power within the NAWSA. Catt's Organization Committee of 1894 called for the systematic study of government and the study of property taxes paid by women to reveal "taxation without representation." It also called for women to be "visible and vigilant" and to "go to all county and state political conventions and make themselves known to all office holders and candidates to convince them that women were valuable helpers to their friends."[124] Woman suffrage, the NAWSA leaders had agreed at their 1890 convention, "can be gained only through the assistance of men in all parties."[125] The problem was how women should present themselves when they went to these conventions.

Partisan alignments and endorsements were a clear problem in the 1894 Kansas and 1896 California campaigns for suffrage.[126] Kansas had granted women the right to vote on educational issues in 1861 and had extended municipal suffrage to women in 1887. Ordinarily a Republican state, Kansas was swept by the Populists in 1892, and now Republicans were seeking to regain their seats. Kansas Republican women established the Kansas Republican Woman's Association and elected the state suffrage president, Laura Johns, as its president. Republicans and Populists both promised to support a referendum on woman suffrage and to place a woman suffrage plank in their platform. These promises were enough to bring the national NAWSA organizers to the state.[127] Foster also arrived and declared, "I care more for the dominant principles of the Republican party than I do for woman suffrage."[128]

When the national NAWSA organizers, including Anthony, Stanton, and Catt, arrived in Kansas, it became evident that different ideas about partisanship existed between national and local suffrage workers. It was a difference not only about activism but also the identity of the overall suffrage movement and the relationship between the national organization to the state organizations. The national suffrage organizers saw the issue as suffrage first and party second; national party leaders, like Foster, saw the issue as party first and suffrage second. The state suffragists found the situation more complex. Laura Johns, a longtime suffrage and temperance activist and close ally of Judith Ellen Foster who held the politically difficult position of president of both the Kansas State Suffrage Association and the State Republican Woman's Association, became the center of the controversy about loyalty. National suffrage organizers suggested that her loyalties were divided, and charges that Johns embezzled suffrage campaign funds led to confrontations that were publicized in the temperance and suffrage press. The *Chicago Times* focused on the source of the controversy and quoted a "Miss Harding, M.D.," who stated that it was not right "for Laura Johns, after she had been made President of our non-partisan suffrage organization to stray away and organize a woman's Republican League and take the best women we had in our organization. . . . She has simply betrayed the cause of suffrage."[129]

But Laura Johns did not betray the cause of suffrage, at least not in her own eyes. She believed that Kansas women could work for the Republican party and its candidates as well as for the issue of suffrage. Relations between the national organizers and the state workers were further strained when the NAWSA was refused a hearing before the Republican party convention, while Johns and Foster were "permitted to present the claims of the women."[130]

In the end, the state suffrage referendum was a failure, and woman suffrage was not expanded. The failure in Kansas and the bitterness between the national and state suffragists substantiated Anthony's "deep-seated distrust of 'partial' suffrage such as the school or the municipal ballot. . . . The difficulty was that the women promptly aligned themselves with a political party."[131] Anthony wrote to Henry Blackwell during the Kansas campaign, arguing that "the difference between yourself and me, and Mrs. Johns and me, is precisely this—that you two are and have been Republicans *per se,* while I have been a Republican only in so far as the party and its members were more friendly to the principle of woman suffrage."[132] Of course, the picture was more complex. Many women, including Anthony, identified as Republicans even as they promoted paths of nonpartisanship.

Elizabeth Cady Stanton died in 1902. Susan B. Anthony attended her last woman suffrage convention in February 1906, and one month later she too was dead. The relationship between these two suffrage pioneers was strained at times by their differences on various issues, including their partisan differences; in 1888 and again in 1892 Anthony chose to stand by the Republican party. Stanton finally joined the Prohibitionists and had moved on to other projects, such as writing the *Woman's Bible.* Anthony remained at the center of the woman suffrage struggle, but she too moved on. As she wrote to her cousin in 1896 from the trenches of the California campaign, women needed "to hold themselves nonpartisan—or better all-partisan—so as to be free and able to ask of all parties." As for herself, she wrote, "Oh, I have been through the partisan battle and don't want to see it again."[133] Carrie Chapman Catt and Anna Howard Shaw, who succeeded Anthony to the NAWSA presidency, agreed. Women's political party affiliations were a problem because they divided women's loyalties.

The lack of victories for the NAWSA and the declining influence of the WCTU came, ironically, at a time when women's social and reform activism, and even their political activism, was actually increasing. By the end of the nineteenth century, women could take numerous paths as they worked for political change; they had broadened their political horizons, translating their social and reform activism into political terms and engaging male politicians more directly. As these women reformers, profoundly interested in the political process, increased the pace and scope of reform, they were again challenged by the question of whether they could hold "divided loyalties" without being disloyal. The reality of women's partisan and nonpartisan activism raised a special concern about women's limited political power, expressed in internal discussions about whether women have enough time or resources to work for both an issue—temperance or suffrage—and a party, even when it advances the issue. As influential women attempted to sort out this matter, they raised questions about how best to lobby; about what would be at the top of the agenda; and about who ultimately creates and controls the agenda.

The Limits of Partisan Rewards for Women

As the leading Republican woman organizer of the day, Foster was often invited to give speeches at important events, such as the 1898 July 4th Celebration at Washington Grove, Maryland, located a few miles outside of Washington, D.C. She accepted these invitations gracefully but knew they were simply honorific gestures. She was constantly disheartened by the fact that Republican men often ignored the women who had helped in the campaigns. In 1900, as she got ready to accompany Theodore Roosevelt for a campaign swing through the West, Foster wrote Ida Husted Harper that a new Board of Charities for the District of Columbia had just been created by Congress. Everyone assumed a woman would be appointed to the board, but McKinley "sent in the names of *five men* and *no woman!* A Jew, a Catholic, a colored man—but no woman!" She was appalled that a board to "inspect . . . poor, crushed and wicked women and girls" would not have a woman, and she regretted that it was "our noble and good and true McKinley" who had made the decision. Ever resourceful, she asked Harper to use the woman suffrage press to publicize that "a fine woman" who was in line for a position had been passed over. Ever the partisan, she warned Harper not to use her name or that of the "fine woman." "I don't want her to appear as a defeated candidate," and Foster did not want to appear critical of McKinley.[134]

Foster knew that if she could not get rewards for women from the men who controlled her party, she could turn to women outside party frameworks. She wanted to cooperate as much as possible with political men, and she believed that women and men needed to "supplement each other's quality of ability" in the political realm.[135] But her actions indicate that she was also aware that women needed to rely on each other in politics. To maintain that reliance, create unity out of diversity, and see their issues become legislation, women cut across partisan lines. They joined together in nonpartisan organizations. Individual women could act in partisan ways and join political parties, but sometimes women's political impact was stronger by using nonpartisan methods.

There is no direct evidence that Foster believed only women should use nonpartisan means to advance their political interests; men might have been part of her vision of how the political process worked. In her first arguments against the affiliation of the WCTU and the Prohibition party, she stated that it was "the people" who should use "non-partisan agencies" for their reforms. Then a party looking out for the interests of the people, convinced by the education and agitation of the people, would protect the legislation from the varying fortunes of party politics. Foster's fight with Willard and her subsequent work with the NPWCTU and the Republican party occurred in an era when civil service reform, contests to machine politics, and new electoral laws were only beginning to have an impact in limiting, or diminishing, men's partisanship.[136] It was a time when men as well as women promoted "disinterestedness," defined as working for the collective good. Parties were still central to political culture, but strong partisanship was no longer central to men's sense of their total political experience. However, Foster's aim was to advance women in the partisan world, not to bring men into the nonpartisan world. The promotion of nonpartisanship for men was a challenge taken on by others. Foster wanted women to work with men in the partisan arena, but she also knew that women's collective presence made a difference in politics. As women sought inclusion in political parties, and as they struggled for greater citizenship rights, Foster was always concerned that they not lose themselves, or what they had already developed and achieved, in the process.

During the final years of her life, Foster continued her work for the Republican party. She was also active in the suffrage movement and guided the efforts of the NPWCTU in its moral reform efforts and crusade for constitutional prohibition.[137] She died in 1910, ten years before the passage of the Eighteenth and Nineteenth Amendments to the U.S. Constitution and at the height of Republican dominance of national politics. Yet in two years, a schism in the party would lead to the creation of the Progressive party and the loss of the White House to Democrats. In response to the strategic needs of a close three-way race in 1912, Helen Boswell transformed the WNRA into a more vigorous vehicle for women's influence in the party. The WNRA of 1912 was, according to the *New York Times*, "as well entrenched as the regular Republican machine . . . and it is no difficulty for them to reach just the kind of woman who can influence votes, if they don't actually cast them."[138] Being an integral part of the Republican machine was just what Foster was aiming for. And yet, in 1912 the issue of women's nonpartisanship again was prominent in the campaign, as suffragists like Ida Husted Harper carried on Susan B. Anthony's crusade of nonpartisanship and spoke out against women's affiliations with political parties. The tension between women's partisanship and nonpartisanship would take women into the postsuffrage era.

4. The Progressive Spirit, 1910–12

IN 1910 THE *Outlook,* a self-avowed "progressive" magazine editorially controlled by Lyman Abbott and Theodore Roosevelt, explored recent changes in political culture as the country moved from the era that historians call the "Gilded Age" into the one called the "progressive era."[1] It reported that an individual "accustomed to the torchlight processions of the campaigns . . . might have considerable difficulty in finding himself as much exercised emotionally as he was then," because "the country has passed from the emotional to the intellectual stage."[2] The extravagant displays of strong partisanship that dominated the nineteenth-century political world were on the decline. These rituals of popular politics, once seen as symbolic illustrations of people's loyalties and shared beliefs, became instead equated with corruption and the deterioration of the social fabric. Political parties in the late nineteenth and early twentieth centuries instead championed themselves and their candidates through educational and then, in an attempt to increase participation, advertising forms of campaigning.

Changes in campaigning were the result of greater transformations in party composition and power as the nineteenth century came to an end and an economic depression forced people to realize that industrialism failed to provide for social and economic progress. New solutions to social and economic problems had to be found, and because traditional party leaders and their corporate allies were slow to respond, they found their political power challenged by party bosses and then by party independents and social reformers.[3] These women and men had created social reform movements and institutions that gave them spaces to work out new relationships to partisan politics. They concentrated on building independent paths within the major parties and challenging existing party machinery. They used extra-party strategies and legal means to regulate the power of parties. There was a two-sided nature to the party evolution that resulted; changes were forced on those within and outside of party structures.[4] These changes represent crucial steps toward women's greater involvement in the political culture of the early twentieth century.

In 1901 the Republican president William McKinley was shot, bringing to an end a long career of public service that began during the Civil War when he was an aide to Colonel (later President) Rutherford B. Hayes. He was succeeded by his vice president, Theodore Roosevelt, whose political path to the White House had been paved by the political bosses of the New York Republican machine, including Thomas Collier Platt, who wanted him out of the New York governor's mansion.[5] Platt's vision of politics was grounded in ideas of strong partisanship and the avoidance of civil service reform and nonpartisanship in municipal elections. When Republicans became the party in power after 1893, he moved to expand state authority over the large Democratic cities of New York, Brooklyn, and Buffalo. Through Albany, he encouraged and increased legislative investigations, charter changes, and bipartisan police boards, all enhancements to the party in power. He also filled the party campaign chest with money from wealthy men and large corporations, providing certain classes of big business with "regular access to political representation."[6]

The genius of party bosses like Platt was that they absorbed independents and other marginal actors into the party machine, allowing for its transformation in ways beyond their control but guaranteeing the survival of parties and partisanship even as partisan political culture was transformed.[7] By 1894, Platt and other party bosses across the country were forced to recognize party independents, mainly educated, professional men who were dissatisfied with the old party loyalties that sustained the bosses and machines. Networks of reformers worked together to advance specific reforms and, at the same time, establish thousands of clubs and associations that supported their party. They believed in the party system and the power of partisanship and took on party labels, but they contested the idea of absolute party loyalty.[8] Independents began to win offices and accelerated the transformation of the makeup of parties by bringing new issues to the front of political struggles. Significantly, Roosevelt became the first progressive Republican governor of New York through this process in 1898. In 1900, when Platt came to prefer a less independent governor, Roosevelt became vice president under McKinley, and when McKinley was shot in 1901, Roosevelt became president of the United States.

Challenges by reformers led to important political reforms in New York and across the nation. The Pendleton Act of 1883 for civil service reform was expanded to include more federal workers, thus limiting the influence of patronage. Civil service acts were also passed by state legislatures. The Australian ballot system gave parties legal status by providing for government ballots containing party labels or columns. Stricter laws about campaign contributions were passed. Mandatory state-administered direct primary laws were passed by some states. And there were municipal reform campaigns for nonpartisan ballots. These political reforms were championed by critics of the parties, of course, but also by the growing numbers of reformers who had won political office. Reformers not only reshaped the political landscape with these changes; they reshaped their own parties as well.[9]

Nonpartisan social reformers concerned about the growing problems of municipal life supported party reformers in their revolts against political bosses and machines. These reformers argued that a city was "'simply a business corporation' . . . and expansion of city services enhanced the need for nonpartisan government. National party principles had nothing to do with street cleaning."[10] To these public-spirited individuals, machine-dominated parties were illegitimate. They had become by definition corrupt because their "members worked for the spoils of office instead of for programmatic causes."[11] The solution was not simply to increase state governance over the parties. It included a mandate to instill within parties new principles that transcended the scurry for power. Party independents had paved the way; now reformers also demanded that parties work for meaningful principles that rose above the scurry for power. These reformers formed alliances between their organizations and political parties and engaged parties directly as members.

Recognition of the limitations of their power, coupled with a belief that parties were more available to them as independents gained positions of power, propelled many nonpartisan reformers into party arenas. They understood that, in the end, they "were forced to go hat-in-hand to the partisan politicians who actually controlled government."[12] Working through numerous organizations—such as the National Municipal League, National Conservation Association, National Consumers' League, and National Child Labor Committee—social reformers represented a wide range of issues and concerns. They became political activists who moved with great deliberation and thought, but without hesitation, from the municipal to the state and then to the federal level. They moved from being party critics to being party activists. Like Frances Willard years earlier, they wanted to be in at the birth of new ideas and initiatives.

Individuals like Theodore Roosevelt made political parties more attractive to independents and nonpartisan activists. He was seen by women and men as embodying the hope of the era, a symbol of a new emphasis on principles over blind partisanship in politics. In 1882 he described his partisanship in a letter to Josephine Shaw Lowell, the first woman member of the New York State Board of Charities whose family had long and deep connections to the Republican party. "I thoroughly believe in the Republican party," Roosevelt wrote, "when it acts up to its principles—but if I can prevent it I never shall let party zeal obscure my sense of right and decency."[13] Louise Ward Watkins made connections between the past and present in her assessment of his promise. Active in California woman suffrage politics, she remembered the "parades and torchlight processions" of the 1896 and 1900 campaigns. Strongly Republican, she noted in her autobiography that McKinley's "death was almost a personal blow," but "with the advent of Roosevelt the old order changed somehow and another was born."[14]

Throughout his career, Roosevelt cultivated independents to keep them in the Republican coalition. Initially his tactic was to challenge the power of party bosses, and he "carefully fashioned political rhetoric that combined support for the party with skepticism of the machine's claims."[15] As governor of New York and as president of the United States, he always scorned the alliance between machine politicians and business, or, to use the language of the day, "special interests." But he never challenged political party activism. He believed that parties directed and controlled the political game.

The calls for less bossism in politics were calls for greater participation. The *Outlook* made clear that citizens might feel confused by all the denunciations of conventions, special interests, and bosses and machines. Such confusion would be clarified if individuals could remember that "it is the duty of every citizen in the Republic to exert all the influence that he can exert consistently with other duties on behalf of the principles and the party he believes in. . . . We have done well to economize on brass bands and torchlight processions. . . . But the money expended in public meetings is well expended. The campaign of education is worth all its legitimate cost."[16] The refrain held. Political parties were legitimate entities.

In another article, "The Municipal Problem: The Ideal City," Roosevelt's *Outlook* expressed the hopes of reformers. "In the ideal city the multitude of problems that arise from the congestion of population will not be abandoned to the inhumanity of commercialism or to the chance of philanthropy. They will be taken up by the city itself." Who is to lead the city? In 1909 the *Outlook* only hinted at the answer with the statement that in the ideal city, "the whole people will take self-respecting care of themselves. . . . It cannot have

an oligarchical or inefficient government."[17] In Roosevelt's scheme, an engaged citizenship, politicians following an independent path, and reformers
engaging the partisan lens were interchangeable as long as political parties
retained primacy. Partisanship as an essential political identity must survive.

There was an exception to Roosevelt's call for an inclusionary political
culture. Southern black men were systematically disfranchised in the 1890s,
and racial segregation became the law of the land.[18] Northern blacks were not
immune to the climate of racism that produced this political reality; like some
southern blacks, they were able to craft their own political successes. They
formed their own political clubs, participated in campaigns, and voted. They
too sought inclusion in political parties, but they were excluded from most
of the organizations that were laboratories of the new independent political
movement.[19]

Some of the most important of these laboratories were in Wisconsin, Illinois, and California, where good-government movements had succeeded in
getting legislation passed that limited the unbridled influence of political
parties. County and local offices were made nonpartisan, and direct primary laws were passed.[20] As the Los Angeles reformer Charles D. Willard stated, people believed that the old politics of "loyal partisanship," a politics "run
and managed almost entirely by professional politicians," needed to be sup-
planted by a new politics and a new class of voters who formed opinions for
themselves. "We shall still have partisanship," he stated, "but the welfare of
the nation will not be subordinated to that of party."[21]

The legislative and rhetorical promotion of a new type of politics based
on an independent partisanship allowed parties to be political conduits for
women who wanted or needed to move from the status of disfranchised
public activist to voter to politician. Women could act politically without
having to take on the designation "politician," a label that implied bossism,
the control of corporate leaders, and a subservient public.

Women Reformers

In this larger political culture, women carved a unique place for themselves.
They were in the forefront of the ranks of social reformers, leading campaigns
for playgrounds, wage and hour reforms, better working conditions, separate prisons for women, and social purity. Arguing for more rather than less
government to meet these challenges, women transformed benevolence into
reform and reform into political activism.[22] In the process, they reinvigorat-
ed their own relationship to the electoral world, making stronger arguments

for the right to vote and redefining their relationship to partisan politics. This redefinition hinged on the more wide-reaching changes in the political sphere but also on women's own political evolution. Women social reformers began to understand, as their male counterparts had, that nonpartisanship was a political roadblock.[23]

In 1897 Judith Ellen Foster published an article in the *North American Review* that traced her view of "Woman's Political Evolution" and summed up her ideas about women's political position at the end of the nineteenth century. Women, she argued, are not "sheltered home-keepers" but are "everywhere in the industrial world." They provide essential labor in and outside the home, and they benefit from the opening of educational avenues such as coeducational schools and women's colleges. Educated women had created careers for themselves by establishing new institutions to meet the needs of people in a growing urban and industrial era. Their benevolent activism had become efforts of social reform, and women's interest in politics, as Foster saw it, was a result of their participation in this public world.[24]

Women's political activism, for Foster, revolved around the struggles for specific reforms such as temperance and woman suffrage but also on the fulfillment of citizenship duties—of participation in the political world at every level. With flourish, she argued that "women are acknowledged by political leaders to have been an effective and, in many instances, a controlling element in late national elections and in many local political contests." She believed the evolutionary moment had come for men to recognize that they needed women in politics, but she also softened her argument that women were influential by stating that "men and women with experience and consequent power will supplement each the other's quality of ability." "The present political influence of women is proportionately more intelligent than that of men; by this I mean that there are so few political emoluments possible to women as a return for political service that they are not tempted to think and act from hope of personal reward. In proportion as political action is intelligent and disinterested, it is independent. The present political influence of woman is intelligent, and should be so dealt with."[25] In an era when independence had been cornered within the confines of partisanship and the spirit of nonpartisanship was being promoted by both men and women, Foster again divided women's and men's political efforts and justified women's political participation through arguments of gender difference. Still, her evolutionary analysis was a challenge to political parties and their male leaders to look beyond the realm of traditional rewards when dealing with women. Women were participating in elections and political parties, especially in states where they

held the right to vote, and men must recognize their participation and capture their allegiance and activism. The end result would be the greater benefit
for society.[26]

Foster's partisanship and her political relationships with men placed her
within a political culture that was exceedingly diverse. She was a politician,
and saw herself as such, but it was still common for some women activists
to deny that their works were "political." For example, the Mother's Club of
Cambridge, Massachusetts, "refused to admit it was in politics long after the
reality of its political influence was visible for all to see."[27] Directly facing the
issues before their communities, club women worked to ameliorate social and
economic ills, but their view of their work as nonpolitical was informed by
a strong tradition that equated women's public work with virtue and principles. At the same time, the expanding argument, used by women and men
reformers, that municipal problems needed to be solved without interference
from corrupt or potentially corrupt political parties and their leaders encouraged women to espouse a rhetoric emphasizing the nonpolitical.

The Woman's Municipal League, established in New York City in 1894,
highlights the complexity of this political culture. The league was a "political club" for women concerned with "education, sanitation, public health,
and police and fire protection." League women argued that their greater
moral sensitivities made their participation in discussions of these issues
essential. They were there, they stated, not to engage the "dirty" business of
partisan politics but the "'clean' arena of nonpartisan work on city problems.
. . . And since this nonpartisan territory was meant to include City Hall, campaign work was not off limits." Holding themselves independent from men's
political groups was part of their strategy; they refused to become an auxiliary to a men's club, including a political party.[28]

Josephine Shaw Lowell, one of the founders, denied that league women
were involved in politics. According to one historian, she "believed that she
could suppress the controversial issue of women's relation to politics even
while League women campaigned for candidates."[29] New York City politics
made this possible, because politics was defined as "partisan maneuverings
for power," and "reform rhetoric insisted that partisan concerns had no place
in the conduct of city affairs and represented the coalition's candidate as
'nonpartisan.'"[30] By defining politics narrowly, these women sought to rec-
oncile, for themselves and for men, their actions with traditional ideas of
womanhood to extend the scope of their political duties.[31]

The Woman's Municipal League and similar women's organizations continued to be important for women, but they were not in the vanguard of re-

form in the early twentieth century. That was a new arena of settlement houses, established by educated women seeking a new training ground and career path. Motivated by a desire to help communities function more efficiently, residents of the settlements, what one historian calls a "female dominion of reform," contributed to building the new American state.[32] Settlement residents were influential in reform circles because they were willing to innovate and their networks were so extensive. A few settlement residents and supporters were also influential in creating a bridge that allowed aspects of women's reform work to engage the electoral sphere in more direct ways.

By 1906, there were about two hundred settlements with almost four thousand workers. The reformers who established the settlements, including Jane Addams and Ellen Gates Starr of Hull-House in Chicago and Lillian Wald of Henry Street in New York City, were crucial links in establishing and re-establishing relationships of reform.[33] Motivated by various desires and goals, they became actors searching for ways to ameliorate the harsh working and living conditions in their communities. Their promises of reforms and their successes in achieving them gave these reformers authority as well as the power to undertake an ideological and practical search for a new order for society.[34]

Reformers in Chicago, especially those connected to Hull-House, engaged their work in four steps. They investigated specific problems; they publicized issues and offered solutions; with public support, they lobbied the government for programs to enact solutions; and they attempted to prove their own expertise and demand their own appointments to administer the new programs.[35] Their investigations were grounded in a belief that the world, as Jane Addams put it, "must be faced with a knowledge of its actuality." Addams argued: "To be of value in the delicate process of social adjustment and reconstruction a man must have a knowledge of life as it is, of the good as well as of the evil; he must be a patient collector of facts, and furthermore, he must possess a zeal for men which will inspire confidence and arouse to action."[36]

Jane Addams

Jane Addams, the founder of Hull-House, dominated the Chicago reform scene. Although she does not represent all women who became interested in political party activism in the early twentieth century, she was a great political thinker and activist, and her influence on the developing political discourse was far-reaching.[37] Addams was born in Cedarville, Illinois, in 1860. Her mother died when she was two. Her father built a small fortune as a miller and banker. He was also a politician, serving as a state senator for the Whig and then the Republican parties. Republican politics was a part of Jane Addams's life from the day she was born.

Graduating from Rockford Seminary in 1882, she spent the next years asking herself questions about women's opportunities and evaluating the limitations set on them by their family obligations.[38] A second trip to Europe in 1887 provided her with the answer.[39] With her friend Ellen Gates Starr, she would establish a settlement house similar to the one she had visited in London, Toynbee Hall. Hull-House became the most famous settlement in the world. Located in Chicago's Nineteenth Ward, its residents served an immigrant population and, in turn, attempted to learn from their situation and their community.[40]

The women of Hull-House were social workers—Alice Hamilton, Florence Kelley, Julia Lathrop, and other highly educated women—and they contributed crucial services to the settlement and the community. Kelley probably more than anyone helped transform the settlement into a vehicle for reform. She was a socialist and active in Socialist party politics in New York and Chicago. Hull-House in Chicago and Henry Street in New York City provided her and her colleagues with strong institutional frameworks in which they could meet with male reformers and yet pursue independent political action. Women's separate reform and political organizations provided a space apart from the public sphere dominated by men where women could debate the extent and content of their nonpartisanship and partisanship. It also allowed them a place to discuss the impact political party activism would have on their own political actions. While women created women-only organizations and institutions, they also worked in alliances with men more than has been generally acknowledged. These alliances were necessary because women could not achieve their goals on their own.[41]

At the same time, no reformers could achieve their goals without engaging politicians. To direct public policy they needed to influence the politicians and political party officials who fronted legislation. Reformers collected data and wrote reports before seeking out politicians. In the best of cases, the politicians were themselves reformers interested in the same policy aims; in the worst of cases, they were seen as corrupt officials disinterested in the welfare of their constituency and lacking a vision for their communities. In either case, alliances had to be built or contests over power had to be waged.

As women social reformers began to build alliances with politicians, they benefited from the fact that reform-minded men—independents and former nonpartisans—had won elected office and had appointed women to positions, and not only on school boards. For example, Illinois's reform governor, John Altgeld, appointed Sarah Stevenson to the Board of Health, Mary Kenney to the Board of Labor Commissioners, and Julia Lathrop to the Board of Charities in 1893. Florence Kelley was appointed factory inspector, and Alzina Stevens was appointed assistant inspector. These appointments were praised by social reformers and provided women with the understanding that the extent of their success depended in part on the party in power. Chicago women began to think about patronage and its power and danger. Many of the Hull-House residents believed that their ability to reach their goals was hampered by their own male political allies, who were themselves tied to or influenced by the spoils system. Their first step was to have certain positions freed from the patronage circle using the Civil Service Law of Illinois.[42]

When Lathrop was appointed to the Illinois Board of Charities, she found in her studies of poorhouses and asylums for the disabled and insane that most executive positions in these public charitable institutions were political appointments. Within two years she was arguing that appointments "should occur not in closed political caucuses testing for loyalty to party but in the open labor market, for fitness, by examination."[43] When the governor, Richard Yates, ignored her recommendations and made other political appointments, Lathrop resigned. She returned to her position in 1905, when the new governor, Charles Deneen, promised changes, but it took until 1909 for the state to abolish the Voluntary Board of Charities and establish the Charities Commission, made up of salaried experts rather than political appointees.[44] Kelley also grew "disgusted with the practice of political patronage." She had been appointed factory inspector in 1893, but in 1897 she was replaced by a "political crony" of the new governor. She discovered that her "cherished laws" were "gutted by the appointments of lackadaisical administrators." It was patronage, she believed, "which blocked them from competition for any position within governmental agencies."[45]

Patronage also influenced Jane Addams. Two years before Judith Foster wrote of women's political evolution, Addams began to contest the power of the city's boss and his machine. Angry at the laxity of garbage collection in her ward, she convinced the mayor to appoint her as garbage inspector. When her efforts did not contribute to better garbage collection, which meant that the city's services were still not being equally distributed, she blamed John Powers, the city's political boss. Powers was chairman of the Finance Committee of the Chicago City Council, and to challenge his control over services, Addams and the Hull-House Men's Club began a campaign to reduce his influence.[46] They nominated Frank Lawler to run for ward alderman, and although he won the race, he soon became a supporter of Powers or, at least, refused to challenge him on issues. Addams continued the campaign against Powers, and in 1896 and 1898 he was challenged by forces organized out of Hull-House. Both campaigns were unsuccessful, but they had forced the women and men of Hull-House to direct their political thinking and practices in a new direction.[47]

Addams's ideas about women's relationship to politics are contained in a group of essays based on lectures she gave in New York and Vermont. Published as *Democracy and Social Ethics* in 1902, these essays challenged people to broaden their ideas about politics and think seriously about democracy; she argues that "most people interpreted democracy too narrowly." In the last chapter she explores the failures to challenge the power of the ward boss. "Would it be dangerous to conclude that the corrupt politician himself, because he is democratic in method, is on a more ethical line of social development than the reformer, who believes that people must be made over by 'good citizens' and 'governed by experts'? The former at least are engaged in the mass energy and wisdom to the community as a whole." She acknowledges that the situation is complicated, about more than good versus evil, principles against corruption. The boss is not "elected because he is dishonest. He is elected because he is a friendly visitor," but he brings with him the "evils of corrupt government" that "are bound to fall heaviest upon the poorest and least capable."[48] Addams acknowledged the complexity of the situation while at the same time reaching for a pragmatic solution. When writing of the corrupt politician, she attempted not only to understand his appeal to voters but reformers' lack of appeal to the public. Their "'goodness is not dramatic,'" she reasoned, "'it is not even concrete and human.'"[49] She was searching for a way to make politics good, principled, active, concrete, and human. She understood that politics had integrity only when grounded in daily life.

Campaigns like the one undertaken by Addams and the women of Hull-House were mounted in cities across the nation. These campaigns and a growing intellectual discourse about parties contributed to a shift in reformers' focus from the local to the state and then the national level. The lesson of the municipal campaigns was that the city, state, and nation were tied together and that one of the crucial links was political parties.[50] During the first decade of the twentieth century, women activists created their own organizations, worked with men, and attempted to bridge class and race differences in their efforts at reform. In 1899 the National Consumers' League was formed to champion better working conditions and hours and wage reforms. Moving beyond consumer action, the Women's Trade Union League was founded in 1903 and mobilized working-class and middle-class women to champion changes on the shop floor. The work arena and the private sphere overlapped when women reformers sought to abolish child labor. This activism expanded into one of the largest female reform efforts, to reduce infant and maternal mortality. In all of their actions, women increasingly recognized that they needed to be professionals and that they needed to turn to the state.[51]

It was clear to Addams by 1909 that the federal level had to be addressed. In her autobiography, she traces her political journey and targets 1909 as a year of division in the thought and work of those interested in reform. Hull-House was beginning its third decade, and there was an "insurgent mood" that allowed individuals to reexamine the "social institutions upon which they have been relying and renew their faith in human volition as a power which may really direct and shape social conditions."[52] That reexamination led to increased activism by women and men at the local level. The results included studies like the *Pittsburgh Survey,* which changed public opinion about reform, challenged elected officials to remedy their corrupt practices, and brought the attention of reform politicians to the social workers' agenda. Through national organizations like the National Conference of Charities and Corrections, of which Addams became president in 1909, social reformers became convinced that reform had to take place at the national level and that the national government needed their guidance.

It was failures as well as successes that convinced the reformers of the need to focus on the national level. In the spring of 1912, Congress passed a bill prohibiting the import and export of poisonous phosphorous matches and placing a revenue tax on their manufacture. Reformers had championed this bill, and they were dismayed that the same legislature failed to pass a law regulating the interstate carriage of commodities produced by child labor. The failure placed another success, the establishment of the Federal Children's Bureau with Julia Lathrop appointed as its chief, into perspective.[53]

Woman Suffrage and Women's Influence

Ongoing work with suffragists also shaped Addams's rhetoric and political agenda. Illinois was one of the states where partial suffrage allowed women to participate in limited ways in the electoral arena. In 1873 Illinois women won the right to hold school offices, and in 1891 the School Suffrage Act gave them the right to vote in the election of school offices created by the legislature. Addams's belief in a participatory democracy was enhanced by her active suffrage work as a "partial voter" and a champion of greater voting rights for women. But she did not throw her energies fully into the suffrage movement until 1911. Until that time, suffrage had been a social reform to her; after that time, she expanded her definitions of social and political reform. As one biographer has written, she feared that "government was becoming remote and unreal because it refused to deal with the actual life of the mass of men," and this fear led her to espouse woman suffrage as an instrument of good government, an instrument of politics, rather than as a right.[54] Her personal engagement of municipal problems, her limited suffrage rights, and her need for alliances with male reformers to unseat male politicians helped her understand the promise and limits of her political influence and power.[55] Woman suffrage was important to this fusion of ideas because it demanded that women see themselves as engaging the political sphere directly.

In March 1912 a delegation from the NAWSA followed the tradition set in the 1860s and traveled to Washington, D.C., to meet with legislators and lobby for woman suffrage. The women who argued before a joint Senate and House committee hoped to persuade the members to act on a resolution for a woman suffrage amendment to the Constitution. According to their own accounts, their reception by the committees was extremely positive. As Jane Addams, a vice president of the NAWSA, noted, the women speakers were given a warm welcome and not simply the perfunctory five minutes that had been allocated them in earlier years.[56]

There were two reasons for this warm welcome. First, the delegation included male members of the House of Representatives who were willing to speak in support of the suffrage resolution. Suffragists had always had male allies, but now they included a wide range of partisan leaders and nonpartisan reformers. The second reason was the growing competition among political parties for the loyalties of voting women.[57] And yet the women did not have high hopes. The climate for woman suffrage continued to be hostile or, at best, full of ridicule.[58]

While almost all of the ten speakers before the committees emphasized the justice inherent in giving women the vote, their overt arguments fell into two categories. First, a majority of them argued on behalf of women's ability to participate in political decision making.[59] "The time has come," said a speaker, "when the home and the State are one." An equally important argument concerned the handicaps of women's disfranchisement. This argument had two parts. First, while women were encouraged to have opinions about public policy matters, they had also been told they could "influence legislation only in indirect ways." Why, one speaker asked, should they even bother, when the government "makes no record whatever of the opinions which we express in our women's clubs and our prayer meetings?" The futility of indirect influence was evident to these suffragists.

Another speaker stated that even when women had attempted to speak to legislators their voices had gone unheard, because legislators were only interested in the voices of those who "have the power to take the legislator's political ladder away from him, a power that we, who have no votes, do not have." Another woman speaker also pointed out how women's indirect influence handicapped their usefulness, and yet she astutely argued that the committee members should remember "not that women succeed" in their social service work, but that "where they do succeed it is at tremendous and needless expenditure of energy and vital strength and at the cost of dignity and self-respect." She argued that "no intelligent man in this scientific day would try to do anything by an indirect and wasteful method if he could accomplish his purpose by a direct and economic method." The tragedy, she pointed out, was that once women succeeded in their goals—and here she used the example of the establishment of school gardens and playgrounds—and the "city or State adopts these institutions the management is immediately and entirely taken out of the hands of women and placed in the hands of men."[60] This is the second part of the argument about the handicaps of women's disfranchisement. The very success of their activities was a failure for them, as they lost influence.[61]

This argument was echoed by Jane Addams. "A good many women with whom I have been associated," she stated, "have initiated and carried forward philanthropic enterprises which were later taken over by the city and thereupon the women have been shut out from the opportunity to do the self-same work which many had done up to that time." The extension of governmental activities into areas that were once the domain of families, communities, and charity organizations, therefore, necessitated the equal extension of women's political power. Another speaker made the argument more succinctly. Woman, she stated, "asks for the vote in order to do her woman's work better."[62] These women recognized that "social policy"—formerly the province of women's voluntary work—had become public policy. As men took up what had been women's issues and causes, and as the issues themselves evolved in the changing social and political structures, women were increasingly "shut out," as Addams put it, but they were also increasingly interested in new ways to directly influence policy.[63]

As if to prove the women correct about the limits of their political influence, the members of the congressional committees chose not to consider the arguments any further after the delegation left the meeting rooms. In the end, as the editors of the *History of Woman Suffrage* would later assess, the suffrage question was not considered or resolved, "as no report, favorable or unfavorable was ever made by either committee. In so far as bringing the Federal Amendment before Senate or House for action was concerned, the hearings might as well never have taken place."[64] By the midsummer of 1912, women activists had evidence that a new opportunity for direct political action had arisen with the birth of a new political party, and many seized the moment.

The Progressive Bolt

In late June 1912, hundreds of progressive Republicans, including delegates on the floor and the many supporters viewing the scene from the gallery areas, walked out of the fifteenth Republican National Convention at Chicago's Coliseum in protest over the nomination of William Howard Taft as the party's candidate for the presidency. After months of campaigning, finding enormous popular support for his candidacy, and winning a majority of committed delegates in state Republican primaries, Theodore Roosevelt lost his party's nomination when 235 of the 254 contested delegates to the convention went to Taft.[65]

Roosevelt, angry and confrontational as always, but with his finger correctly taking the pulse of assembled supporters, announced the immediate formation of a new Progressive party and welcomed into it all those who considered themselves progressives.[66] Claiming that Taft had won the majority of delegates through foul play and "steamroller" methods, Roosevelt's delegates and supporters immediately held a rump convention on June 22; set up an Organizational Committee chaired by Joseph Dixon, a senator from Montana; and released a nationwide call for the new party.[67] Throughout July, supporters of the new Progressive party regularly met with Roosevelt in Oyster Bay, New York, and with Dixon in Chicago to draw up a platform. Others across the country set up state party organizations.[68] By early August, the Progressive party was ready for its national convention, and the campaign of 1912 became a three-way race between Roosevelt, Taft, and the Democratic nominee, Woodrow Wilson.

The bolt from the Republican party and the formation of the new Progressive party was the result of an intense factionalism between progressives and the "Old Guard" within the Republican party, a factional fight that began rumbling in 1910 and intensified during the years of the Taft presidency. When Roosevelt returned from nearly two years of hunting big game in Africa, he saw the Republican party as ravaged by political disputes and the country being injured by weak leadership. The Republican party, he believed, had strayed from its true calling as the party of progress. The newspaper of the NAWSA, the *Woman's Journal*, commented that if women acted like Taft and

Roosevelt when they disagreed on policy, they would put the women's rights "cause back fifty years."[69]

Roosevelt's strong stance on progressive reforms made him an appealing candidate in a presidential race where all the candidates declared themselves to be progressive.[70] At a time of declining cohesiveness in the electorate, an issue-based agenda thrust Roosevelt to the forefront, as progressive Republicans looked beyond Taft for a candidate. The other progressive Republican candidate was Robert LaFollette of Wisconsin. Most insurgents in the Republican party, organized as the Progressive Republican League, backed LaFollette until Roosevelt agreed to become the standard bearer. In early February, LaFollette had an apparent physical and mental collapse and dropped out of the race, and the Republican contest was between Roosevelt and Taft.

On the evening before the start of the Republican National Convention, Roosevelt told his supporters, in what is called one of the greatest speeches of his political career, that the 1912 Republican contest had "become much more than an ordinary party fight"; it had become a fight for the "rights of humanity" and would "go on whether we win or lose." In calling for support of progressivism, he concluded: "We fight in honorable fashion for the good of mankind; fearless of the future; unheeding of our individual fates; with unflinching hearts and undimmed eyes; we stand at Armageddon, and we battle for the Lord."[71]

Assemblies of Women

Women's attendance at the Republican convention followed tradition, but the excitement about women that year was exceptional. According to a reporter from the *New York Herald*: "With a suddenness and force that have left observers gasping women have injected themselves into the national campaign this year in a manner never before dreamed of in American politics." These women "constituted the famous 'purple row' which distinguished the Republican convention for the beauty and elegance of its speakers."[72]

At the convention, women supporters of the Republican candidates cheered from the balconies and the floor, as involved as the men in the "delirium" of the hotly contested convention. There was a diversion when a "pretty young woman in the west balcony" waved a picture of Roosevelt and began cheering "in a shrill voice."[73] The "high thin voice" of Ottila Davis, aged twenty-nine and the wife of a Chicago lumber merchant, "somehow carried through the hall like a faint wisp of a breeze. . . . aimed in a kind of mute appeal to the Taft men on the platform as if asking them to be fair to her hero." The California delegation then sent her their gold bear atop a tall pole, and she waved that. Then they "carried her down from the balcony, pushed past the police, paraded her up the hall, put her on the platform. . . . The California delegation served as the woman's personal flying wedge, swept her down the aisles past the jam of howling men, lifted and dragged her to the reporters' tables."[74] She told the reporters that she "couldn't help leading the stampede" but that "women ought not to go into politics. They have enough to do at home."[75]

The attendance of Helen Varick Boswell, now president of the WNRA, caused much less interest.[76] Working alone after Judith Ellen Foster's death in 1910, Boswell had kept the organization alive, but it had not grown in number, and she and her auxiliary seem to have had little influence on the national party overall. When other Republicans bolted from their party, Boswell and the WNRA stayed. Throughout the campaign, she was in charge of organizing Republican women for Taft.

Attending the convention in an official capacity were two women delegates-at-large from California, Florence C. Porter and Isabella Blaney.[77] Republican women in California had aligned themselves with the Lincoln-Roosevelt League, "promising support in the election of 1910 in return for a constitutional amendment in 1911 giving women the vote."[78] When women got the vote, they also won places for themselves in the state Republican party because of their continuing willingness to use the energies of their organizations on behalf of candidates in return for support on specific issues.[79] These women, according to a contemporary observer, "were no longer a novelty" and did not attract the attention women did a few years before.[80]

It was suffragists, not the female party activists, who captured the most attention at the Republican convention. They had come once again to the national convention to present a proposed suffrage plank for inclusion in the national platform. Following what was now their routine, the suffragists attended the national nominating conventions after their meetings with congressional representatives. As the first national convention of the year, featuring a hotly contested race between Roosevelt, who had recently become more vocal in his support of woman suffrage, and Taft, who continued to oppose the extension, and as the party with numerous male supporters of woman suffrage, the Republican convention was of special interest to the suffragists.[81] Jane Addams was in charge of the eight-woman delegation that met with the Resolutions Committee.[82]

They stated their case in the seven minutes allocated to them, but, in the end, the platform adopted by the convention did not contain a woman suffrage plank or make any mention of support for women's enfranchisement.[83] The suffragists were profoundly disappointed in their hearing before the

Resolutions Committee and in the final draft of the Republican platform. NAWSA representatives who attended the Democratic National Convention were equally disappointed. They too were allotted a few minutes before the Resolutions Committee, and there was no suffrage plank in the Democratic platform.[84] The suffragists' attendance at the Republican National Convention had its rewards, however. Upon losing the nomination, Roosevelt found himself unable or unwilling to back out of the race. He bolted from the Republican party, took his backers with him, and the Progressive party was born.[85]

The roots of the Progressive party were well nurtured by male Republicans and nonpartisan reformers, but once the party was initiated many women rushed in to fill the vacuum that is an inevitable part of any new political structure. Men and women who held different traditions and ideas struggled together, for a time, to reshape the partisan landscape. In the process, the women attempted to educate the public about the role women could play in politics and to educate women in the role they should play. Thus, the election of 1912 was a critical one for women. While it did not introduce a new political system, it allowed women an opportunity to create closer and more permanent ties to state political party organizations and leaders and, as they did so, to extend the public debate about women's proper political sphere.

As the supporters of the new Progressive party met in Chicago during the last days of June to discuss the structure and policies for the new party and to build a list of supporters, they anxiously watched the proceedings of the Democratic National Convention in Baltimore. Support for their party would be determined in part by whether or not the Democrats nominated a progressive candidate. When Woodrow Wilson was nominated as the party's presidential candidate, the Progressives decided to go ahead with their new party. Wilson was a progressive, and the Democratic platform was seen by many to embody clear progressive principles, but Roosevelt's supporters determined that the differences between the parties' and candidates' views were still great.[86] They expected their platform and the organizational structure of their party to convince the voters of this difference.

On July 7, a public call announcing the new Progressive party was released. It stated that the time had come for a national progressive movement, where the people rule themselves through agencies of the government that they control. It pledged that the movement would concentrate on the passage of legislation "demanded by the modern industrial evolution" to promote and secure the "better and more equitable diffusion of prosperity" and to "avert industrial revolution."[87] The need for workers and eye-catching activities in what was predicted to be a close three-way race contributed to party men's interest in women. Women's interest was determined by their individual professional and personal connections, including a desire to increase their influence in a changing political culture. From the time of the call, the Progressive party actively encouraged women's participation by making it clear from the beginning that women would be welcomed in all party councils and the party's platform would endorse woman suffrage.[88]

On June 25, 1912, just after Roosevelt's bolt from the Republican party and as the Democrats were beginning their national convention, Jane Addams wrote to Judge Ben Lindsey of Denver, Colorado, a founder of the juvenile court system and soon to be a member of the Progressive party Executive Committee, and thanked him for bringing an appeal for woman suffrage before the National Republican Convention, thus making it a national issue. She told him to let her know "if I can be of any service in pushing it forward in the new party, where your council will have so much weight!"[89] Addams initially supported Robert LaFollette, who was nationally known for his leadership on progressive principles such as open nominating primaries and nonpartisan civil service laws. When William Kent, a Republican representative from California, wrote to Addams in May 1911 asking her to speak to well-to-do women about making a contribution to LaFollette's campaign fund, she responded that she had delivered his letter to someone she hoped would help and that "You may be sure if there is an opportunity I shall try to advance the cause." At the beginning of 1912, Addams kept up a correspondence with Belle LaFollette, working out how politically active women would advance causes dear to them as the campaign was heating up.[90] Lindsey did not have to bring Addams to Roosevelt's notice, for she was well known to the male reformers who worked with Roosevelt throughout July in preparation for the National Progressive Party Convention, and they understood that she would not only be a real leader in the party but also a symbolic leader of women.

One reason Addams moved to the Progressives was the woman suffrage issue. On July 6, 1912, Ben Lindsey wrote to assure her that Roosevelt had had a "change of heart . . . I have been trying to get him to see the necessity, the right and justice, of taking a strong affirmative stand for suffrage and I flatter myself to believe he has been quite convinced that this is the proper attitude from now on."[91] Whether or not Roosevelt was personally convinced of the right or justice of woman suffrage, during the campaign of 1912 he pledged himself and his party to the issue. Addams told the press: "I regard Col. Roosevelt as a convinced suffragist, not as an ardent suffragist, and of the two types I prefer the former always."[92] "Convinced" seems to refer to those who had been persuaded by rational arguments, whereas "ardent" suggests a passionate or emotional basis for support, and the pragmatic Addams embraced the convinced Roosevelt.

The unfolding political drama led to correspondence between Addams and Lillian Wald. Addams wrote Wald that she had heard that they were to be "sworn enemies in the future" because Wald had done the "unspeakable" in pledging herself to the Democratic party and its nominee, Woodrow Wilson, the governor of New Jersey. Wilson's nomination had "unsettled" her, Addams wrote, because she believed that he personally supported "many of the things that appeal to us but I cannot feel that his party does." As a result, she had chosen to stay within the Republican party, where she supported Roosevelt. When Roosevelt left to form the Progressive party, she was already there, in effect, as a supporter of the candidate.[93] Politics was, Addams argued, "much like everything else in some way, one follows one's cause whither it leads."[94]

Two of Roosevelt's most important male backers came from the world of business. George Perkins was a millionaire who had made his money working with J. P. Morgan; Frank A. Munsey was a millionaire magazine and newspaper owner. Both became the party's chief financial backers, and Perkins was one of its most controversial members.[95] These men were joined by men and women who had until then chosen to stay outside of political party work, working instead on behalf of specific issues through nonpartisan organizations. Social workers dominated this group of nonpartisan political activists, and the Progressive party was able to get the support of many of the most influential of them, including Addams; Raymond Robins, a millionaire who dedicated his life to social work in Chicago; Margaret Dreier Robins, of the Women's Trade Union League; Medill McCormick, whose family controlled the *Chicago Tribune* and who worked for labor reform; Ruth Hanna McCormick, the daughter of the Republican leader Marcus Hanna; and Paul Kellogg of the *Survey* magazine.[96]

Although these mainly Republican men and women of the new Progressive party differed in their stands on substantial political issues and varied in their political goals, they were joined together by the fact that crucial differences separated them, as a group, from those who stayed within the Republican party. Their dedication to formulating and implementing a progressive agenda that focused on a government for and by the people bound them together for a short and intense period of time.[97]

Plans for the platform and for the organizational structure of the national party were drawn up during July by this diverse group in Chicago and at Roosevelt's home in New York. During the same month, state parties were rapidly formed, and state nominating conventions quickly met. Here the delegates to the national convention were chosen. Women immediately answered the call to be part of the state conventions and delegations.[98] A brief overview cannot do justice to the importance of these political meetings to women. Women focused not only on the upcoming national convention but also on creating places for themselves in state parties. They also used the state conventions to build or strengthen alliances with political men. Many of these politically active women were already working alongside men on commissions and boards and in private and state institutions. Party conventions where women were promised full participation provided a new and unique opportunity. Women filled the convention halls.

New York State's convention and its delegation were the largest, best organized, and featured the most women. Seven women delegates and alternates from New York attended the national convention, chosen from the fifteen hundred delegates who attended the state Progressive party's nominating convention on August 3 in Buffalo, where about 10 percent were women.[99] A headline in the *New York Times* declared, "Women Rule Moose State Convention," and it introduced its readers to the women who would play a major part in the upcoming campaign.[100] New York women were also in attendance at the New York State convention, held on September 5. Women were appointed to the Resolutions Committee, which wrote the state party's platform, the Committee on Presidential Electors, and the Assembly and County Committees. Two women, Anna Brown and Mary Elisabeth Dreier, were elected as delegates by districts to the state committee, and nine women were elected by judicial districts.[101] While the *Times* saw fit to remark that "it is to be a woman's convention" and called the party a "skirt," they missed the obvious. It was the uniqueness of the women's presence that made them so prominent. While their numbers were impressive at the New York State convention, it was, in the end, dominated by the men. Still, the New York State chair, William Hotchkiss, told the *New York Times* that women would have, at least in the 1912 primary, the same power as men—because "under the present law the members of the new party will have nothing to do with the primaries this year, and in fact for two years, and because of this the women will be able to do the same work as the men." In Hotchkiss's view, the fact that both men and women could not vote meant they had equal power.[102]

While Jane Addams was the most famous woman in the Progressive party overall, Frances Kellor became the most important worker not only in the New York group but also at the national level; she was certainly the most dedicated worker from the party's founding until its demise in 1916. An 1897 graduate of Cornell Law School and a sociologist who was well known in settlement and social welfare circles for her work on women and employment, Kellor built her power within the Progressive party on her past associations with reformers and politicians.

Kellor moved to Chicago in 1900 and began to participate in the settlement culture dominated by Hull-House women and men. By 1902 she was back in New York City, working with Margaret Dreier through the Woman's Municipal League and the Inter-Municipal Committee on Household Research, a coalition of reformers in New York, New Jersey, and Pennsylvania. The committee was a clearinghouse that distributed information on the problems of women and waged housework; their efforts allowed Kellor to publish her study, *Out of Work*.[103] In 1908 she was appointed by the governor, Charles Evans Hughes, to be secretary of the New York State Immigration Commission, which lobbied for the creation of a Bureau of Industries and Immigration. When it was created, Kellor directed it until early 1913, when she resigned because of a conflict of interest with her work for the Progressive party. She then worked for the Legislative Committee of the North American Civic League for Immigrants.[104] Moving from investigations for reforms to establishing innovative structures to implement or further the reforms was a trait that links Kellor's early work to her Progressive party work and her subsequent work for the Republican party in 1916. And it was a link that required her to build strong relationships with reformers and politicians and, additionally, to think of herself as both.

Kellor used the Progressive party to get power beyond what she could have gotten from working through nonpartisan networks. Her ability to do so was in part a result of Roosevelt's own desire to bring reformers into his partisan fold. Roosevelt's interest in reformers was often tempered by a belief that as politicians they were less than able. He often referred to "well-meaning but head-in-the-air reformers who insist on taking such an impossible position that we lose all benefit from them."[105] Kellor, in Roosevelt's eyes, did not have her head in the air. She had given him advice on immigration laws as early as 1906, and by 1911 they were corresponding regularly about political and legal matters.[106] Kellor's interest, the party's needs, and Roosevelt's support all contributed to Kellor being offered three positions in the party: national committeewoman at the first national convention, director of the Publicity and Research Committee, and chair of the Progressive Service, which was formed after the election.

Roosevelt's interest in social and labor reforms had also brought him into contact with Mary Elisabeth Dreier and Maud Nathan, two other members of the small circle of influential New York women who were engaged in political lobbying for maximum hour and minimum wage legislation, disability and unemployment legislation, and other efforts to help working women.

Mary Dreier was the president of the New York Women's Trade Union League from 1906 until 1914. Maud Nathan, a founder and then president of the National Consumers' League, first met Theodore Roosevelt when he was governor of New York and she guided him on a tour of sweatshops in New York.[107]

Nathan's history in politics is typical of the female reformers who worked with male politicians. She claimed that her "first experience in the game of politics" was as a member of the Board of Managers of the New York Exchange for Women's Work in their effort to oppose the Dingley Tariff Bill. Nathan and the board believed that women would lose well-paid home work if the bill passed. The successful crusade against the tariff encouraged her to participate in the Woman's Municipal League, the Women's Auxiliary to the Civil Service Reform Association, and finally the Consumers' League. Nathan's work in these organizations provided for two things. One was the experience of working with male politicians; in New York, she championed Roosevelt, whom she believed to be interested in labor problems. She also began to take a greater interest in woman suffrage. Thus, when Roosevelt asked her to work for the party, she accepted.

Roosevelt chose Nathan to head the Suffrage Committee of the party. He stated that the head of the committee "must be a convinced suffragist eager for the cause, but she must also be identified in the public mind with other movements—that is she must embody our principle, that we are for suffrage because women are not merely entitled to it as a right, but are entitled to it as a means of rendering more efficient service to the community as a whole."[108] She accepted and recalled that Alice Carpenter's help was essential on the committee.[109]

Carpenter was one of six women delegates elected by the Massachusetts state nominating convention at the end of July.[110] The delegation achieved notoriety when it suggested that a woman should be named as Roosevelt's running mate.[111] Also on that delegate roster was Eleanor Garrison, "a demure, prim-appearing lady, with a lurking twinkle in her eye and a general air of being a pretty nice sort of person," according to the *New York Times*.[112] She was accorded special attention at the Massachusetts and New York conventions because of her heritage. The granddaughter of William Lloyd Garrison, she was represented as the living embodiment of the connection between the new party and the Republican party during the era of the abolitionist crusade. As Roosevelt asserted in 1912, "every honest Republican who is true to Lincoln's principles must vote with us."[113]

California women, who had just won the right to vote in the May primaries and whose governor, Hiram Johnson, became Roosevelt's running mate, sent one woman delegate. Isabella Blaney had been a delegate from California at the Republican convention and bolted into the Progressive camp; she became a member of the National Committee. Florence Porter, who with Blaney had been a delegate at the Republican convention, became a member of the Roosevelt Progressive League of California and vice president of the Los Angeles County League.[114] The suffrage states of Utah and Colorado also sent women delegates to the national convention. Wyoming women seem to have been absent.[115]

One could speculate that the low number of delegates who were women voters was a result of their hesitation about leaving positions they had found in the Democratic or Republican parties. Some women, especially those with long partisan histories, may have found it difficult to give up their positions for a temporary interlude in a third party that might not last beyond the election. The low number might also be a result of women's absence in state party networks, or possibly the auxiliary mode may have kept women in positions that prevented them from challenging men for delegate slots. Women voters may also have been perceived as more politically threatening than disfranchised women, and thus they may have already been relegated to honorary or unimportant party positions. Partial suffrage may have made the choice more difficult for women voters than for nonvoters.

Illinois women were probably the most active organizers. Chicago was the site of the Republican and Progressive conventions as well as the Provisional National Committee headquarters and then the Progressive National Committee headquarters, until it moved to New York City. Jane Addams and Mary Hawes Wilmarth were chosen as Illinois's two women delegates to the National Progressive Party Convention.[116] Abba Bass wrote to Addams in early July that Cook County had thirty-six women willing to work on behalf of the party, but she was looking beyond the county level to establish an advisory committee of women to give her advice, which she would then pass on to Joseph Dixon, who was chairing the Provisional Committee. Bass suggested Sophonisba Breckinridge, Frances Kellor, a Mrs. Treadwell, and a Mrs. Bennett, who was *"colored,"* as well as representatives from the Political Equality League and the Illinois Equal Suffrage headquarters. She informed Addams that Dixon had already expressed interest in moving "fast to organize the women or it will be too late."[117] Bass's letter to Addams indicates a number of important things. It shows that women were keenly interested in organizing as quickly as possible, that they sought recognition from the party, and that they expected the other parties to organize women into their ranks. Further, Bass's list of women may be representative of the network used in Illinois and other states.

Women were active at the New Jersey nominating convention, but there are no indications that they held any official positions. What the New Jersey evidence does show is the enthusiasm and wonder that the women felt in a politically charged milieu. According to Mina C. Van Winkle, when the plank for woman suffrage in the New Jersey platform was read at the state convention, "Our small group of twelve women who thought themselves the only suffragists present were surprised to find scores of women on their feet in all parts of the hall. It was an unforgettable moment. Then followed a long round of applause by the men. There was unspeakable joy in every woman's countenance."[118] The delegates and alternates who were chosen by state parties all participated in the proceedings of the National Progressive Party Convention which met in Chicago from August 5 through 7. They arrived to find a city and nation eager to watch them participate. It was a "strange sight," the *New York Times* reported, to see these women take on the role of politician. It was stranger still to see how their presence changed the normal course of things. The chartered train from New York had "every car half full of women," according to the *Times,* and for once men "were not going down the aisles with their hats on, flicking cigar ashes on the carpet; no indeed." Decorum ruled the day. Although "about a quarter of the seats" at the convention "were taken by women," "Nobody smoked."[119] The *Times* did not overestimate the fact that women felt comfortable at the convention, but it was not decorum that was the cause of their comfort. It was a feeling of power.

Anna E. Dickinson (Engraving by G. E. Perine & Co.,
New York, N.Y.; #00140, Chicago Historical Society)

Mary Ann Shadd Cary (Moorland-
Spingarn Research Center, Howard
University)

Judith Ellen Foster (Photograph by Jno. Buell, Geneseo, Ill.; Aldrich Autograph Collection, State Historical Society of Iowa, Des Moines)

First International Convention of Women, Washington, D.C., 1888 (Photographer unknown; ICHi-09222, Chicago Historical Society)

Mary Church Terrell (Photograph by Scurlock
Studios; Moorland-Spingarn Research Center,
Howard University)

Alice Carpenter (Photograph by Alman &
Co., 590 Fifth Ave., New York, N.Y.; Sophia
Smith Collection, Smith College)

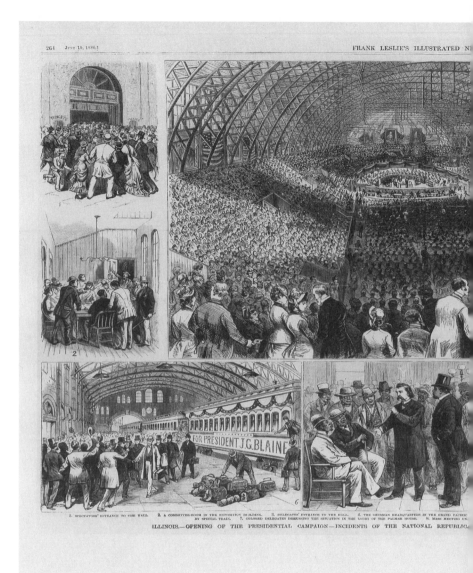

1. SPECTATORS' ENTRANCE TO THE HALL.   2. A COMMITTEE-ROOM IN THE EXPOSITION BUILDING.   3. DELEGATES' ENTRANCE TO THE HALL.   4. THE SHERMAN HEADQUARTERS IN THE GRAND PACIFIC
BY SPECIAL TRAIN.   7. COLORED DELEGATES DISCUSSING THE SITUATION IN THE LOBBY OF THE PALMER HOUSE.   8. MASS MEETING ON

ILLINOIS.—OPENING OF THE PRESIDENTIAL CAMPAIGN—INCIDENTS OF THE NATIONAL REPUBLIC.

"Opening of the Presidential Campaign—Incidents of the National Republican Convention
at Chicago" (*Frank Leslie's Illustrated Newspaper*, June 19, 1880, 264–65, from sketches by W.
Parker Bodfish): (1) "spectators' entrance to the hall"; (2) "a committee-room in the exposition building"; (3) "delegates' entrance to the hall"; (4) "the Sherman headquarters in the
Grand Pacific Hotel"; (5) "Hon. Geo. F. Hoar, temporary chairman, addressing the delegates, June 2d"; (6) "arrival of the Maine and New Hampshire delegations by special train";

TEMPORARY CHAIRMAN, ADDRESSING THE DELEGATES, JUNE 2D.   6. ARRIVAL OF THE MAINE AND NEW HAMPSHIRE DELEGATIONS
NAL WOMAN'S SUFFRAGE ASSOCIATION AT FARWELL HALL, JUNE 1ST.

CHICAGO.—FROM SKETCHES BY W. PARKER BODFISH.—SEE PAGE 267.

(7) "colored delegates discussing the situation in the lobby of the Palmer House"; and (8) "mass meeting under the auspices of the National Woman's Suffrage Association at Farwell Hall, June 1st." (ICHi-02011, Chicago Historical Society)

(*Left to right*) Isabella Blaney, Mary Hawes Wilmarth, and Jane Addams, in the "Votes for Women" car, 1912 (Jane Addams Collection, Swarthmore College Peace Collection)

National Progressive Convention, Chicago, August 4–5, 1912 (Photograph by Moffatt Studio and Kaufmann, Weimer; ICHi-01993, Chicago Historical Society)

Jeannette Rankin (*standing, right*), Carrie Chapman Catt (*standing, left*), and several other women prepare to depart from the National Suffrage Headquarters, Washington, D.C., April 12, 1917 (Leslie Woman Suffrage Commission, 171 Madison Ave., New York, N.Y.; Sophia Smith Collection, Smith College)

Alice Paul (*second from the left*) and other members of the National Woman's Party hold a banner with a quotation from Susan B. Anthony. (AP/Wide World Photos)

Republican National Convention, June 10, 1920 (Photograph by Moffett Studio and Kaufmann, Weimer & Fabry Co.; Prints and Photographs Division, Library of Congress)

New York Women's Republican Club with President Coolidge, 1924 (National Photo Company Collection, Prints and Photographs Division, Library of Congress)

5. A Contest for Inclusion:
    Gender, Race, and the Campaign of 1912

IN THE MIDDLE of August 1912, Theodore Roosevelt wrote Jane Addams that
he wished her to write articles on the "new movement and what we Progressives are striving for in the way of social justice, especially for the women and
children and those men who have the hardest time in life."[1] Writing campaign literature had been a function of partisan women since the founding
days of the Republican party, and Roosevelt's letter was therefore an invitation for Addams to continue this political tradition. At the same time, her
prominent position in the central ritual of the Progressive party—the national convention—strengthened and magnified the representation of women as
symbols of political virtue and principles. The Progressive party offered them
new political opportunities even as it reinforced long-held political ideas of
the proprietary boundaries of political womanhood.

Addams accepted the offer and took it as an opportunity to expand her
own role in national politics. She understood that men like Roosevelt would
offer prominent women carefully defined campaign roles to fill organizational voids but also to create an image for the party. The party looked more
principled with principled men, and women, in it. Women like Addams accepted the offers given by the party not only to build the party itself but also
to build on its promises to create more expansive political roles for women.
To do so, Progressive women and men had to negotiate not only who would
write campaign literature, give speeches, and create organizational groups;
they were involved in a renegotiation of the meanings of gender and race in
party politics.

In early August 1912, supporters of the newly founded Progressive party
traveled to Chicago for their first national convention. The election was three

months away. As they were gathering, the Provisional Committee was meeting at Chicago's Congress Hotel to organize the party's structure and to finalize the platform for presentation to the convention delegates. There was to be no bossism or corruption at this convention and, it was hoped, no controversy over delegates. In the thirty days between the announcement of the formation of the party and the first meeting of the Provisional Committee, Roosevelt spent a good deal of time on organization. From the start, he held firm to his belief that each state Progressive party was an autonomous organization and would choose its own delegates, structure its own organization, and write its own platform. Forty-eight states responded. This was to be a national party strengthened by local and state organizations championing local and state candidates. It was not to be a party by and for Roosevelt's political fortunes only.[2]

Three women worked with the Provisional National Committee and were members-at-large of the National Committee: Jane Addams, Frances Kellor of New York, and Isabella Blaney of California. Jean Gordon of Louisiana declined the offer of a position on the National Committee, and her place was not filled. Alice Carpenter, who sat on the Platform Committee, was the only other woman to be given an important position. Eleanor Garrison, who accompanied Carpenter to Chicago, was "filled with pride" by Carpenter's position on the committee.[3] Working with the committee, these women sought to influence the structure of the party and the formation of the platform. Although the writing of the platform had been underway since late June, it was only finalized during the convention. By then, women were in places from which they had some influence over specific planks. Eleanor Garrison wrote her mother that she and Carpenter were leading "a thrilling life" and that the "women in this convention are perfect stars" and have "real status. You feel it every minute and they are going to keep it or else leave the party."[4]

The Progressive party platform was written as the new party quickly moved to gather supporters, workers, and volunteers. The desire to be a part of the creation of a party platform based on long-standing policy goals led many women social reformers into the ranks of the party. Aspects of the platform and the party deliberations frustrated some Progressives, but the inclusion of its many important planks for social welfare concerns won party members' final endorsement. They believed that the party would survive beyond the election, whether Roosevelt won or lost, and that the structure of the organization would be used toward the service of these goals.

The belief that party platforms could be transformed from uninteresting or ignored promises or rhetoric into principled and practical agendas for social justice drew many people into the new party and accounts for their dedication. The Progressive party platform was based on decades of research by social scientists, as well as the experience of social workers and practicing politicians.[5] Roosevelt may have controlled the final draft of the platform, but the team he helped assemble and gave initiative to was responsible for its life. As Paul Kellogg wrote in the *Survey,* "minority parties ultimately write the platforms for all parties. In time, the causes which they have the temerity to espouse are taken up by the established organizations when direct appeal to the latter may have proven fruitless."[6] The reformers understood both the short- and long-term implications of their work.

Articulated and argued in lofty, almost religious terms, the platform was first presented on the second day of the national convention, after Roosevelt exhorted his "Confession of Faith." Calling the platform a "contract with the people," Roosevelt's "confession" was a vivid description of the written platform and included a discussion of the key issues of the campaign. He concluded: "Our cause is based on the eternal principle of righteousness; and even though we who now lead may for the time fail, in the end the cause itself shall triumph."[7]

Addams, Kellor, and Carpenter, in their work with the Provisional Committee, found that there was almost no discussion of the woman suffrage plank, and it appears that it went through only three drafts. The final plank read: "The National Progressive party, believing that no people can justly claim to be a true democracy which denies political rights on account of sex, pledges itself to the task of securing equal suffrage to men and women alike."[8] According to a report from the pro-Progressive *Philadelphia North American,* there was a widespread tendency to attribute women's support for the party to suffrage alone. The paper declared that women like Addams looked "upon the suffrage plank as . . . important because of its genuine programme for the aid of those . . . now overwhelmed in the flood of economic error and social wrongs."[9]

Overall pleasure with the Progressive party platform was a major reason women and men energetically supported the party. This pleasure also allowed Addams to compromise on planks and convention decisions she disagreed with. According to her own account, for days and nights she agonized over the plank endorsing a stronger navy and army. She wrote in 1932 that her disappointment over the battleships equaled that of other women pacifists attending the convention. She found solace and support from Mary Hawes Wilmarth, who expressed "gay comments as to how frail a barrier woman's influence seemed to be in spite of its vaunted power, even in a new party which had welcomed us so enthusiastically."[10]

Addams's place as a member of the Provisional National Committee taught

her new lessons about political compromise and bolstered her belief that individuals, especially women, needed to rethink their political strategies. Central to this process was an understanding of the role of expediency in political party survival. This understanding informed women's views of Roosevelt's
support for woman suffrage and of their own power and status within the
party. Motivated by expediency, many women chose to support the party *and*
Roosevelt as a way to further women's rights and social justice.

Because of her prominence and commitment to women's participation in
public and political life, Addams dedicated much of her work on behalf of
the party to explaining why individuals should support the Progressive party. She explained that she had come to the gradual conviction that there was
a need for "a new political organization committed to a well-defined program
of social legislation with resolute leaders of courage and political experience,
if America is to carry out the most fundamental obligation of self-government,
that of making the legal order an adequate expression of the common good."
She argued that people should be "consciously committed to the same program and organized to reduce it to political action," and that the Progressive
party served that end. Above all, the platform served that end.[11]

Addams's work to promote the party went beyond Roosevelt's mandate,
as she attempted to explore and interpret why women should engage in partisan activism. Women, she argued, should be especially interested in the new
party because they were losing influence as power shifted and the state grew.
She testified to the fact that she had seen "philanthropic enterprises carefully
developed by public-spirited women, such as industrial schools and juvenile
courts, when they were made an integral part of government, languish and
fail of their highest usefulness because their founders and promoters could
have no further part in them." Women needed to accept the fact that political power was situated in political parties and work with them. Otherwise, all
that they had worked to create would be lost. Party politics was necessary to
counter the bureaucratization of social services. Parties, in turn, should recognize women's influence and knowledge in building these enterprises.[12]

Coupled with her argument about the changing locale of political power
was the argument that indirect influence did not work and that women should
not rely on it any longer. In newspaper articles and through the official paper
of the party, the *Progressive Bulletin*, Addams traced how her own social activism had led her to the party. She argued that reformers first identified problems and tried through philanthropic means to solve them, but in that effort
they recognized that solving an individual's problem did not remedy the larger
problem. Helping one person to find work did not solve the problem of unemployment for thousands more. In what she called the "wavering line" that

divides philanthropy from politics, women became involved in political activism when they went to the state to ask for changes in laws. At this stage, philanthropic activities supported by women were taken over by politics, and many women lost influence.[13] It was important to emphasize, Addams argued, that women "are not changing their interest in taking up politics." Women were making the same demands and speaking for the same things as always. The "interest of women in philanthropy is exactly the same but they find that they can reach the desired ends more directly through a political party," she argued.[14]

In her autobiography, *Second Twenty Years at Hull House,* Addams wrote that the founding of the Progressive party provided for "a curious moment of release from inhibitions, and it did not seem in the least strange that reticent men and women should speak aloud of their religious and social beliefs, confident that they would be understood."[15] She embraced the Progressives because of what the party stood for and because she believed the time had come for men and women to engage each other's political ideas in the partisan arena. So she welcomed Roosevelt's invitation, and she and the other women, on behalf of the party, engaged in a unique political conversation in the campaign of 1912.[16]

A Celebration of Womanhood

Reports on the number of women delegates and participants at the National Progressive Party Convention vary.[17] The *Woman's Journal* reported that there were between thirty and forty women delegates from different states and a number of women alternates.[18] The *Progressive Bulletin* listed thirty-four women as "A Few of the Women Progressives" in its first issue, but it is difficult to get an exact number because the convention roll is incomplete and only the first and middle initials for the majority of individuals were given.[19] An examination of Progressive party records for the national convention indicates that the sixteen women delegates and five alternates included: one delegate from Colorado and two alternates; two delegates-at-large from Illinois; six delegates-at-large from Massachusetts; one delegate-at-large, one alternate-at-large, two district delegates, and three district alternates from New York; and one delegate and one alternate from Utah.[20]

The convention roll is probably more accurate than press reports, because the press's fascination with the women led them to give women power and positions they did not possess. Newspapers reported that "the women who identify themselves with the Bull Moose movement are not to work in any auxiliary capacity; they are to have a say in everything that is going on."[21]

Another problem with press reports was the confusion about whether indi-viduals were delegates to the state or to the national conventions.[22] The *New York Times* reported in one article that Mrs. W. H. Felton of Cartersville, Georgia, was a delegate, while another stated that she declined on account of her age. Rebecca Felton, who did attend the convention, would have been a member of Georgia's white delegation, the "Roosevelt White League of Georgia."[23]

The women assembled at the Chicago Coliseum just after noon on August 5 for the opening of the National Progressive Party Convention. Joseph M. Dixon called the convention to order and introduced the keynote address by Albert J. Beveridge, a senator from Indiana who would become the conven-tion chairman. According to the *Outlook,* at least one midwestern newspa-per reporter believed that the speeches given at the convention were as im-portant as the platform that was to be voted on. Everywhere, the reporter wrote, "the people read Mr. Beveridge's speech. They remember it. . . . On the other hand, does anybody happen to remember anything in the 'keynote' speeches delivered by Elihu Root or Judge Alton B. Parker at the two old party Conventions?" The keynote of Beveridge's speech was that the "people's government has been taken away from them and must be restored."[24]

On the afternoon of the second day of the convention, William A. Pender-gast of New York nominated Theodore Roosevelt as the party's presidential candidate. His speech was followed by a seconding speech by Ben Lindsey, a judge from Denver. Jane Addams gave the next seconding speech. Arthur Ruhl, writing for *Collier's* magazine, observed that a delegation of women escorted to the convention hall "its one figure perhaps—next to the protagonist him-self—of greatest interest and significance." "Some were girls in cap and gown, some 'our very best people,' . . . Most of them carried 'Votes for Women' flags; most were for the new party, and two or three were not, but all were there to do honor to Miss Jane Addams, who had consented to be a delegate at large from Illinois and to second the nomination of Colonel Roosevelt. She sat—this first citizen of Illinois—in the center of the front row."[25] According to the *New York Times,* Addams ascended to the platform and "was promptly followed by a Georgia woman, Mrs. W. H. Felton. . . . Following her, Miss Dreier . . . Miss Alice Carpenter of Boston and a lot of women from Massachusetts, including Mrs. Elizabeth Towne, Mrs. Richard Washburn Childs, Mrs. Lew J. Johnson, Miss Helen Temple Cook, and Miss Mabel Cook."[26]

Addams held the spotlight. She stood on the stage of the Chicago Colise-um, a "gracious figure in white," as one reporter remarked, and seconded the nomination of Theodore Roosevelt as the Progressive party's candidate for president of the United States.

I rise to second the nomination stirred by the splendid platform adopted by this convention. Measures of industrial amelioration, demands for social justice, long discussed by small groups in charity conferences and economic associations, have here been considered in a great national convention and are at last thrust into the stern arena of political action. A great party has pledged itself to the protection of children, to the care of the aged, to the relief of overworked girls, to the safe guarding of burdened men. Committed to these human undertakings, it is inevitable that such a party should appeal to women, should seek to draw upon the great reservoir of their moral energy so long undesired and unutilized in practical politics. . . . I second the nomination of Theodore Roosevelt because he is one of the few men in our public life who has been responsive to the social appeal and who has caught the significance of the modern movement. Because of that, because the programme will require a leader of invincible courage, of open mind, of democratic sympathies, one endowed with power to interpret the common man and to identify himself with the common lot, I heartily second the nomination.[27]

Arthur Ruhl wrote that "never before, at a national convention, had a woman seconded the nomination of a candidate for President; never before had men shouted 'Good! Good!' as she spoke of things hitherto remote from ordinary politics. . . . It was a new sound at a national convention, this woman's voice speaking of the relief of overworked girls. . . . a new sound, more strange and stirring, even, than the moo of the bull moose."[28] According to Eleanor Garrison, after her speech Addams "took a votes for women banner, carried it across the platform and then through the whole auditorium and back, followed by admirers of both sexes."[29]

Addams's speech, like others given at the convention, was greeted with cheers by the ten thousand Progressives who gathered in the Coliseum. According to a reporter for the *Outlook*, "ten thousand people, American men and women, stood in the flag-draped Coliseum at Chicago . . . many wearing red bandannas. . . . spots of red against the prevailing black, . . . worn around the neck or the crown of the hat. It seemed as if most of the delegates were wearing them."[30] To the assembled Progressives these red bandannas represented the fighting spirit of the Rough Riders, the cavalry Roosevelt had led in Cuba during the Spanish-American War.

Addams was a symbol of the part all women were taking, "for weal or woe," in political activities, reports stated, and she was heralded as the first American woman to give a nominating speech at a national party convention.[31] She was seen as the perfect woman for this honor. Reporters noted that she was the type of political woman most acceptable to a public greatly aroused by the exciting three-way presidential race of 1912. She was a celebrity for her great work for immigrants and the poor; she was a suffragist and a vice president of the respectable NAWSA; she was not seeking the reward of office for her partisan loyalty; she was simply fulfilling her public responsibilities.

When women moved into the Progressive party they were represented—and represented themselves—as moving from a nonpartisan sphere of influence. They could do this because of the weak public awareness of women's work in the Republican and Democratic parties. Republican women's auxiliaries were well established, and Democratic women had their clubs, but these organizations were marginalized in the parties, in the public's awareness, and in the public memory. Newspaper reports stated that the WNRA was an integral part of the Republican machine but also claimed that it was the Progressive party that was bringing women into partisan politics in ways never seen before.[32] Republican women had moved into the campaign with an organization, but the public came to it without a social memory of women's partisanship. It was as if women moved into the campaign of 1912 without any history in partisan politics. Progressive women, in turn, did not draw on strong female partisan images or examples to argue for a place in the party. That absence worked to women's advantage and to the advantage of the party. It was the disinterested, virtuous (read uncorrupted), and principled woman that the Progressive party wanted to use to capture the public's imagination and support. It may also have worked to their disadvantage, as the party moved from celebrating its emphasis on the common good at the national convention and moved into the trenches of campaign warfare.

The public representation of Addams as a disinterested and principled political woman built on an image she had carefully crafted for herself. Her self-creation for the public included her important autobiography, *Twenty Years at Hull House,* published in 1910. In it, she addresses the question of political or public corruption. She explains that she had been offered a bribe by a businessman during a Hull-House drive for a sweatshop bill. Her courage to resist the bribe had come, in part, from her family memory of Abraham Lincoln, which was reinforced by walks to Lincoln Park, where she gazed at St. Gaudens's monument of her hero. Lincoln's vision of tolerance and "charity towards all" fueled her moral perceptions, coexisted with her intellectual preparations, and guided her in her search for new ways to help the "nation's resource," its people.[33] Now Addams was in the Progressive party, which she envisioned as a party of the people, for the people. "In the unceasing ebb and flow of justice and oppression," she wrote in her autobiography, "we must dig channels as best we can." These channels, she understood after twenty years of agitation, needed to be made in the partisan sea of politics.[34]

Press reports noted that Addams had dignity, a womanly dignity, and the theme of the uncorrupted woman was overt in the campaign.[35] Addams was wrapped in the memory of Lincoln and was seen by the public as the "Mother Emancipator of Illinois." The party itself promoted her in Lincoln's image. The "burden of the sorrows of the world shows in her face as it did in the face of Abraham Lincoln," said the *Progressive Bulletin* in its first edition.[36]

The perception of women as uncorrupted, virtuous activists who could add shine to the new party helped Progressive women gain a place inside the party. This was not a new image for political women; it benefited from long-held ideas about why women engaged in political activities, ideas that were promoted by both women and men in different political milieus. This image fit perfectly into the new Progressive party, which was intended to formulate and carry out a progressive agenda that focused on a government for and by the people.

After her speech, Addams returned to Hull-House and found many congratulatory telegrams praising her appearance at the national convention. She also received critical telegrams, including one from William Monroe Trotter, the editor of the African-American *Boston Guardian,* who wrote, "Woman suffrage will be stained with Negro Blood unless women refuse all alliance with Roosevelt."[37]

Oppositional Voices

When the nationwide call for the new Progressive party was issued in late June 1912, many African-American political leaders hoped that it might be a political home during an era in which the Republican and Democratic parties were increasingly indifferent to the African-American voter and hostile to African Americans in general. They worked in southern and northern states to organize African-American voters for Roosevelt. It was not an easy task because of the strong hold the Republican party had over the African-American voter, a hold that was reinforced by federal appointments—jobs. Patronage kept the Republican party strong in the North and alive in the South.[38]

T. Thomas Fortune, the editor of the African-American newspaper the *New York Age,* was a Republican loyalist and no fan of Roosevelt. He was critical of anyone who supported the new party, including African Americans, thus leaving the Republican party that "gave them opportunity to make themselves all that they are." Fortune was also responding to the increasing tendency of African Americans to hold their votes independent of the Republican party and take an independent path in politics. The aim was to protect and strengthen the black vote by building it into an influential political bloc that could be brokered, if needed, for rights and protections.[39]

Fortune strongly criticized the Progressive party, but his criticism was more than a partisan attack. He focused on the red bandannas that the Progressives waved so enthusiastically as representations of their fighting spirit. To him, the red bandannas represented something else. An article in the *Age* explained: "In our youth, when the memory of the days of slavery was more than a fact to joke by, the black woman everywhere in the South, and very generally, wore the red bandana, a big handkerchief, as a head covering. It was really the sign of the black woman, and stood for the good nature and good cooking. . . . For sentimental reasons we have a kindly feeling for the bandana as headgear." Now, the article went on, it was time to let go of this sentimental association and let it be associated with Roosevelt. Fortune even argued that the new party should be called the "Bandana party" rather than the Progressive party. For this to occur, the bandanna would have to be transformed even more. Painted in the center of the bandanna would be "Mingo Saunders, dressed in the uniform of a United States Soldier, dead, with his arms stacked beside him, with this sign pinned to his bosom, 'Killed by the Brownsville order!'" It would "symbolize," the *Age* concluded, "the reckless contempt of law and public opinion for which the Bandana Party stands."[40]

The reference to Brownsville alludes to Roosevelt's discharge in 1906, when he was president, of three African-American companies of the Twenty-Fifth U.S. Infantry. The discharge came after none of the soldiers claimed responsibility or would accuse others for a night of crime in the town of Brownsville, Texas, which left one white person dead. Three of those soldiers were Medal of Honor winners; many of them had served in Cuba longer than the Rough Riders. The timing of the discharge made Roosevelt's actions even worse. The night of crime occurred on August 13; by October 30, Roosevelt had told confidants of his decision to discharge the soldiers; but not until November 7, after elections where Republicans depended on the African-American vote, did the decision become public. No evidence was ever presented to prove the guilt of any of the discharged soldiers.[41]

Fortune's transformation of the bandanna from a sentimental image of the African-American woman's headcovering to a cloth inscribed with the image of the Brownsville soldier was an attempt to associate the red bandanna with people who do not belong in politics. Who was perceived as having less right to a place in politics than the African-American woman? Progressives also became outsiders, as the red bandanna connected Roosevelt and the Progressives to an episode considered shameful by many African Americans and whites.

Fortune's rejection of the way the Progressives symbolically used the red bandanna was a common theme in the cartoons printed in the *New York Age*. The rejection is especially clear in the cartoon of September 26, 1912, which depicts Roosevelt, wearing the bandanna around his neck, being pursued by the ghost of the Twenty-Fifth Infantry. Below this cartoon is another article on the red bandanna to reinforce Fortune's point, claiming that waving or wearing the bandanna means subscribing to a value system that promotes opportunism.

The editorials and cartoons in the *Age* were directed toward African-American readers, but events at the Progressive convention broadened the criticisms and made them more public. It was within this context that the Progressives sought to assert positive symbols for the party—and where the pragmatic reasons for women's inclusion in the party were reinforced by symbolic benefits. Addams was one of those positive symbols, standing in white, a legitimizing, stabilizing force on the stage of the Coliseum.

Much of what is public about politics—about the political process—is a careful manipulation of images and words. Political parties, especially, must have symbols that are easily readable and digested by their supporters and the public. This is why the cartoon representations of elephant and donkey have become stock symbols for the Republican and Democratic parties. They were first created in 1874 by Thomas Nast for readers of *Harper's Weekly*. An elephant, representing the Republican voter, was being frightened by an ass wearing a lion's skin. Over time, the elephant came to represent the party, the ass became the Democratic donkey, both became shared symbols that could be easily manipulated and read, and these symbols contributed to the creation of a shared culture. Viewers as well as the creators constructed, and continue to construct, the meanings of these symbols.[42]

The experiences of those who participated in politics were always more than symbolic; they were real, and this is certainly true of Jane Addams. As a founding member of the fledgling National Association for the Advancement of Colored People (NAACP) and a believer in racial justice, she had a difficult time in the Progressive party. That difficulty began when it became clear that Roosevelt was going to employ a lily-white strategy to win the White House.

The term "lily-white" was coined by Norris Cuney, an African-American political leader in Texas, in the 1880s. It refers to the establishment of all-white political clubs in the South.[43] It was a sectional Republican strategy to make the party appealing to Democrats, and it came about simultaneously with the passage of disfranchising laws. When they occurred together, the result was the formal exclusion of African Americans from party politics. Because political parties in the early twentieth century were coalitions of representatives of state parties, the development of lily-whiteism influenced the shape and direction of national political activities, including national party conventions.[44]

To succeed with his new party and win the presidential race, Roosevelt planned for the party to dissociate itself from Republican traditions. Decades earlier the Republican party stopped waving the bloody shirt and promoted itself as the party of tariff reform and industrial democracy.[45] Now Roosevelt was free of the Old Guard Republicans and ready to build the Progressive party into a national party, unconstrained by "war issues." He was ready to challenge the Democratic domination of the South and win the votes of southern whites, including Democratic businessmen. The strategy was to support efforts to make southern Progressive organizations "lily-white." To put it another way, to win the presidency he needed to cast a wide but not indiscriminate net to gather supporters and workers. Women like Addams fit in that net. Southern African-American men did not; African-American women were not even in his vision.

Lily-White Politics and the Exclusion of African-American Men

Roosevelt's lily-white strategy was supposed to work itself out at the state level, and in most southern states it did. However, African-American Progressives from three southern states refused to bow out of the new party and sent delegations to Chicago demanding recognition from the party's Provisional National Committee. The arrival of both lily-white and "black-and-tan" delegations from the states of Alabama, Florida, and Mississippi led one Progressive to declare that the issue of race "may haunt us; it may destroy us in this movement."[46]

The tone for the committee's deliberations was set by the discussion about the representation of the territories. Delegates from Hawaii demanded equal representation, and discussion followed about whether Hawaii's delegates should be granted a vote since it was a territory and not a state. In the middle of this discussion Frances Heney of California proclaimed the "fact that these foreigners will be in a majority in the islands." The foreigners in question were spelled out by another member of the committee, who described Hawaii as a "colony built of Japanese and Chinese laborers" and stated, "as I understand it, gentlemen, this is to be a white man's party."[47] In the end, Hawaii, Alaska, and the District of Columbia were permitted to seat three delegates each, but they were refused the right to vote. Immediately after this issue was settled, the committee heard a motion that all delegations whose credentials were not contested be placed upon the temporary roll. This done, the committee quickly moved to discuss the cases of Alabama, Florida, and then Mississippi.[48]

In the Alabama case, Dr. Joseph Thomas spoke for twelve African Americans who claimed they had been promised that they would be included in the Alabama delegation of twenty-four but the white state chair, Oscar Hundley, had excluded them. Upon exclusion, they chose their own delegates. The committee had a severely limited discussion and voted to seat the all-white delegation. In Florida, two Progressive state conventions had been held; one was black, the other was white. Both were organized by the white state chair, H. L. Anderson. Charles Alston, a lawyer from Tampa, explained that he and the other African-American delegates went to the white convention in Ocala when they realized that it was the "official" convention. The confusing and clearly corrupt events in Florida led the committee to exclude the state as a whole from the proceedings (though Anderson was allowed to retain his committee chairmanship).[49]

The Mississippi case was the most important, because the African-American delegation was led by Perry W. Howard, and because it was now evident that this was not about individual cases; it was about establishing a lily-white policy for the national party.[50] Howard had a long history in the Republican party, and he had been one of the Republican delegates who sat stoically for Roosevelt as Taft's name was placed in nomination in June at the Republican National Convention.[51] Now he was asking for recognition from the Progressive party. He knew the chances of gaining recognition were limited. Roosevelt and Dixon supported the white state chair, B. F. Fridge, and his lily-white organization and had failed to recognize the black-and-tan group organized by Sidney Redmond and Howard. Howard's appeal to the committee invoked the past: "Would you have Roosevelt the cause of taking from us liberty that Abraham Lincoln has given us?"[52] The debate was intense. John Parker of New Orleans argued that white southerners knew "how the Negro for more than forty-five years not only had done nothing whatsoever for the Republican party but there is not a gentlemen here that does not know that with the negro it is a physical absolute impossibility to do anything."[53] In the end, the answer to Howard's question was yes. Charles Alston, one of the African-American delegates from Florida, asked Dixon to approach Roosevelt to see if concessions could be made for the black delegates. Roosevelt refused to negotiate the matter.[54] The Mississippi delegation was excluded.

After the delegate contests were resolved, Jane Addams and Henry Moskowitz issued a protest stating that they were disturbed that a party that "stands for human rights, should even *appear* not to stand for the rights of negroes." They asked how a party that stands for the rights of working men and women and the protection of children could deny "the right of the negro to take part in this movement."[55]

The protests continued. Frank Garrison wrote to his niece Eleanor asking her to "withdraw at once and formally" from the party. He reminded her that her "grandfather refused to enter an antislavery convention from which women were excluded" and told her that the family regretted that she would "follow an unprincipled humbug who cares nothing for suffrage except as it will win him votes and is not to be trusted on that or any other question."[56] Eleanor Garrison wrote her mother that she thought her uncle had "overstepped the bounds considerably" with his telegram and that she considered herself "old enough to decide such things." She wrote that she was in "wonderful society" and told her mother about Addams's speech, the planks of the platform, and that "the feeling toward the black people is most friendly, there are many of them scattered through the delegations." Referring to her grandfather's support of the right of American women to be delegates to the 1840 international abolitionist conference, she concluded that "the case is not parallel with Grandpa in London, though I don't like the idea of exclusion. Perhaps if the antislavery people had backed the women as they promised to do, we shouldn't be in our present position." She chose to stay in the party because, she wrote, it made her feel like a "political entity," and because she wanted to cast her lot with the women who stayed put.[57]

Working with W. E. B. Du Bois, Henry Moskowitz, and Joel Spingarn, all directors of the NAACP, Addams attempted to convince the party to endorse a platform statement that called for the repeal of unfair discriminatory laws and the right of all citizens to vote on equal terms. Drafted by Du Bois, the statement reads: "The National Progressive party recognizes that distinctions of race, or class, or sex in political life, have no place in a Democracy. Especially does the party realize that a group of 10,000,000 people, who have in a generation changed from slavery to a free labor system, re-established family life, accumulated $1,000,000,000 of real property, and reduced their illiteracy from 80 to 30 percent, deserve and must have justice, opportunity, and a voice in their own government."[58] The Resolutions Committee rejected the statement, and Progressive party supporters found themselves with two immediate choices: stay and accept the party's policies (maybe with the hope of making changes from within) or leave.

Exodus and Explanations

Du Bois left. He had never really been a Roosevelt supporter, even though he found the Progressive agenda "irresistible."[59] He could not forgive him for the Brownsville episode. Du Bois then supported the Socialist party, seeing it as the only "party which openly recognizes Negro manhood," but by early November he had come out for Woodrow Wilson.[60] Redmond, Alston, and

William Monroe Trotter also went over to the Democrats and supported Wilson. The exodus from the Progressive party by northern African Americans included African-American women who joined Florence Harriman's Women's National Wilson and Marshall Organization.[61] This move by African Americans into the Democratic party forever changed the contours of American politics.

Other African Americans returned to the Republican fold and supported William Howard Taft. Among them was Perry Howard.[62] African Americans who remained loyal to the Republican party were given party resources to publicize the reasons for their loyalty. A sixty-four-page pamphlet, "The Republican Party and the Afro-American: A Book of Facts and Figures," which had been first prepared in 1908, was reissued. Written by Cyrus Field Adams, a prominent African-American Republican who held the position of assistant register of the treasury, it emphasized the long history of the association of African Americans with the party as well as the party's recent efforts on behalf of African Americans. In 1908 the party also included a strong statement on the "Rights of the Negro" in the national platform. It praised the long friendship, proclaimed support for the Reconstruction amendments, and condemned all efforts toward disfranchisement. The Republican platform of 1912 had a weak plank denouncing lynching and was silent on the Fourteenth and Fifteenth Amendments. At the 1908 convention and again in 1912, contrary to tradition, no African-American Republican was invited to make a seconding speech.[63]

Addams chose to stay. While Trotter was appalled, his was only one of many telegraphs she received during and after the convention. Some criticized her.[64] Others thanked her for her "firm stand," for her "just and admirable stand," for her "courageous stand."[65] Some questioned what had happened and what she had done. As one person wrote, the "colored people look upon you as one of their best friends and will believe what you said or say." He told her that the newspapers reported that she had something of interest to offer them, and it would go into the Progressive platform. Did she do that? If not, or if it did not get in, why not?[66]

Explanations for the Progressive party's actions began immediately. Black delegates from northern states who remained loyal to the party spoke out in a pamphlet prepared by the National Committee. They emphasized the point that there were more African-American delegates at the Progressive convention than at either the Republican or Democratic conventions. No one pointed out that the Progressives failed to revive the Republican tradition of honoring an African-American as nominating speaker, a move that would have changed the symbolic construction of the convention and the party.[67]

Roosevelt used the *Outlook* and the *Progressive Bulletin* to explain the party's racial exclusion, a policy that was entirely consistent with his political strategies, since he first became president in 1901.[68] Roosevelt argued that southern African Americans were easily bribed (corrupted), and therefore they harmed the party's attempt to build a nationwide movement. Further, he argued, they were of "very grave harm, to their own race." The solution was that they would be protected and guided by whites, by the "best white men in the South."[69] Only this program would ultimately bring justice and gradual reenfranchisement. Northern African Americans, the "best colored men," were welcome in the party because they were not manipulated by white politicians.

To put it another way, Roosevelt and those who supported his strategy believed that southern African Americans would tarnish the image of the new party. Compare this to the party's decision to include women and celebrate their inclusion. Women were seen to have something to give to the party because they were represented as uncorrupted and incorruptible. Southern and northern African-American men, in alliance with some white Progressives, attempted to contest the image of the corrupted African American without effect. Their lack of success may have resulted not only from race constructions within the party but also gender constructions; standing next to the image of the corrupted southern African-American man was the image of the uncorrupted, now white, Progressive woman. Addams symbolized the legacy of the virtuous Republican mother, the nonpartisan temperance worker, and the disfranchised woman looking to vote but not to hold office.

Addams used the NAACP's *Crisis* for her explanation. She had originally submitted the article published in the *Crisis* to *McClure's* magazine, but its editors rejected it as too controversial.[70] She told *Crisis* readers that she wondered if her abolitionist father would have participated in a political convention that excluded African Americans. She recalled that as a child she had once made a mistake when she tried to do what she thought her father would do rather than follow her own course. In response, her father warned her not to "complicate moral situations, already sufficiently difficult, by trying to work out another's point of view. You will do much better if you look the situation fairly in the face with the best light you have." She concluded, a "war on behalf of the political status of the colored man was clearly impossible at the moment, but that there might emerge from such federal action as the interference with peonage, perhaps, a federal system of federal arbitration in interracial difficulties." The party's success was in taking "the color question away from sectionalism" and putting "it in a national setting which might clear the way for a larger perspective."[71]

Another public response by Addams came at a Carnegie Hall symposium.

She stated that a meeting was held at Hull-House after the convention with "prominent Negroes in Chicago," who agreed that there should be a new party in the South, "which should not be based on war issues, and which would allow them [African Americans] to build up strength and independence for themselves." She concluded that "we might have put more glittering phrases in our glittering platform but we did not wish to fool the negro any longer." She did not address the fact that she and others had attempted to get the Resolutions Committee to accept the Du Bois statement.[72]

McClure's did finally grant Addams space to discuss her experiences as a Progressive delegate. Her article concentrated on the unique role women could play in partisan politics. She argued that women belonged in all political arenas, because they had long ministered "to big human needs," and listed women's efforts. Included in that list was "women's support for the families of the convict whose labor is adding to the profits of a prison contractor." A major issue for the NAACP as well as other southern and national African-American organizations in 1912 was the convict-leasing system. This was the closest she could come to using the party as a vehicle for promoting racial justice.[73]

The emphasis in the *McClure's* article was on how the party furthered women's political influence and, in turn, how women benefited the party process.[74] Because of the Progressive party, she wrote, "the old-line politician will be surprised to find . . . that politics has to do with such things [as human needs], so philanthropic women, on their side, will be surprised to find that their long concern for the human wreckage of industry has come to be considered politics." Addams concluded by stating that during the convention she felt not only the breakdown of the old issues of past elections but the emergence of a "new code of political action . . . formulated by men who are striving to express a sense of justice."[75] Those men were ready to hear her when she talked of gender justice, but they were not ready to hear her, or many others, express their sense of racial justice.

Addams was described as a female Lincoln by the press and the party during the campaign. She was seen to share with Lincoln the burden of race relations. Her burden was not shared by Roosevelt and those in the party who supported his lily-white policy. In an essay about Roosevelt written after his death, John Dewey wrote:

> There are those who think that morality does not enter into action until morality has become a problem—until, that is, the right course to pursue has become uncertain and to be sought for with painful reflection. But by this criterion Roosevelt rarely if ever entered the moral sphere. There is no evidence that he was ever troubled by those brooding questions, those haunting doubts, which

never wholly leave a man like Lincoln. Right and wrong were to him as distinctly and completely marked off from one another in every particular case as the blackness of midnight and the noonday glare.[76]

As Roosevelt stated during the campaign, "We have made the Progressive issue a moral, not a racial issue."[77]

The Progressive party's simultaneous inclusion of white women and a woman suffrage plank and its exclusion of southern African-American men and silence on racial justice made it clear that (once again) white women would be united with white men in opposition to African-American women and men—no matter Addams's own personal views or burden.[78]

During the 1912 campaign the Progressive party established special bureaus in New York and Chicago to attract African-American voters and supported the formation of separate African-American organizations within the party.[79] These were surprisingly effective. According to Kelly Miller, 60 percent of the African-American vote went to the Progressives.[80] May Martel, writing in the *New York Age,* observed that "Colored women have taken a comparatively insignificant part in campaign activities, but this is no indication that they are not thinking along political lines. I heard a number of heated arguments among women as to women's voting and the merits of the respective parties." Martel reported that Lydia Smith of Brooklyn was the "only woman of color" who attended the New York State Progressive party convention in Syracuse.[81] Grace Johnson organized Progressive women in the Boston area, including ten "colored women."[82] Two African-American women, Irene McCoy and Hulette M. Barnett, were reported to be among the "efficient stenographers and secretaries" who worked at the Progressive party headquarters in Chicago.[83] Most prominent African Americans, however, including Booker T. Washington, supported Taft.[84] Included in those ranks were undoubtedly African-American women who would have been organized by the WNRA. Mary Church Terrell, as well as other prominent African-American women, actively worked on behalf of the Republican party during this time.[85]

Campaigning for Votes

After the national nominating conventions were over, the *New York Times* reported that the 1912 presidential campaign had "suddenly become feminized," because women, as voters and vote gatherers, were of interest to all political parties. The Progressives "set the pace," declared the *Times,* because they endorsed woman suffrage, welcomed women into the party ranks, and pledged themselves to equal representation on committees. The New York state chairman, William Hotchkiss, speaking from the office of the Men's Bureau of the Progressive party in New York City, stated that the Woman's Bureau across the hall, under the leadership of Alice Carpenter, "will have an equal voice with men in every phase of party management."[86]

Jane Addams, the acknowledged leader of the women Progressives, told reporters that women's self-interest in suffrage was balanced by the overall long-term goals of the campaign. Women would benefit if suffrage was advanced by a Progressive victory, but, more importantly, the campaign was serving an "educational purpose. . . . People are learning things about social reforms, of which many were ignorant. It amounts to a tremendous campaign of education."[87] Mary Dreier wrote Lillian Wald, "We are going to have the biggest educational campaign the country has ever seen except perhaps before the Civil War."[88]

To translate activism into education, and to help their candidates, women Progressives set out to give speeches and interviews and write pamphlets and press releases. They also downplayed their self-interested motivations by using varying approaches in their presentation of themselves as political party activists. This variety indicates that they understood that their political expressions on issues, and how and to whom they were made, were important. The press and the public followed women's activities diligently all through the campaign. How women presented themselves was as interesting as the candidates. Women understood this and used it to their advantage, but they also tried not to let public expectations determine their actions.

Not surprisingly, initial press reports consistently equated the women with the issue of suffrage, and that issue dominated the press reports about the women Progressives throughout the campaign. The suffrage plank and women's celebration of the party's endorsement of a reform they dearly desired accounted for that domination. Party leaders pointed out that neither the Republicans nor the Democrats endorsed suffrage for women, and women Progressives cheered the Progressive party's endorsement. The newspapers, however, may have overplayed the suffrage issue. It was without a doubt crucial to women's motivations, but the campaign of 1912 was not a single-issue campaign for women reformers.

Women's work for political parties provided the press with a new angle on the suffrage story. The press had a field day with stories of women who did not support the same candidates or hold similar views, although suffragists were pledged by tradition to be nonpartisan. A *New York Times* reporter asked Addams about the fact that so many women were interested in working in the current campaign but for different candidates. She replied that their interest was inevitable and continued, "it is only natural that women should divide into different camps in politics just as men do."[89]

Suffragists put the idea of a female voting bloc to rest in the pages of the NAWSA newspaper, the *Woman's Journal*. The editor, Alice Stone Blackwell, noted that women as individuals were using their freedom to take sides in the campaign and that the *Journal* was receiving many letters endorsing the Progressives, Republicans, or Democrats, but it would not publish any of them.[90] She stated that the president of the NAWSA was against Roosevelt, the first vice president was for Roosevelt, and "now the Treasurer has accepted a nomination for a judgeship in New York City on the Socialist ticket." She pointed out that these women's choices offset each other, as did men's, and that "any man who is not willing that they should so differ would not be likely to vote for an equal suffrage amendment in any case." Blackwell understood women's differing partisan views as a benefit to the suffrage cause.[91]

To follow up on this argument, she sent out a questionnaire concerning voting preferences to state presidents of suffrage associations. When she announced the results in the *Woman's Journal,* she declared that "the outcome ought forever to set at rest any fears that all the women would vote one way." A few women refused to respond, because they believed it to be "inconsistent with strict nonpartisanship to express any opinion." Of those who responded, seventeen supported Wilson, thirteen supported Roosevelt, and three were for Taft. The Prohibition and Socialist candidates received one vote each, and four women were in doubt. The lesson from the survey was twofold, Blackwell informed *Journal* readers. No one, not even the national organization of suffragists, could "deliver" the woman's vote. And the divided opinions of its members shows how "absolutely necessary" it was that the NAWSA remain nonpartisan.[92] The press returned to the story of the women's voting bloc in 1919 and 1920, as the federal suffrage amendment was passed.

Suffragist partisanship was a much larger issue than the voting bloc and not so easily dismissed. When the press picked up on the issue it touched a nerve because of earlier debates within the suffrage and antisuffrage press about suffrage and partisanship. Ida Husted Harper initiated the ensuing controversy about suffragists acting in partisan ways when she wrote a letter to the editor of the *New York Times* just after the Progressive party's national convention in which she noted that to the press all women in the limelight are identified as suffragists, but only two women in the limelight of the convention held positions in suffrage organizations. Mrs. Robert Elder of Brooklyn was one, and Harper noted that Elder had defected to the Democratic camp. Jane Addams was the other, and Harper believed that she should resign from the NAWSA because of her position in the party. Harper was also disturbed that the Chicago suffragists had used their offices to organize a parade to support the Progressives during the convention. That violated the "tradition and unwritten law" of the NAWSA.[93]

For a few weeks of the campaign, the press reveled in suffragists fighting suffragists. The *Outlook* called it the "Crisis of the Woman Suffrage Party." According to its account, the crisis was caused not by Addams but by suffragists who refused to allow women to express their partisan positions as individuals and still hold office in suffrage organizations. Some demanded that new rules be instituted whereby officers were forbidden to affiliate in any way with a political party.[94]

Harriot Stanton Blatch, writing in the newsletter of the Woman's Political Union, stated that she believed it was "suicidal" for women to affiliate with a political party and work for political candidates.[95] She believed women's partisanship would harm the suffrage movement. Antisuffragists also believed that the "women's campaign clubs . . . meant to boost individual candidates" were wrong, but for a different reason. The *Women's Protest* declared that women should steer clear of "outworn political schemes" because it was their business to "prove the argument their friends among men made for them—that they would bring needed decency into politics."[96]

Addams met the criticisms head on. To the public and to the suffragists she explained why she seconded Roosevelt's nomination, stating that individuals should be allowed to join political parties but "should, in no case, urge their suffrage associations to such action." She merely claimed her right to act as an individual when she became a delegate to the Progressive convention.[97] She also could not help noting that Harper, in her public criticism of Roosevelt and the Progressive party, had herself "departed from the nonpartisan attitude."[98]

In private Addams moved more cautiously. She wrote to Anna Howard Shaw asking her for advice and proposing that she resign her position or stay away from the upcoming NAWSA national convention.[99] Shaw responded with a letter saying that she "rejoiced" in Addams's nominating speech but that she did not herself support Roosevelt. She told Addams to take note of the fact that "no matter what criticism comes . . . it is always made by persons strongly partisan in some other way."[100]

Here Shaw was responding to Harper's criticism but also to criticism directed at Addams from Mabel Boardman, the president of the National Red Cross, who accused her of unfairly using the influence of Hull-House for a political cause. Boardman had been approached by the Republican National Committee to direct women's work for Taft's reelection. She refused on the grounds that no "woman whose name has been closely associated with any great nonpolitical work should permit the use of her name," because it would carry the influence of their organization. Addams publicly responded to the criticism, claiming "the right as an individual to sit as a delegate in a convention whose platform embodies the measures for which I have worked for many years. . . . those who know Hull House realize that it has little value to the community save as it has been able to express certain principles and thus it has always stood for freedom of speech."[101] In the end, Boardman became the chair of the WNRA's Advisory Bureau and was starting a chain letter to raise one-dollar subscriptions from Republican women.[102]

Publicly, the partisan women had won the debate. Women's partisanship was legitimate, the press reported, now that even former critics were taking a role in the campaign. The suffragists would deal with the issue again after the campaign was over. By a vote of ten to one, the board of the NAWSA defeated a resolution introduced by Mrs. George Howard Lewis and presented by Ida Husted Harper that called for all officers of the association to remain nonpartisan. An alternative resolution was proposed and passed. It reaffirmed that the NAWSA was an "absolutely non-partisan, non-sectarian body" and that the "association must not declare officially for any political party." The vote formalized the public victory.[103]

There are different ways to look at these controversies over suffrage and partisanship. The debates helped the NAWSA clarify its position in relationship to political parties and provided women with the opportunity to exchange ideas about women's evolving relationship to a changing political sphere. At the same time, they presented the public with a particular view of women who took themselves seriously as politicians, advancing public ideology about women and politics. John Kingsbury thought there would also be an impact among male nonpartisan reformers, and he thanked Addams, stating that it would help all social workers "forced into the arena to fight for their ideas."[104]

Frances Kellor was concerned that the debates would have a more negative impact. She wrote Addams to express her concern that in pitting suffragism against partisanship, the press would weaken the already strong role she believed women were playing in the campaign. Women would be seen as unruly or concerned with the single issue of suffrage, and so she suggested that they broaden their appeal. Reports and documents of written appeals and speeches given by female Progressives indicate that they did so, and probably with little prodding. These women Progressives were, after all, influential and committed social reformers who had dedicated decades of their lives to social and industrial justice. They spoke about child labor and the needs of children; the development of domestic policy for the protection and education of immigrants; conservation legislation; and the expanding role of government in society. They also discussed the cost of living and economic issues.[105] For example, one woman Progressive told a Philadelphia audience that women do not want to hear a discussion of the tariff and states' rights, as they are not interested in those topics. "Tariff is the football of politics," she stated, "nobody seems to know who is right, but the Payne-Aldrich bill was certainly a game against the people." After making such a strong statement, she continued: "We believe that the tariff should be studied and adjusted by experts. As for that old bogie of states' rights, we women settled that fifty years ago, when we made lint bandages for our loved ones maimed in the Civil War. It is this new declaration of rights in which we are interested."[106]

Addams also discussed trusts and tariffs. Before the State Federation of Women's Clubs, she argued: "In federal legislation, what was it that the last Congress talked about most but Schedule K? Who buys the wool and spends the money for household needs? The whole question of the tariff comes back to the home. The food manufacturers have been obligated to put labels on their packages announcing their contents and now we are trying to have the pure food law enforced. Who buys the food good or bad? The government is constantly extending these fields of influence."[107] At a mass meeting for the Progressive party at Carnegie Hall, Addams told her audience that she wanted to say a word about trusts, "although that is not generally regarded as a woman's subject," and went on to argue that "we must have concentration in our industries just as we have concentration in our cities. We need control of business, however, and that is what the Progressive party is seeking."[108]

Addams traveled the country throughout October giving speeches for the Progressive party. She received requests from many other groups, including suffrage groups, when it became known that she was arriving in a certain location. When Julia Kent from Swarthmore, Pennsylvania, wrote asking Addams to speak at a suffrage meeting there, Addams declined, stating that while she would be doing some suffrage speaking, she was confining it to the western states in which suffrage amendments were pending.[109] Addams carefully split her time between suffrage-only work and party work. She made rules for herself. She refused to speak to women-only groups after the national convention and before the election. She believed that such groups were useful only for organization around specific issues. Addressing and working alongside men was a step in translating those issues into legislation.

In her speeches on behalf of the party and its platform she was very careful as well. When she was booked to give a speech for the party, she discussed the platform, praised its woman suffrage plank, and generally brought up one other issue to highlight the fact that suffrage alone did not dominate her partisanship. But when she went on her western tour for suffrage, she did not mix in party campaigning. Thus, she kept party and issue separate and yet joined.[110] Addams was dedicated to the suffrage movement. Like the Kansas women of the 1890s, she did not think it disloyal to work for a political party as well as suffrage. However, unlike them, she was working at the national level. At the state level, in both suffrage and nonsuffrage states, political maneuvering was more difficult.

During the campaign the Progressive party issued numerous pamphlets to bring its cause before the public. Among them was "Why Women Should Vote for . . . Roosevelt," directed at California's new women voters.[111] The party's Publicity Bureau coordinated the writing and dissemination of party literature, much of it written by Frances Kellor and reflecting her idea that women needed to follow three steps into partisan politics. First, women were to be educated on the issues; then they were to be motivated; motivation would lead to activism. In pamphlets and in the party's newspaper, the *Progressive Bulletin,* Kellor attempted to tell readers "What Women Can Do." Women's work "is but begun with the defeat or election of Mr. Roosevelt," the first issue of the *Bulletin* announced in September. They were organizing at the state level with the goal of helping to elect Progressive candidates, getting the platform's planks enacted into law, and "in educating the public where legislation is not the remedy."[112]

Kellor noted that the "method of neutrality" that women had so long cherished to get woman suffrage had failed "not at the polls but by the manipulations inside the old party lines." Women were now on the inside, she declared, participating "in party affairs before the vote is won," and as women do their daily work for the party, they have the "practical opportunity of answering forcibly many of the objections to the vote" for women. Women in the old parties could go on "as women have always done, with their philanthropic, welfare, and civic work and have the chivalrous support of their political friends. . . . They will be a good deal like the unorganized laborer, dependent."[113] Progressive party women were the opposite: organized, activist, and independent. Emphasized over and over again in the literature was the idea that, by working within political lines, women could benefit from a "tremendous education and moral opportunity and force before the votes are obtained."[114]

A pamphlet issued just after the convention was probably the most important source of information from and to women. "From the Women Delegates to the National Convention of the Progressive Party to the Women of the United States" included a quote from Albert J. Beveridge, the chair of the convention, arguing that women deserve the right to vote because they are a part of "economic and social life." The pamphlet also included the platform, the plank on equal suffrage, Addams's seconding speech, and a telegram from Roosevelt to Addams thanking her for the speech. It called on women to join the Progressive party, educate themselves on the issues, and work through the party on their behalf.[115]

The literature also connected the party's platform with the right of women to act in partisan ways. The platform emphasized social reform issues and "political footballs" like the tariff, but it also asserted that the old parties had become corrupt and that the alliance between corrupt business and corrupt politics needed to be dissolved. Toward that end, the Progressive party called for direct primaries, presidential preference primaries, direct election of senators, the short ballot, and the initiative, referendum, and recall. It also called for woman suffrage. In the literature that promoted the platform alongside the call for women's activism, the link between female partisanship and non-corrupt or participatory politics was implicitly clear.[116]

More details were given to women supporters of the party in the form of two fliers that served the campaign. The first, "Women! Do Something!" took on the issue of women's partisanship directly. Three-quarters of the flier's space lists suggestions for "What to Do in the Party," telling women to "Enroll as members of the Party. Do not form auxiliaries or separate clubs, and thereby lose the training and advantages of party work."[117] Another flier informed members of the "Program for Women's Organization within the Progressive Party in Non-suffrage States." The goal of the organization was gender integration. A woman, "advisedly more than one woman," was to be a member of each state committee or central committee of each county. Subcommittees were to have women members. Women were to be asked to work in election districts and attend primary meetings and conventions, and all "educational work should be taken up with the women generally to get their interest and support."[118] Fliers were distributed telling women how to organize a Jane Addams Chorus. Others told them that there were plans to form schools of oratory for women to make them spellbinding speakers.[119]

Were men and women following this organizing advice? The Progressives seem to have had better success with meetings than committees. For example, Vermont's Progressive state chairman, Charles H. Thompson, arranged an organizational meeting in the town of Stowe in early September, only days after the state primary election. Thirty men attended. At a second meeting later that month the "hall was packed" not only with men but, as the *Progressive Bulletin* described them, "the wives of the men there." The women "provided the supper, which proved to be of banquet proportions. Fifteen new members were added to the roll that night." Thompson reported that the "wives of the club members were as much interested as their husbands" and that club meetings were attended by women as well as men. The Progressives did well in Stowe, Vermont. Out of four hundred eligible male voters, the Progressives polled 146, the Republicans 144, and the Democrats 100.[120]

After getting off to a slow start, California had the most success with gender integration.[121] Women sat on important committees in New York, Connecticut, and Maryland.[122] Other states also wrote in to the *Progressive Bulletin* praising the inclusion of women on their committees.[123] It is clear, however, that a limited number of women in each state dominated committees or became token members on different committees. Even though integration was the goal, separate women's organizations sprang up everywhere, as women and men separated their labor. Sophonisba Breckinridge told Addams that Boston women had formed a Women's Progressive Committee with the plan of "separate work—that is women's meetings, teas, and social functions."[124] Breckinridge was not happy about the separation. A Women's National Finance Committee of the Progressive party was founded in October 1912. Women's financial contributions to the campaign were especially important and may account for why women created their own separate finance committee. Women solicited and collected money from women. Men did the same from men.[125] Throughout the campaign, while a few women like Addams and Kellor had positions on the National Committee, and a few women held positions on state committees, most positions of power or influence were held by men. This lack of recognition by the party, plus their tradition of separate gender organizations, contributed to the formation of these women's committees within a party dedicated to gender integration.

One issue surprisingly absent from press reports about the Progressive party and from Progressive party literature during the campaign was the question of women holding elective or appointive political offices and whether or not the Progressive party, in welcoming women as members, would become a vehicle for female officeholders. The *Independent* seemed to put the issue to rest with the statement that there arise "from time to time exceptional women better qualified than men for administration and legislation and they should not be debarred from any offices. . . . But it should be made plain in this campaign that women are asking for votes, not for offices . . . in order that they may cooperate with men in the promotion of measures in the interests of both."[126]

There may be good reasons for this lack of questioning about women's officeholding. First, women may have downplayed the issue to present themselves as nonthreatening to men. They were seeking inclusion in political parties but did not demand that men relinquish the power represented by offices. However, they may have felt that their ability to demand those positions was weak. Even the Progressive party could not live up to its promise that women would fully participate in all party councils. Most importantly, for Progressive women, this campaign was not about individual victories. It was dedicated to the issues written into the party's platform. The history of women's enfranchisement in western states had demonstrated already that voting rights did not necessarily translate into the right to hold office. It was an issue that women and men would revisit again and again, before and after 1920.

Serious internal problems contributed to the party's failure to win the presidency in 1912 and may have been another reason why women did not promote themselves as office holders more than they did within the party. Despite the dedication of time and energy by a remarkable number of women and men, the Progressives could not counter the problems of running a campaign that was hastily organized and plagued by external controversy and internal crises. From its founding, the Progressive party scrambled for volunteers and money.[127] During the course of the campaign, the party encountered problems not faced by the two established parties, with their carefully nurtured political alliances that brought in workers and money. As Margaret Robins wrote to her sister in September, "If you are poor in New York, I can assure you that we are paupers in Chicago. It is incredible how little money is coming in."[128] Progressives would go from the joy of working for the party to the despair of the reality of their political situation. The Progressive party had unique difficulties, but they occurred at a time when all political parties were troubled, as fewer people seemed inclined to engage in partisan and electoral politics. Only the dedication of the party's workers and the appeals of the party account for the its second-place showing and victories at the state level.[129] Among the victors was Dr. Nena Jolidon Croake, a Progressive from Tacoma, Washington. Only two years after women won the right to vote in Washington, she joined Frances C. Axtell, a Republican from Bellingham, as the first women elected to the Washington House.

6. Partisan Women, 1912–16

No POLITICAL PARTY believed it could take women's support for granted in 1912; neither could the parties completely ignore women. This was true not only at the national level but also at the state level and not only in suffrage states but also in nonsuffrage states. Like the Progressive party, or maybe because of that party's overtures to women, the Republican and Democratic parties sought women supporters. They used existing party machinery and formed new organizations to bring women into their parties. As a *New York Tribune* reporter put it, "each party now has Corps of Feminine Assistants to Win Votes," and these women were making "the political world hum."[1] And amid this buzz of activity, the discussion of the appropriateness of women's partisanship retreated, and other questions come to the forefront of debates. At the state and national levels, people discussed and faced with new vigor the old issues of the relationship between women's independent political organizations and political parties and when and how women should hold political office.

The Conclusion of 1912

The WNRA had a tradition of transforming itself into a campaign organization, and it did so again in 1912. The *New York Times* reported that the Women's Bureau of the Republican National Committee—the campaign organization of the WNRA—was the best equipped of the coming campaign, "because it has been organized for years and it knows just how to go about to get the best results with the least amount of effort." Republican women, the *Times* continued, were "as well entrenched as the regular Republican machine of which their bureau is an integral part, and it is no difficulty for them to reach just the kind of woman who can influence votes, if they don't actually cast them."[2]

Helen Boswell led the Republican women's forces. According to one report, her chief advisor was Mabel Boardman, who brought to the organization a long friendship with the Taft family; William Howard Taft was the honorary president of the Red Cross.[3] Notable defections from the Republican camp included Anna Brown, who had long been a member of Boswell's New York West End Woman's Republican Club.[4] In press reports Boswell made clear why she remained a staunch Republican supporter. In words that echoed Judith Ellen Foster, she called the Republican party "the party of action; its breath is progress, its speech is the language of the world, its dialect the rhetoric of the home and the farm and the shop."[5] She stated that the "issues of 1912 cover a wide range and demand a high level of knowledge" and that the Republican party could "stand pat on the records of its achievements in national development and what it has done and it will do and can do, for its platforms and its principles are broad enough and strong enough to meet the needs of the hour, no matter at what rate those needs may grow."[6]

Boswell set up a bureau within the offices of the Republican national headquarters at the Times Building in New York City. She had initially wanted to establish her bureau at the Astor Hotel, where women "are accustomed to go to teas and lectures, and where they would feel more at home."[7] It was at the behest of the men of the party, who "decided that their fair assistants must be closer at hand," that the WNRA moved into the Times Building. Boswell was assisted there by Mary Yost Wood as general secretary and Mary C. Francis as office secretary.[8]

In early September, Boswell stated to the press that the WNRA would have meetings at some later date, "but it would be a waste of time to have them now. It is too long before election." She commented that "in the last campaign we didn't even open our headquarters till more than a week after this date."[9] In spite of their slow pace in bringing the women's side of the campaign to the public, the WNRA offices filled up with volunteers, so much so that when the president of the International Peace Propaganda (the American Peace and Arbitration League) went to Europe, the WNRA took over her office to accommodate overflow work.[10] One report stated that thirty-five people worked in the WNRA office.[11]

To organize Republican women, Boswell and the WNRA focused on the suffrage states, setting up committees of women to "work in harmony with the respective county chairman."[12] Boswell told one reporter that letters had been sent to western women voters "to act as leaders," and while she counted

herself as "an old stager in this work, I am constantly amazed by the prompt-
ness with which timid women respond to the call." Women's major task, according to Boswell, was in influencing men to register and vote.[13]

Organizing women was only half of the work. Boswell stated that the
WNRA's "particular labor in both suffrage and nonsuffrage states is not
with the women, but with the men."[14] In the campaign of 1892, Judith Foster
had put Boswell in charge of organizing the efforts of Republican women
in New York City. Now that she was leading the WNRA, Boswell was mapping a new course and expanding the organization's efforts beyond wom-
en. The reason she shifted emphasis is not immediately clear. It could have
been a reaction to the Progressive party's emphasis on gender integration
or to the increasing belief that women should move away from indirect
political methods, such as "influencing" men, to direct methods, such as
working with men in every political way. It could also have been a mandate from the RNC or her own attempt to increase the WNRA's role within the Republican campaign machinery. Whatever prompted her, Boswell
traveled across the country to organize women and men into the Republican party during this campaign.[15]

Republican efforts could not overcome the problems created by the party
split. Republicans and Progressives were both defeated by the Democrats in
1912, as Woodrow Wilson carried forty of the forty-eight states in the union.
Theodore Roosevelt and the Progressives carried six, and William Howard
Taft and the Republicans carried only Vermont and Utah. The Socialist candidate, Eugene Debs, had a spectacular showing with about 6 percent of the
popular vote. Roosevelt declared that it was a "'phenomenal thing to bring
the new party into second place and to beat out the Republicans.'"[16]

The Progressives lost five of the seven suffrage states and carried California by only 174 votes. Roosevelt claimed he was "amused" that women in
suffrage states "voted exactly like the men," even though the Progressives were
the only party to endorse woman suffrage.[17] In spite of the fact that he perceived women as only doubling the vote, he recognized that women had
proven themselves as loyal party workers by their hard work and dedicated
participation. As he wrote Jane Addams, women had shown they have a place
"to fill precisely as men have, and on an absolute equality. It is idle now to
argue whether women can take their part in politics, because this convention saw the accomplished fact . . . and we have a right to expect that wom-
en and men will work . . . with the same high sincerity of purpose and like
efficiency."[18]

Roosevelt wrote to Margaret and Raymond Robins that the Progressives
had "done a good work in this campaign, because we have forced our peo-

ple to look the great problems of the day straight in the face and we have laid the foundations, at least, for a great movement toward securing social and industrial justice."[19] As Addams wrote to Roosevelt, the campaign had given "tremendous impulse" to "social reform measures in which I have been interested for many years, but which have never before seemed to become so possible of fulfillment as at the present moment. I had never dared hope that within my lifetime thousands of people would so eagerly participate in their discussion. . . . you have been in a large measure responsible for this outcome."[20] So too had the hundreds of other women and men who had come into the partisan fold with the founding of the Progressive party. They were now ready for new challenges. Some moved carefully, as indicated by a resolution issued by Progressive women of Pennsylvania: "Inexperienced as we are in political life, we believe that our practical common sense and our high ideals deserve recognition, and we pledge ourselves to work as willingly in the more peaceful fields of education and organization in the coming years, as we have in the strenuous campaign of the past weeks."[21]

Others believed that it was necessary to continue on the strenuous path and began a discussion about how to transform the party into an organization that would formulate and direct social policy. Unlike the bureaus of the two major parties, including the WNRA, which closed their doors at the end of the campaign season, the Progressives saw their work as only beginning. Most Progressives had no hesitation about keeping the party alive, and they discussed organizational concerns rather than fusion with the Republicans. It was decided that the leaders of the campaign organization would hold on to their positions. George W. Perkins was appointed chair of the Executive Committee, while Joseph M. Dixon was appointed national chair of the party. Oscar King Davis was placed in the position of secretary to the Executive Committee, which included nine individuals. Of the women members of the Provisional National Committee—Jane Addams, Frances Kellor, and Isabella Blaney—only Addams was appointed to a seat on the Executive Committee. No written debate or discussion indicates the reason for this sole female appointment.

Four committees were established under the Executive Committee, and women found more places on them, but their numbers were again minimal. The Publicity Committee and the Organization Committee had no women members, but the five-member Finance Committee included Mrs. Kellogg Fairbank of Illinois, and the Progressive Service Committee was chaired by Frances Kellor. The structure of the new party made it immediately clear that, at the national level at least, the number of women holding seats would be low and the party would rely on the most visible women for the most visible slots.

Eleanor Garrison, now working at Progressive headquarters in New York City, wrote her mother that she "thought everyone was going to stop and breathe after the election, but all the plans are being made for the permanent organization and there is any amount to attend to."[22] The office, she wrote, "has turned into a bureau of education," and she described her own job as "kind of an errand boy." When she had a moment to sit still, her task was to go through newspaper clippings and create a state-by-state catalogue of "all the women workers and tell what office they filled."[23]

The Progressive Service, led by Kellor, was the most innovative structure created within the party after the election. Addams served as the chair of the subcommittee, which formulated its "Plan of Work."[24] The Progressive Service dealt with "measures" while the other committees of the party dealt with "candidates and election machinery." As the educational/lobbying arm of the party, the Progressive Service had the mandate of carrying out Roosevelt's Contract with the People by drafting legislation and publishing recommendations in advance of legislative sessions. In a sense, the Progressive Service was replicating the structure and goals of civic leagues.

Kellor oversaw a volunteer board of six members working through different bureaus and departments. She was dynamic in this position and perceived herself to be responsible for organizing the process whereby the party's major mandate could be fulfilled. Party supporters were reminded, as they were introduced to the plan, that "what brought these leaders together was primarily a program, not a partisanship."[25] All her past organizing, investigative, and political skills came together in this post, and she crafted a structure and put together a coalition of extremely knowledgeable and dedicated individuals to carry out her plans. She opened an office on Forty-Second Street in New York City and hired Alice Carpenter, the lawyer Donald Richberg, and the writer Paxton Hibben to assist her.[26] Partisan politics was moving out of the back room.

Initially, two women sat on the seven-person Board of the Progressive Service: Kellor, who was the chair, and Addams. By March 1913, the board, now called the Council of Chairmen, was expanded to thirteen and included four women. There was one woman on the sixteen-person Bureau of Education. The Bureau of Legislative Reference included eleven men and two women, Jane Addams and Isabel Giles, who was listed in 1913 as the assistant to the director, Donald Richberg. They all reported to Kellor. Addams was also appointed director of the Department of Social and Industrial Justice, which had four committees, one of which was headed by a woman. The Departments of Conservation, Popular Government, and Cost of Living were all directed by men.[27] The Suffrage Committee was in the Department of Popular Government and was still headed by Maud Nathan.

The overlapping positions held by Kellor and Addams and the low numbers of women in other leadership positions indicate that the Progressive party, while pledged to equal representation of women in its councils, did not live up to its promise of gender equality at the national level. Women disappear from the rolls of the National Committee between 1912 and its last meeting in June 1916. As early as November 1913, when the Progressive National Committee met, the idea of gender equality seems to have been forgotten. From this time on, only men sat on the National Committee. Addams, Kellor, and Catherine Hooker of San Francisco—who replaced Isabella Blaney—are listed as members-at-large in 1913. No women are listed in 1914, 1915, or 1916. In the same years, women did not capture any new appointments on subcommittees.[28]

The reasons for the small numbers of women in national positions are unclear. In part, factionalism within the party and the party's overall poverty contributed to an unwillingness by many to share any power or resources they had gained. Equally, the noteworthiness of the Progressive party's dedication to equality in gender representation waned after the election. Women gained a foothold when the party benefited, but when this story was no longer newsworthy the press and the party itself gave women less notice.[29]

Simultaneously, women became a sideline story in the press and sideline participants in the party. Their strongest showing was in the Progressive Service, but as organizational decisions were made and positions reallocated, women were increasingly excluded. In the nonelection years of 1913 and 1915 and the off-year election of 1914, the focus was on keeping the party alive through organizational efforts. The grand plans of the Progressive Service were put on hold, and by the time of the 1916 election, women's exclusion was complete. The country entered the campaign of 1916 with a focus not on gender integration as an aspect of partisan good but new issues, including the war in Europe.

Part of the problem for women may have been Addams's retreat from the partisan spotlight. She was trying to resign from the Executive Committee even before the November 1912 election but was convinced that her resignation would harm the party.[30] She held her seat but almost never attended the Executive Committee meetings of the National Committee. Frances Kellor, and later Harold Ickes, usually held her proxy.[31] In March 1914, Addams finally resigned from her position as a member of the Legislative Reference Bureau.[32] With her resignation women lost a key partisan role model. Women like

Frances Kellor and Isabella Blaney did not have Addams's cachet, and it is unclear whether or not they may have wanted to replace her on the Executive Committee. Addams may have also chosen to shift her focus and energies to peace work. As early as November 1912, magazines and newspapers were covering the war in the Balkans. It would be two more years before Addams and other women would commit themselves to almost full-time activism in pacifist organizations like the Woman's Peace Party, but the trend toward this change had been coming for some time.[33]

Progressive women's activism was more vibrant at the state than the national level. Progressive party records and private correspondence indicate that women were active workers during and after the campaign, organizing and attending meetings, giving speeches, establishing clubs, and even winning office. Nena Jolidon Croake was elected in 1912 to the legislature in Washington State. Her slogan during the campaign was "Consideration for Women is a Measure of the Nation's Progress," and she argued that since women were now enfranchised in Washington, "it is only just and fair that [they] be given a trial."[34]

Washington State was one of the places where Maud Howe Elliott, the daughter of Julia Ward Howe, spoke in 1913 during a swing west that included a five-state conference of northwestern Progressives in St. Paul, Minnesota.[35] Ethel Roosevelt, the daughter of the candidate, took part in an outdoors campaign in New York City organized by women Progressives. In Illinois and Connecticut, women established their own state Progressive Services and appointed women as chairs.[36] The aim was to find ways to move more women into positions of power at every level. Their success was limited by the unwillingness of the male leadership to work for the same goal. Just after the election, Thomas Robins presented to Theodore Roosevelt a "Pennsylvania Plan" that he and Edwin Van Valkenburg had formulated. The plan was to be a "practical method of giving power to the women" who worked in the campaign. Disfranchisement, Robins argued, kept most women "outside the breastworks," and he proposed giving women within the party the vote and schooling them in practical political work. Women would then hold actual power on par with men, because all decisions would be determined by a vote of all members of the party.[37]

Roosevelt rejected the idea. One could speculate that concern over formulating a party that would endure led him to believe the best course was a hierarchical organization with hand-picked leaders. He had given a great deal of thought to the organization of the party, and he may have decided that such a departure would be harmful. He may also have thought that the dedication the party had already demonstrated on the question of women's equal representation was enough. If women wanted positions, they would seek them out. This argument would be similar to the one he made about suffrage.[38]

The example of Alice Carpenter highlights the difficulty women had in the party.[39] She had campaigned for the party during the 1912 election and was then hired as an assistant in the Progressive Service. In 1913 she traveled all over the country speaking on behalf of the Progressives.[40] In 1914 she was hired in a new position as a speaker for the party and moved from working for Kellor to working for George Perkins. As the campaign season began, she wrote to Perkins stating that she would have to stop her work if they could not afford to raise her salary.[41] She asked for permission to make an arrangement with the suffragists whereby she would speak for them a few times a month. Perkins agreed.

Perkins was less agreeable about Carpenter's association with the Working Man's Progressive Party League.[42] Correspondence between Carpenter and Perkins indicates that he was concerned that Carpenter was making promises that "a labor man should and would be the Progressive candidate in any specified district." He thought such promises would cause future problems, and he made it clear that Carpenter had crossed a line because she had "been requested not to take up political organization work in connection with [her] speech-making work."[43]

Relations between Carpenter and Perkins deteriorated as their correspondence continued. In early August, Carpenter told Perkins of her plans: "I shall give my efforts to those districts where the political organization has backed the labor candidates. . . . I shall endorse no candidate not endorsed by the political organization nor shall I use my influence to secure the endorsement of any candidate, labor or otherwise."[44] Perkins responded that she was describing it as "your work, as your labor organization and what you must do as an individual." He explained to her that she was a regular salaried employee of the party hired to do the work of the party as determined by the office. He warned her to "leave the question of political organization entirely to Mr. Robinson and Mr. Bird."[45]

Carpenter saw her position differently. She informed Perkins that the initiative and idea for organizing laboring men was hers, that she did not see her work as political organization work, and, "in view of the recent developments in the Progressive party here in the State of New York," she would therefore resign. She submitted a bill for services of $108, and Perkins accepted her resignation.[46] By the end of September, the disagreement between them was resolved. She took back her resignation and was now speaking before, but not organizing, groups of laboring men. The exchange between Carpenter and Perkins shows how clearly women were excluded from the organizational side of the party. Only men worked in the organizational arm. When women were approached by individuals or groups about campaign or organizational matters, they sent the requests to Perkins or Hooker.[47] As much as women and men may have made alliances outside the Progressive party in nonpartisan organizations, within the party there was little confederation.[48]

The greatest problem with women's representation within the party resulted from the party's evolving dual purpose. As the Progressive National Service attempted to establish State and Local Services, Kellor explained that their role was to "organize to fight for principles, not for candidates."[49] Queries about whether the party was simply a vehicle to enhance Roosevelt's personal power opened up the question of the party's purpose. Eleanor Garrison, in response to her mother's questions about Roosevelt's place in the party, stated that the Progressive party "is about as much a 'one man' party as suffrage is a one woman party. They are both great democratic educational movements, parts of the same thing in fact."[50] The first quarterly report of the Progressive National Service stated that it was "a political organization in the highest sense of that term," and it was "non-partisan in the sense that it nominates no candidates and makes no campaigns based upon individuals." The aim was to place "the burden not upon voting on election day but upon civic responsibility and duty" throughout the year and at the local and national levels. The result would be that voting "becomes one expression of patriotism rather than a sum total of civic expression."[51] In off-election years there was room to ignore the candidates and the partisan purpose of a political organization, and there was room for the emphasis on principles over candidates, but as the party geared up for the campaigns of 1914 that space diminished. The Progressive Service was a logical step in reformers' attempts to redefine partisanship and reorient the purpose of political parties themselves. However, because the service was the women's arm of the party, when the party went from emphasizing civic responsibility to strategizing for electoral success women found themselves relegated to the sidelines. As the correspondence of Theodore Roosevelt, George Perkins, and Amos Pinchot shows, the power of the Progressive party was in the organizational arm.

Whether or not Progressive party women like Kellor and Addams felt that their political innovations had given them, for a time, power on the inside is not clear.[52] The finances of the Progressive party diminished crucially in 1914, and the Progressive Service was one of the first casualties. Kellor attempted to keep it alive and proposed that it survive with its own fundraising efforts. It was still to be connected to the party, but it would be financially autonomous, as all funds raised would remain within the service and could not be touched by the party.[53] The effort failed. In late December 1914, Perkins told

Kellor that her office space was needed for organizational work and that she must vacate it immediately. Kellor, by using her continuing good relations with Roosevelt, decided the only option for keeping the service alive was to separate it completely from the Progressive party. By 1915 the Progressive Service was completely autonomous, all ties to the party were cut, and it became "just another organization with an ambitious reform agenda."[54] With separation, the final act of women's attempts to achieve power with the Progressive party failed.

Partisan Choices

In 1914, Marcus M. Marks, the president of the Borough of Manhattan, told the women who had just created a Woman's Republican Club that Republican women should be admitted "on equal footing" in all Republican clubs. He argued that if men's clubs took in women, they "would make the word 'politician' a term of honor and distinction."[55] He was cheered for his comments, but women were rarely integrated into men's political clubs. Instead, it was more common for women to be invited as guests in recognition of "the broader sphere into which women have forced their way," as the toastmaster at the headquarters of one New York Republican club stated.[56] And Republican women reciprocated by inviting men to the meetings of their separate clubs. The rare challenges to the auxiliary mode by women, and the rarer challenges by men like Marks, only made it clearer that the party would be dominated by men.

The auxiliary mode that women found themselves in did not give them equal power within political parties, but it did give them an independence that they could appropriate and manipulate in some circumstances. In a primer for "practical politics" published in 1917, P. Orman Ray explained that in Chicago the Republican and Democratic parties maintained "women's clubs wherever they have men's organizations. They are frequently called the 'women's auxiliary.'" As in New York, Illinois partisan women possessed a "strong disposition to organize and act quite independently."[57]

Independence produced positive results for the Seventh Ward women's Republican organization in Chicago's aldermanic election of 1914. A Republican woman's committee picked a candidate they wanted to support, but their choice was rejected by the party. The women put him in as an independent candidate and used "machine politics" to win the election. They canvassed houses across the ward, sent out letters, ran a pledge campaign, gave teas, and used automobiles on election day to get people to the polls. The result was not only the candidate's victory, but the women's organization was welcomed into the old Republican machine. In the same election, women in the Twelfth Ward "organized a write-in campaign for Mrs. Naperalski as the Progressive party candidate." According to one report, she received the nomination with forty-seven votes, forty-two of which came from women.[58]

African-American women in Illinois also organized independent political clubs to have an impact in partisan politics. At a time when many white suffragists and reformers were concentrating on the national level of politics, African-American women were becoming more "disillusioned by national politics, after struggling so hard to support woman suffrage and the Republican party over two generations," and turned to establish strong local and state organizations.[59] The woman suffrage and partisan clubs in Chicago included the Colored Women's Party of Cook County, the Third Ward Political Club, the 25th Precinct Political Club, and the influential Alpha Suffrage Club organized by Ida Bell Wells-Barnett.[60] The Alpha Suffrage Club was instrumental in championing the black independent William R. Cowen in the 1914 primary and the Republican Oscar Stanton DePriest in 1915. DePriest's victory made him the first African-American alderman in Chicago; it "fulfilled rising African American expectations" in politics and helped make black women "integral players on the black political landscape."[61]

As women worked on specific campaigns for candidates and issues, they crossed party lines. One example is the 1914 New York Women's Temporary Committee for Representation in the Constitutional Convention. Correspondence between Anne Rhodes, the secretary, and Lillian Wald, the chair of the organization of 175 women, demonstrates that women crossed party lines to "secure for the women of the state who are working for social and civic betterment a voice" in the upcoming constitutional convention and thus in the "formation of the fundamental law under which work is done."[62] The aim of the Women's Temporary Committee was threefold: to get women to agree to run for a place in the convention; to get male party leaders to accept and support the women; and to get women through their parties to launch a campaign to win the primary and the regular elections. The success of the campaign, as Rhodes presented it to Wald, was in getting each county's party organization to accept a woman candidate. In some counties Democratic women accepted and ran. In others, Progressives or Republicans ran. Lillian Wald, Frances Kellor, Katharine Bement Davis, and Josephine Goldmark were chosen by the committee as candidates for delegates-at-large. These delegates-at-large candidates lost, as did three women from the Prohibition party.[63]

The New York and Chicago cases show the variety of approaches used by women after 1912 as they sought to influence the political sphere. In both cases, women identified their partisanship. They identified themselves by

their gender and used gender as an organizing tool because of their continuing lack of influence in parties. Gender organization was a way for women's
voices to be heard in a partisan culture dominated by men.[64] African-American women continued, as they had since the late 1860s, to be "torn between
identifying with racial priorities or with gender priorities."[65] While successful in some cases, separating their work by gender also perpetuated and reinforced the auxiliary mode for women in partisan politics, which limited
their power and influence. Since they were peripheral to the party, auxiliaries could create the impression that women were less dedicated to their
parties and less interested in voting than men, because they reinforced the
idea that women were not fully integrated into the partisan political process.
Partial integration meant partial independence, which, while potentially
powerful, could also be limiting. Independence meant women might be less
loyal to the party than men and therefore should not or could not be trusted with positions of power.

Whether organized in party auxiliaries or on behalf of candidates through
"nonpartisan" organizations, partisanship was an expected and accepted
political identity for women by 1916. The importance of this identity can be
seen in a biographical index of prominent women compiled and published
by John Leonard in 1914. A significant number of the women identified their
party affiliations, and the index lists Democrats, Republicans, Progressives,
Socialists, and Prohibitionists. Some of the women were very specific. Harriet Alexander of Salida, Colorado, for example, identified herself as a Republican voter in national elections and an independent voter in local politics.
She was also the chair of the State Institutions Committee of the Colorado
Federation of Women's Clubs, whose purpose was to "endeavor to show the
necessity of eliminating partisan politics from the management of our state
institutions."[66]

Florence Collins Porter and Women's Partisanship in California

At the same time that California women won the vote, political leaders in
the state were succeeding in removing state and local political offices from
the partisan arena. Regulation of political parties began in the late nineteenth
century, and by the early part of the twentieth century, the good-government
movement, including the influential Lincoln-Roosevelt League, had succeeded in getting legislation passed that limited the influence of political parties.[67] This effort influenced California women's understanding of and opportunities in politics. How this worked can be seen in the political career

of Florence Collins Porter, one of the most prominent Republican women in the state.

Porter, of Los Angeles, and Isabella Blaney, of San Jose, were delegates-at-large to the Republican National Convention in 1912 and followed the Republicans who bolted into the new Progressive party. Porter became a member of the Roosevelt Progressive League of California and a vice president of the Los Angeles County League. The Progressive-Republican domination of state politics and the alliance with the national Progressive party worked to her political advantage.[68] She was elected as one of California's thirteen presidential electors, casting the first woman's electoral vote in the country, and she held a prestigious position as one of three women on the Progressive party's National Committee.

Even after the decline of the Progressive party, the new politics of the progressive era strengthened rather than challenged Porter's ideas about women's place in politics. Between 1912 and 1914 she continued to promote the idea that the meaning of politics was different for women than for men. At the heart of this difference was her understanding that nonpartisanship worked differently for women than for men. She believed that women needed to continue to organize separately from men, even as they worked alongside them in some political milieus. She also believed that women must not be self-seeking or self-serving in their political actions. If nonpartisanship for men was about confronting corruption, for women it was about preserving a state of virtue already in existence. For women with a strong Victorian legacy, like Porter and others of her generation, this state of virtue was seen as natural.

Porter had a long political career by the time she moved to Los Angeles in 1900 to become an editor of the *Los Angeles Herald*. She was born in Caribou, Maine, in 1853.[69] In 1873 she married the Reverend Charles William Porter, a Congregational minister, and in addition to her duties as a minister's wife, she was a charter member of the Woman's Literary Club in Caribou and helped establish the Children's Aid Society and the Girls' Home of Belfast. She also became a politician's wife when Charles served as Caribou's Republican representative to the state legislature. Together they worked for temperance and prohibition.

Florence Porter became involved in the WCTU and was part of the political crisis that split the organization in the late 1880s. She allied herself with Judith Ellen Foster, became the recording secretary of the NPWCTU, and when the WNRA was formed, she campaigned for Harrison in 1888.[70] Her work with the NPWCTU and WNRA enlarged her political world, as did her work as a schoolteacher, which she took on after her husband died in July

1894. Her widowhood status, especially her high status as a clergyman's widow, allowed her to transform the purpose of her work. She connected work and politics by advancing from schoolteacher to school trustee to the elected position of school superintendent, all acceptable jobs for women. Republican motherhood had taken on not only public housecleaning in the dirty, corrupt world of politics but also public childrearing in local school politics.

After four years as superintendent, Porter resigned to pursue another career. She purchased the *Aroostook Republican,* a Caribou newspaper, which she edited for a year. Then, at the urging of her uncle, Wallace L. Hardison, who had recently purchased the *Los Angeles Herald,* she accepted a position on the editorial staff of his paper and in the summer of 1900 moved to South Pasadena, California. In addition to being an editor, Porter also held a position on the Board of Directors of the *Herald* and was an editor and writer for the *California Outlook.*[71]

In Los Angeles, Porter continued her club work and her involvement in politics. She was a member of the Friday Morning Club, president of the Los Angeles District of Federated Women's Clubs, and vice president of the Ebell Club. She also served two terms as president of the Los Angeles County Equal Suffrage League. Her work for woman suffrage and her loyalty to progressive Republican politics connected her to influential Republican women and men around the state.[72] Porter's ideas about women's political responsibilities were influenced by her long partisan career and might best be summed up with the Ebell Club's creed: "No woman should seek or use official positions for self-aggrandizement or club affiliations for a stepping stone only, but . . . she should utilize her opportunities for the altruisms of life." It was a creed that Porter was living even before she moved to California and joined the Ebell Club; she sought inclusion and recognition for women in political parties and the electoral world, but she remained committed to the maintenance of gendered boundaries in politics. In this effort, she engaged in a political dialogue with women and men to promote her vision (or version) of women's politics.

From a secure political position in the Progressive party and then the Republican party with the *California Outlook* as her sounding board, Porter addressed the women of California, for whom, she said, there existed "much confusion as to the meaning of the terms 'partisan' and 'nonpartisan.'" The confusion resulted from the efforts of women's groups, especially the Woman's Progressive League, to restrict the right of an individual woman "to be as active as she pleases in the political party of her choice." Created out of the disbanded suffrage organizations, the Woman's Progressive League wanted to enact a rule that "no woman holding an appointive or elective office under any of the national parties will be eligible to hold office in the League."[73]

The *Woman's Bulletin*, the organ of the Woman's Progressive League, asked its readers: "Is it possible for a body of citizens to take part in political life and remain nonpartisan?" The answer was yes. Women could be citizens and voters and join in political alliances as nonpartisans, "not merely only because they happen to be women, but because they enter the arena untrammeled with party ties or traditions. And, moreover, they come into the field . . . trained in the doing of civic work, which has for its sole object the welfare of the community." While this argument is unique in its denial of some sort of essentialist nature of women's politics, it is false in its claim that women moved into a state of enfranchisement "untrammeled with party ties or traditions." This version of women's political history was told by a group of women (and some men) who wanted to ensure that nonpartisanship would continue to be a dominant feature of women's politics.[74] As Eliza Tupper Wilkes, a Democrat, stated in 1914: "I believe in party, not as the master, but as the instrument. Partisanship of the old sort is dying out. 'My party, right or wrong,' is no longer the cry. I claim the right to vote independently when the principle demands it. I believe the day for party politics in municipal affairs is gone."[75]

Porter believed in women's separate political organizations, and she believed those should be nonpartisan, but she was also concerned that the Woman's Progressive League's rule, which she described as "arbitrary and narrow," would keep "capable and desirable officers" out of leadership positions. In her estimation, the rule would force women to avoid working in political parties or force them out of their separate organizations. As a vice president of the Roosevelt Progressive League of Los Angeles County (a party organization), Porter may have been referring to herself. But what she was trying to keep alive was a balance for women between partisanship and nonpartisanship.[76] The balance would then keep alive the idea that women have a special place and role in politics as the virtuous politician serving a nonpartisan political ethic and helping to redefine partisanship and citizenship.

Porter was also concerned about women's discussions about running for political office, and she believed that women's political advancement would be harmed if their qualifications were questioned as they "scrambled for political offices."[77] Women would be seen as self-seeking and self-serving rather than enlightened and disinterested. They could, should, and would hold political appointments and offices in California just as they were doing in other suffrage states, but they must always do so for the right reasons, and they had to be the right offices, at the right level, at the right time. In the broadest terms, experienced women would hold office to advance important (shared) principles. So, for example, when Clara Foltz announced that she was a candidate for the state senate in 1912, she carefully stated that she wanted "to win for women justice before the law," because justice was a key word in the rhetoric of the principled partisan woman.[78] When the California Civic League encouraged the candidacy of Dr. Adelaide Brown for a vacancy on the State Board of Health in 1914, it emphasized her expert training.[79]

More controversial was Helen Williams's run for lieutenant governor in 1914 on the regular Republican ticket.[80] Porter spoke out against Williams, but her criticism was more than a partisan attack. She did not believe Williams had the political or civic record required of a woman for such a position, and she implied that no woman should look to such a high office so soon after enfranchisement. There were many women candidates running for office in 1914, and Porter was not opposed to those races as long as they were at the bottom of the political ladder. It is more logical, she wrote, for women "to begin at the bottom and work up than at the top and work down." Porter's view was similar to that of the Democrat Mary Foy, but Foy's strategy was to encourage women to attend party committee meetings.[81]

Porter also opposed the idea that women should receive the support of other women simply because of their sex. A woman's candidacy was not and should not be regarded as a "woman's cause." Nor should male politicians place women candidates in the field to garner the women's votes. "When there is a demand for women legislators the women themselves, not politicians who seek to snatch victory from threatened defeat, through woman's vote, will lead the movement, and the woman candidate will receive the vote of both men and women," Porter wrote. "Until then all sporadic, self-seeking efforts on the part of women are an injury to their permanent advancement."[82] As another Progressive woman put it, if women never heeded the "call of selfishness and personal ambition," then "we will not need to dread women in politics."[83]

Politics is about rewards and favors, selfishness and personal ambition, as much as it is about ideals and justice. Nowhere is this more evident than in the political conversation between the progressive Republicans Meyer Lissner and Hiram Johnson about the place of women in party politics. After 1911, Lissner kept up a continual correspondence with Johnson about the need for women's appointments to political offices. These women deserve attention, he argued, to "keep our books straight" and because they are "of great value to us, especially among the women's clubs and with women audiences."[84] As Lissner and Johnson decided which women to include, to listen to, or to reward with an office, they compared the women to each other rather than to men.

Johnson, who held the keys to appointments, listened closely but moved slowly. If Porter wanted women to start at the bottom and slowly work their way up the political ladder, Johnson seems to have had a ladder longer at the bottom.[85] In his responses to questions about women holding office, he sounds more like Porter than Lissner, however. He had no sympathy, he said, "with the demand that emanates from certain women constantly asking not the appointment of the best in official position, but the appointment of a particular sex." The women who held office, he declared, had been "called into service of the state, just as men have been called, because of their peculiar fitness and ability. To adopt any other rule would not only lower the standard of the state service, but it would result ultimately in the very thing that [women] would wish to prevent—the lowering of the standard that women should maintain."[86]

As Porter and Johnson continued to emphasize a promotion of the disinterested woman and the idea of women's gradual political advancement, Lissner grew concerned. If organizing women was a race, then the progressive Republicans seem to have taken the lead position after 1911, but Lissner knew that the Democrats, because they expected a struggle to win women's loyalty, were making a concerted effort to include women in meetings of the party's central committees and, where possible, making prominent appointments.[87] He was also aware of the increasing hostility of women within the party who believed they were being unfairly excluded from important meetings.[88] In 1916 he told Johnson that the Republicans were "a little bit too cavalier" in their "treatment of women politically, and have taken a little too much for granted." Women, he argued, "have been good soldiers," and some were "important enough" to be included in the preliminary conferences held by party leaders.[89] Johnson was, of course, a pragmatic politician aware that strategy as well as culture needed to be considered in political equations. He did listen.

The voices of women dissatisfied with their place in the Republican party of California continued to grow louder after 1914, and even more so after 1916. This increase was due in part to the growing criticisms of nonpartisan election bills and the belief that legislation had not only weakened the influence of parties but had left the electoral process in chaos. Nonpartisan elections continued, but the movement for nonpartisanship in politics was coming to an end; it was no longer an advantage in political culture. The increase of women's dissatisfaction was also due to the declining political influence of women like Porter, whose political star fell or, more accurately, dimmed with age, and the rise of a new generation of California political women who held ideas about women's place in politics that were shaped out of the debates of the twentieth century, not the late nineteenth century.

Porter continued to be politically active in California politics. After the passage of the Nineteenth Amendment, she became the leader of the Los Angeles Republican Study Club, a woman's party organization. In 1924 she was a delegate to the Republican National Convention and delivered a seconding speech nominating Calvin Coolidge for president. She died on New Year's Eve 1930.

The Crisis of the Suffrage Movement

In 1914 the NAWSA was again challenged by partisanship, but this time the challenge came not from women wanting to work for their parties but from members wanting to work against the party in power. Many suffrage supporters were dismayed that their movement had become so "conservative" even as it had grown nationally and internationally. New ideas and new strategies were shared by women interacting in this international crusade, and some of these proposed that the time had come for women to use direct action to advance their cause. Calls to militancy were especially strong from British suffragists (or "suffragettes"), and American women who traveled to Britain returned to the United States with new ideas for activism and founded new organizations to energize the movement. Among them was Harriot Stanton Blatch, the daughter of Elizabeth Cady Stanton, who founded the Equality League for Self-Supporting Women in 1906, renamed the Woman's Political Union in 1910.[90] This organization arranged spectacular events such as suffrage parades. A new mood was in the air.

Adding to this new mood were the women of the National Woman's Party (NWP). Calling itself a "party" rather than an "association" or "union," the NWP was organized in 1913 when members of the NAWSA's Congressional Committee split off from the parent organization in an attempt to create a more militant suffrage organization. They employed the strategy and tactics its founders, Alice Paul and Lucy Burns, had learned from the British Women's Social and Political Union.[91] The NWP targeted the party in power as responsible for failed efforts on behalf of suffrage and mobilized women to work against the Democrats. "By putting suffrage first and party affiliations second," the NWP claimed, "women can make the suffrage issue a deciding factor" in the presidential campaign.[92] Their political strategy was denounced by the NAWSA because it went against their policy and was seen as militant and partisan. NAWSA leaders also feared that the NWP's approach would hurt suffrage efforts to convert Democratic politicians, especially in the South, where there were few Republicans in power.[93]

In an attempt to clarify the NWP's attitude, Lucy Burns asserted that their policy was nonpartisan because the NWP was applying its policy to all political parties. However, because the Democratic party was the party in power, it was being held responsible for the lack of progress on woman suffrage. Mrs. Russell Malcolm MacLennan, in an attack on the NWP's policy, saw the issue differently. She believed that it was a partisan policy and argued that it was "only just that individual members of all parties be held to an accounting for their attitude on the question of the franchise for women."[94] According to her reasoning, the party leaders and not an entire party should be targeted, because suffrage supporters within the parties could influence a party's official stand on suffrage. But the NWP was moving beyond the individual lobbying efforts that had become much of the work of the NAWSA. They were following Blatch's lead into the streets, and there it was hard to distinguish between a person and a party, as members of the New York Woman Suffrage Party found when they demonstrated outside Republican and Democratic clubs in 1914.[95] Throughout 1915, the NAWSA repudiated the NWP's campaigns against Democrats. Responses to the NWP's actions increased in late 1915, when Carrie Chapman Catt reaffirmed the NAWSA's commitment as an organization to nonpartisanship with an acknowledgment of individuals' partisan rights.[96]

The NWP's focus on the Democratic party raised another issue for suffragists. It demanded that all women vote against all Democrats solely on the issue of woman suffrage. Since 1912, the NAWSA had denied that women would vote as a bloc and promoted women's different individual partisan identifications. The small numbers of women who supported the NWP's policy and the disruption it caused in suffrage circles indicates how important partisan choices were to women. Later, women would dismiss the NWP for other reasons—including its militant tactics and its attacks on the president—but in its early days it was, in part, partisanship that led to its rejection.[97]

The End of the Progressive Party

Throughout the early months of 1916, Progressives met in Chicago and New York to discuss the upcoming election. Progressive National Committeemen—and they were men; no women are included in the lists of 1916—talked about which candidates would remain loyal to the party, whether new members might be tempted to join the party, and their chances for victories at the local and national levels.[98] After the election of 1914, most Progressives believed that the party could not survive. It had lost elections in every state except California, where Hiram Johnson was reelected as governor.[99] It had trouble keeping its coalition together, as new issues were addressed and old ones were taken over and successfully co-opted by the winning Democrats.

Local, state, and national leaders left the Progressive party, as the Progressives declared for prohibition and preparedness in 1914 and 1915.[100]

A core group of Progressives decided that victories were possible, and again the National Committee voted to run a national campaign, hold a national convention, and work against any efforts at national fusion with the Republicans. Theodore Roosevelt was still their leader but, known only to some of his followers, he had carefully questioned and lobbied Republican friends about their party's interest in his candidacy on the regular Republican ticket. He was determined to win the 1916 election because of new issues before the country, most prominently the war raging in Europe, and his firm conviction that he was best qualified to direct foreign policy in an era of increasing international tension fueled his determination. Probably nothing more conveyed the change in issues, tone, and style of the 1916 campaign, compared to the 1912 campaign, than a cartoon that showed Roosevelt standing next to a placard on which the boldfaced word "PREPAREDNESS" was printed diagonally over the message, "My Policies: Social Justice, Recall, Initiative and Referendum, Presidential Primaries, Etc."[101]

Women struck out on their own while Roosevelt and the Progressive party made their plans. In February 1916, forty prominent women met in New York City to make arrangements for an organization of women to work in the presidential election. Alice Carpenter, who had survived her conflicts with George Perkins, headed the committee of seven that arranged the conference.[102] She had by then succeeded Kellor and Addams as the most prominent and influential woman in the Progressive party, but women's place in the party had dramatically changed since 1912. There was no discussion of gender equality within the party, the decline of the Progressive Service had left women without a base of support for their work, and their numbers and influence remained small.

There was no discussion of racial inclusion or equality in the party; there were no black women at the 1916 meetings.[103] S. Willie Layton, the president of the Black Baptist Women's Convention, had supported the Progressives in 1912, but in 1916 she "expressed her disillusionment" in a letter to the Republican Mary Church Terrell. Layton chose to follow the course that had often been taken by partisan women discouraged with their party. She decided to support the efforts of the NWP in 1916.[104]

The *New York Times* reported that a group of women meeting in New York had decided that "the women should work as members of a political party, but the decision as to which party and the methods of work were left for action later."[105] Those questions were resolved within the next month by different groups of women around the country. In April, women from six states met and pledged their support to Roosevelt and began plans for an organization of women on his behalf. Their plans were halted when George Perkins wired them from Chicago that the Women's Roosevelt Club of Chicago was starting a national organization and that "it would be better for women voters to take the lead."[106] At the same time, the Roosevelt Republican League and the Colored Roosevelt Headquarters geared up to champion Roosevelt's candidacy.[107]

On June 7, 1916, the Progressive and Republican conventions began deliberations in Chicago. Considering the care with which Roosevelt planned the 1912 convention, to ensure that it would be "unbossed," his absence from its initial deliberations was striking. Roosevelt instead devoted his time to behind-the-scenes maneuvers for his nomination. He was in touch with the nominating committees of both conventions, and his name was presented to both. At the Auditorium Theater, the Progressives nominated Roosevelt, but to their shock he declined the nomination. He hoped to win the Republican nomination. When the telegram he had sent was read to the assembled crowd, "there was silence. Then there was a roar of rage. It was a cry of a broken heart such as no convention ever had uttered in this land before."[108] Less than a mile away, Republicans meeting at the Coliseum chose Charles Evans Hughes, a former progressive Republican governor of New York and Supreme Court justice, as their presidential nominee for the Republican party, and when Hughes declared his support for preparedness, Roosevelt endorsed his nomination.[109]

The Progressive party died with Roosevelt's rejection of the nomination, but there were men who were still committed to keeping something of the party alive. There were attempts to run other candidates and complete a platform. Women also wanted the party to continue, and in the middle of June, just after the conventions adjourned, Progressive women met in Chicago to organize a national Progressive Women's League that "would work separately from the men." At this meeting, chaired by Harriet Vittum, a difference of opinion developed about the "wisdom of a separate campaign by the women." There was also a question about whether or not the women had received permission for their organization from the National Executive Committee.

Alice Carpenter argued that Roosevelt had endorsed the organization, probably a reference to her earlier contacts with him. Katherine Bement Davis said that he had endorsed the idea of an organization of Progressive women in the East, not a national organization of women, and she claimed that the women had called on George Perkins, but "they barely received a graceful reply from him which did not contain consent for such a step as they planned taking."[110]

Not surprisingly, considering the overall disarray of the party and the defections of prominent men and women, nothing came of this meeting of women. Thus, women ended their careers in the Progressive party. It is significant that women's final discussions in the party were debates about a separate women's organization and that they were divided about whether or not this was needed, allowed, or desired. In a party that had pledged itself to gender equality, that had met such drastic failures in its elections and organizational work, and at a time when women's auxiliaries were coming into more prominence in the other two major parties, the fact that women continued the discussion at all is noteworthy.[111]

Richard Hofstadter has written that "third parties are like bees: once they have stung, they die."[112] The Progressive party, especially its platform, had an impact on progressive-era politics. Women's partisanship was changed by the opportunities the party had offered to women. They took their place within the party and raised public awareness about the relationship between women and politics. Now that the party was dead, it would remain to be seen how long the sting would last. The question for women was where they would go. The choices were to go into one of the two dominant parties, into another third party, leave the partisan path altogether, or just sit out the election.[113]

Some Progressive women, including Frances Kellor, Alice Carpenter, Margaret Dreier Robins, Katherine Bement Davis, Maud Howe Elliott, and Cornelia Pinchot, joined Roosevelt in the Republican party. Compared to the Democrats, the Republicans had two things going for them. The first was Roosevelt's endorsement of the nomination of Charles Evans Hughes. Second, the Republican party platform of 1916 finally included a woman suffrage plank, which favored "the extension of suffrage to women but recognizes the right of each state to settle this question for itself." The plank did not endorse a constitutional amendment and thus was not as strong an endorsement of suffrage as the Progressives had given.

On June 28, Roosevelt met with Hughes to discuss the campaign, and they agreed that the prominent issues would be preparedness and Wilson's foreign policy.[114] The next day, Roosevelt wrote Carpenter a confidential note stating that he had also urged Hughes to endorse the federal amendment for woman suffrage. Hughes assured him, Roosevelt told Carpenter, that he was "unequivocally" for suffrage and would "say so when he gets the opportunity."[115] Hughes gave a public declaration for woman suffrage that cheered most of the women at the time of the national convention, but many expected him to do more. At the urging of the Nevada suffragist Anne Martin, Cornelia Bryce Pinchot wrote to Hughes expressing her concern that he, if not the party, needed to rethink the stand on supporting a federal amendment for suffrage.[116] Hughes proclaimed his support for a federal suffrage amendment in early August.

The Democrats also dealt with the issue of woman suffrage in 1916. At the national convention, where Wilson was nominated for reelection, the press was amazed not by the twenty-three women delegates or the members of the women's campaign organizations but by the women in the galleries who were there to hear the roll-call acceptance of a woman suffrage plank.[117] It read: "We favor the extension of the franchise to the women of this country, State by State, on the same terms as men." The acceptance followed a bitter floor debate, to which the assembled suffragists responded with cries of support or disagreement. The *New York Times* reported that it was the "first time that one of the great cheering demonstrations of a National Convention had been a women's cheer, the first time that the gallery menace to a National Convention had ever been a women's menace."[118]

The Republican convention also saw the presence of woman suffragists from the NAWSA and the NWP who marched in from a massive parade. One might question how Susan B. Anthony would have responded to the proceedings and what Judith Ellen Foster would have thought about the fact that fourteen women attended as delegates and alternates. Olive Cole, Abbie Krebs, and Frances Keesling came as part of the delegation from California; Louise Lusk represented Montana; and Minnie Bunnell represented Minnesota. Nine additional women attended as alternates. Maybe Foster would have seen progress, but women were not given positions on any committees. Abbie Krebs and Mrs. W. T. Moran of Nevada were accorded the honorary positions of notifying Charles Fairbanks of Indiana of his nomination as vice president. Anthony and Foster might only have been thinking of the next step.

Will Hays of Indiana, who would become the national party chairman in 1918, was also thinking about how to build on lessons from past campaigns for the next step and claimed that one of the most crucial lessons from the campaign of 1912 was the need to develop "strong appeals to the voters" through the "use of women speakers," and he mentioned Ruth Hanna McCormick.[119] While the men wanted the women as speakers and voters, the women wanted to participate as well. In early March, Republican women were again transforming their clubs into auxiliary campaign organizations. Helen Varick Boswell took the lead and traveled widely to organize Republican women at the state level, pledging her organization to "work in co-operation with the Republican National and Campaign Committees."[120] During the campaign, her Woman's National Republican Association was called the National Women's Campaign Committee of the Republican Committee.

The Republican Challenger

It was a newcomer into the Republican party that challenged Boswell and her organization. Frances Kellor brought with her lessons from the Progressive party when she decided to join the Republicans. She founded the Women's Committee of the National Hughes Alliance, organized solely as a vehicle for the election of the Republican candidate, Charles Evans Hughes. The Women's Committee was dominated by women from New York, New Jersey, Pennsylvania, and Connecticut. Only one woman not from the east coast, Harriet Vittum, who had given up on organizing Progressive women, had a place as a committee member.[121] The committee was structured along the lines of the other political campaign clubs of the day, but where they worked for candidates at the local and state levels, the Women's Committee concentrated on the national level.

The Women's Committee declared itself to be nonpartisan, and Kellor was careful to explain what she meant by nonpartisanship. The committee sought to "work in entire harmony and cooperation with party committees and other organizations" pledged to Hughes. It was nonpartisan because it would take no part in primary or factional contests and would make no nominations or endorse any candidates for any office.[122] Nonpartisanship did not mean that women would stay out of politics. To do so, Kellor argued, "means the same thing in our national life as refusal on the part of American men to defend the country. Women have the same opportunity to conserve the ideals, traditions, standards, and honor of the country as men have to defend them, and the highway is national service."[123]

In making the Women's Committee nonpartisan, Kellor was emphasizing her autonomy from the Republican National Committee and the WNRA. While the press consistently called the organization the Women's Auxiliary of the Hughes Alliance, Kellor did not see the organization as an auxiliary to anything. She would be in charge, and she was. In the campaign of 1912 she had been schooled in the dangers of bossism and machines. She now made herself a political boss, of women.[124]

Kellor now had to build a constituency. The Women's National Wilson and Marshall Organization and the new Women's Democratic Bureau, headed by Elizabeth Bass, were busily recruiting women into the party.[125] Because of what they saw as a weak suffrage plank, the NWP had declared a full-out war against Wilson and the Democrats. Wilson's speech at the NAWSA National Convention in September, when he asked the "conservative" suffragists to be patient, created more antipathy.[126] The NAWSA reaffirmed its nonpartisan stance after Margaret Dreier Robins introduced a resolution to have the convention delegates support Hughes, explaining that she did not consider this a "partisan resolution, but the best means to work for votes for women." Instead, the convention reinforced its nonpartisan stance by accepting another resolution declaring that only "nonpartisan methods" would be used in state and national work. This resolution drew clear distinctions between the NAWSA, the NWP, and the women's partisan organizations.[127] Illinois women took a different tack. At a special meeting of the Illinois Equal Suffrage Association in August, the members adopted a resolution stating that the association "does not stand for the policy of attacking or indorsing political parties. . . . The Illinois Equal Suffrage Association includes representatives from all parties, all sects, all people. It is all partisan."[128] One can almost hear the echo of Susan B. Anthony's words from the 1880s.

Other women focused their energies in single-issue organizations or new national pressure and policy-making groups. In 1915, Jane Addams, Lillian Wald, Crystal Eastman, Florence Kelley, Fanny Garrison Villard, Anna Garland Spencer, Alice Hamilton, Grace Abbott, and many other prominent women had joined together to call for Wilson to mediate the European war. They founded the Woman's Peace Party and traveled to The Hague to meet with an international group of women and call on the leaders of the warring countries to cease hostilities. In their efforts, they had crossed party lines. Now, with a new election before them, and with Wilson declaring that he would keep the United States out of war—even though he had moved toward endorsing preparedness—the women's political choices were formed, in part, on the basis of this issue.[129] The 1916 election was not a one-issue election for men or women, but the European war was crucial in determining the responses of politicians and their supporters before and after the national nominating conventions.

Kellor attempted to get women to support Hughes by advertising his progressive record as governor of New York. Margaret Dreier Robins cited it as her reason for supporting the Republicans.[130] Kellor had long-standing ties to Hughes. He had given Kellor her first patronage appointment as secretary of the New York State Immigration Commission in 1908. She may have also seen that her chances for striking out on an independent path were better in the Republican party than with the Democrats. Hughes heartily endorsed her plan for a Women's Committee of the National Hughes Alliance.[131]

Kellor and her women allies built a unique organization within the Republican party to secure power for women as much as to secure the White House for Hughes.[132] Their stated objective was to "safeguard the splendid service and recognition which women had achieved as a result of the Progressive movement of 1912." They saw the campaign of 1916 as one of "general confusion" and feared that "the woman's movement in politics was likely to lose its national significance without some definite conservation movement."[133] Just after the election, the Women's Committee published a thirty-eight-page report titled *Women in National Politics* to explain their history and accomplishments. According to the report, the alliance may have failed to get Hughes elected, but it had succeeded in its efforts to advance women's participation in party matters to the degree that "the party that reckons without them in the coming elections will fail of success."[134] The organization's impact on the campaign and election is debatable, but it is clear that Kellor believed she had accomplished her goal of proving that "the women's movement in national politics has come to stay."

The report carefully explains the background of the alliance. It notes that Republican party women were without national representation and were unorganized before the campaign began. This was, of course, not true, but it shows that Kellor viewed the WNRA as a nonentity. The report claimed that the party had only a Republican Woman's Bureau, which was founded at the Chicago convention, and Kellor found fault with it because it was "under the direction of a man" and "failed to satisfy anyone." Her unwillingness to trace the history of the WNRA and Republican and Democratic women's tradition of transforming their clubs or associations into campaign organizations may have stemmed from her competitiveness within the party, her belief that these women's auxiliaries were ineffective and outdated, or her hope that the Women's Committee would absorb the other women's organizations.[135]

Addressing the history of women's separate organizations within the Republican party may have also weakened Kellor's own argument for why the Women's Committee was necessary. According to the report, the first question that the women faced was whether to have a separate organization of women or to join the Hughes Alliance, which had just been established by men in the party. The report argued that women chose to become a separate committee of the alliance because they recognized that "women can secure individual recognition and equal opportunity to work with men only when they are part of a collective body with power and purpose." The report noted that the experience of the campaign "emphasized the wisdom of our choice."[136]

The report also explained why the women had chosen to focus their work at the national level. The major political weakness of the country, the report stated, was an "insistent localism and sectionalism." Kellor may have been responding to her earlier experiences within the Progressive party, especially her frustration that individuals were willing to give money to local or state candidates but not the national party. She was also continuing to reinforce the social workers' belief that legislation and political action had to take place at the national level. As she wrote to Narcissa Cox Vanderlip, the issues of "Americanization, preparedness, social and industrial justice laws for workers and a united citizenship are national and Hughes' stand on the federal amendment [for woman suffrage] assures us that if elected he will deal with them as national matters."[137]

The committee had two separate budgets for its two main tasks. The first was the work of researching Hughes's record, writing reports, and furnishing information to speakers. With a budget of $132,836.95, all raised by the committee, the women used publications and speakers to achieve what Kellor called the aim of politics: education and enlightenment. Politics, she wrote, "may be and must be 'civics' at its best."[138]

In addition to following the standard method of educational campaigning by contrasting Hughes and Wilson's records as governors, Kellor innovated. The committee published a weekly twelve-page publication, "The Campaign Service," disseminating facts, or what would today be called "talking points," instead of reprinting long speeches. This information helped keep distant states and organizations in touch, gave speakers material to argue the issues, and furnished propaganda "adapted to general readers and independent voters." Kellor argued that the "Campaign Service" put the women's organization in closer touch with local Republican organizations and prominent campaign workers than did the Republican National Committee.[139]

A separate budget of $48,873.32 was established for Kellor's more controversial innovation, a Campaign Train whose purpose was to stimulate "local committees of women . . . to undertake the work of political organization, often for the first time, and to raise their first independent political funds."[140] Press reports sent by the Women's Committee reinforced the idea that the Campaign Train was not a suffrage vehicle.[141] Key speakers were selected on the basis of their ability to counter a campaign of disinformation about Hughes's record. Margaret Dreier Robins spoke on labor questions to counter charges that Hughes "was against labor"; Rheta Childe Dorr countered the charge that Hughes was "against human interests in America and for Wall Street"; Katherine B. Davis countered the belief that he was "against suffrage"; Elizabeth Freeman was chosen because she could address "colored audiences at specially arranged meetings."[142]

Six hundred women attended the breakfast that celebrated the send-off of the Campaign Train from New York City on October 2.[143] The eight-car train traveled from New York to California, stopping along the way so that the speakers could address audiences and organize women. Kellor wrote Narcissa Cox Vanderlip that women had "shown the value of parades and publicity in our cities" and asked, "is not the time ready to march across the continent and back talking the things women believe in halls and at cross-roads?"[144] The goal was to convince women to move beyond or above specific issues and local politics and join together East and West to elect Hughes.

The Campaign Train had problems from the beginning, and Kellor spelled them out in the report. First, the press dealt with it as "society copy" and called it the "Billionaires' Special."[145] The Women's Committee tried to minimize this negative reporting with carefully crafted press releases, but to no avail.[146] The curiosity and respect shown by the press to the new partisan women of 1912 had turned into indifference or hostility in 1916.[147] Another problem was the "indifference of the Republican organization to its women voters." Coupled with the "desire of Republican leaders to limit the train's activities to suffrage states," the party leaders had shown their "inability to grasp the idea that women can do campaign work without arguing for or against suffrage as a sole issue." Kellor argued that the train's speakers refuted the belief that "women are supposed to have inalienable tendencies like pro-hibition and suffrage which they cannot keep out of politics."[148] Again, as in 1912, the party and the press seemed unable to look beyond suffrage when it looked at women.[149]

It was not only men who created problems for the women. Kellor point-ed out that the train was hurt by two groups of women. First, they were hurt by the "silent opposition of suffragists" who still held to the belief that only a nonpartisan stance could help the suffrage cause. Second, club women "who put club above country and club methods ahead of party and who consider civic work as of a higher order than political work" were a problem. In striv-ing to organize women for Hughes, Kellor had illuminated the complexity of women's political culture. Women held different positions on political issues, different partisan identifications, and different ideas about the role of politics in female activism.[150]

Kellor also noted that the "able organization which the Democratic party put behind its women leaders, who pursued a highly personal, bitter campaign of insult and misrepresentation," contributed significantly to the problems the Campaign Train encountered. While the Democratic party certainly ral-lied its women, Democratic women were already poised for a fight before the Republican women organized the train. They were ready to fight the NWP. Instead, they also used their arguments, tactics, and organization against the Women's Committee of the Hughes Alliance.

At almost every stop the Hughes Train was met by Wilson supporters. At some stops only one or two Democratic women waited silently with banners supporting Wilson, while at others large gatherings of male and female Democrats jeered the Republicans. Things got worse as the train went farther west. In Helena, Montana, the governor's wife, Mrs. Samuel V. Stewart, declared that it was "simply ridiculous" for nonvoting eastern women to attempt to give western women voters political instruction. Katherine Philips Edson, watching from California, was disturbed by the "lack of dignity" given the women and cited the horror of the train being "rotten-egged at Minneapolis."[151] Tension between western women voters and eastern women who did not have the vote was only fueled by the train. Regional and gender differences, as well as internal state fighting between conservative and progressive factions within the Republican party, contributed to the difficulties faced by the Women's Committee of the Hughes Alliance on its western journey.

What did the Campaign Train accomplish? It traveled over 11,075 miles, and the women organized 328 meetings. They believed they had influenced voters, especially women. Kellor argued that, more importantly, "it opened the political door to women's independence, self-respect and resourcefulness." It made "national issues and American conditions" a chief topic of conversation for women. Further, the train countered the suffrage focus of women's political work, especially in the nonsuffrage states, where "there is no political organization through which a woman can seek to obtain the civic improvement she wants, except a suffrage or anti-suffrage party." Women, Kellor argued, do not regard "getting or opposing suffrage as the chief end of existence and as yet have no other entry into political activity." As such, the train gave male politicians, blinded by suffrage, "a new insight into women's powers of organization, resourcefulness, and ability to do teamwork."[152]

Kellor's report on women's work for the 1916 campaign ended on an optimistic note, with a list of suggestions for future party work. Most of the suggestions were for new organizational measures such as new kinds of campaign literature, careful selection of speakers, and consideration of foreign literature press services, but three issues were of most importance. At the top of the list was a call for educating voters on national issues. Education must be based on an "awakened national feeling," or what the report termed "nationalized citizenship." Equally important was the suggestion that women be taken "into account in all political reckonings and all political work," for "women have demonstrated their ability to hold up their end."[153]

The report also called for "a new spirit in party organization" and noted the tendency in the West and among women voters to vote for individuals rather than parties on national tickets. "This tendency," the report stated, "contains both danger and promise." The danger was in losing the "sound national principles upon which valid political parties are founded." The country needed parties, the report declared, but people needed to make parties "express their principles." With attention to principles, "the 'nonpartisanship' of a large percentage of our present voters" would become the "greatest asset in securing the new spirit in party organization" because it is the source not of party disaffection but of party control and regeneration.[154]

For the Hughes campaign itself, the Campaign Train and the Women's Committee were of little help. Even Kellor recognized that the campaign was "lifeless." Still, she believed that the women were able to "put ginger and interest" into it and "cracked the surface of the selfish, material, wholly complacent issues of the campaign and restored to some the faith and courage that put national honor above prosperity."[155] The fact that the Campaign Train dominated press reports about partisan women, however, may have kept women from advancing within the Republican party. Helen Boswell's Woman's Campaign Committee of the Republican National Committee received little notice, although this may have also resulted from her tendency to move slowly and carefully during the campaign season.[156]

Republicans overall, in their newly united but still deeply divided party, could not garner enough votes to unseat Wilson.[157] The Democrats won the election of 1916. Wilson received 49.4 percent of the popular vote. Charles Evans Hughes received 46.2 percent. Eleven of the twelve suffrage states went to Wilson, including the traditionally Republican states of California, Kansas, Utah, and Washington. Only the suffrage state of Illinois went to Hughes.[158]

The *New York Tribune* reported in the week following the election that leaders of the Democratic and Republican women's organizations had decided that the help of the women in the campaign had been too great a value to permit their organizations to disband and that they would become permanent bodies for future campaigning.[159] Women may not have captured the spotlight as they had in 1912, and may in fact have been ridiculed more than they had in many other campaigns, but party leaders, within the women's organizations and in the national committees, had new evidence of the importance of women's partisan commitments.

The most notable evidence and achievement was the election of Jeannette Rankin of Montana to the U.S. House of Representatives.[160] "The Lady from Montana speaks not merely for the eternal feminine in Montana, but for all women, and all women are not of the same mind," claimed the NAWSA's "Headquarters News Letter." According to the suffrage line, she "is in the limelight not to glorify herself nor merely to proclaim a triumph for the cause of woman suffrage. She stands in her place to give battle for ameliorative measures that are higher than political interest."[161] Rankin ran on a "progressive Republican platform calling for woman suffrage, protective legislation for children, tariff revision, prohibition, and 'preparedness that will make for peace,'" and she represents a link between generations of women political activists.[162] She was schooled in the politics of progressive reform, active in the woman suffrage struggle, and joined forces with the women's peace efforts. Once elected, one of her earliest tasks was to vote on the entry of the United States into World War I. As a Quaker, she voted no, but once war was declared she supported the war effort through the Liberty Bond drives. The war work done by women around the country provided further proof of their necessary contribution to the common good and bolstered support for woman suffrage.

Knowing that because of redistricting she would lose another run for the House, in 1918 Rankin unsuccessfully sought the Republican nomination for the Senate. Her loss was usually explained by her antiwar vote. She may also have been seeking a too powerful or prominent political office. In 1940 she was again elected to the House of Representatives, but when she voted against the entry of the United States into World War II her partisan career came to an end, and she returned to reform politics, working for women and for peace. In 1968, at age eighty-eight, she joined a group of five thousand women calling themselves the "Jeannette Rankin Brigade" to protest the war in Vietnam in a march on Washington. She died five years later.

7. Claiming Victory, 1918–24

JUST AFTER HE lost his bid to recapture the White House in 1912, Theodore Roosevelt wrote a letter to the prominent British suffragist Millicent Garrett Fawcett indicating that, if he had won, Jane Addams might have been the first woman to hold a cabinet-level position. It was his intention, he wrote, "to put women in two or three places in my administration, with the ultimate hope of getting one of them, probably Miss Jane Addams, into the Cabinet." He then qualified this vow by concluding that he would "not have put her in at the start."[1] It took twenty-one years for the first woman cabinet member to be appointed (Frances Perkins, secretary of labor), and then it was by another Roosevelt from a different party.

People are appointed to political office for many reasons. Appointments are given as rewards for long service in a party or special service in a campaign. They are a way to bring people who are dedicated to a specific agenda or expert in a certain field into politics. They can be about money, friendship, or even revenge. Political appointments can come from an individual or be decided on by a committee, and they are often the result of partisan maneuvering. The history of Republican women seeking and receiving political appointments begins in the late nineteenth century, with women postmasters and party loyalists like Judith Ellen Foster, and extends into the early twentieth century, with the women of Jane Addams's circle. These women challenged the idea that women's struggle for greater political influence stopped at the ballot box, and they paved the way for new efforts within the Republican party to expand women's roles and create gender equality.

The story of women's advancement into elective office is also rooted in the nineteenth century. Even without the vote and before they were considered eligible, women ran for political office, including president of the United States, on third-party tickets.[2] Their first successes came at lower levels in towns and counties and usually in offices considered appropriate to women. They reached the state level when three Republican women were elected in Colorado in 1894. Jeannette Rankin of Montana took women to the next level when she was elected to the Sixty-fifth Congress in 1916. Alice Mary Robertson of Oklahoma followed in 1920. In 1921 Winnifred Sprague Mason Huck of Illinois was elected to fill her father's seat after his death, and Mae Ella Nolan of California filled her husband's seat in 1923.[3] All were Republicans.

Alice Mary Robertson was born in 1854 in Indian Territory to missionary parents; her grandfather was Samuel Worcester. She attended Elmira College in New York, taught at the Carlisle Indian School, was involved in the Lake Mohonk Conference of Friends of the Indian, and was appointed by Theodore Roosevelt to be federal supervisor of Creek Indian schools in 1900. Five years later, he appointed her postmaster of Muskogee, Oklahoma, but when the Democrats moved into office in 1913 she lost the appointment. She then adopted a daughter, established a farm, ran a cafeteria, was active in antisuffrage activities, and worked for the Red Cross during World War I. After taking her congressional seat, she was assigned to the Committee on Indian Affairs, broke with her party to oppose the Sheppard-Towner Bill, and was defeated for reelection in 1922.[4]

Winnifred Sprague Mason Huck got to Congress in 1922 after winning a special election that had been called after her father, William Mason, a congressman-at-large from Illinois, died in 1921. She ran in the next regular election but lost her bid for a full term. She then joined the NWP and became a journalist. Although a daughter rather than a wife, she was the first Republican woman in a line of political accommodation at the congressional level that would be called the "widow's succession."[5] Mae Ella Nolan was the second. Her husband, John Nolan, died a week after being reelected to his sixth term in Congress. He had entered the House as a Progressive Republican, and Mae Ellen Nolan announced she would carry on his work in the area of labor legislation. She was the first woman to chair a House committee, the Committee on Expenditures in the Post Office Department. She did not seek another term and left office claiming "'politics is man's business.'"[6]

Electing women to office had never been high on the suffrage agenda. In fact, suffragists worked hard to explain that, as the *Woman Voter's Manual* put it in 1918, the "female of the species has proved herself rather fundamentally adverse to office-seeking." The exceptions, the authors claimed, were school offices and those connected to the welfare of women and children. Women's "special training" and "marked ability or experience in these lines"

made them qualified for some positions, but overall women were not looking to gain offices. The *Woman Voter's Manual* claimed that men should be
reassured by the facts and rid themselves of their "obsession" with the idea
that women voters might immediately "untie all the neat packages into which
political parties have tied their inherited traditions."[7] In 1917 the NAWSA
publicized the fact that of the eleven women in the lower houses of state legislatures, all were wives and most were mothers. The "mother-capacity," as
they called it, "withstands all political, social and economic innovations.
. . . Women know it and carry it along with them into each and every new
sphere that opens up."[8] Coexisting with the evidence of the "mother-capacity" were statistics that proved "rather conclusively that women are attracted principally to the public educational positions."[9]

The suffrage agenda did include an encouragment for women to join political parties. Carrie Chapman Catt, as she looked to the future of a nation
of women voters, told women that the "only way to get things in this country, is from the inside of political parties. More and more parties have become agencies through which powerful things have been accomplished. It is
not a question of whether it is right for us but rather a realization of the fact.
They are powerful."[10]

Both parties knew that the increasing number of states with woman suffrage laws meant potential votes, volunteers, and victories. In 1917, North
Dakota, Nebraska, Rhode Island, New York, and Arkansas enfranchised wom-
en, bringing the number of suffrage states to seventeen. Four more states
followed in 1918, and eight more in 1919. A national woman suffrage victory
seemed imminent. It was logical for the parties to look to enroll these new
women voters, and they did, but to provide women with greater opportunities to participate, institutional structures also had to be changed. About this
there was more resistance.

The Democrats moved first to change policies and allow women greater
access to party structures. In 1916 the Democratic party began to incorpo-
rate women systematically into the party with the establishment of a Wom-
en's Bureau of the Democratic National Committee (DNC). Elizabeth Bass
of Chicago was appointed as its first chair.[11] The Women's Bureau recruited
women volunteers during and after the election, but Bass also worked with
Democratic women leaders in different states as well as with DNC members
on a plan for incorporating women into all party councils. In late 1917 the
Women's Bureau became the Women's Division of the DNC, and women
from suffrage states were appointed as members.[12] There was discussion
about enacting a fifty-fifty rule for the DNC and the Democratic National
Executive Committee. This discussion derived from the actions of state par-

ties, especially Colorado, which paved the way when its state parties passed the first fifty-fifty rules in 1906. Four years later the Colorado legislature passed a fifty-fifty law.[13] A fifty-fifty rule went into effect for the DNC in 1920.

Republican women found that the RNC was not willing to move as quickly as the DNC. The *New York Times* announced the "Republican Plan to Enlist Women" on January 23, 1918, but the next month the Republican National Executive Committee (RNEC) tabled a motion to appoint a campaign advisory committee of women.[14] At almost the same time, the woman suffrage victory seemed even nearer when the Susan B. Anthony amendment was passed in the House of Representatives with the required two-thirds majority, by a vote of 304 to 89. Of the sitting Republicans, 200 voted in favor and 19 voted against the amendment; the Democrats voted 102 in favor and 70 against.[15]

Soon after these events, Cornelia Bryce Pinchot wrote to Will Hays, the new chairman of the RNC, that it was with "considerable anxiety" that she had been observing his work since his election. She was especially disturbed that no women were included in the meetings he was having with Republican leaders, and she contrasted this neglect with the moves being made by the Democrats. This neglect was a "serious political mistake," she stated, and was "one from which the Republican party has already suffered heavily in the past." The party needed to be bold if it was going to keep women's loyalties from drifting into the Democratic party, which "has taken the women in with great bon homie, and with a great show of 'liberty, equality and fraternity.'"[16]

Pinchot also warned Hays that it would not work to organize women at the last moment before an election with the hopes that such "a hasty attempt to marshal their interest and support will offset the results of this neglect."[17] Here she may have been referring to the work of the WNRA in the last election. By 1916, Pinchot was well acquainted with progressive Republican politics. Born into a wealthy political family in 1881, she was surrounded in her early years by anti-Tammany Democrats and reform Republicans as she grew up in Rhode Island and New York; her father was an advisor to Theodore Roosevelt. She married Gifford Pinchot at the height of his unsuccessful 1914 campaign as a progressive Republican candidate for the Senate from Pennsylvania. She was also active in the woman suffrage movement and served as secretary of the Pennsylvania Woman Suffrage Association from 1918 through 1919.[18] Her awareness of Republican policies and actions was built on this history.

Singled out by Pinchot for criticism were "the old political hacks among the women" who, she claimed, were being allowed to set the policies for women's inclusion in the party. These "hacks" of the "Women's Auxiliary

Committees of the Republican Organization" were behind the times, she said, and none "stands for vigorous social and political conviction among the women." She was especially critical of Helen Varick Boswell, calling her "a typical auxiliary committee type" who "has had no experience in the most important social and political measures of the past twenty years at least, and she could in no way stand in any position of leadership with reference to the women of the nation."[19]

Pinchot situated herself in a new generation of women political activists in her letter to Hays and made it clear that the Republican leaders must be guided by the ideas of what she called this "great group of women interested in civic and political affairs." To make her point, she informed Hays about what was happening in New York, where Republicans had decided on equal representation in party councils, but they were making blunders, including appointing Reta Yawger as "Associate Chairman" of a "Women's Republican State Committee."[20] Yawger was the president of the New York City Federation of Women's Clubs, and Pinchot acknowledged that fifty years ago, "in their grandmothers' times," this might have been a logical choice, but now it was laughable and even dangerous for the party. "To thus establish arbitrarily, a weak and non-representative leadership, is the best possible way to alienate the new and vigorous blood among women that ought to be flowing right now into the Republican party."[21]

She argued that the Republican party needed to change its policies, its institutional arrangements, if it was to win women's loyalties. She understood she was challenging tradition. As Emily Newell Blair, the vice chair of the DNC in the 1920s, stated, "'before suffrage was extended to women, the law, in some states, used the word "man" or "male," thus limiting eligibility to these committees. Precedent always did.'"[22] Election laws and party rules had to be changed at the same time that perceptions of the proper political place for women needed to be challenged. It would be a big job, Pinchot reasoned, because both men and women needed to work against traditions. For men, it meant relinquishing some powers of office. For women, it meant coming to terms with what she called the "vice" that was one of the legacies of decades of disfranchisement—women's nonpartisanship.

In spite of her conviction that the "most practical and most powerful women, no matter in what field, have a keen value of the need of party strength," basic steps needed to be taken to overcome women's long enthusiasm for working through nonpartisan organizations. To explain the circumstances that needed to be faced, Pinchot gave the examples of Colorado and Wyoming, on the one hand, and California and Chicago, on the other hand, and then put forth her recommendations. In Colorado and Wyoming there were two groups of politically active women, the "feminists" and the "paid hacks." The "feminists" were nonpartisan and kept to themselves as "a group of women," but it was due to their work that some important pieces of legislation had been passed in Colorado. The "paid hacks" were "women whom the men are sure they can use and control." They might be party regulars, but they were a problem in Pinchot's estimation. In California and Chicago party women were more independent, but they did not go so far as to separate themselves and promote nonpartisanship. They combined their efforts with party men, but "the women's political interest is tied less to the idol of party organization . . . than it is to party function as a means of getting through important social and national measures." It was this model that the party should embrace. She recommended the following: women from "really representative groups" should be the ones to negotiate with the men on the party committees; a woman representative from every full suffrage state should be appointed to the RNC; and women should be represented in state and county committees only in exactly the same way as the men were represented and without special provision for a separate women's organization.[23]

While equal representation and cooperation were the goals, Pinchot observed that at the present time "it will be necessary to make some special arrangement by which women are enabled to have representatives on the committees." In the end, however, she stated that the women on whose behalf she spoke "positively repudiate the wisdom of dealing with women through separate or auxiliary committees. To do so is at once to take advantage of women's inexperience in politics, and to prevent the women's vote from working out to any permanent good either to themselves or to the body politic." She had made it clear that her ideas were not hers alone; they were the result of a political conversation among women that extended across the nation and across party and organizational lines.[24]

Hays responded to her letter with a carefully worded public declaration. "The time has long passed," he stated, "when political parties should be used for personal aggrandizement by any individual or for the advancement of any small group of individuals. Political parties exist in order that men and women of certain well-defined political faiths should come together and impress that faith upon the government under which they live." In conclusion, he stated, "there is no reason why women should not have the fullest participation in all affairs of the political parties." With his response and in statements to the press, he consistently affirmed his belief that women should work side-by-side with men in the party.[25] At the same time, however, he stated that the national Republican party would not dictate state policy with reference to the organization of women voters, making it clear that male party leaders of state and local organizations would control the bulk of the appointments.[26]

To move forward on Pinchot's resolutions, Hays asked Ruth Hanna Mc-Cormick of Illinois in early September 1918 to head a new women's organization in the party, the Republican Women's National Executive Committee (RWNEC).[27] It would be the partner of the RNEC. McCormick, like Pinchot, had family connections to progressive Republican party politics. Her father, Marcus Hanna, a senator from Ohio, was chairman of the RNC from 1896 to 1904, and her husband, Medill McCormick, was elected to the Illinois House in 1912, the U.S. House of Representatives in 1916, and the U.S. Senate in 1918.[28] McCormick was active in the 1912 Progressive party campaign and in Illinois and national woman suffrage politics. Her connections with women and men across generations allowed her to represent the loyal party woman and the new generation of women in politics. She moved cautiously. Women, she stated, "do not want jobs, but want good men in office. They have come into politics with their knitting to stay."[29]

The six-member RWNEC was approved by the RNC in September 1918.[30] Working with McCormick were Florence Collins Porter of California, Corinne Roosevelt Robinson of New York, and Mary Garrett Hay.[31] Robinson was the sister of Theodore Roosevelt and had been active in the 1912 Progressive and 1916 Republican campaigns. Hay was, like Hays, a native of Indiana and had a long career in temperance and suffrage organizing. She moved to New York in 1895 and served as president of the New York State Federation of Women's Clubs and the New York City Woman Suffrage Party. Hay, who had been living with the NAWSA president Carrie Chapman Catt since the death of Catt's husband in 1905, moved up the Republican party ladder and was chosen to chair the platform committee of the New York State Republican convention in 1917, the year that New York women won the vote.[32]

The RWNEC women were given the daunting task of creating a plan of action for organizing women into the party. Pinchot had spelled out the challenge. The problem of the women party "hacks" had to be dealt with, nonpartisan women needed to be brought into the partisan fold, the competition from the Democrats had to be faced, and party rules had to be addressed. The problem of the "hacks" who worked at the national level seemed to be taken care of when Boswell was not appointed to the RWNEC. Instead, she moved back to the state level and became the woman's chair of the Republican Committee of New York County. Her base was again, as it had been since the mid-1890s, the West End Republican Club.[33]

When the RWNEC was created, McCormick stated that their plan was "to organize women within the party and not to maintain any separate Republican clubs for women." Republican women would work "in association with men and under the leaders of the party."[34] Robinson reiterated that women would go "shoulder to shoulder with men" but also stressed that they would go slowly in accepting appointed political positions and would certainly not support women nominees for high elective positions such as lieutenant governor.[35]

Despite the emphasis on cooperation, when the men appointed antisuffragists to the RWNEC, McCormick began to work on a plan of action that removed the women's appointments from men's control.[36] The plan stated that the "Chairman of each State Committee shall appoint in consultation with the Women's National Executive Committee, a State Executive Committee of women numbering from five to fifteen members to act with the State Central Committee." This plan would then be followed down the chain from the state level to the precinct or election district. On January 10, 1919, the plan was ratified by the RNC, and a copy was sent to the chair of each state committee.[37]

At the end of May 1919, "the first joint political conference of men and women" of the Republican party was held in Washington, D.C.[38] Almost every state sent representatives to work on the implementation of the plan to bring women into the party. The first aim was to identify and inform Republican women that they would have a voice in the selection of their representatives within the party. The second was to bring the plan to the attention of all women nationwide.[39] There would be "no separate women's organizations except for temporary purposes" allowed in the Republican party, they told the public, essentially repeating Pinchot's initial formulation.[40] Republican women, Will Hays declared, "are part of the party membership, not as women but as voters entitled to participate and participating in so far as present legal limitations permit, just as other voters. Their activity is not supplementary, ancillary or secondary at all. They are not to be separated or segregated but assimilated and amalgamated with just the full consideration due every working member of the party."[41] By the time of the national convention, the RWNEC had organized women in thirty-eight states.[42]

The RWNEC was renamed the Women's Division in late 1919, as it underwent a change in leadership. McCormick resigned and was replaced first by Mary Garrett Hay and then by Christine Bradley South of Kentucky.[43] As she relinquished her position, McCormick told the men of the RNC, "I marvel at the apprehension of some of you regarding our citizenship. It is not that there is imputed to us smaller patriotism than yours but one somehow different, wanting in quality, stamina and virility if you will. . . . This is our country no less than yours, gentlemen."[44] She would continue to try and help men understand women's citizenship for decades to come. Harriet Taylor Upton succeeded South. From Warren, Ohio, Upton, like so many of the women who gained early positions in the party, was a suffragist, temperance activist, and from a political family. Her family moved to Warren in 1861 when Harriet was eight years old. Just before her father was elected to Congress to fill James Garfield's seat when he became president, her mother died, and so Harriet became his "official hostess" for four years until she married George Upton in 1884. Her husband joined her father's law firm, and they all lived in Washington, D.C., when Congress was in session and in Warren for the rest of the year. In 1893 Upton began a new phase of her political career, moving from being her father's hostess to being a lobbyist for the NAWSA on Capitol Hill. She was also the NAWSA treasurer, editor of the organization's paper, the *Progress,* and president of the Ohio Woman Suffrage Association. In 1898 she was elected to the Warren Board of Education.[45]

The Women's Division lasted until 1952, when it was abolished by the chair of the RNC.[46] While women's "temporary" separation into the Women's Division was being instituted, discussion arose about increasing the membership of the RNC to include one man and one woman from each equal suffrage state.[47] The larger aim was to institute a fifty-fifty rule to double the size of party committees at every level, but the immediate idea about doubling the committees of the suffrage states was introduced to the Rules Committee at the national convention in June. The committee offered a counterproposal. Instead of the RNC being doubled with representatives from the suffrage states, the RNEC was enlarged from ten to fifteen members, with seven of the seats going to women. The first battle for fifty-fifty was lost. As the *New York Times* put it in a headline, "Women Not Content but Remain Loyal."[48]

The fight for fifty-fifty would move to the state level in the 1920s, and its function and usefulness would be debated for years to come.[49] New York passed fifty-fifty legislation in 1922, after a bill was introduced by Russell Livermore, the son of Henrietta Livermore. Henrietta Livermore's career in New York demonstrates how women built political alliances and found ways to hold themselves independent in Republican politics, and reflects the overlap that existed between local and state committees, national committees, and the Republican women's clubs. She also provides another example of the overlap of the suffrage leadership and the Republican party.[50]

Henrietta Livermore graduated from Wellesley College in 1887, married a prominent New York lawyer in 1890, managed a school for the Russell Sage Foundation, helped found the Women's University Club of New York City, and was a vice president of the New York State Woman Suffrage Association. When women won the vote in 1917, she was appointed to the Republican State Executive Committee. After the RWNEC was created and began organizing state committees, she was chosen as chair for New York.[51] The *Woman Re-*

publican, the paper of the New York Republican women, reported that the women's state committee was "appointed by the State Chairman of the Party."[52] It is not clear whether women were included in the decision-making process. At the end of 1923, Livermore congratulated "the men of the National Committee . . . for the women associate members that you have selected."[53] There is a vagueness to her statement, but it indicates that men were either choosing the women members or were perceived as choosing them.

Livermore's other political cap was as founder of the Women's National Republican Club. Established in 1921 as a meeting place for women voters, the club's first headquarters were on West 30th Street in New York; it opened at its present location at 3 West 51st Street in 1934. The New York club is unusual in that it calls itself a national club; most Republican women's clubs defined themselves as local, county, or state, and it was in those divisions that the RNC and RWNEC/Women's Division positioned women as they worked on organizational strategies.[54] The "brief history" posted on the club's website claims that it is not only the "oldest national club for Republican women and the only one to provide its members with a Clubhouse," but it is also "a separate entity not officially or legally associated with any other organization, although its members work closely with the Republican party."[55]

The creation of separate women's Republican clubs was explained and justified by their founders as proper or practical. Even McCormick's "idealism gave way to practicality," and she spent these transition years organizing Republican women's clubs.[56] Some saw the division as temporary; others sought permanence in the form of buildings. The persistence of the clubs can be explained in part by the fact that few women were able to gain real power in the parties, and those who did had few guarantees that they could hold on to or build that power. As the historian William Chafe has written, "party leadership was ever ready with flowery honors. But when it came to the formation of party policy, women's place remained that of an outsider."[57] Clubs were therefore a way for women to come to the aid of their party while also establishing structures where they would determine how that assistance would be accomplished.[58] Republican club women wanted equal representation on party committees but also needed, as much as wanted, their separate party clubs as institutional supports that the rest of the party did not give.[59] These clubs could be retreats. They could be building blocks or transfer points to power within the party, and they kept women organized during and after elections, which had been Boswell's aim for the West End Republican Women's Club in 1895. In 1937 the RNC created the National Federation of Women's Republican Clubs as a new women's auxiliary to organize clubs around the country, which became the National Federation of Republican

Women (NFRW) in 1948, in a move that made it "completely independent" of the RNC. Today the president of the NFRW is an ex-officio member of the RNEC.[60]

Nonpartisanship: A Vice or Virtue?

According to a newspaper report, while women were being welcomed into the party, a "skeleton in the closet of national politics" was causing some fear.[61] The skeleton was women's nonpartisanship, and Mary Garrett Hay had forced it out of the closet. In spite of her position in the Women's Division and in state Republican politics, she was organizing New York women across party lines to work against the reelection of the Republican senator James Wadsworth Jr. "That the Republicans of New York should even contemplate the placing of Senator Wadsworth's name in nomination is astounding when viewed in connection with their interest in the women's vote," these women stated in their flier, "Oppose Wadsworth!" His no votes on the federal suffrage amendment "rang out the loudest of any in the Senate Chamber," they claimed. "There is nothing partisan in women's opposition" to Wadsworth, because Democratic and Republican women had joined together to defeat this man who is "*non grata* to the women" not only because of his record on woman suffrage but also on child labor.[62]

The New York City Woman Suffrage Party, which Hay led, became the first state League of Women Voters (LWV) in April 1919, following the move by the NAWSA to ready women for the postsuffrage era and to transform its body into a new organization, the National League of Women Voters (NLWV). The NAWSA had passed a resolution in March 1919 that the organization would "not affiliate with any political party nor endorse the platform of any party nor support or oppose any political party unless such action shall be recommended by the Board of Directors in order to achieve the ends and purposes of this organization as set forth in the constitution."[63] The New York LWV declared its intention to "oppose candidates for public office, irrespective of their political affiliations, when the records and policies of such candidates are at variance with the objects set forth in the Party's constitution."[64] Hay saw Wadsworth as an obstacle to the aims of the New York league. When the NAWSA became the NLWV in February 1920, it too joined the fight against Wadsworth.

As one influential woman Democrat was reported to have said, "No woman would last a week in that position in opposition to the men on that committee."[65] She was right. Wadsworth was reelected, but Hay was forced out of her position in the Women's Division.[66] To women and men, the founding of the NLWV and Hay's actions had raised an old fear, now represented in the form of a skeleton. How could women be loyal to their party if they also remained loyal to their nonpartisan organizations? Since the eighteenth century women were seen to have embodied civic virtue and principles. In the nineteenth century that embodiment took the form of nonpartisanship. The politics of women's nonpartisanship, because it was shrouded by disfranchisement, meant that men could choose to ignore women, praise them, or accept their offers of cooperation. Now the shroud of disfranchisement was replaced by the status of voter, and people were forced to look at women's nonpartisanship in a new way. The newspaper reporter got it wrong about the "skeleton in a closet." It was not a skeleton that was creating fear; it was the realization that the NAWSA had created a lean political machine that was changing the Constitution and the gendered boundaries of the political world.

Men were not the only ones concerned about the continuing institutionalization of women's nonpartisanship through the NLWV. The question of nonpartisanship and the related question of women's partisan loyalty were addressed by women throughout 1919 and the early 1920s.[67] According to the *New York Times,* "party politics overshadowed all other issues on the eve of the fifty-first convention of the National American Woman Suffrage Association," which met in Chicago in February 1920. Illinois Republican women had placed a full-page paid advertisement in the program of the convention that declared: "To the Republican party you owe the passage of the Federal suffrage amendment and it will be responsible for the ratification soon to come." Democratic women issued a statement criticizing the advertisement, and Elizabeth Bass spoke for the Democratic women to defend their party. She stated that the Democratic party in Congress and in the states had done more for suffrage than any other party. Wilson, she declared, "is the only President who has lifted his voice and his influence in the cause of suffrage." Bass also criticized an earlier statement by Will Hays in which he claimed that the victory for suffrage should go to Republicans. As if conceding that the Republicans might have some right to the victory, Bass stated that the more important issue was how the parties were now responding to the women. She said that the "mere act of giving woman suffrage does not automatically give them all the privileges of party management. . . . Some changes in party rules and election and primary laws are necessary to give women equal representation with men."[68]

The suffragists eventually adopted two resolutions to settle the conflict. The first congratulated the Republican party "for having a Chairman who is astute enough to recognize the certain trend of public affairs and to lead his party in step with the inevitable march of human progress."[69] A similar resolution issued by Democratic women at the convention was then introduced and adopted. Carrie Chapman Catt made it clear that while women could and should be partisan activists, the new League of Women Voters, like the NAWSA, would be a nonpartisan organization. Women needed their nonpartisan organizations to create political agendas, she argued, but the "only way to get things in this country, is from the inside of political parties."[70]

The *New York Times* stated that the NAWSA was to be congratulated for its party divisions, especially "if it is really true that there is a 'danger' of its dividing over party politics."[71] The *Times* took the position that the real danger had always been that women would not divide and would instead create a woman's bloc or a "woman's party," whereby women and men would be separated in politics "not over principles, but as members of different sexes." Thankfully, it concluded, "feminism, a different thing from suffrage, does not yet brood over the United States, at least politically."[72] The *Times* would have been cheered to learn that the California LWV, like other state leagues, described its organization as "nonpartisan, nonsectarian and not a woman's party as in contradistinction to a man's party."[73]

In 1919 and the early 1920s, women did, and did not, divide politically.[74] At the same time that they found places for themselves in the parties, they held firm to their own separate political organizations, including the NLWV.[75] Although she called women's nonpartisanship a "vice," Cornelia Pinchot actually supported the formation of the league. Ruth Hanna McCormick and Frances Kellor were among those who regarded it as more harmful than helpful for women.[76] According to Kellor, the league was the result of the personal weakness of suffrage leaders who could not bear to see "their child adopted by the political organizations." She singled out the league's belief that women needed instruction on political questions before they decided on what party to join. Not only would this slow down the process of women's political incorporation, it was based on men's faulty premise that women did not possess the "clarity of thought or expert skills" necessary for politics. Kellor argued that women were wrong to think they had to slowly educate themselves and work their way up to power. Men, after all, were "called to high office by distinction in business or professions." Influential women should demand and take the same right. To achieve that end, it was necessary for men and women to increase their contacts in "practical impersonal affairs."[77]

Kellor's view contrasts with that of Corinne Roosevelt Robinson, who wrote that, even though she had lived with politics all her life, she considered herself unfit in many ways politically because of a lack of practical knowledge. She thought women should go through an "apprenticeship" stage.[78] The emphasis on moving slowly was important, because it kept women from accepting positions in parties that were offered to them. Lucy Miller, the chair of the Pennsylvania LWV, wrote to Pinchot that she knew several league women had already been approached by the Republican party and was "now beginning to realize that perhaps every member of the Board may be asked to serve in some capacity." Miller stated that because women were "so new it might seriously undermine the confidence of the community in us if we immediately became officially a member of either party." She made it clear that she was speaking of women in leadership positions, not "the rank and file of our members."[79] Pinchot responded to Miller, stating that her letter had "opened up a variety of questions I had not considered sufficiently before." In the end, she wrote, complications might arise if league women accepted political appointments, but "the idea of not functioning politically does not appeal to me, personally at least, as either desirable or practical."[80] Pinchot worked for both the Republican party and the LWV in Pennsylvania.

As league women worked out their relationships to the parties and responded to criticisms from women and men, they made it clear that it was not their aim to challenge the power of parties but to "mobilize public opinion behind reform programs and to instruct women in the tasks of citizenship."[81] By organizing along sex lines, they argued, the LWV brought women of different political parties together to work for common goals. In 1920 the league presented a "Woman's Platform" to both party conventions, which included a call for maternity- and infancy-protection legislation. This legislation, the Sheppard-Towner Act, was the first federally funded social welfare measure in the United States.[82] On the issue of women working with parties, league leaders did not see the organization as an obstacle and were not aiming to create their own political party.[83] As if to prove it would not be an obstacle, by 1924 "NLWV elites made a provisional (and private) decision not to make statements endorsing or opposing candidates for office."[84]

Nonpartisanship took many forms and resulted from many factors in this era. There was rhetoric and reality. Clara Burdette told the press that women were "naturally non-partisan; their inborn tendency is to support the idea and the man; programs cannot hold them to a party with which they do not agree."[85] In New York, at the same time that two African-American women, Gertrude Curtis and Laura Fisher, were delegates to the 1918 Republican state convention, black women in Harlem were forming a Women's Non-Partisan League.[86] After the Ohio legislature defeated the Beatty Equal Rights Bill, the Colored Women's Republican Club of Columbus, Ohio, "severed its party affiliation" and changed its name to the Colored Women's Independent Political League.[87] The use of nonpartisan rhetoric and the formation of nonpartisan political organizations by women was sometimes an act of defiance, sometimes an attempt to gain political leverage, and always an indication to observers that gender mattered in political organizing.

The Republican Conventions of 1920 and 1924

On June 4, 1919, the Senate finally followed the House when sixty-six out of the ninety-six senators voting cast their votes in favor of the Susan B. Anthony Amendment. The majority of the yea votes, forty, were from Republicans.[88] As states were ratifying the amendment, women went to the Seventeenth Republican National Convention, which convened at the Chicago Coliseum on June 8, 1920, to work not only for greater inclusion in party councils but also on behalf of the final push for the woman suffrage victory.

The 1920 and 1924 conventions celebrated women.[89] Women were officially welcomed into the party, as they had been so many times in the past. The 1920 platform statement on women would have warmed the hearts of nineteenth-century Republican women. "We welcome women into full participation in the affairs of government and the activities of the Republican party. We earnestly hope that Republican legislatures in states which have not yet acted on the Suffrage Amendment will ratify the amendment, to the end that all of the women of the nation of voting age may participate in the election of 1920 which is so important to the welfare of our country."[90] In 1920, twenty-seven women were delegates, and 129 were alternates. At the 1924 convention there were 120 women delegates and 277 women alternates.[91] Among them was Helen Varick Boswell. She attended both conventions as a delegate from New York, and she would serve again in 1928 and 1932. During the 1920s she continued her work with the West End Women's Republican Club and was also president of the Women's Forum of New York. In 1929 Coolidge appointed her to represent the United States at the International Exposition in Spain. She died in 1942, five years after stating that the "modern woman—that is, the woman who lives close to life and has to rely on her initiative to make her place in the world—has been with us down through the ages, but never until the present decade has she had a great opportunity to express herself. Today we have that opportunity and let us take advantage of it."[92]

Three women served as assistant secretaries, and Lenna Lowe Yost of West Virginia was the tally clerk at the 1920 convention.[93] Of the four convention committees, women sat on the Committee on Permanent Organization and the Committee on Rules and Order of Business. A special Advisory Committee on Policies and Platform was established; it consisted of twenty women, including Helen Rogers Reid of the *New York Herald Tribune,* who chaired the subcommittee on the High Cost of Living.[94] Among the fifteen specialists advising the Executive Committee were Mary Van Kleeck of the Russell Sage Foundation and Mrs. John B. Andrews, the secretary of the American Association for Labor Legislation.[95] A total of twenty-five women sat on all four convention committees in 1924. It would be the highest number until 1944.[96]

Women were speakers at both conventions. Seventeen seconding speeches were given for presidential candidates in 1920. Six were from women, including Helen Varick Boswell's for Nicholas Murray Butler and Katherine Edson's for Hiram Johnson. Corinne Roosevelt Robinson seconded Leonard Wood. According to a reporter from the *New York Times,* her "gestures, her mannerisms, the intonation of her sentences . . . recalled to the convention the man who might have been its unrivaled candidate for the Presidential nomination had he lived long enough."[97] Robinson was not a replacement for her brother; she was not a candidate. Neither was she a surrogate; Hays's appointment of her to the RWNEC was made in recognition of her previous loyalty and work for the party.[98]

In 1923, women members of the RNC were given the title "Associate Members" of the national committee, and at the 1924 convention Rule XIV was adopted, which stated that "A National Committee shall be elected by each National Convention called to nominate candidates for President and Vice President consisting of two members from each State, Territory or Territorial Possession."[99] The rule would be modified in 1952, when state party chairmen were placed on the committee. As a result, women lost equal representation, because most of the chairmen were, and are, men.[100] In 1968, as the second wave of feminism swept politics, equality in representation was restored, but the evidence had been given that equal numbers did not necessarily mean equal power.[101]

The 1924 platform might have made women who had long associations with the Republican party contemplate how many times women needed to be welcomed into the party and ponder the concept of equality and the meaning of the expression "more complete." It included the following:

> We extend our greeting to the women delegates who for the first time under Federal authorization sit with us in full equality. The Republican party from the beginning has espoused the cause of woman suffrage, and the presence of these women delegates signifies to many here the completion of a task undertaken years ago. We welcome them not as assistants or as auxiliary representatives but as co-partners in the great political work in which we are engaged, and

we believe that the actual partnership in party councils should be made more complete.[102]

The 1920 platform endorsed the establishment of a Women's Bureau in the Department of Labor, the principle of equal pay for equal work for federal workers, the special needs of women workers for vocational training, and legislation regulating working hours for women in certain industrial jobs.[103] It passed by voice acclamation. Warren Harding, a senator from Ohio, had more trouble winning the nomination for the presidency; it took ten ballots before he had enough votes to overcome his rivals, including Major General Leonard Wood. Calvin Coolidge, the governor of Massachusetts, took the vice-presidential nomination on the first ballot.[104]

The Ratification Fight

As the country geared up for the 1920 campaign to elect the Republicans Warren Harding and Calvin Coolidge or the Democrats James Cox and Franklin Roosevelt, Carrie Chapman Catt led the suffrage forces for ratification of the Nineteenth Amendment. She expected that the ratification battle would be one of the most intense in the long war for suffrage, despite the facts that both parties had endorsed the amendment and in twenty-eight states women had full or at least presidential suffrage. Thirty-six states were needed for ratification, and the NAWSA pledged that not one state, one state suffragist, one legislator, one governor, or one political party leader would be off the hook until the final vote was taken in the final state. Catt wrote daily to state suffrage leaders with suggestions on how to proceed in their state. She discussed how to lobby legislators and the governor. These were not soft suggestions. She demanded that suffragists march constituencies of women through legislative halls and expected women to be aggressive and vigilant. In return, she promised to open and drain the NAWSA's war chest to provide financial support for materials and publicity. She arranged for suffragists from neighboring states to cross borders when more workers were needed.

Suffragists hoped that Wyoming would be among the first states to ratify, thereby bringing the suffrage struggle full circle. In Wyoming, however, as in many other states, there was one enormous problem. Its legislature was out of session and was not scheduled to meet again until January 1921.[105] Catt reasoned that when governors saw that it was right and necessary to call special sessions, they would do so. Many governors, including Wyoming's governor, Robert Carey, were reluctant and cited a myriad of reasons for not doing so. Carey told Catt that the cost of a special session would be a "burden" on the people of Wyoming, who would have "no direct benefit," presumably because Wyoming citizens already had equal suffrage rights.[106]

Catt was furious at his myopic view, and she telegraphed back that a special session might be of no benefit to Wyoming, "but this is now a national and not a state question."[107] Carey was not convinced, so Catt tried another approach, informing him that the governor of Kansas was also reluctant to call a special session but was polling members of the legislature to see if they would be willing to attend a single day's session. What she did not tell him was that Henry Allen, the governor of Kansas, had long supported the NAWSA's efforts, even stumping for them in the New York referendum campaign of 1915, and that he would call the session no matter what the outcome of his poll.[108]

Wouldn't Carey, she asked, also be willing to poll the legislators? He finally responded that yes, he would, but he assumed that the Kansas legislators were bearing their own expenses for the one-day session. He also wanted her assurance that Wyoming's session would not be in vain, that she knew with certainty that enough legislatures would convene and give the necessary number of states needed for ratification.[109] Of course, she assured him, legislatures across the nation were lined up like ducks in the water, and the sacrifice of Wyoming's politicians would not be in vain.

Catt wrote to a Minnesota suffrage supporter that the NAWSA women were "disturbed by the slow action in the West," and so they were sending "emissaries to find out what is the matter."[110] Republican women like Christine Bradley South and Marjorie Shuler and Democratic women like Minnie Fisher Cunningham were sent into the western states. These partisan women were asked to identify themselves and "take care" of the legislative members of their parties.[111] Catt told Carey that the problem in his state was that the "women of Wyoming long ago retired from the struggle," and they "feel little sense of connections with the great nation-wide battle." However, she concluded, "millions of women throughout the country are looking to the Republican state of Wyoming for action and we hope we shall not be disappointed."[112] Catt and others wrote similar letters to Democratic governors.

In a private letter to the University of Wyoming professor and historian Grace Raymond Hebard, Catt stated that she found the lack of interest in Wyoming "embarrassing," and she put enormous pressure on Hebard to correct this matter.[113] Hebard's hard work could not help Wyoming gain another new "suffrage first." Wyoming's special session convened in January 1920, making it the twenty-seventh state to ratify the Nineteenth Amendment. Overall, it took fifteen months, with state and national suffragists working in concert—demanding, pleading, and begging their state legisla-

tures to ratify—before the final state, Tennessee, was won, and the U.S. secretary of state declared the amendment ratified on August 26, 1920.

At the mass meeting held in Washington the next day to celebrate, the
secretary of state, Bainbridge Colby, told the new women voters, "Let the
party serve you but not dominate you. Do not let party feeling cast a film before your eyes. . . . Vote your convictions."[114] They were words, similar to so
many others, that many women took with them into the campaign of 1920.

The Republican Campaigns of 1920 and 1924

The party structures created before 1920 were incredibly resilient, even as more
and more women were incorporated into the Republican party. In spite of the
new effort to establish equality in party organizations from the national down
to the precinct levels, women and men organized separately in 1920 and again
in 1924. The party fed this separation.[115] A public relations machine was set
up at the Chicago headquarters in 1920, and every week thousands of bulle-
tins were sent out. Harriet Taylor Upton was in charge of creating and dis-
tributing over three and a half million leaflets, the writing of a national bulletin for women, and the recruitment of women into a speakers' bureau, party
clubs, and committees. She made sure that newspapers were given plenty of
copy about why women supported Harding and Coolidge. The literature directed at women together with press releases about women's activities in the
party showed them as an entity to be addressed with special rhetoric.[116] Harding made it clear that women were welcomed into the party and spoke of
his admiration for the "'voice of womanhood.'"[117] Coolidge, in his acceptance
speech at the 1924 convention, stated, "'I know the influence of womanhood
will guard the home, which is the citadel of the Nation. I know it will be a
protector of childhood, I know it will be on the side of humanity. I welcome
it as a great instrument of mercy and a mighty agency of peace. I want every
woman to vote.'"[118] Delegations of women were received by Harding at his
home in Marion, Ohio. A "Social Justice Day" celebrated the "protection of
the motherhood of America."[119]

During the 1920 campaign Upton organized women from headquarters
in Chicago; afterward she moved to Washington, D.C., to continue to organize women in her new position as vice chair of the RNEC.[120] In the 1920s
women organized women and men organized men—with one exception.
African-American women were considered to be outside the province of the
Women's Division. Instead, they were organized by male Republican leaders through African-American churches and community organizations.[121]
In 1920 these party leaders hired Mary Church Terrell to direct the work of

African-American women in the East. She was born in Memphis, Tennessee, into a wealthy family, graduated from Oberlin College in 1884, taught, and moved to Washington, D.C., where she married Robert H. Terrell. She became the first president of the NACW in 1896, was active in the suffrage movement, and wrote and spoke about race relations. In spite of the fact that she began her work for the party in New York with some hesitation—because she was a southern woman who would be in charge of experienced northern political activists—she was successful in her organizing work. The African-American women in the East were vigorous Republicans in the early 1920s.[122]

Lethia C. Fleming was the party's appointed leader of African-American women in the West, and she worked out of Chicago in 1920.[123] Fleming, whose husband was a Cleveland, Ohio, councilman, issued an open letter urging black women to vote for Harding and Coolidge, stating, "We as Colored women have prayed for a better day, a day when we would be in a position to demand fair play and an equal chance. We must not now neglect the opportunity given us to serve the party of Lincoln, McKinley and Roosevelt."[124] Terrell in New York and Fleming in Chicago found women around the country willing to answer the Republican call. Among them was Laura Brown of Pittsburgh, Pennsylvania. A temperance worker and club woman, Brown became a member of her county's Republican Women's Executive Committee, one of the thousands of such committees around the country that were organized by the Women's Division. Two years later, she became the first African-American woman to run for the Pennsylvania legislature.[125]

Not all African-American women followed the directives of the party. For example, Hallie Quinn Brown, the vice president of the Ohio Council of Republican Women and the president of the NACW, criticized the party for its weak stand in opposition to lynching, and the association did not endorse the Republican party in 1920.[126] Brown was born around 1845 in Pittsburgh to former slaves. In 1873 she graduated from Wilberforce University in Ohio, taught, served as dean of women at Tuskegee Institute in 1892, and then returned to Wilberforce as a professor of elocution. As a club woman she moved quickly from the local to state and national work. She served as president of the Ohio Federation of Colored Women's Clubs from 1905 to 1912, and in 1920 she became president of the NACW.[127]

Hallie Quinn Brown's challenge to the Republicans in 1920 did not seem to hurt her. In 1924 she spoke at the Republican National Convention in Cleveland and directed the party's efforts to organize African-American women through the new National League of Republican Colored Women, which adopted the slogan, "We are in politics to stay and we shall be a stay in politics."[128] The NACW also supported the Republicans in 1924; Maria C. Lawton transformed the NACW's *National Notes* into a party organ.[129] The creation of the National League of Republican Colored Women in the summer of 1924 allowed the NACW to minimize partisan differences and divisions in future elections. Nannie Burroughs and Mary Church Terrell took leadership positions in the league, although it was founded by two black Republican national committeewomen, Mary Booze and Mamie Williams.[130] By the end of the decade, the league's importance as an independent place for black Republican women was reinforced not only by their continued position outside of the Women's Division and the unwillingness of those organizing African-American voters to relinquish positions to them but also by the RNC's rejection of Burroughs's request for a permanent headquarters for black women.[131]

Burroughs sent her request to Sallie Hert of Kentucky, who had replaced Harriet Taylor Upton as the chair of the Women's Division in 1924 and would carry on the work of forming women's clubs. Hert takes the history of Republican women forward within the party's national structures. Upton takes it back to the local level. The last of the suffragists to head the Women's Division, Upton had returned to her home town of Warren, Ohio, looking for new political opportunities. In 1898 she had been elected to the Warren Board of Education. Now, at the age of seventy, she sought a higher office and ran for her father's old congressional seat. Three women were elected to Congress in 1924. The first Democrat, Mary Norton, was elected in New Jersey. The Republicans Florence Kahn of California and Edith Rogers of Massachusetts followed the path of the "widow's succession" into Congress.[132] Upton had a harder time trying to regain the seat her father held until his death; she lost the election. She continued working for the Republican party in Ohio and served as a state campaign organizer in 1928. She then received an appointment as a liaison between the office of the governor, Myers Cooper, and the state Department of Welfare. When Cooper left office in 1931, so did she. Soon after, she moved to Pasadena, California, where she died in 1945 at the age of ninety-one.

Claiming the Suffrage Victory

In 1928 Lucy Anthony, the niece of Susan B. Anthony, wrote Carrie Chapman Catt to ask if she had seen a leaflet being distributed by the Republican party claiming credit for the passage of the Nineteenth Amendment. Catt responded that she had not seen that particular leaflet but was not surprised to hear of it and assumed that there existed "another leaflet somewhere saying that the Democratic party gave the vote to women."[133] In the 1920s both parties claimed the suffrage victory by praising past platform planks that mentioned women and honoring party leaders who supported the issue. They also counted numbers—of states dominated by their party that granted suffrage before 1920 and those that ratified the amendment, of women delegates to conventions and women committee members, and the dates of their fifty-fifty plans and the establishment of the women's divisions. All these "proved" their party was justified in claiming the suffrage victory.[134] It was "natural" for the parties to claim credit, Catt wrote Anthony, "but we know who got the backache."[135]

The passage of the Nineteenth Amendment made the political situation of the early 1920s different from earlier decades. So too did the larger cultural climate. The aftermath of war, the Red Scare, the resurgence of the Ku Klux Klan, the birth control movement, a new consumerism, and many other variables changed political and cultural moods and patterns. But there was also continuity. Before and after 1920, the people questioned how women would vote, in what numbers, and women's suitability for holding political office. Before and after, women were "welcomed" into political parties. As the political scientist Anna Harvey explains, disfranchisement shaped women's political activism before 1920 and created a political legacy that conditioned it for fifty years after the passage of the Nineteenth Amendment, as women felt "the consequences of not having had that right in the first place."[136] Catt wrote in the mid-1920s that the fact that women were not taken into party councils on equal terms, the "unwillingness to give women even a small share of the political positions which would enable them to score advantage to their ideals," might mystify some women but not "any old time suffragist."[137] It was politics as usual.

Catt claimed that she expected women would be disappointed with politics after the suffrage victory, because they would miss the thrill and camaraderie that came from working so closely with other women in such an intense political struggle.[138] She wrote Grace Hebard of Wyoming that the suffrage struggle had created a "great companionship which kept us continually pressing forward when all the world doubted and we alone had faith."[139] Catt and other women found companionship in new women's organizations like the NLWV, the International Woman Suffrage Alliance, the Committee on the Cause and Cure of War. Catt left party politics to others but encouraged women to act in partisan ways. In a 1928 letter written in response to an inquiry about what women had done with the vote, she wrote that women had engaged in "agitation concerning their own place in political parties which is not yet completed." Was she satisfied with woman suffrage now that it had been achieved? Her answer was yes, and she stated that women were optimistic about their place in politics and were determined to challenge all circumstances of women's political exclusion, subordination, and silence.[140]

Notes

Abbreviations

BWA	*Black Women in America: An Historical Encylopedia,* ed. Darlene Clark Hine et al.
DAB	*Dictionary of American Biography,* ed. Dumas Malone
DuBois, ed., *Correspondence*	Ellen DuBois, ed., *Elizabeth Cady Stanton–Susan B. Anthony: Correspondence, Writings, Speeches*
Gordon, ed., *Selected Papers*	Ann D. Gordon, ed., *Selected Papers of Elizabeth Cady Stanton and Susan B. Anthony,* vol. 1 and 2
Harper, *LWSBA*	Ida Husted Harper, *Life and Work of Susan B. Anthony,* 2 vols.
HWS	*History of Woman Suffrage,* 6 vols., ed. Elizabeth Cady Stanton, Susan B. Anthony, Matilda Joslyn Gage, Ida Husted Harper.
LC	Library of Congress
NAW	*Notable American Women, 1607–1950: A Biographical Dictionary,* 3 vols., ed. Edward T. James, Janet Wilson James, and Paul S. Boyer
NAW: The Modern Period	*Notable American Women: The Modern Period,* ed. Barbara Sicherman and Carol Hurd Green
NAWSA	National American Woman Suffrage Association
SSC	Sophia Smith Collection
WCTU Papers	Woman's Christian Temperance Union Papers. Francis X. Blouin Jr., ed., *Temperance and Prohibition Papers: A Joint Microfilm Publication of the Ohio Historical Society, Michigan Historical Collections, and Woman's Christian Temperance Union.*

Introduction

1. Curtis, *History of the Republican Party,* 1:176.

2. Gienapp, *Origins of the Republican Party,* 105.

3. Qtd. in ibid., 193, 205.

4. "History of the Republican Party," available at <http://www.vbe.com/bsimons/ripon/birth.htm>. See also Curtis, *History of the Republican Party* 1:1–2; Rutland, *Republicans,* 1.

5. Cott, "Across the Great Divide," 154.

6. Harvey, *Votes without Leverage,* 1.

7. Although I refer to women's political culture and women's political networks in minimal ways in the narrative, I am in agreement with Kathryn Kish Sklar that the concept of "women's political culture" provides a way to order and help explain the forms and meanings of the gender-segregated institutions women created to promote their participation in public culture. Such a concept does not mean that women and men lived and worked in "separate spheres" even as they emphasized gender difference. I am most interested in the aspect of this culture that nurtured women's campaigns for greater political inclusion and equality of representation in partisan and electoral politics. As such, my emphasis is on the political interactions between women and men. Sklar, *Florence Kelley and the Nation's Work,* xiii. For a different conceptual approach using the idea of women's political networks, see Ware, *Beyond Suffrage.* On historians' use of "separate spheres," see Kerber, "Separate Spheres, Female Worlds, Woman's Place"; and Hewitt, "Beyond the Search for Sisterhood."

8. Not all women gained access to the ballot with the passage of the Nineteenth Amendment. Black women in the South, women in Puerto Rico, and Native-American, Asian-American, and Hispanic women in the West were denied the right to vote by various laws and tests, as well as violent and coercive measures.

9. Louise Graham, "Mrs. Upton Sees Big Field for Women in U.S. Posts," clipping, April 16, 1921, Burdette Collection, Huntington.

10. Kunin, *Living the Political Life,* 205.

11. For example, Emily Newell Blair recollected in 1940 that when she went to National Democratic Headquarters in February 1922 to take her position as the new chair of the Women's Division of the Democratic National Committee, she discovered that "not so much as a scrap of paper remained from all of the splendid work" of Elizabeth Bass. After the defeat of the Democrats in 1920 all files were destroyed, and Blair was forced to begin her organization of Democratic women "from scratch." Blair, "Advance of Democratic Women," 15.

Chapter 1: Loyal Republican Women, 1854–65

1. *New York Tribune,* September 27, 1860. See also *New York Herald,* September 19, 1860; *New York Times,* October 3, 1860. On the Wide-Awakes, see Curtis, *History of the Republican Party,* 1:343; McPherson, *Battle Cry of Freedom,* 202–33; and Dinkins, *Before Equal Suffrage,* 51.

2. Greeley and Cleveland, comps., *Political Text-Book for 1860,* 22; Johnson, *National Party Platforms,* 31–33.

3. *New York Tribune,* September 27, 1860. The *Tribune* reported his name as D. B. Murray; Ann D. Gordon identifies him as John B. Murray. See Gordon, ed., *Selected Papers,* 1:444. In 1864, Elizabeth Cady Stanton wrote, "Had I been asked who should be President in '61, I should have said, William H. Seward." Elizabeth Cady Stanton to Caroline Healey Dall, May 7, 1864, in Gordon, ed., *Selected Papers,* 1:518. This letter was published in *The Liberator,* June 3, 1864, and the *National Anti-Slavery Standard,* June 11, 1864.

4. Susan B. Anthony to Henry B. Stanton Jr. and Gerrit S. Stanton, September 27, 1860, in Gordon, ed., *Selected Papers,* 1:441–44.

5. On popular politics, see McGerr, *Decline of Popular Politics;* Baker, *Affairs of Party;* Ryan, "American Parade"; and Ryan, *Women in Public.*

6. Varon, *We Mean to Be Counted,* 148. For more information on southern white women and partisan politics during this era, see Olsen, "Respecting 'The Wise Allotment of Our Sphere.'"

7. "Laura," 1859, qtd. in Terborg-Penn, *African American Women in the Struggle for the Vote,* 13.

8. *New York Tribune,* June 16, 1854; September 19, September 29, October 18, October 19, October 26, and November 3, 1860. Roseboom, *History of Presidential Elections,* 153; Kleeberg, *Formation of the Republican Party,* 15; Dinkins, *Before Equal Suffrage,* 44.

9. *New York Tribune,* October 20, 1860.

10. Isenberg, *Sex and Citizenship in Antebellum America,* 29; Kerber, *No Constitutional Right to Be Ladies,* chap. 3.

11. *New York Tribune,* September 27, 1860.

12. Zagarri, "Gender and the First Party System," 118–34.

13. Kerber, *Women of the Republic;* Lewis, "Republican Wife"; Cott, *Bonds of Womanhood.*

14. "One of the first items of business, once the club was organized, was to invite 'the ladies' to meetings." Altschuler and Blumin, "Limits of Political Engagement in Antebellum America," 873.

15. Zagarri, "Morals, Manners, and the Republican Mother."

16. Fahs, "Feminized Civil War," 1466–67. The theoretical scholarship about how the public and private spheres are separated and linked is extensive. For an overview, see Kerber, "Separate Spheres, Female Worlds, Woman's Place." See also Cott, *Bonds of Womanhood;* Epstein, *Politics of Domesticity;* Ryan, *Cradle of the Middle Class;* and Isenberg, *Sex and Citizenship in Antebellum America.*

17. The idea of women as purifying or housecleaning politics and the public sphere changed over time. Regarding women's and men's use of the idea, see Baker, "Domestication of Politics"; Baker, *Moral Frameworks of Public Life;* and Lebsock, "Women and American Politics."

18. Silbey, *Partisan Imperative,* 56.

19. Varon, *We Mean to Be Counted,* chap. 3; Zboray and Zboray, "Whig Women, Politics, and Culture in the Campaign of 1840."

20. For an argument that questions the pervasiveness of people's political engagement in antebellum America, see Altschuler and Blumin, "Limits of Political Engagement in Antebellum America"; and Altschuler and Blumin, "'Where is the Real America?'" They challenge William E. Gienapp's view of widespread political engagement. See Gienapp,

"'Politics Seem to Enter into Everything.'" For further discussion of this debate, see Formisano, "'Party Period' Revisited"; and Voss-Hubbard, "'Third Party Tradition' Reconsidered."

21. McGerr, *Decline of Popular Politics*, 13.

22. Silbey, *Partisan Imperative*, 55.

23. Ginzberg, *Women and the Work of Benevolence*, 68–69; Hewitt, *Women's Activism and Social Change;* Ryan, *Cradle of the Middle Class.*

24. Qtd. in Baym, "Women and the Republic," 4–5.

25. Sklar, *Catharine Beecher,* xiv.

26. Brown, "Negotiating and Transforming the Public Sphere"; Brown, "To Catch a Vision of Freedom"; Richardson, *Maria W. Stewart;* Giddings, *When and Where I Enter.*

27. Wilentz, *Chants Democratic.*

28. For a discussion of the different woman suffrage arguments, see Kraditor, *Ideas of the Woman Suffrage Movement;* DuBois, "Outgrowing the Compact of the Fathers," 96–98; and Buechler, *Transformation of the Woman Suffrage Movement,* 108–17.

29. Silbey, *Transformation of American Politics,* 7.

30. Foner, *Free Soil, Free Labor, Free Men,* 78–81; Gienapp, *Origins of the Republican Party.*

31. Silbey, *American Political Nation,* 92.

32. Grimke, *Letters on the Equality of the Sexes and the Condition of Woman;* Lerner, *Grimke Sisters of South Carolina.*

33. Marilley, *Woman Suffrage and the Origins of Liberal Feminism in the United States,* 41; Sewell, *Ballots for Freedom,* 37; Perry, *Radical Abolitionism.* Kathryn Kish Sklar also makes the point that antislavery men and women cooperated "to achieve what neither could have accomplished separately." Sklar, *Florence Kelley and the Nation's Work,* 23.

34. Qtd. in Ginzberg, *Women and the Work of Benevolence,* 84; Kraditor, *Means and Ends in American Abolitionism.*

35. Lydia Maria Child to James Miller McKim, January 26, 1842, in Meltzer and Holland, eds., *Lydia Maria Child,* 157.

36. Foner, *Free Soil, Free Labor, Free Men,* 78.

37. Ginzberg, *Women and the Work of Benevolence,* 109, 116.

38. Bogin and Yellin, "Introduction," 12.

39. Hershberger, "Mobilizing Women, Anticipating Abolition," 26.

40. Sklar, "'Women Who Speak for an Entire Nation,'" 329.

41. Ginzberg, *Women and the Work of Benevolence,* 82.

42. Qtd. in Bogin and Yellin, "Introduction," 17.

43. Marilley, *Woman Suffrage and the Origins of Liberal Feminism in the United States,* 28.

44. Kerber, "'Ourselves and Our Daughters Forever,'" 31.

45. Kerber, "Meanings of Citizenship"; Isenberg, *Sex and Citizenship in Antebellum America,* xviii. The temperance movement, undergoing a revival in this era as many women became active supporters of the crusade against alcohol, also began to take a turn away from moral suasion toward legal reforms and electoral politics. Maine led the way in 1851 when state temperance advocates were able to get passed the first statewide law prohibiting the sale of liquor. DuBois, ed., *Correspondence,* 16.

46. Isenberg, *Sex and Citizenship in Antebellum America,* 16.

47. Griffith, *In Her Own Right*, 90.

48. DuBois, *Feminism and Suffrage*, 34; Ginzberg, "'Moral Suasion Is Moral Balderdash.'"

49. Elizabeth Cady Stanton to Elizabeth Pease, February 12, 1842, in Gordon, ed., *Selected Papers*, 1:29.

50. Antoinette Brown Blackwell to Lucy Stone, September 21, 1851, in Lasser and Merrill, eds., *Friends and Sisters*, 108.

51. Howe, "Evangelical Movement and Political Culture in the North during the Second Party System."

52. Swisshelm, *Half a Century*, 112. The Liberty party's willingness to include women varied by locality and leadership. See Jeffrey, *Great Silent Army of Abolitionism*, 164–65.

53. Swisshelm might have had more luck later in the 1840s with one faction of the Liberty party. By 1846, the Liberty League had endorsed women's rights. Isenberg, *Sex and Citizenship in Antebellum America*, 19. See also Johnson, "Liberty Party in Massachusetts," 237–65.

54. Swisshelm, *Half a Century*, 91.

55. Ibid., 135 and 158.

56. Harper, *LWSBA*, 1:133.

57. Roseboom, *History of Presidential Elections*, 161; Booraem, *Formation of the Republican Party in New York*; Gienapp, *Origins of the Republican Party*.

58. Trefousse, "Republican Party," 1151, 1200.

59. Gienapp, *Origins of the Republican Party*, 375.

60. Lydia Maria Child to Sarah Shaw, August 3, 1856, in Meltzer and Holland, eds., *Lydia Maria Child*, 291.

61. Swisshelm, *Half a Century*, 159.

62. *Republican Campaign Edition for the Millions*; *NAW*, 1:668–71; Herr and Spence, eds., *Letters of Jessie Benton Frémont*.

63. Errett, "Republican Nominating Conventions of 1856 and 1860"; *Proceedings of the First Three Republican National Conventions of 1856, 1860, and 1864*; Roseboom, *History of Presidential Elections*, 161.

64. Isely, *Horace Greeley and the Republican Party*, 191.

65. Qtd. in Silbey, *American Political Nation*, 98; Varon, *We Mean to Be Counted*, 100.

66. Edwards, *Angels in the Machinery*, 63; Jeffrey, *Great Silent Army of Abolitionism*, 169.

67. Lydia Maria Child to Sarah Shaw, August 3, 1856, in Meltzer and Holland, eds., *Lydia Maria Child*, 290.

68. Gienapp, *Origins of the Republican Party*, 376.

69. Isely, *Horace Greeley and the Republican Party*, 161.

70. Ibid., 164.

71. Qtd. in Trefousse, "Republican Party," 1151. In the electoral college, Buchanan won 174 votes and Frémont won 114. Buchanan had 1.8 million popular votes to Frémont's 1.3 million. Roseboom, *History of Presidential Elections*, 166–67.

72. Gienapp, *Origins of the Republican Party*, 246, 439; Trefousse, "Republican Party," 1149.

73. Gienapp, *Origins of the Republican Party*, 447.

74. Ibid., 377.

75. The Frémonts did not completely fade from political life after 1856. When Republicans won the White House in 1860 and the Civil War broke out, John Frémont took a military command, and Jessie Frémont worked with the Sanitary Commission in St. Louis and New York City. She also helped found the Women's Loyal National League and continued to play a crucial role in her husband's political, military, and writing careers until he died in 1890. After his death she moved into a house presented to her by the women of the city of Los Angeles. Jessie Frémont died in 1902 at the age of seventy-eight.

76. Nichols was a suffragist, temperance advocate, and journalist from Vermont, writing for the *Windham County Democrat* in Brattleboro. She married, had three children, divorced, remarried, and had another child. She moved to Kansas in 1854. Child published "An Appeal in Favor of That Class of Americans Called Africans" in 1833 and "The Duty of Disobedience to the Fugitive Slave Act: An Appeal to the Legislators of Massachusetts" in 1860. From 1841 to 1843 she was editor of the AASS's *National Anti-Slavery Standard*. On Nichols, see *Woman's Tribune*, May 5, 1888; *HWS*, 1:171–200; Dinkins, *Before Equal Suffrage*, 45; Edwards, *Angels in the Machinery*, 29 n. 55; Gambone, "Forgotten Feminist of Kansas"; and Gordon, ed., *Selected Papers*, 1:327. On Child, see Karcher, *First Woman in the Republic*.

77. Elizabeth Cady Stanton to Susan B. Anthony, November 4, 1855, in DuBois, ed., *Correspondence*, 59.

78. In the 1840s and 1850s, Henry Stanton supported the Liberty party, Free Soil party, and Democratic party before he joined with Republicans in 1855. Two years after the Stanton family moved from Boston to Seneca Falls in 1847, he was rewarded by the Democrats for his campaigning on behalf of other candidates with a nomination to a New York State Senate seat. He remained active in the Democratic party, but in 1852 he refused efforts by the party to enlist him for higher office and returned to his law practice. Always politically active in party politics and in abolitionism, Henry Stanton moved easily through his political commitments and into the Republican party after it was established in 1854. Griffith, *In Her Own Right*, 48.

79. Gienapp, *Origins of the Republican Party*, 379, 397.

80. DuBois, *Feminism and Suffrage*, 12, 17, 26; Griffith, *In Her Own Right*, 76, 81.

81. Elizabeth Cady Stanton to Susan B. Anthony, September 10, 1855, in DuBois, ed., *Correspondence*, 58.

82. Griffith, *In Her Own Right*, 85; DuBois, *Harriot Stanton Blatch and the Winning of Woman Suffrage*, 10.

83. Griffith, *In Her Own Right*, 107.

84. There are various versions of this letter. See Elizabeth Cady Stanton to Susan B. Anthony, [ca. December 15, 1859], in Gordon, ed., *Selected Papers*, 1:400; DuBois, ed., *Correspondence*, 69; and Harper, *LWSBA*, 1:181–82.

85. Greeley and Cleveland, comps., *Political Text-Book for 1860*, 26–27.

86. Willard and Livermore, eds., *Woman of the Century*, 467; Hanaford, *Daughters of America*, 305–17; Logan, *Part Taken by Women in American History*, 325–26.

87. Susan B. Anthony to Elizabeth Cady Stanton, November 23, 1860, in Gordon, ed., *Selected Papers*, 1:449–50.

88. Susan B. Anthony to Elizabeth Cady Stanton, August 25, 1860, in ibid., 439–41.

89. Foner, *Free Soil, Free Labor, Free Men*, 10.

90. Trefousee, "Republican Party," 1160.

91. Baker, "Mary (Ann) Todd Lincoln," 179; *NAW*, 2:404–6.

92. Baker, "Mary (Ann) Todd Lincoln," 179.

93. Qtd. in ibid., 180.

94. *Providence Journal,* obituary, July 31, 1889, available at <http://pweb.netcom.com/rilydia/chase/kate.html>; Belden and Belden, *So Fell the Angels.*

95. *NAW*, 3:339–40; Belden and Belden, *So Fell the Angels.*

96. Swisshelm, *Half a Century,* 159–201.

97. Ibid., 214–16.

98. *NAW*, 1:475–76; *HWS*, 2:40–50.

99. *HWS*, 2:41.

100. Clarkson Hall was owned by the Pennsylvania Abolition Society. Bacon, "By Moral Force Alone," 289.

101. This is similar to the way her early political mentor, William Kelley, got his political start and may have contributed to their political bond. See Sklar, *Florence Kelley and the Nation's Work,* 8.

102. Qtd. in Chester, *Embattled Maiden,* 21.

103. Sarah Pugh, Florence Kelley's aunt, also attended this school. A close friend of Lucretia Mott, she was president of the Philadelphia Female Anti-Slavery Society for most of its existence, from 1838 to 1870. Sklar, *Florence Kelley and the Nation's Work,* 15, 17.

104. Chester, *Embattled Maiden,* 12–15.

105. Ibid., 14.

106. Willard and Livermore, eds., *Woman of the Century,* 471–72; Bacon, *Valiant Friend.* Longshore's daughter Lucretia married Rudolph Blankenburg, who became mayor of Philadelphia in 1911, so for a continuation of one thread of this story, see VandeCreek, "Unseen Influence," 33–43.

107. Chester, *Embattled Maiden,* 15; *HWS*, 2:41.

108. *HWS*, 2:41.

109. Chester, *Embattled Maiden,* 27.

110. Anna Dickinson to William Lloyd Garrison Jr., March 16, 1862, Dickinson Papers, LC.

111. See correspondence between Chace and Dickinson, and Garrison and Dickinson, for 1861 and 1862, Dickinson Papers, LC; Willard and Livermore, eds., *Woman of the Century,* 241.

112. Willard and Livermore, eds., *Woman of the Century,* 242. Livermore most likely had heard Dickinson speak before inviting her to the 1863 Northwestern Sanitary Fair. Elizabeth Cady Stanton wrote, "'There have been many speculations in public and private as to the authorship of Anna Dickinson's speeches. . . . Those who know Anna's conversational power,—who have felt the magnetism of her words and manners, and the pulsations of her generous heart, who have heard her impromptu replies when assailed,—see, at once, that her speeches are the natural outgrowth of herself, her own experience and philosophy, inspired by the eventful times in which she lived.'" Qtd. in Hanaford, *Daughters of America,* 319.

113. "Call for the first anniversary meeting of the Women's Loyal National League, May 12, 1864," in Gordon, ed., *Selected Papers,* 1:483–86.

114. *HWS*, 2:81.

115. "Meeting of the Loyal Women of the Republic," [May 14, 1863], in Gordon, ed., *Selected Papers,* 1:487–93.

116. Ibid.

117. *HWS,* 2:85.

118. Ibid., 50.

119. Dinkins, *Before Equal Suffrage,* 56.

120. *HWS,* 2:85.

121. Ibid., 84.

122. Curtis, *History of the Republican Party,* 1:398.

123. Berkeley, "Partisan Politics Makes for Strange Bedfellows," 1.

124. Fahs, "Feminized Civil War," 1469–70.

125. Benjamin Franklin Prescott to Anna Dickinson, February 3, 1863, Dickinson Papers, LC.

126. See letters from Clarissa Olds of Hampton, New Hampshire, and Mary J. Tappen of Bradford, New Hampshire, in *HWS,* 2:875–76.

127. Chester, *Embattled Maiden,* 45–60.

128. Willard and Livermore, eds., *Woman of the Century,* 241.

129. Chester, *Embattled Maiden,* 45–60.

130. J. G. Battenson to Anna Dickinson, April 9, 1863, Dickinson Papers, LC.

131. Lillie B. Chace to Anna Dickinson, March 30, 1863, Dickinson Papers, LC.

132. *HWS,* 2:44.

133. Elizabeth Cady Stanton to Susan B. Anthony, November 4, 1855, in DuBois, ed., *Correspondence,* 59.

134. Qtd. in Chester, *Embattled Maiden,* 61.

135. *HWS,* 2:45–46.

136. Anna Dickinson to Susan Dickinson, April 28, 1862, Dickinson Papers, LC; Berkeley, "Partisan Politics Makes for Strange Bedfellows," 3.

137. Chester, *Embattled Maiden,* 68. According to Sklar, "Speaking on this issue on July 6, 1863, Kelley became the first elected official in Philadelphia to join black leaders in addressing a predominantly black audience." Sklar, *Florence Kelley and the Nation's Work,* 333 n. 31.

138. See Kelley and Dickinson correspondence in Dickinson Papers, LC.

139. Mary Livermore to Anna Dickinson, August 17, September 12, and October 1, 1863, Dickinson Papers, LC.

140. Berkeley, "Partisan Politics Makes for Strange Bedfellows," 4.

141. Lillie Chace to Anna Dickinson, September 19, 1864, Dickinson Papers, LC.

142. Qtd. in Chester, *Embattled Maiden,* 81.

143. Griffith, *In Her Own Right,* 105; Lutz, *Susan B. Anthony,* 86.

144. Belden and Belden, *So Fell the Angels,* 114.

145. *NAW,* 3:339–40.

146. Dinkins, *Before Equal Suffrage,* 64.

147. Roseboom, *History of Presidential Elections,* 215. Elizabeth Cady Stanton and Susan B. Anthony attended the Democratic convention, and Anthony was given a place on the stage as a clerk read her woman suffrage appeal. Privately, Anthony stated her hope that Chase would present himself as an independent candidate for the presidency. See

Susan B. Anthony to Anna E. Dickinson, June 29, 1868, and July 10, 1868, in Gordon, ed., *Selected Papers*, 2:150–53.

148. Elizabeth Cady Stanton to Caroline Healey Dall, [April 24, 1864], Caroline Wells Healey Dall Papers, Massachusetts Historical Society. This letter is catalogued under May 1863 in the chronological arrangement of the microfilm edition of the Dall Papers. The date of ca. April 22, 1864, is cited in Gordon, ed., *Selected Papers*, 1:514–15.

149. Elizabeth Cady Stanton to Central Frémont Club, May 14, 1864, and Elizabeth Cady Stanton to Jessie Benton Frémont, [1864], *Selected Papers of Elizabeth Cady Stanton and Susan B. Anthony*, microfilm.

150. Susan B. Anthony to Charles Sumner, March 1, 1864, in Gordon, ed., *Selected Papers*, 1:511–13.

151. Elizabeth Cady Stanton to Caroline Healey Dall, May 7, 1864, in ibid., 518–22.

152. Wendell Phillips to Elizabeth Cady Stanton, April 25, 1864, Alma Lutz's Records, Schlesinger Library; Gordon, ed., *Selected Papers*, 1:515–16.

153. McPherson, *Battle Cry of Freedom*, 715–17.

154. Anna Dickinson to Elizabeth Cady Stanton, July 12, 1864, Harper Collection, Huntington; Trefousse, "Republican Party," 1170–72.

155. *HWS*, 2:42; Chester, *Embattled Maiden*, 81–82.

156. Curtis, *History of the Republican Party*, 1:441.

Chapter 2: The Entering Wedge

1. Kerr, "White Women's Rights," 64.

2. *HWS*, 2:88. Lori Ginzberg writes that the women leaders of the Civil War organizations "helped introduce a new class-based ideology of gender sameness that would exist alongside the older one of gender difference that had sustained antebellum movements." Ginzberg, *Women and the Work of Benevolence*, 174.

3. *HWS*, 2:85.

4. The Reconstruction Act of 1867 required the former states of the Confederacy, except Tennessee, to call constitutional conventions. Additionally, states around the nation were revising their constitutions. Ibid., 320.

5. Ibid., 87; Harper, *LWSBA*, 1:265.

6. DuBois, *Feminism and Suffrage*, 187.

7. *HWS*, 2:320.

8. Susan B. Anthony to Sidney Clarke, January 21, 1866, in Gordon, ed., *Selected Papers*, 1:573.

9. "Preamble to the Constitution of the American Equal Rights Association," in Gordon, ed., *Selected Papers*, 1:586.

10. See Gordon, ed., *Selected Papers*, 1:549 n. 2; and Kerr, "White Women's Rights," 64–65.

11. *HWS*, 3:340–44; Marilley, *Woman Suffrage and the Origins of Liberal Feminism in the United States*, 75; Buhle and Buhle, eds., *Concise History of Woman Suffrage*, 17.

12. Elizabeth Cady Stanton to the editor, *National Anti-Slavery Standard*, December 26, 1865, in Gordon, ed., *Selected Papers*, 1:564–65.

13. "Elizabeth Cady Stanton for Congress. To the Electors of the Eighth Congressional District, October 10, 1866," in Gordon, ed., *Selected Papers*, 1:593–94, and *HWS*, 2:180–81.

14. Ibid.

15. Gordon, ed., *Selected Papers*, 1:597.

16. *HWS*, 2:166.

17. Frederick Douglass to Anna Dickinson, May 1867, Dickinson Papers, LC; Kerr, "White Women's Rights," 68; *HWS*, 2:328.

18. Harper, *LWSBA*, 1:317; *HWS*, 2:327.

19. *New York Tribune*, June 19 and June 28, 1867.

20. *HWS*, 2:350.

21. Kerr, "White Women's Rights," 64–68; Buhle and Buhle, eds., *Concise History of Woman Suffrage*, 17.

22. Kerr, "White Women's Rights," 68.

23. Marilley, *Woman Suffrage and the Origins of Liberal Feminism in the United States*, 67.

24. Lillie Chace to Anna Dickinson, May 29, 1868, Dickinson Papers, LC.

25. *HWS*, 2:309–12.

26. *Chicago Tribune*, February 13, 1869, in Gordon, ed., *Selected Papers*, 2:213–21.

27. Ibid. See also Harper, *LWSBA*, 1:315; and Gordon, ed., *Selected Papers*, 2:143–47 and 2:368.

28. *HWS*, 2:320.

29. Isenberg, *Sex and Citizenship in Antebellum America*, 193. Isenberg points out that abstract rights also did not always include all men.

30. Edwards, *Angels in the Machinery*, 35.

31. Collier-Thomas, "Frances Ellen Watkins Harper," 49–51. In a serialized novel, *Minnie's Sacrifice*, published in the *Christian Recorder* in 1869, Harper reiterated her belief that African-American women needed the vote, but she did not propose to place women's claims before those of African-American men. Boyd, *Discarded Legacy*, 127.

32. Qtd. in Gordon, *Selected Papers*, 2:293 n. 7.

33. Newman, *White Women's Rights*, 63.

34. The paper became more controversial because it was funded in part by George Train. DuBois, *Feminism and Suffrage*, 103.

35. The AWSA was committed to organizing state suffrage campaigns, but it also supported work for a federal amendment. The NWSA rejected state work for its first twelve years and focused its energies on obtaining woman suffrage at the national level. According to Kerr, the difference between the two organizations was less about national versus state agitation than it was about "representation, size, membership, budget, tactics, and political impact." The AWSA was always larger, it had a greater influence, and, she argues, its work at the state level led to victories for partial suffrage. Kerr, "White Women's Rights," 71.

36. DuBois, "Outgrowing the Compact of the Fathers," 94–95. See also Ginzberg, *Women and the Work of Benevolence*, 183–85.

37. Elizabeth Cady Stanton, "Address to the National Woman Suffrage Association, Washington, D.C., January 19, 1869," qtd. in DuBois, "Outgrowing the Compact of the Fathers," 95. See also Elizabeth Cady Stanton, "Miss Becker on the Difference in Sex," *Revolution*, September 24, 1868.

38. Susan B. Anthony to Elizabeth Harbert, September 23, 1879, Harbert Collection, Huntington.

39. *Congressional Globe,* 41st Cong., 3d sess., December 21, 1870, 272; Harper, *LWSBA,* 1:314.

40. *HWS,* 2:340–44.

41. Ibid., 514.

42. Ibid.

43. Harper, *LWSBA,* 1:365–66; Elizabeth Cady Stanton to Isabella Beecher Hooker, February 3, [1871], in Gordon, ed., *Selected Papers,* 2:411–14.

44. *HWS,* 2:811.

45. Ibid., 368.

46. *HWS,* 4:496, 506; Hafen, *Colorado and Its People,* 1:350, 2:569. Ruth A. Gallaher groups woman suffrage into five categories: complete, school, municipal, tax, and presidential. See Gallaher, *Legal and Political Status of Women in Iowa,* 163.

47. In addition to granting women full suffrage in 1869, the Wyoming territorial legislature passed a married women's property act, providing for equality in the pay of teachers and including a resolution that permitted women to attend the deliberations of the legislature. Larson, *History of Wyoming,* 78.

48. Larson, "Petticoats at the Polls," 75.

49. Van Wagenen, "Sister-Wives and Suffragists," 48.

50. Henry Blackwell was especially angry that the Republican Senate had passed a bill disfranchising the women of Utah the same year that the Republican platform pledged a "respectful consideration" of women's rights demands. Ibid., 121–23.

51. Buhle and Buhle, eds., *Concise History of Woman Suffrage;* Flexner, *Century of Struggle,* 179–80.

52. D. J. Pierce, letter to the editor, *Laramie Sentinel* [1870], qtd. in *HWS,* 3:739–40, and Flexner, *Century of Struggle,* 164.

53. The many publications of the suffrage associations are filled with this rhetoric. For examples, see the *Woman's Journal,* NAWSA "Headquarter News Letter," and other papers located in the NAWSA Papers, LC. See also "The Elective Franchise," *Woman Suffrage Leaflet* (AWSA), September 15, 1889; Brown, *History of Equal Suffrage in Colorado;* Howe, "Woman and the Suffrage"; Hebard, *How Woman Suffrage Came to Wyoming;* Gail Laughlin, "Woman Suffrage and Prosperity" and "Fruits of Equal Suffrage," in *Political Equality Series* (Warren, Ohio: National American Woman Suffrage Association, [1904]); Plunkett, "Working of Woman Suffrage in Wyoming"; Pitman, "Woman as a Political Factor"; and Robinson, *Massachusetts in the Woman Suffrage Movement.*

54. *HWS,* 2:343.

55. Larson, *History of Wyoming,* 85.

56. Qtd. in Harper, *LWSBA,* 2:897.

57. Elizabeth Van Lew of Richmond, Virginia, received her appointment in 1869 for her services as a Union spy during the Civil War. *HWS,* 4:462. According to Harriet Robinson, Salmon P. Chase appointed the first woman postmaster in 1862. She also claims that there were 44,140 post offices in 1881, and four thousand of these were managed by women, but with a new law making married women eligible, their numbers were increasing. Robinson, *Massachusetts in the Woman Suffrage Movement,* 157.

58. Cox, *Women State and Territorial Legislators,* 276.

59. For women's jury service in other states, see Mary Sumner Boyd, "Must Women Voters Serve on Juries?" NAWSA "Headquarter News Letter," February 15, 1916, 6, NAWSA Papers, LC.

60. Larson, *History of Wyoming,* 84–89.

61. Ibid., 88; *Cheyenne Leader,* November 8, 1876, and March 3, 1880.

62. Van Pelt, "Estelle Reel."

63. Susan B. Anthony Interview, *Cincinnati Times and Chronicle,* May 1, 1872, *Selected Papers of Elizabeth Cady Stanton and Susan B. Anthony,* microfilm; Harper, *LWSBA,* 1:415.

64. Susan B. Anthony Interview, *Cincinnati Times and Chronicle,* May 1, 1872, *Selected Papers of Elizabeth Cady Stanton and Susan B. Anthony,* microfilm; *Proceedings of the Liberal Republican Convention.*

65. Harper, *LWSBA,* 1:415–16.

66. Braude, *Radical Spirits;* Underhill, *Woman Who Ran for President,* 71; Goldsmith, *Other Powers,* 288.

67. *Woodhull and Claflin's Weekly,* March 23, 1872. See also Elizabeth Cady Stanton to Isabella Beecher Hooker, February 2, [1872], Isabella Beecher Hooker Collection, Stowe Center; and Gordon, ed., *Selected Papers,* 2:478–81.

68. *Woodhull and Claflin's Weekly,* April 6, 1872; *HWS,* 2:517.

69. Susan B. Anthony to Elizabeth Cady Stanton and Isabella Beecher Hooker, March 13, 1872, in Gordon, ed., *Selected Papers,* 2:485. See also Harper, *LWSBA,* 1:413.

70. *New York World,* May 10, 1872.

71. Frisken, "Sex in Politics"; Horowitz, "Victoria Woodhull, Anthony Comstock, and Conflict over Sex in the United States in the 1870s."

72. Cherny, *American Politics in the Gilded Age,* 22–23.

73. *Proceedings of the National Union Republican Convention . . . 1872,* 11, in Blaine Papers, LC.

74. Ibid., 33–34.

75. Ibid., 12–13.

76. Ibid. The statement is similar to a resolution Blackwell presented to the Massachusetts Republican convention in 1870, which read that the "Republican party of Massachusetts is mindful of its obligations to the loyal women of America for their patriotic devotion to the cause of liberty" and thanked the party for making women eligible for state political offices. The resolution was defeated in 1870 but passed in 1871. Robinson, *Massachusetts in the Woman Suffrage Movement,* 72.

77. Henry Blackwell to Elizabeth Cady Stanton, June 8, 1872, Blackwell Family Papers, LC.

78. *HWS,* 2:517–18.

79. Harper, *LWSBA,* 1:417. See also Susan B. Anthony to Martha Coffin Wright, June 13, 1872, Garrison Family Papers, Sophia Smith Collection (SSC).

80. Elizabeth Cady Stanton to Henry Blackwell, June 13, 1872, NAWSA Papers, LC.

81. Harper, *LWSBA,* 1:415–18; Buhle and Buhle, eds., *Concise History of Woman Suffrage,* 23.

82. Elizabeth Cady Stanton to Henry Blackwell, June 13, 1872, NAWSA Papers, LC.

83. Elizabeth Cady Stanton to Susan B. Anthony, July [16], 1872, qtd. in Harper, *LWSBA,* 1:420.

84. Henry Blackwell to Elizabeth Cady Stanton, June 8, 1872, Henry Blackwell to Susan B. Anthony, June 10, 1872, Blackwell Family Papers, LC.

85. Harper, *LWSBA*, 1:417; Susan B. Anthony to Elizabeth Cady Stanton, July 10, 1872, in Gordon, ed., *Selected Papers*, 2:516.

86. Susan B. Anthony to Henry Blackwell, June 14, 1872, Blackwell Family Papers, LC.

87. Susan B. Anthony to Elizabeth Cady Stanton, July [12], 1872, qtd. in Harper, *LWSBA*, 1:420.

88. Buhle and Buhle, eds., *Concise History of Woman Suffrage*, 275–79; *HWS*, 2:517.

89. *HWS*, 2:517–18; *Rochester Democrat and Chronicle*, July 20, 1872; *Woman's Journal*, July 27, 1872.

90. Susan B. Anthony to Henry Blackwell, July 22, 1872, Blackwell Family Papers, LC.

91. William Chandler, secretary, Republican National Committee, to Henry Blackwell, September 22, 1872, NAWSA Papers, LC. The New York Republican party also gave Anthony five hundred dollars. Harper, *LWSBA*, 1:421.

92. Susan B. Anthony to Henry Blackwell and Lucy Stone, September 4, 1872, Blackwell Family Papers, LC.

93. *HWS*, 2:520; *Cincinnati Daily Gazette*, September 13, 1872; *Rochester Democrat and Chronicle*, September 21, 1872; *Rochester Evening Express*, September 21, 1872.

94. Henry B. Blackwell to Susan B. Anthony, September 7, 1872, Garrison Family Papers, SSC; Gordon, ed., *Selected Papers*, 2:518–21.

95. Harper, *LWSBA*, 1:509.

96. *New York Times*, October 5, 1872.

97. *New York Times*, October 4, 1872.

98. Buhle and Buhle, eds., *Concise History of Woman Suffrage*, 24; *New York Herald, New York Times,* and *New York Tribune*, October 8, 1872.

99. Chester, *Embattled Maiden*, 121.

100. Anthony, *Susan B. Anthony*, 274.

101. Chester, *Embattled Maiden*, 129–33.

102. Ibid., 136.

103. *New York Tribune*, October 26, 1872.

104. Susan B. Anthony to Elizabeth Cady Stanton, November 5, 1872, Harper Collection, Huntington.

105. For evidence of women registering and voting collected by Susan B. Anthony, see Gordon, ed., *Selected Papers*, vol. 2, app. C.

106. Babcock, "Clara Shortridge Foltz," 1231–85.

107. For a comparison of the voting in Washington, D.C., and Rochester, see Terborg-Penn, *African American Women in the Struggle for the Vote*, 40.

108. The date of her law degree is unclear. She finished law school in 1870, which would make her the first black woman lawyer in the country. However, her degree was not conferred until 1883. *BWA*, 1:224–26; Rhodes, *Mary Ann Shadd Cary*.

109. Rhodes, *Mary Ann Shadd Cary*, 195–205.

110. *HWS*, 2:628–47.

111. Ibid., 2:690.

112. Griffith, *In Her Own Right*, 155; Cott, "Women's Rights," 382–96.

113. Chester, *Embattled Maiden*, 140–43.

114. Edwards, *Angels in the Machinery*, 30–31.

115. Hoar sponsored many suffragists in their attempts to get hearings and present resolutions to Republican conventions and committees. For his role at the 1870 Massachusetts Republican convention, see Robinson, *Massachusetts in the Woman Suffrage Movement*, 72–75.

116. *Proceedings of the Republican National Convention . . . 1876*, 31; Van Wagenen, "Sister-Wives and Suffragists," 160–65.

117. Van Wagenen, "Sister-Wives and Suffragists," 160–61.

118. Qtd. in ibid., 164; *HWS*, 2:587–99.

119. Van Wagenen, "Sister-Wives and Suffragists," 165.

120. *Proceedings of the Republican National Convention . . . 1876*, 32–34.

121. Ibid., 57. In reprinting the plank in the *HWS*, the editors placed an exclamation point in parentheses between the words "Republican" and "Legislatures." *HWS*, 4:436.

122. Edwards, *Angels in the Machinery*, 33.

123. Geer, *First Lady*, 113, 147–55.

124. *New York Times*, October 31, 1884.

125. According to Lola Van Wagenen, Spencer's optimistic evaluation probably resulted from the fact that, as the first woman to address a national political convention, her appearance brought her "personal celebrity." Van Wagenen, "Sister-Wives and Suffragists," 166.

126. Abigail Scott Duniway of Oregon, qtd. in ibid, 166; Harper, *LWSBA*, 1:476.

127. Dinkins, *Before Equal Suffrage*, 72.

128. Robinson, *Massachusetts in the Woman Suffrage Movement*, 77–78.

129. Qtd. in Griffith, *In Her Own Right*, 153, 171.

130. *Woman's Journal*, November 6, 1880.

131. Susan B. Anthony to Elizabeth Harbert, August 5, 1880, Harbert Collection, Huntington.

132. *HWS*, 4:436.

133. Harper, *LWSBA*, 2:518.

134. Peskin, "Lucretia (Rudolph) Garfield," 237.

135. Ibid., 237. Sprague and Conkling's affair contributed to the Spragues' divorce in 1882. Kate Chase Sprague died in 1899 at the age of fifty-eight, after being supported in the last years of her life by a small trust fund from her father's friends.

136. *Boston Evening Journal*, August 8, 1884; *Woman's Journal*, August 9, 1884; Harper, *LWSBA*, 2:594.

137. *HWS*, 2:320.

138. McGerr, *Decline of Popular Politics*, 13–14.

139. Harper, *LWSBA*, 2:594.

140. Qtd. in Terborg-Penn, *African American Women in the Struggle for the Vote*, 41; Rhodes, *Mary Ann Shadd Cary*, 205.

141. Susan B. Anthony to Elizabeth Harbert, March 19, 1882, Harbert Collection, Huntington.

142. *Woman's Herald of Industry*, July 1882.

143. Davis, *Life of Marietta Stow*, 171; Schuele, "In Her Own Way."

144. Lockwood, "How I Ran for the Presidency."

145. Susan B. Anthony to Mrs. Katie R. Addison, September 20, 1897, *Selected Papers of Elizabeth Cady Stanton and Susan B. Anthony*, microfilm.

146. *New York Times*, December 14, 1884. Dodge was born in 1833, graduated from the Ipswich Female Seminary in 1850, and taught there, at the Hartford Female Seminary, and at Hartford High School. In 1858 she moved to Washington, D.C., worked as a governess, and began writing. She moved back to her home town of Hamilton, Massachusetts, to care for her mother during the Civil War. After her mother's death she returned to Washington, where she lived in the Blaine household. Coultrap-McQuin, ed., *Gail Hamilton*.

147. Qtd. in Harper, *LWSBA*, 1:365–66.

Chapter 3: Devotions and Disharmonies, 1881–1910

1. *Woman's Tribune*, April 1, 1888.

2. Ibid.

3. Foster, "Woman's Political Evolution."

4. Adams and Foster, *Heroines of Modern Progress*, 248. Unless otherwise noted, information on Foster's background comes from Adams and Foster, *Heroines of Modern Progress; NAW*, 1:651–52; Lender, ed., *Dictionary of American Temperance Biography*, 175–76; Hanaford, *Daughters of America*, 653–59; and *Inter-Ocean*, September 29, 1888, 9. Warren Foster was Judith Foster's grandson. See "Warren Dunham Foster," in Marquis, ed., *Who's Who in New England*, 424.

5. Her sister is identified by Hanaford as "Mrs. Pierce, wife of a wealthy business man of Boston." Hanaford, *Daughters of America*, 654. Mrs. Charles W. Pierce's daughter is identified as Elizabeth F. Pierce, who was active in the Foreign and Home Missionary Societies of the Methodist Episcopal Church. She and her mother moved to Washington, D.C., after her father's death, where she became the recording secretary general and chaplain general of the Daughters of the American Revolution. J. E. Foster was also involved in the Missionary Societies and the Daughters of the American Revolution. Logan, *Part Taken by Women in American History*, 410–11. Elizabeth F. Pierce is listed as treasurer on the 1901 letterhead of the WNRA.

6. Qtd. in Hanaford, *Daughters of America*, 657.

7. Willard, *Woman and Temperance*, 323.

8. Adams and Foster, *Heroines of Modern Progress*, 263. Barbara Epstein argues that WCTU members supported the Republican party due to sectional political allegiances. Epstein, *Politics of Domesticity*, 122.

9. Judith Ellen Foster to Susan B. Anthony, May 10, 1881, *Selected Papers of Elizabeth Cady Stanton and Susan B. Anthony*, microfilm. According to Barbara Epstein, in 1874 "temperance became an issue in a series of local elections throughout Ohio," and Republicans ran for office on the issue but were generally defeated. Epstein, *Politics of Domesticity*, 99. It was also an issue in Iowa and Kansas. See Bader, *Prohibition in Kansas;* and Bordin, *Woman and Temperance*.

10. Cherrington, *Evolution of Prohibition in the United States of America*, chap. 6; Epstein, *Politics of Domesticity*, chap. 4.

11. Epstein, *Politics of Domesticity*, 115–17.

12. Bordin, *Frances Willard,* 326.

13. Ibid., 134.

14. Ibid., 374–75; Willard, "President's Annual Address," 1888 National WCTU Meeting, WCTU Papers.

15. Martha Brown was influential in the formation of the party and sat in the first party caucus in 1869. Eliza Stewart and Anna Gordon joined the party during its efforts in 1874 to organize women. Brown was nominated for the first presidency of the WCTU in 1874 but was "reminded" that she had affiliated with the Prohibition party and withdrew her nomination. From 1877 until 1882, she worked for both the party and the nonpartisan National Prohibition Alliance, which was discontinued when the WCTU and Prohibition party joined forces. Willard and Livermore, eds., *Woman of the Century,* 127–28.

16. Ginzberg, *Women and the Work of Benevolence,* 204; Bordin, *Frances Willard,* 136.

17. Adams and Foster, *Heroines of Modern Progress,* 257.

18. Willard, *Glimpses of Fifty Years,* 324. See also a similar quote in Hanaford, *Daughters of America,* 658.

19. Judith Foster to unknown correspondent, April 2, 1884, WCTU Papers; Adams and Foster, *Heroines of Modern Progress,* 253.

20. Judith Ellen Foster to Frances Willard, April 2, 1884, WCTU Papers.

21. *Woman's Tribune,* March 31, 1888; Adams and Foster, *Heroines of Modern Progress,* 263.

22. *Woman's Tribune,* March 31, 1888; Foster, "Influence of Women in American Politics."

23. Adams and Foster, *Heroines of Modern Progress,* 263; Foster, "Constitutional Amendment Manual"; Foster, "Constitutional Amendment Catechism".

24. Foster, "Republican Party and Temperance."

25. Ibid.

26. Ibid.

27. Foster, "For God and Home, and Native Land."

28. Foster, *The Saloon Must Go,* 22.

29. Annual Report of 1885 and Minutes of the 1885 Annual Meeting, WCTU Papers; Bordin, *Frances Willard,* 374–75.

30. Willard, "President's Annual Address," 1888 National WCTU Meeting, WCTU Papers.

31. The controversy can be followed in the minutes of the annual meetings, ser. 3, reel 2, WCTU Papers. See also Letter by J. E. Foster, *Boston Journal,* September 9, 1884.

32. Minutes of the 1885 Annual Meeting, WCTU Papers.

33. Ibid.

34. Ibid.

35. Ibid.

36. Ibid.

37. On Anthony's position, see chap. 2.

38. Judith Ellen Foster to Frances Willard, April 2, 1884, Judith Ellen Foster to Frances Willard, November 16, 1888, WCTU Papers; *Boston Journal,* September 9, 1884.

39. *Union Signal,* June 12, 1888; Foster, "For God and Home, and Native Land."

40. Avery, ed., *Transactions of the National Council of Women of the United States,* 135–41.

41. On Porter, see chap. 6. Address by Ellen Phinney, President of the NPWCTU, *Temperance Tribune,* February 15, 1894, Nonpartisan National WCTU Records, SSC.

42. Willard and Livermore, eds., *Woman of the Century,* 104–5. The NPWCTU had at least two national conventions. The first was in Chicago in 1889; the second was in Cleveland, Ohio, in 1890. In May 1896, the Polk County, Iowa, NPWCTU held its twenty-eighth annual convention. *Des Moines Register,* May 6, 1896.

43. Nonpartisan National WCTU Collection, SSC.

44. *Woman's Tribune,* April 1, 1884, and March 31, 1888; *HWS,* 4:19, 443.

45. *Woman's Tribune,* October 1885.

46. *Union Signal,* May 17, June 21, June 28, and September 13, 1888.

47. Judith Ellen Foster to James Clarkson, n.d., Clarkson Papers, LC; "Permanent Republican Clubs," *North American Review* 146 (March 1888): 241–65.

48. McGerr, *Decline of Popular Politics,* 79.

49. Qtd. in ibid., 80.

50. Ibid., 80–81.

51. It was also known as the Woman's Republican Association of the United States. The first secretary was Mrs. Thomas Chace of Rhode Island. *New York Tribune,* August 18, 1888; *Woman's Journal,* September 1, 1888.

52. Judith Ellen Foster to Benjamin Harrison, July 19, 1888, Harrison Papers, LC.

53. It is unclear whether the WNRA became an official member of the National League of Republican Clubs. In 1893 the National Convention of Republican Clubs, meeting in Louisville, Kentucky, endorsed woman suffrage by adopting a resolution presented by Henry Blackwell. It read: "We recommend to the favorable consideration of the Republican Clubs of the United States, as a matter of education, the question of granting to the women of the State and nation the right to vote at all elections on the same terms and conditions as male citizens." *HWS,* 4:713.

54. "California's Tribute to Its New Voters," *California Outlook,* May 4, May 13, and May 21, 1912, Gifford Pinchot Papers, LC; Ryan, "Clubs in Politics," 172–77.

55. *Woman's Journal,* September 18, 1880; *Woman's Tribune,* November 3, 1888; *New York Herald,* October 1, October 21, and November 2, 1888. ·

56. The estimate of a thousand clubs comes from Adams and Foster, *Heroines of Modern Progress,* 266, and Dinkins, *Before Equal Suffrage,* 94. More information is in the *New York Tribune,* September 29, 1892; and Willard and Livermore, eds., *Woman of the Century,* 10–11. How many women make a club? Foster traveled the country to mobilize Republican women, and it is likely that in some communities only one or a few women may have constituted a "club" after meeting Foster or attending a rally. I have been unable to find any membership lists for the WNRA. As the National League of Republican Clubs was being formed in 1888, William Chandler wrote, "In any canvass if three men alone wish to organize themselves as a Republican club, one to be president, another secretary, and the third treasurer, by all means encourage them to do it." Chandler, "Permanent Republican Clubs," 247.

57. Adams and Foster, *Heroines of Modern Progress,* 267.

58. *New York Herald,* October 23, 1888.

59. *New York Tribune,* September 27 and October 3, 1892; October 31, 1894.

60. Scrapbooks 13–16, WCTU Papers. See also Gilmore, *Gender and Jim Crow;* Brown, "Negotiating and Transforming the Public Sphere."

61. James Clarkson to Anna Dickinson, August 18, August 23, 1888; Anna Dickinson to James Clarkson, November 5, 1888; *New York Press,* November 8, 1888, all in Dickinson Scrapbooks, Dickinson Papers, LC.

62. James Clarkson to Anna Dickinson, August 28, 1888, Dickinson Papers, LC; *New York Herald,* May 14, 1892.

63. H. S. Hull to T. S. Pritchard, October 9, October 12, 1888, Dickinson Papers, LC.

64. See correspondence between Anna Dickinson, James Clarkson, and others for October and early November 1888, Dickinson Papers, LC.

65. *New York Herald,* November 9, 1888.

66. Anna Dickinson to James Clarkson, November 5, 1888, Dickinson Papers, LC.

67. Ibid.; *New York Tribune,* November 9, 1888.

68. Anna Dickinson to Benjamin Harrison, June 1, 1889; E. M. Halford, secretary to Benjamin Harrison, to Anna Dickinson, June 6 and June 10, 1889, Dickinson Papers, LC.

69. For all these law suits see "Legal File" and Anna Dickinson Scrapbooks, Dickinson Papers, LC.

70. Anna Dickinson to Senator William Allison, December 10, 1907, and May 7, 1908; Anna Dickinson to Charles Evans Hughes, October 2, 1907; Robert Fuller, secretary for Charles E. Hughes, to Anna Dickinson, October 3, 1907, Dickinson Papers, LC.

71. Foster, "Republican Party and Temperance."

72. Edwards, *Angels in the Machinery,* 86.

73. Foster, "Republican Party and Temperance"; *Union Signal,* October 4, 1888.

74. *New York Times,* March 8, 1891; *Chicago Times,* June 28, 1890.

75. Judith Ellen Foster to Elijah W. Halford, secretary to Benjamin Harrison, May 30, 1889, and undated notation by Halford, in the "President's Private Files," n.d., Harrison Papers, LC. Issues of the *Congressional Directory* from 1889 to 1893 and 1898 to 1906 list Elijah Foster's appointments.

76. J. E. Foster to Benjamin Harrison, December 24, 1888, January 1 and May 30, 1889, Harrison Papers, LC.

77. "Why They Suffer: Working Women and Working Men's Wives. How the Tariff Affects Them" (pamphlet, Chicago[?], 1894[?]). See also Edwards, *Angels in the Machinery,* 86–87.

78. John Porter to Judith Ellen Foster, July 1, 1898, McKinley Papers, LC.

79. Theodore Roosevelt to Judith Ellen Foster, June 25, 1907, Roosevelt Papers, LC; J. Ellen Foster to D. A. Tompkins, May 20, 1907, and Tompkins to Foster, May 25, 1907, Tompkins Papers, LC. Tompkins, of the National Manufacturers Association, was the chair of the Child Labor Committee.

80. Correspondence between Foster and Taft is located in the Taft Papers, LC. Also see Roosevelt Papers, LC. Information on the WNRA can be found in these collections under Foster's name, Helen V. Boswell, and the Women's National Republican Association.

81. Judith Ellen Foster to Mr. Brigham, September 18, 1891, Letters of Judith Ellen Foster, State Historical Society of Iowa, Des Moines.

82. "Republican Women: Please Take Notice," Woman's Republican Association of the

United States, flyer, 1892, SSC; *New York Tribune,* September 16, 1892, includes the names of the women who attended the league convention in Buffalo, New York.

83. *Woman's Exponent,* July 1, 1892. Women were also elected as delegates to the Populist National Convention the same year, and Mary Elizabeth Lease raised the bar on women's participation by seconding James Weaver's nomination for president.

84. *New York Tribune,* September 16 and September 29, 1892.

85. Beach, comp., *Women of Wyoming,* 1:226. Jenkins's daughter later recalled that people could hear her mother four blocks away because she practiced her speaking skills "on the open prairie, with her husband riding off in a buggy to greater and greater distances and shouting back, at intervals, 'Louder.'" Larson, *History of Wyoming,* 260. By 1895 Jenkins was the president of the state suffrage association. Harper, *LWSBA,* 2:823.

86. *Woman's Exponent,* July 1, 1892.

87. Harper, *LWSBA,* 2:725.

88. Terborg-Penn, *African American Women in the Struggle for the Vote,* 88.

89. It is also unclear if they were attending a convention of African-American Republicans.

90. *BWA,* 2:759–61, 1157–59, 1233–35.

91. Ibid., 2:994–97.

92. Qtd. in White, *Too Heavy a Load,* 51–52.

93. Ibid.

94. Giddings, *When and Where I Enter,* 130; Beatty, "Perspectives on American Women," 39–50.

95. *HWS,* 4:439; Sautter and Burke, *Inside the Wigwam,* 107; Good, *Republican Womanpower,* 8. While providing a useful outline, Good includes a number of mistakes about women delegates, including naming Frances E. Warren as the woman delegate from Wyoming in 1900. (Warren was the Republican governor of Wyoming and a U.S. senator.)

96. Judith Ellen Foster to Benjamin Harrison, September 6, 1892, Harrison Papers, LC.

97. Judith Ellen Foster to Mrs. Callanan, August 17, 1893, Letters of Judith Ellen Foster, State Historical Society of Iowa, Des Moines.

98. *New York Tribune,* September 27 and October 3, 1892; September 8, 1900; *New York Times,* November 8, 1892; October 5, 1895; *Woman's Tribune,* December 28, 1895; June 29, 1907; *Woman's Standard* (Des Moines, Iowa), August 1896; *Woman's Journal,* October 24, 1896; Scrapbooks, reel 32, WCTU Papers; *HWS,* 4:444; Brown, *History of Equal Suffrage in Colorado,* 30.

99. Brown, *History of Equal Suffrage in Colorado,* 31–33.

100. James Clarkson, "How Women Voted in Colorado," *Woman Suffrage Leaflet* 6:6 (December 1894), from an article published in Clarkson's *Iowa State Register,* November 16, 1894, Clarkson Papers, LC; *New York Tribune,* September 13, 1896.

101. *Woman's Journal,* November 10, 1894; Edwards, *Angels in the Machinery,* 105; Muncy, "'Women Demand Recognition,'" 46.

102. Clement, "Women at Past National Conventions," 28; Bass, "Advance of Democratic Women," 17, 39.

103. Robinson went on to be the "first woman Co-Leader in Bronx County" when New

York women got the vote. Boswell, "Political Episodes" (June 1935), 5. According to Boswell, the first New York Republican club was established in Brooklyn in 1895. Boswell, "Political Episodes" (May 1935).

104. Logan, *Part Taken by Women in American History,* 420–21; Boswell, "Promoting Americanization"; *New York Times,* January 6, 1899; "Men Dug the Canal . . . But Women Played a Vital Role," *Panama Canal Review* (Spring 1976), available at <http://www.serve.com/CZBrats/Builders/women.htm>.

105. Boswell, "Political Episodes" (May 1935).

106. Boswell, "Political Episodes" (March 1935).

107. The Women's National Republican Club was founded by Henrietta Wells Livermore in 1921. "A Brief History" of the Women's National Republican Club of New York, available at <http://www.wnrc.org/history/html>; Livermore, "New York State Republican Women," 3–4. The California Federation of Republican Women, organized in 1925, traces its roots to "the Los Angeles Republican Study Club with Mrs. Florence Collins Porter as leader." "History of the California Federation of Republican Women," available at <http://www.cfrw.org/history>. The League of Republican Women of the District of Columbia traces its presidents back to 1912 but was incorporated in 1923. "Certificate of Incorporation," League of Republican Women of the District of Columbia Records, courtesy of Kerry Stowell; "D.C. League of Republican Women," available at <http://users.erols.com/leaguelady/index.html>.

108. Born in Llandudno, Wales, Martha Hughes Cannon came to Utah as the fourth wife of Angus M. Cannon. A physician who trained at the University of Michigan Medical School, she left Utah for England in 1888 rather than testify in federal court against her husband for their polygamous practices. Returning to Utah and her family, she became involved in the woman suffrage movement, and when Utah women were granted the vote in 1870 she became the first woman voter (or so it is claimed). Van Wagenen, "Sister-Wives and Suffragists," 469–74.

109. Gustafson, "Partisan Women," 164–69.

110. Logan, *Part Taken by Women in American History,* 395–96, 477.

111. Ibid., 397.

112. Colby's was a fascinating life and is deserving of a full biography. She was born in 1846 in England, moved with her family to Wisconsin in 1849, graduated from the University of Wisconsin (but had to fight for her degree), and married Leonard Colby in 1871. They moved to Beatrice, Nebraska, in 1872, where he practiced law and served in the state senate. In 1891 they adopted Lost Bird, or Zintkala Nuni, after she was found in her dead mother's arms after the battle of Wounded Knee. For more on Colby, see Norma Kidd Green's entry in *NAW,* 1:355–57.

113. Sautter and Burke, *Inside the Wigwam,* 107.

114. Boswell, "Political Episodes" (December 1935).

115. Qtd. in Miller, *Ruth Hanna McCormick,* 43.

116. Epstein, *Politics of Domesticity,* 145.

117. Odegard, *Pressure Politics,* 89.

118. Ibid., 38.

119. Ibid., 95.

120. *HWS,* 4:173.

121. Ibid., 4:437.

122. Ibid., 4:443–44.

123. Harper, *LWSBA,* 2:928.

124. Van Voris, *Carrie Chapman Catt,* 43–44.

125. *HWS,* 4:173.

126. For a fuller treatment of the situation in Kansas, see Goldberg, *An Army of Women.* For California, see Gullett, *Becoming Citizens.*

127. Flexner, *Century of Struggle,* 179.

128. Qtd. in Harper, *LWSBA,* 2:785. Or, "'I care more for Republican principles than woman suffrage.'" Qtd. in Edwards, *Angels in the Machinery,* 107.

129. "Women Who Vote," undated clipping, WCTU Papers.

130. *HWS,* 4:645.

131. Flexner, *Century of Struggle,* 229.

132. Harper, *LWSBA,* 2:793–94.

133. Susan B. Anthony to Jessie Anthony, August 1, 1896, Anthony Memorial Collection, Huntington.

134. Judith Ellen Foster to Ida Husted Harper, July 14, 1900, Harper Collection, Huntington.

135. Foster, "Woman's Political Evolution," 608.

136. For an examination of these changes, see Clemens, *People's Lobby.*

137. *Woman's Journal,* February 21, 1903; *HWS,* vol. 4.

138. *New York Times,* August 11, 1912.

Chapter 4: The Progressive Spirit, 1910–12

1. On the origins of the term "Gilded Age," see Cherny, *American Politics in the Gilded Age,* 3. On the progressive era in general, see Rodgers, "In Search of Progressivism." Throughout this and subsequent chapters, "progressive" will only be capitalized when it refers to the Progressive party.

2. "Campaign Methods," *Outlook,* November 5, 1910, 523.

3. Thelen, "Social Tensions and the Origins of Progressivism"; Thelen, *New Citizenship;* Kloppenberg, *Uncertain Victory,* 164; Cooper, *Pivotal Decades,* 82.

4. McGerr, *Decline of Popular Politics,* 58–68; McCormick, "Prelude to Progressivism," 293–97; VanderMeer, "Bosses, Machines, and Democratic Leadership"; Trowbridge, "Political Machine," 287. On the importance of regional identity, see Berman, "Political Culture, Issues, and the Electorate"; For Marcus Hanna's important role, see Croly, *Marcus Alonzo Hanna;* and Miller, *Ruth Hanna McCormick,* 9–35.

5. Keith Polakoff argues that Platt was a "manager," not a boss, because he wanted party success as much as personal success and was "flexible enough to do what the party wanted." Polakoff, *Political Parties in American History,* 245.

6. McCormick, "Prelude to Progressivism," 296.

7. In New York specifically, the machine's first concession to independents was the adoption of the primary election statute in 1898, providing for "rigid state regulation of primary elections" and explicitly allowing "party members to join nonpartisan municipal organizations." Ibid., 299.

8. Skowronek, *Building the New American State;* McCormick, *From Realignment to Reform;* Aron, *Ladies and Gentlemen of the Civil Service.*

9. Epperson, *Changing Legal Status of Political Parties in the United States.* Philip Vandermeer argues that "party critics in various places deliberately used anti-party rhetoric, which developed in big cities and even there was only partly appropriate. Besides strengthening their position and nationalizing their political struggle, they obscured the democratic nature of parties and party leadership, thus adding to the confusion about the nature of this era." Vandermeer, "Bosses, Machines, and Democratic Leadership," 422.

10. McCormick, "Prelude to Progressivism," 298.

11. Epstein, *Political Parties in the American Mold,* 159; Hays, "Politics of Reform in Municipal Government in the Progressive Era." For a contemporary view, see Brooks, *Corruption in American Politics and Life.*

12. Gable, *Bull Moose Years,* 6; Huthmacher, "Urban Liberalism and the Age of Reform."

13. Theodore Roosevelt to Josephine Shaw Lowell, February 24, 1882, in Morison, ed., *Letters of Theodore Roosevelt,* 8:1425.

14. Louise Ward Watkins Autobiography, Watkins Collection, Huntington.

15. McCormick, "Prelude to Progressivism," 300. Roosevelt used almost every campaign to increase the rhetoric about the need for a cleaner government. See Roosevelt, "Fight for Clean Government and Popular Rule," 342–44.

16. *Outlook,* November 12, 1910, 575–76.

17. "Municipal Problem: The Ideal City," *Outlook,* September 25, 1909, 141–42.

18. Kousser, *Shaping of Southern Politics;* Woodward, *Strange Career of Jim Crow;* Lewinson, *Race, Class and Party.*

19. Gosnell, *Negro Politicians.*

20. Cresap, *Party Politics in the Golden State,* 116. The good-government movement included the Municipal League, the Direct Legislation League, and other groups that formed the vanguard of the Lincoln-Roosevelt League. See Woods, "A Penchant for Probity," 99–113. The Lincoln-Roosevelt League was founded during the efforts of progressives in Los Angeles to take partisanship out of local affairs. The first success came in Berkeley, which made all municipal offices nonpartisan. The Berkeley Plan had been adopted, or was about to be adopted, by all of the chartered cities of California by 1911. By 1913, state and county offices were also nonpartisan. Only eleven officers of the state were elected on a partisan basis. MacRae, "Rise of the Progressive Movement in the State of California," 151.

21. Willard, "Old and New Politics."

22. For the distinction between benevolent workers and reformers, see Boylan, "Women in Groups"; Ginzberg, *Women and the Work of Benevolence.*

23. For background, see the essays in Frankel and Dye, eds., *Gender, Class, Race and Reform in the Progressive Era;* Buhle, *Women and American Socialism;* and Davis, *Spearheads for Reform.*

24. Foster, "Woman's Political Evolution."

25. Ibid., 609.

26. While this may sound like broad rhetoric, Mary Dietz writes that the key idea of a feminist vision of citizenship is that "citizenship must be conceived of as a continuous activity and a good in itself, not as a momentary engagement . . . with an eye to a final goal or a societal arrangement . . . this is a vision fixed not only on an end but rather in-

spired by a principle—freedom—and by a political activity—positive liberty." Dietz, "Context Is All," 16.

27. Scott, *Natural Allies,* 126. When the Republican Carrie Harper-White was elected to the Idaho legislature in 1919, she stated, "I am not a politician but I wanted to accomplish certain things and this legislative position seemed to be the only avenue. . . . One of my objects is to wake up women to their responsibility of citizenship. . . . Another message I have for women is [they] . . . must remember always to elect womanly women to office, not the masculine types. We want men to understand we wish to cooperate, not dominate." "Legislative Women of Idaho," clipping from *New West Magazine* [1919?], Burdette Collection, Huntington.

28. Monoson, "Lady and the Tiger," 101. On "metaphors of filth," see Lebsock, "Women and American Politics," 35–62.

29. Monoson, "Lady and the Tiger," 101. See also Villard, *Women in the New York Municipal Campaign of 1901,* 8. Villard wrote that the women's effort against Tammany Hall was "primarily a fight for honest municipal housekeeping and for economic management of the city's business, and next a fight for decency and morality, of which women ever have been and ever must be the natural guardians."

30. Monoson, "Lady and the Tiger," 104–5. Ellen DuBois notes a similar argument by suffragists during the New York Constitutional Convention of 1894. "Focusing on political corruption, Anthony and her allies argued that women were the political reformers' best allies. . . . everyone knew that women were naturally nonpartisan." Woman suffrage was "therefore a solution to the power of the party bosses." DuBois, "Working Women, Class Relations, and Suffrage Militancy," 179.

31. DuBois, *Harriot Stanton Blatch and the Winning of Woman Suffrage,* 92. Clara Burdette of California was criticized for acting like a politician because she set up campaign headquarters to run for the presidency of the General Federation of Women's Clubs (GFWC) in 1902. According to the *Los Angeles Times,* "This is one feature of politics as done by men that is particularly in disfavor with women. They believe implicitly that the office should seek the woman and not the woman the office." *Los Angeles Times,* May 6, 1902, qtd. in Miller, "Within the Bounds of Propriety," 115. The major question in the GFWC campaign that year concerned admitting black women's clubs.

32. Muncy, *Creating a Female Dominion in American Reform;* Davis, *Spearheads for Reform;* Breckenridge, *Women in the Twentieth Century;* Beard, *Woman's Work in Municipalities.*

33. Coss, *Lillian D. Wald;* Daniels, *Always a Sister;* Addams et al., *Philanthropy and Social Progress;* Addams, *Twenty Years At Hull House.*

34. Chambers, "Toward a Redefinition of Welfare History."

35. Muncy, *Creating a Female Dominion in American Reform,* 30; Sherrick, "Private Visions, Public Lives."

36. Addams, *Excellent Becomes the Permanent,* 6, 40.

37. For background on Jane Addams, see *NAW,* 1:16–22; Lasch, ed., *Social Thought of Jane Addams;* Davis, *American Heroine;* Farrell, *Beloved Lady;* and Levine, *Jane Addams and the Liberal Tradition.*

38. Addams, "Domestic Service and the Family Claim"; Addams, "College Woman and the Family Claim"; Antler, "'After College, What?'"

39. On the transfer of information between Europe and the United States, see Rodgers, *Atlantic Crossings*.

40. Addams, "Subjective Necessity for Social Settlements"; Addams, "Objective Necessity for Social Settlements"; Taylor, "Jane Addams' Twenty Years of Industrial Democracy," 405; Abbott, "Grace Abbott and Hull House," 502.

41. Sklar, "Hull House in the 1890s"; Sklar, *Florence Kelley and the Nation's Work*. For assessment by contemporaries, see Lathrop, "Florence Kelley," 677; and Perkins, "My Recollections of Florence Kelley."

42. For Illinois, see Muncy, *Creating a Female Dominion in American Reform*; and Sklar, "Hull House in the 1890s." For New York, see Perry, *Belle Moskowitz*; Dye, *As Equals and as Sisters*; and Payne, *Reform, Labor, and Feminism*. See also Trolander, *Professionalism and Social Change*.

43. Muncy, *Creating a Female Dominion in American Reform*, 33. For views of contemporaries, see Addams, *My Friend, Julia Lathrop*; Chenery, "Great Public Servant," 637–38; and Wald, "Right Woman in the Right Place."

44. Muncy, *Creating a Female Dominion in American Reform*, 33; Harmon, "Altgeld the Suffragist"; Larsen, *Good Fight*.

45. Muncy, *Creating a Female Dominion in American Reform*, 31. Church, *History of the Republican Party in Illinois*.

46. Davis, *American Heroine*, 122; Baker, "Hull House and the Ward Boss," 769–70; Nelli, "John Powers and the Italians."

47. Addams, *Second Twenty Years at Hull House*, 13–14; Levine, *Irish and Irish Politicians*; Green and Holli, eds., *Mayors*.

48. Davis, *American Heroine*, 127; Addams, *Democracy and Social Ethics*, 270–76; Addams, "Ethical Survivals in Municipal Corruption"; Boyer, *Urban Masses and Moral Order in America*.

49. Qtd. in Davis, *American Heroine*, 123.

50. Diner, *A City and Its Universities*; Flanagan, *Charter Reform in Chicago*; Ostrogorski, *Democracy and the Party System in the United States*; Macy, *Party Organization and Machinery*.

51. Kessler-Harris, *Out to Work*; Rosen, *Lost Sisterhood*; Ladd-Taylor, *Raising a Baby the Government Way*; Hine, *Black Women in White*.

52. Addams, *Second Twenty Years at Hull House*, 12–13.

53. Koven and Michel, "Womanly Duties."

54. Farrell, *Beloved Lady*, 122–23. Catherine McCulloch wrote to Alice Park to help her prepare California women for a campaign to increase mothers' rights over children: "If you fail to pass your bill and your associated women are indignant and complain that they really need the ballot to accomplish anything important for women, well you have taught the women a splendid object lesson. If you succeed, you have one law to your credit which will encourage you to press on." Catherine Waugh McCulloch to Alice Park, November 5, 1908, Park Collection, Huntington. See also Winter, *Alice Park of California*.

55. Buenker, "Urban Political Machine and Woman Suffrage."

56. *HWS*, 5:354; Scott and Scott, *One Half the People*; Davis, *American Heroine*, 188; Park, *Front Door Lobby*; Hackett, "Lady Who Made Lobbying Respectable"; Merk, "Early Career of Maud Wood Park."

57. *The Nation* tabulated the voting power of women. Colorado had 213,425 women of

voting age; Idaho had 69,818; Wyoming had 28,890; Utah had 85,729; and Washington had 277,727. By May, 671,396 women could also vote in California. *The Nation,* September 5, 1912, 201.

58. Only one year earlier Anna Howard Shaw, the president of the NAWSA and one of its most eloquent speakers, was prompted to note in a speech that it was a common belief that women would have "boxes of bonbons" as part of their platforms and that they would only vote for "handsome men or put ugly men in jail." Thus, even though women were making great strides in social reform circles, their connection to politics still brought ridicule. *New York Times,* January 30, 1911.

59. Aileen Kraditor states that suffragists in general moved from arguing on the basis of natural right and justice to arguing that women should be granted the vote for expedient reasons—where suffrage was a means to the principal goal of social reform. See Kraditor, *Ideas of the Woman Suffrage Movement,* for an overview of the changing suffrage movement. I agree with scholarship that emphasizes how both arguments coexisted after 1910. For an early example, see Nichols, "Votes and More for Women."

60. *HWS,* 5:346–63. See also Addams, "Why Women Should Vote," 21–22.

61. Sophonisba Breckinridge stated the "ballot is a labor saving device like the biscuit-machine. . . . Reforms will be gained even without the ballot. . . . but these things will be done much more wastefully, with much more labor, while women are limited to indirect methods. Life is too short and work too heavy for any talent to be overworked unnecessarily." *Woman's Journal,* May 18, 1912.

62. *HWS,* 5:346–63.

63. According to McCormick, the growth of government's involvement in social policy areas can be measured by the cost of government. "From 1894 to 1910, the yearly cost of government quadrupled from some $15 million to about $60 million." McCormick, "Prelude to Progressivism," 291.

64. *HWS,* 5:363.

65. *Official Report of the Proceedings of the Fifteenth Republican National Convention.* For background, see Mowry, *Theodore Roosevelt and the Progressive Movement;* Mowry, *Era of Theodore Roosevelt and the Rise of Modern America;* and Gable, *Bull Moose Years.*

66. *Progressive Bulletin,* December 7, 1912, 3; Pinchot, *History of the Progressive Party.*

67. Roosevelt, "Two Phases of the Chicago Convention," 620–30.

68. Davis, "Social Workers and the Progressive Party."

69. *Woman's Journal,* June 29, 1912.

70. Before and after the Republican convention, Roosevelt built his agenda around the term "New Nationalism" and called for stronger railroad regulation, a workmen's compensation law, prohibition of child labor, graduated income and inheritance taxes, the direct primary, the initiative and referendum, conservation, and welfare legislation. He believed these reforms could be obtained without class conflict and with responsible leadership provided by a restrained Republican insurgency. Cooper, *Warrior and the Priest,* 145–47. For the specific progressive goals that he saw abandoned by Taft, see Youngman, ed., *Theodore Roosevelt,* especially Roosevelt's "What is a Progressive?" address at Louisville, Kentucky, April 3, 1912.

71. Hagedorn, ed., *National Edition of the Works of Theodore Roosevelt,* 17:204–31.

72. *New York Herald,* August 11, 1912, Harriman Scrapbook.

73. *New York Herald,* June 20, 1912.

74. Martin, *Ballots and Bandwagons*, 153–54.

75. *New York Herald*, June 20, 1912.

76. *New York Times*, August 20, 1912.

77. *Official Report of the Proceedings of the Fifteenth Republican National Convention*.

78. Starr, *Inventing the American Dream*, 259.

79. "News Release, Los Angeles, March [1912?], A Great Rally, especially in the interests of women voters. . . ." Gifford Pinchot Papers, LC. See also *New York Times*, May 17, 1912.

80. Harger, "Two National Conventions," 6.

81. Roosevelt was not always a strong supporter of woman suffrage. He wrote to Carrie Chapman Catt in 1910 that, although he believed in suffrage, he did not consider it a question of "great practical importance in America." Theodore Roosevelt to Carrie Chapman Catt, NAWSA, May 6, 1910, Catt Papers, New York Public Library. In an article published in the *Outlook* in early 1912, Roosevelt stated that women should have the vote when they wanted it, but he did not believe it to be a vital issue. It would neither cause the "damage prophesied or bring the benefits promised." Roosevelt, "Women's Rights," 262 and 266. See also *New York Times*, February 24 and June 6, 1911.

82. The NAWSA group included Addams, Louise DeKoven Bowen, and Mary Barthelme of Chicago; Sophonisba Breckinridge of Kentucky; Mary Mumford of Virginia; Lillian Wald and Mary Kingsbury Simkhovitch of New York City; and Helen Todd of Illinois, but representing California.

83. *Woman's Journal*, June 29, 1912; *HWS*, 5:705.

84. *HWS*, 5:707. That the suffragists did not expect to be the center of attention in Chicago is evident in the fact that they decided to cancel their planned parade. As Jane Addams reported to the Official Board of the NAWSA, "there was little chance of press publicity for any issue outside of the convention proper." "Minutes of the Official Board Meeting of the NAWSA," June 5, 1912, *Jane Addams Papers*, microfilm. Social workers, who had just met in Cleveland for the National Conference of Charities and Corrections, also decided to attend the Republican convention. They found their "Platform of Industrial Minimums," a "program of minimum standards to help direct public thought and secure official action," also rejected by the platform committee. Davis, "Social Workers and the Progressive Party"; Johnson, ed., *Proceedings of the National Conference of Charities and Corrections*.

85. Collin, ed., *Theodore Roosevelt and Reform Politics;* Crunden, *Ministers of Reform;* Davis, *Released for Publication*.

86. Theodore Roosevelt to Horace Plunkett, August 3, 1912, in Morison, ed., *Letters of Theodore Roosevelt*, 7:591; Democratic National Committee, *Democratic Text-Book*.

87. "The Call for the New Party," *Outlook,* July 20, 1912, 601–2.

88. Jane Addams to Ben Lindsey, June 25, 1912; Ben Lindsey to Jane Addams, July 6, 1912, *Jane Addams Papers*, microfilm.

89. Jane Addams to Ben Lindsey, June 25, 1912, *Jane Addams Papers*, microfilm.

90. William Kent to Jane Addams, May 11, 1912, with enclosure of William Kent to Victor Lawson, *Daily News*, Chicago, May 10, 1911; Jane Addams to William Kent, May 15, 1911; Belle LaFollette to Jane Addams, January 22, 1912; Jane Addams to Belle LaFollette, February 5, 1912, *Jane Addams Papers*, microfilm.

91. Ben Lindsey to Jane Addams, July 6, 1912, *Jane Addams Papers*, microfilm.

92. *New York Times,* October 13, 1912.

93. Jane Addams to Lillian Wald, July 14, 1912; Jane Addams to Lillian Wald, August 17, 1912, Wald Papers, New York Public Library; Lillian Wald to Jane Addams, August 12, 1912, *Jane Addams Papers,* microfilm.

94. *New York Times,* September 26, 1912.

95. *New York Times,* August 18, 1912; George Perkins to Theodore Roosevelt, January 31, 1912, Perkins Papers, Columbia. See also Perkins, "Business and Government"; Garraty, *Right-Hand Man.*

96. The social workers were a "diverse group" because social work in 1912 was "more a cause than a profession." Davis, "Social Workers and the Progressive Party," 672. On the McCormicks, see Miller, *Ruth Hanna McCormick,* 33–57.

97. For the diversity of Progressives and for a comparison to the Republicans, see Gable, *Bull Moose Years,* chap. 2. For reasons why progressive Republicans and then Progressives were against Taft, see Wright, *Progressive Yankees,* 128; and Margulies, "LaFollette, Roosevelt, and the Republican Nomination of 1912."

98. Chauncey Dewey, chairman, Illinois Progressive Committee to Mrs. Raymond Robbins [*sic*], September 9, 1912, *Papers of the Women's Trade Union League and Its Principal Leaders,* microfilm; Catharine Waugh McCulloch to Grace Johnson, August 6, 1912, Johnson Papers, Schlesinger Library.

99. Perry, *Belle Moskowitz,* 77; Gable, *Bull Moose Years,* 267. Women were 25 percent of the 25th Congressional District of New York (White Plains) Progressive party Convention. *New York Times,* July 27, 1912.

100. *New York Times,* August 4, 1912. They included Mary Elisabeth Dreier of the Women's Trade Union League, reported to be the lone woman elected delegate-at-large; Frances A. Kellor, listed as an alternate-at-large; Anna Brown, reported to have been elected secretary of the delegation. Brown, an active suffragist and president of the New York City Federation of Women's Clubs, and Clara B. Morrison, the sister-in-law of Timothy Woodruff, the former Republican boss of Brooklyn, also served as district representatives at the New York County Convention of the Progressive party, held on August 1 at Carnegie Hall. The county convention also elected Augusta C. Houghton and Pauline Goldmark as alternates to the state convention. Goldmark, Mrs. Robert H. Elder, and Madeline Doty joined the other women in attendance at the National Progressive Convention in Chicago. For Dreier, see *NAW: The Modern Period,* 204–6. For Kellor, see *NAW: The Modern Period,* 393–95; and Fitzpatrick, *Endless Crusade,* 130–65. For Brown, see Leonard, comp., *Woman's Who's Who of America,* 132; and *New York Times,* August 1, 1912. Goldmark was chair of the Legislative Committee of the Consumers' League of New York. Martha Wentworth Suffren, vice president of the New York Woman Suffrage Party, wrote to Timothy Woodruff asking for five seats for the suffragists at the Kings County Convention, held July 23. *Woman's Journal,* July 20, 1912.

101. For women elected by judicial districts, see *Progressive Bulletin,* September 1912, 7.

102. *New York Times,* August 11, 1912. Hotchkiss explained that the law required a party to have cast ten thousand votes for governor before it was entitled to an emblem or to go on the primary ballot. Gable argues that the New York ticket was "distinguished" and included men who either possessed political power in the state or who were seeking to regain power by joining the new party. Gable, *Bull Moose Years,* 39 and 47.

103. Fitzpatrick, *Endless Crusade,* 135–37; Kellor, *Out of Work;* Kellor, "Protection of Immigrant Women," 250–54.

104. Bennett, *American Women in Civic Work,* 163–82.

105. See Theodore Roosevelt to William Hulbert, December 23, 1911, in Morison, ed., *Letters of Theodore Roosevelt,* 7:465.

106. Theodore Roosevelt to James Wilson, December 10, 1906, in Morison, ed., *Letters of Theodore Roosevelt,* 5:523; Frances Kellor to Theodore Roosevelt, August 1, 1911; and Theodore Roosevelt to Frances Kellor, August 5, 1911, Roosevelt Papers, LC.

107. Nathan, *Story of an Epoch-Making Movement.* Nathan does not give a date for this meeting. See also Kelley, "Twenty-five Years of the Consumers' League Movement."

108. Nathan, *Once upon a Time and Today,* 142.

109. Described in early press reports as a "prominent club woman," Carpenter was born in Chicago in 1875 and attended Smith College in Northampton, Massachusetts. For three years she worked at the Elizabeth Peabody Settlement House in Boston, and her work there provided her with a bridge to suffrage activism and then to party politics. Leonard, comp., *Woman's Who's Who of America,* 161; *Berkshire Evening Eagle,* February 12, 1912, Garrison Family Papers, SSC.

110. Also elected as delegates were Grace Johnson, a notable suffragist; Mrs. Richard Washburn Child, who was one of the few women to identify herself as an antisuffragist; and Elizabeth Towne. Maud Wood Park was elected, but she declined. *Boston Post,* July 28, August 6, 1912; *Woman's Journal,* August 3, 1912; *New York Times,* July 28, 1912.

111. Another active Massachusetts woman was Clara Cahill Park, a vice president of the Massachusetts branch of the National Congress of Mothers and an appointed member of Governor Eugene Noble Foss's commission to study the needs of widowed mothers. Park, like Nathan, is representative of the diversity of alliances between reformers and politicians in the first decade of the twentieth century. The wife of the sociologist Robert Park, she had also lobbied politicians and received recognition for her work for "child rescue" and mothers' pensions. This work brought her into contact with social workers and led Roosevelt to call the 1909 Conference on the Care of Dependent Children. That conference laid the groundwork for the formation of the Children's Bureau. Leonard, comp., *Woman's Who's Who of America,* 619; Crunden, *Ministers of Reform,* 89. On the crusade for "child rescue," see the *Delineator* magazine for 1908 and 1909. Rothman, "State as Parent"; "T. R. Only President to Halt Grabbers," newspaper clipping, November 2, 1912, in Gifford Pinchot Papers, LC. This clipping also lists progressive women who worked in Philadelphia.

112. *New York Times,* August 4, 1912; correspondence of Eleanor Garrison and her mother, Garrison Family Papers, SSC.

113. "The Roosevelt Party Movement," *Independent,* July 18, 1912, 153.

114. "List of All the States," Progressive Party Papers, Roosevelt Collection, Houghton; *Woman's Journal,* August 3, 1912; *New York Times,* August 5, 1912; Gable, *Bull Moose Years,* 49. On California politics, see Mowry, *California Progressives;* and Olin, *California's Prodigal Sons.*

115. "List of All the States," Progressive Party Papers, Roosevelt Collection, Houghton. Colorado's delegate was Dr. Maud Sanders of Denver; Mrs. Dudley Dorn and Allison Stocker were the alternates. Also attending from Colorado was Gail Laughlin, a lawyer and grad-

uate of Wellesley College and Cornell Law School. She was appointed to the U.S. Industrial Commission in 1900, and, when she moved to Colorado, she was appointed to the Colorado State Board of Pardons. She was also an active suffragist and toured California in 1911 for the cause. In 1912 she was vice president of the Colorado Equal Suffrage Association. Utah's two delegates were Mrs. C. J. Adams of Ogden and Eliza B. Smith of Salt Lake City. Leonard, comp., *Woman's Who's Who of America,* 478. On Gail Laughlin, see *NAW: The Modern Period,* 410–11. Minnie Williams of Park County, Wyoming, is listed in the Progressive party records under the heading "State and County Chairman List, 1912."

116. Mary Hawes Wilmarth was a graduate of Kimball Union Academy and one of the first members of the board of trustees for Hull-House. Another important Illinois woman Progressive was Louise DeKoven Bowen.

117. Abba [Elizabeth?] Bass to Jane Addams, [July 1912], *Jane Addams Papers,* microfilm. Richberg, *Tents of the Mighty,* 36.

118. *Woman's Journal,* August 3, 1912.

119. *New York Times,* August 4, 1912.

Chapter 5: A Contest for Inclusion

1. Theodore Roosevelt to Jane Addams, August 16, 1912, *Jane Addams Papers,* microfilm.

2. William Allen White, "Noted Men Work on Platform," newspaper clipping, [August 5, 1912], Johnson Papers, Schlesinger Library; Washburn, "Roosevelt and the 1912 Campaign"; Rowell, "Building of the Progressive Platform," 5.

3. "Minutes of the National Committee of the Progressive Party," August 7, 1912, Progressive Party Papers, Roosevelt Collection, Houghton; Eleanor Garrison to Mother, August 6, 1912, Garrison Family Papers, SSC. According to the *Boston Post,* Carpenter was the "first of her sex" to hold this honor. *Boston Post,* July 28, 1912.

4. Eleanor Garrison to Mother, August 6, 1912, Garrison Family Papers, SSC.

5. Gable, *Bull Moose Years,* 76; "Progressive Party," *Literary Digest,* August 17, 1912; "A Comparison of the Platforms of the Progressive Party and of the Social Scientists—As to Social and Industrial Justice," Progressive Party Papers, Roosevelt Collection, Houghton. The platform of the social scientists was based on the Committee on Standards of Living and Labor of the National Conference of Charities and Corrections and was written at the Cleveland, Ohio, meeting of June 1912. Addams's speech there was "The Child at the Point of Greatest Pressure." Johnson, ed., *Proceedings of the National Conference of Charities and Corrections.*

6. *Survey,* August 24, 1912, 668–770.

7. Gable, *Bull Moose Years,* 82–85; *Independent,* August 15, 1912, 391; *Progressive Bulletin,* September 1912.

8. The writer and origins of the plank are unclear. According to the *Woman's Journal,* Victor Hugo Duras of Lincoln, Nebraska, asked the New York Woman Suffrage Party to prepare the suffrage plank, and they forwarded the letter to Anna Howard Shaw of the NAWSA. *Woman's Journal,* July 20, 1912. Other information suggests that numerous women had a say in the writing of the early drafts. See Elizabeth Piper to Grace Johnson, July 22, 1912, Johnson Papers, Schlesinger Library; "Platform Drafts," Progressive Party Papers, Roosevelt Collection, Houghton. The equal suffrage plank was different in state Progressive party platforms.

9. "Following the Campaign," *Outlook,* August 24, 1912, 912–16.

10. Addams, *Excellent Becomes the Permanent,* 97, 106; David Starr Jordan to Jane Addams, November 25, 1912, *Jane Addams Papers,* microfilm. The battleships were part of a thirty million dollar naval appropriations bill passed by the House and under consideration in the Senate (H.R. 24565).

11. Addams, "Progressive's Dilemma"; Addams, "Communion of the Ballot"; Addams, "Why I Went into Politics"; Addams, "Politics and Philanthropy."

12. Addams, "Progressive's Dilemma"; Addams, *Second Twenty Years at Hull House,* 23–45.

13. Addams, "What the Progressive Party Means to Women," *Progressive Bulletin,* October 21, 1912, 7, Progressive Party Papers, Roosevelt Collection, Houghton; "Jane Addams Relates the Steps by Which She Became a Progressive," *Progressive Bulletin,* December 28, 1912, 2; "Explains Aid to Colonel," *Chicago Daily Tribune,* August 15, 1912, clipping, Johnson Papers, Schlesinger Library; Addams, "Pragmatism in Politics."

14. *Woman's Journal,* September 27, 1912.

15. Addams, *Second Twenty Years at Hull House,* 32.

16. Elizabeth Piper to Grace Johnson, July 22, 1912, Johnson Papers, Schlesinger Library; Victor Hugo Duras to Anna H. Shaw, *Woman's Journal,* July 13, 1912.

17. No roll call votes were taken at the convention, and the platform and nominees were accepted by acclamation.

18. *Woman's Journal,* August 10, 1912.

19. *Progressive Bulletin,* September 1912, 11; Gable, *Bull Moose Years,* 267.

20. For a list of the delegates, see Gustafson, "Partisan Women," 227–28.

21. *New York Times,* August 11, 1912.

22. *New York Times,* July 26, 1912.

23. Felton, the widow of a Georgia congressman, became famous in 1922 when she was appointed as the first woman U.S. senator to replace Tom Watson. Her appointment lasted less than a day. Chafe, *Paradox of Change,* 33–34; Wheeler, *New Women of the New South,* 191–92.

24. "Following the Campaign," *Outlook,* August 24, 1912, 912–16.

25. Ruhl, "Bull Moose Call," 20–21.

26. *New York Times,* August 7, 1912.

27. Jane Addams, "Seconding Speech for the Nomination of Theodore Roosevelt, Proceedings of the National Progressive Party," *National Progressive Program, 1912,* Progressive Party Papers, Roosevelt Collection, Houghton; Abbott, "Progressive Convention," 857–64; Lowry, "With the Bull Moose in Convention."

28. Ruhl, "Bull Moose Call," 20–21. See also Belmont, *Fabric of Memory,* 101–2.

29. Eleanor Garrison to Mother, August 6, 1912, Garrison Family Papers, SSC.

30. Abbott, "Progressive Convention." On the earlier use of red bandannas in campaigns, see Thieme, "'Wave High the Red Bandanna.'"

31. Ruhl, "Bull Moose Call," 20. Ruhl's claim of Addams as a first for women was inaccurate. Mary Elizabeth Lease seconded the nomination of James Weaver at the Populist convention in 1892.

32. *New York Times,* August 11, 1912.

33. Addams, *Twenty Years at Hull House,* 39.

34. Ibid., 44; Addams, *Second Twenty Years at Hull House,* 23–45; *New York Times,* Sep-

tember 26, 1912; *Progressive Bulletin,* December 28, 1912; clipping [*Boston Journal,* n.d.], in Johnson Papers, Schlesinger Library; *Woman's Journal,* November 2, 1912.

35. *Munsey's,* November 1912. This editorial states that Addams was "the proper kind of recruit for the big battle of national politics. The campaign gets added dignity and distinction because of her cooperation." See also Addams, "Why Women Should Vote," 21–22; Abbott, "Progressive Convention"; Lowry, "With the Bull Moose in Convention"; "Following the Campaign," *Outlook,* August 24, 1912; and *New York Times,* August 7, 1912.

36. The "Mother Emancipator" is from the *Boston American,* February 15, 1911. See also *Progressive Bulletin,* September 1912; Davis, *American Heroine,* 162–65; and Crunden, *Ministers of Reform,* 68.

37. William Monroe Trotter to Jane Addams, telegram, August 6/7, 1912, *Jane Addams Papers,* microfilm. For information on the relationship between African-American and white suffragists, see Harley and Terborg-Penn, eds., *Afro-American Woman;* Wheeler, ed., *Votes for Women!*

38. Gilmore, *Gender and Jim Crow;* Casdorph, *Republicans, Negroes, and Progressives in the South;* Woodward, *Strange Career of Jim Crow;* Kousser, *Shaping of Southern Politics;* Lewinson, *Race, Class and Party.*

39. W. E. B. Du Bois began calling for a "black exodus from the Republican party" in 1908. Lewis, *W. E. B. Du Bois,* 34. See also *Boston Guardian,* July 27 and November 2, 1907, February 29 and August 15, 1908. William Monroe Trotter stated that the Republican hold over the ballot made the black vote like a "chained elephant." Fox, *Guardian of Boston,* 36.

40. *New York Age,* July 18, 1912.

41. On Brownsville, see Thornbrough, "Brownsville Episode and the Negro Vote." Early in his presidency Roosevelt garnered African-American support when he invited Booker T. Washington to dine at the White House; appointed Dr. William Crum to the influential post of collector at the Port of Charleston, South Carolina; and refused to appoint a white person to the post office at Indianola, Mississippi, after Minnie Cox was run out of town by whites. As early as 1903 William Monroe Trotter was writing in the *Boston Guardian* that African-American criticism of Roosevelt was on "race grounds, not on partisan grounds." *Boston Guardian,* December 26, 1903. See also Gatewood, *Theodore Roosevelt and the Art of Controversy.*

42. For the notion of "shared culture," see Levine, *Highbrow/Lowbrow,* 1–22. For a good overview of cultural theory, see Walters, *Material Girls.*

43. White Republican clubs grew slowly in the South between 1888 and 1892 but grew rapidly after 1896. See Walton, *Negro in Third Party Politics,* 47; Mowry, "South and the Progressive Lily-White Party of 1912."

44. Although southern African Americans were disfranchised, they remained active in Republican parties in their states and attended the national conventions of the party. They could not run for office in their states, but they could be delegates to conventions. The move by white southern Republicans to make state parties and conventions lily-white was therefore a move to remove African Americans from politics altogether.

45. Link, "Theodore Roosevelt and the South in 1912"; Hirshson, *Farewell to the Bloody Shirt.*

46. "Official Report of the Provisional National Progressive Committee," 33, Progressive Party Papers, Roosevelt Collection, Houghton.

47. Ibid., 47.

48. The racial construction of the question of Hawaii's representation occurred within the context of political debate in California about Chinese and Japanese exclusion and property rights. Heney was from California and was concerned about the political effect of the "question of oriental immigration" in his state. See James Phelan to William McCombs, March 6, 1912, Phelan Papers, Bancroft.

49. The events in Florida were complicated; neither Anderson nor Alston seems to have played fair politics. Casdorph, *Republicans, Negroes, and Progressives in the South,* 128–30; Green, "Republicans, Bull Moose, and Negroes in Florida."

50. African Americans had been disfranchised in Mississippi by the constitutional convention of 1890 but continued to be active in Republican party politics. Mississippi was called the "model disfranchisement state" because it had a poll tax but no grandfather clause, which limited the vote of illiterate whites. See Woodward, *Origins of the New South,* 321–22.

51. Howard and his half-brother, Sidney Redmond, supported Roosevelt throughout the campaign of 1912, a fact not ignored by Roosevelt. On June 11, just before the Republican National Convention, Roosevelt wrote Redmond and hinted that he wanted Howard to second his nomination as the Republican candidate for President. Theodore Roosevelt to Sidney Redmond, June 11, 1912, Roosevelt Papers, LC.

52. *Chicago Daily Tribune,* August 6, 1912; *New York Times,* August 4, 1912; "Official Report of the Provisional Progressive Committee," Progressive Party Papers, Roosevelt Collection, Houghton.

53. *Chicago Daily Tribune,* August 6, 1912; "Official Report of the Provisional Progressive Committee," Progressive Party Papers, Roosevelt Collection, Houghton; Schott, "John M. Parker of Louisiana and the Bull Moose Progressive Party in State and Nation."

54. Roosevelt, "Progressives and the Colored Man," 909–12.

55. *New York Tribune,* August 6, 1912.

56. Frank J. Garrison to Eleanor Garrison, telegram, n.d., Garrison Family Papers, SSC.

57. Eleanor Garrison to Mother, August 7, 1912, Garrison Family Papers, SSC.

58. *New York Times,* August 7, 1912; "Resolutions Committee," Progressive Party Papers, Roosevelt Collection, Houghton. For a variation on this plank, see box 10, Spingarn Papers, New York Public Library.

59. Lewis, *W. E. B. Du Bois,* 422; "Along the Color Line," *Crisis,* August 1912.

60. *Crisis,* December 1911, November 1912. The NAACP's *Crisis,* under Du Bois's editorial control, encouraged northern blacks to support Wilson. Wiseman, "Racism in Democratic Politics."

61. *New York Times,* August 18 and August 21, 1912. For more on women and the Democratic party in 1912, see Gustafson, "Partisan Women."

62. *New York Times,* August 6 and August 8 1912; *Pittsburgh Courier,* August 9, 1912. For an excellent state-level examination, see Flamming, "African-Americans and the Politics of Race in Progressive-Era Los Angeles."

63. The *Republican Campaign Text-Book, 1912,* had a section called the Afro-American Citizen, which listed black employees of the U.S. government, appointments and retained appointments, officers of the army, the fight against peonage, and the disfranchisement of southerners. See also Sherman, *Republican Party and Black America,* 104; Johnson, comp., *National Party Platforms,* 160; and Casdorph, *Republicans, Negroes, and Progressives in the South,* 7.

64. P. C. Allen to Jane Addams, August 6, 1912; Mary McDowell to Jane Addams, August 7, 1912; Wharton Barker to Jane Addams, August 6, 1912, *Jane Addams Papers*, microfilm. Dr. Reverdy C. Ransom, editor of the *A.M.E. Review* and an influential Republican, said at a mass meeting of African Americans in New York City: "Among other things, I pinned my faith to Miss Jane Addams, whom I have the honor to call my friend. She is one of the choice spirits of all this earth. But even she, one of the rarest and noblest among the daughters of men, surrendered the cause of justice for the colored fellow-citizens to secure things she valued more, in her splendid program of social and civic uplift." *New York Age*, August 29, 1912.

65. George William Cook to Jane Addams, August 17, 1912; N. F. Mossel to Jane Addams, August 8, 1912; Colored Women's Civic Club of Indianapolis to Jane Addams, August 6, 1912; J. F. Ransom to Jane Addams, August 6, 1912, *Jane Addams Papers*, microfilm.

66. Theophile T. Allain to Jane Addams, August 9, 1912, *Jane Addams Papers*, microfilm.

67. "Know the Truth! Statement from the Entire Colored Delegation of the National Progressive Party Convention," Progressive Party Papers, Roosevelt Collection, Houghton. Another pamphlet explaining the party's stand on race, "The Negro Question," reprinted Roosevelt's letter to Harris. "The Negro Question: The Attitude of the Progressive Party towards the Colored Race," Progressive Party Papers, Roosevelt Collection, Houghton; *Crisis*, October 1912; "Negroes against Taft: Conference of Bishops and Clergy Issues an Appeal to Their Race," flyer, March 12, 1912, Gifford Pinchot Papers, LC.

68. *Progressive Bulletin*, October 7, 1912; *Outlook*, August 24, 1912; Gerstle, "Theodore Roosevelt and the Divided Character of American Nationalism."

69. Theodore Roosevelt to Julian Harris, August 1, 1912, in Morison, ed., *Letters of Theodore Roosevelt*, 7:584–90.

70. *Crisis*, December 1912.

71. Addams, "Progressive Party and the Negro."

72. *New York Times*, October 13, 1912.

73. Addams, "My Experiences as a Progressive Delegate."

74. In using press reports for this evaluation I realize that I am actually seeing what the press saw as noteworthy about women's participation. It is clear that most reporters found it difficult to represent Addams as other than a suffragist or a representative of her sex.

75. Addams, "My Experiences as a Progressive Delegate."

76. Dewey, *Characters and Events*, 91–92.

77. Theodore Roosevelt to Julian Harris, August 1, 1912, in Morison, ed., *Letters of Theodore Roosevelt*, 7:584–90.

78. For insights into the connections between nation-building and political struggles, see Cohen, "Nationalism and Suffrage."

79. Sherman, *Republican Party and Black America*, 108.

80. *Kelly Miller's Monographic Magazine*, May 1913. Sherman agrees that never before had so many turned against the Republican party. Sherman, *Republican Party and Black America*, 111.

81. Martel, "Woman's Part in the Campaign."

82. Grace Johnson to Mrs. Child, n.d., Johnson Papers, Schlesinger Library.

83. "Our Brilliant Ladies Recognized," newspaper clipping, Chicago, December 21, 1911, Irene McCoy Gaines Papers, Chicago Historical Society. It is not clear whether they were working only before the convention or continued after. I would like to thank Lisa Mater-

son for sharing this clipping with me. Gaines remained active in Illinois Republican politics; she was president of the Illinois Federation of Republican Colored Women's Clubs from 1924 to 1935 and ran for state representative in 1940. *BWA*, 1:476. For Gaines's work with Ruth Hanna McCormick, see Miller, *Ruth Hanna McCormick*, 92, 131, 207–8, 211.

84. *Pittsburgh Courier,* October 11, 1912.

85. In 1911 Terrell participated in a celebration of Harriet Beecher Stowe as a way to support the memory of Lincoln and the life of the Republican party. Terrell Papers, LC. Higginbotham, "In Politics to Stay."

86. *New York Times,* August 11, 1912; Edith Hooker to Jane Addams, August 6, 1912, *Jane Addams Papers,* microfilm.

87. *New York Times,* September 26, 1912; Addams, "Pragmatism in Politics," 12.

88. Mary Dreier to Lillian Wald, [1912], Wald Papers, New York Public Library.

89. *New York Times,* September 26, 1912.

90. *Woman's Journal,* September 14, 1912.

91. *Woman's Journal,* October 12, 1912.

92. *Woman's Journal,* November 2, 1912.

93. Ida Husted Harper, letter to the editor, *New York Times,* August 10, 1912.

94. "Crisis of the Woman Suffrage Party," *Outlook,* December 28, 1912, 931–34.

95. *Woman's Political World,* January 6, 1913, 2; Harriot Stanton Blatch to Jane Addams, August 12, 1912, *Jane Addams Papers,* microfilm; *New York Times,* September 6, 1912.

96. *Woman's Protest,* May 1915, 14.

97. Addams, "Why I Seconded Roosevelt's Nomination," 257; *New York Times,* August 11, 1912.

98. Jane Addams, letter to the editor, *New York Times,* August 23, 1912; Ida Husted Harper to Jane Addams, n.d., *Jane Addams Papers,* microfilm.

99. Jane Addams to Anna Howard Shaw, August 20, 1912, *Jane Addams Papers,* microfilm; *New York Times,* November 26, 1912.

100. Anna Howard Shaw to Jane Addams, August 16, 1912, *Jane Addams Papers,* microfilm.

101. *Chicago Daily Tribune,* August 15, 1912; *New York Times,* August 15, 1912. When Carrie Chapman Catt asked Lillian Wald of Henry Street to run for the New York state legislature in 1909, she warned Wald: "I do not know the conditions under which your settlement house is maintained and you may need to consult with those who are financial sponsors of it. They may think it a foolish notion." Carrie Chapman Catt to Lillian Wald, [1909], Wald Papers, New York Public Library. See also Sklar, "Who Funded Hull House?" Addams was concerned about the response of Hull-House supporters to her work for the Progressives, but her inquiries led her to believe that supporting the Progressives was not a problem. Charles Hutchinson to Jane Addams, August 5, 1912, *Jane Addams Papers,* microfilm.

102. *New York Times,* August 11 and August 22, 1912; *New York Tribune,* August 14, 1912.

103. *HWS,* 5:332–36; Addams, "Communion of the Ballot"; Carrie Chapman Catt, "Political Parties and Women Voters: Address Delivered to the Congress of the League of Women Voters, Chicago, 1920," History of Women Microfilm Collection, no. 9181, Schlesinger Library.

104. John Kingsbury to Jane Addams, August 15, 1912; Mary McDowell to Jane Addams, August 16, 1912, *Jane Addams Papers,* microfilm.

105. "Ten Reasons Why Women Should Join the Progressive Party," Progressive party pamphlet, Johnson Papers, Schlesinger Library.

106. *Philadelphia North American,* November 2, 1912, clipping, Gifford Pinchot Papers, LC. For women's discussions of the tariff in the nineteenth century, see Edwards, *Angels in the Machinery.*

107. *Woman's Journal,* November 2, 1912.

108. *New York Times,* October 13, 1912.

109. Jane Addams to Julia Kent, December 12, 1911, *Jane Addams Papers,* microfilm.

110. Jane Addams to Alde Blake, July 13, 1912, *Jane Addams Papers,* microfilm; *Woman's Journal,* August 31, 1912.

111. "Why Women Should Vote for Roosevelt," Gifford Pinchot Papers, LC. Publicity was not only about getting supporters; it was also seen as a way to keep parties from being bossed. See Welsh, "Campaign Committees."

112. Kellor, "What Women Can Do," *Progressive Bulletin,* September 1912, 7.

113. Ibid.

114. *Progressive Bulletin,* September 23, 1912, 6.

115. "From the Women Delegates to the National Convention of the Progressive Party to the Women of the United States," *Jane Addams Papers,* microfilm.

116. Ibid. Another example is the pamphlet "Ten Reasons Why Women Should Join the Progressive Party," which claims that the party is the first great political party to seriously consider the needs of women and children; it supports humanitarian laws; it has in its ranks the best people in the nation; it has "made a religion of politics"; it does things practically; it supports equal suffrage; it educates women for politics; it pledges absolute equality of rights to men and women to the full extent of each state's laws; it needs women to become a majority; and it "puts devotion to principle ahead of immediate success at the polls." "Ten Reasons Why Women Should Join the Progressive Party," pamphlet, Johnson Papers, Schlesinger Library.

117. "Women! Do Something!" Flier, *Jane Addams Papers,* microfilm.

118. "Program for Women's Organization within the Progressive Party in Non-suffrage States," *Jane Addams Papers,* microfilm. See also "A Message to All Women (By a Woman): What You Can Do for the Nation," *Progressive Bulletin,* September 30, 1912, 10.

119. Clipping, n.p., n.d., Johnson Papers, Schlesinger Library; "Declaration of Principles," flier, Progressive Party Papers, Roosevelt Collection, Houghton.

120. "Clubs the Best Vote Makers," *Progressive Bulletin,* December 7, 1912, 4–5; "The Political Campaign," *Independent,* September 12, 1912, 583, 623.

121. Florence Porter, Katherine Edson, and Cora Deal Lewis were vice presidents on a board of six. Porter, Edson, and Lewis also sat on the forty-five-member Campaign Committee. Sixteen women, including these three, sat on the 158-member Executive Committee. Florence Porter to Jane Addams, August 16, 1912; "Roosevelt Progressive Republican League," Los Angeles, 1912, *Jane Addams Papers,* microfilm.

122. Juliet Rublee was a state committeewoman from New Hampshire, as was Maud Howe Elliott from Rhode Island.

123. *Progressive Bulletin,* September 16, 1912, 7.

124. Sophonisba Breckinridge to Jane Addams, September 7, 1912, *Jane Addams Papers,* microfilm.

125. Between October 18 and 24, the Women's Finance Committee raised $3950.95; the

People's Dollar Campaign raised $2237.90. Information on campaign contributions can be found in Progressive Party Papers, boxes 3 and 4, Roosevelt Collection, Houghton.

126. *Independent,* August 8, 1912, 333.

127. Elton Hooker claimed that the problem was that people were ready to believe that funding for parties came from corporations, and the Progressives were having a hard time educating the people that they needed to fund the party. Elton Hooker to Joel Spingarn, February 27, 1913, Spingarn Papers, New York Public Library. The Progressive National Committee had about $675,000 to spend on the national campaign, while state and local committees were financially weak. Mowry, "Progressive Party," 2558.

128. Margaret Dreier Robins to Mary Dreier, September 24, 1912, *Papers of the Women's Trade Union League and Its Principal Leaders,* microfilm.

129. Robinson, "Distribution of the Presidential Vote of 1912."

Chapter 6: *Partisan Women, 1912–16*

1. *New York Tribune,* August 14, 1912, Harriman Scrapbook.

2. *New York Times,* August 11, 1912.

3. *New York Tribune,* August 14, 1912, Harriman Scrapbook.

4. *New York Herald,* August 11, 1912, Harriman Scrapbook.

5. Upon the death of Foster, Roosevelt wrote Boswell: "I mourn the death of your mother. I respected her with all my heart; I valued her as a friend, and I admired her as a citizen in the highest sense of the word. Pray accept my deep and sincere sympathy." Theodore Roosevelt to Helen Boswell, August 16, 1910, Roosevelt Papers, LC.

6. *New York World,* August 19, 1912, Harriman Scrapbook.

7. *Milwaukee Sentinel,* October 13, 1912, Harriman Scrapbook.

8. *Shreveport (La.) Times,* August 20, 1912, Harriman Scrapbook; *New York Tribune,* August 22, 1912.

9. *New York Tribune,* September 4, 1912.

10. *New York Tribune,* August 22, 1912.

11. *Peoria (Ill.) Star,* October 18, 1912, Harriman Scrapbook.

12. *Evening Sun,* August 19, 1912, Harriman Scrapbook.

13. *Evening Sun,* September 3, 1912, Harriman Scrapbook.

14. Ibid.

15. Unidentified clipping, Harriman Scrapbook.

16. Qtd. in Mowry, "Progressive Party," 2559.

17. Theodore Roosevelt to Millicent Garrett Fawcett, November 19, 1912, in Morison, ed., *Letters of Theodore Roosevelt,* 7:650–51.

18. Theodore Roosevelt to Jane Addams, [August 8, 1912], in Morison, ed., *Letters of Theodore Roosevelt,* 7:594. See also Theodore Roosevelt to Arthur Hamilton Lee, November 5, 1912, in Morison, ed., *Letters of Theodore Roosevelt,* 7:633: "I have deeply prized [Addams's] support. There were points when I had to drag her forward, notably as regards our battleship program, for she is a disciple of Tolstoi, but she is a really good woman who had done practical work for the betterment of social conditions."

19. Theodore Roosevelt to Mr. and Mrs. Robins, November 7, 1912, *Papers of the Women's Trade Union League and Its Principal Leaders,* microfilm.

20. Jane Addams to Theodore Roosevelt, November 20, 1912, *Jane Addams Papers,* mi-

crofilm; Addams, "Lessons of the Election," 362; Addams, "Larger Aspects of the Women's Movement."

21. Mary E. Mumford to Hiram Johnson, November 15, 1912, Johnson Papers, Bancroft.

22. Eleanor Garrison to Mother, November 10, 1912, Garrison Family Papers, SSC.

23. Eleanor Garrison to Mother, November 12, 1912, Garrison Family Papers, SSC.

24. *Progressive Bulletin,* December 14, 1912, 3–4; *Progressive Bulletin,* December 28, 1912, 4. Charles McCarthy had created the Wisconsin Legislative Reference Library in 1901, a prototype for the Progressive Service. McCarthy, *Wisconsin Idea.*

25. "A Program Not Partisanship," *Progressive Bulletin,* December 21, 1912, 7.

26. Gable, *Bull Moose Years,* 163. The *Progressive Bulletin* was published out of the Munsey Building in Washington, D.C. The Legislative Reference Bureau of the Progressive Service had the task of drafting bills to present to legislatures. A Bureau of Education and Publicity worked to promote the issues. The other four departments were: Social and Industrial Justice; Conservation; Popular Government; and the Cost of Living and Corporation Control. About thirty positions as chairs, directors, committee leaders, and secretaries were created. "Plan of Work," presented to the National Committee, December 11, 1912, Progressive Party Papers, Roosevelt Collection, Houghton.

27. "Progressive Service Documents, 1st Quarterly Report of the Progressive National Service," March 31, 1913, Amos Pinchot Papers, LC; Katherine Coman to Jane Addams, January 1, 1913, *Jane Addams Papers,* microfilm. For names of the members, see Gustafson, *Partisan Women,* 283–86.

28. "Minutes of the National Committee of the Progressive Party," May 23, 1913, Progressive Party Papers, Roosevelt Collection, Houghton.

29. On factionalism within the party, see the Roosevelt letters and Morison's comments for the correspondence of 1913–16, in Morison, ed., *Letters of Theodore Roosevelt,* vols. 7 and 8.

30. Eleanor Garrison to Jane Addams, August 24, 1912, *Jane Addams Papers,* microfilm.

31. "Minutes of the Executive Committee of the National Committee of the Progressive Party," Progressive Party Papers, Roosevelt Collection, Houghton.

32. "Minutes of National Committee, April 13, 1914," Progressive Party Papers, Roosevelt Collection, Houghton.

33. *New York Times,* April 13, 1915.

34. "Nena Jolidon Croake, Mystery Feminist of Tacoma," *Tacoma News Tribune,* August 4, 1994.

35. *Progressive Bulletin,* February 1913, 5.

36. *Progressive Bulletin,* March 1913, 9; Harold Ickes to Jane Addams, January 6, 1912 [probably 1913], and Harriet Lowenstein, "Summary of Work for week ending August 31, 1912," *Jane Addams Papers,* microfilm.

37. Thomas Robins to Theodore Roosevelt, November 27, 1912, *Jane Addams Papers,* microfilm.

38. Silverman, "Reform as a Means of Social Control"; Silverman, "Theodore Roosevelt and Women"; Testi, "Gender of Reform Politics."

39. For another example, see the problems between Donald Richberg and Frances Kellor, Richberg Papers, LC.

40. Eleanor Garrison to Mother, March 13, 1913, Garrison Family Papers, SSC.

41. Some party members revealed a good deal of anger, disappointment, and worry about how much they or others were paid for their work. See, for example, Josephine Stricker to Elon Hooker, April 14, 1916, Progressive Party Papers, Roosevelt Collection, Houghton.

42. Alice Carpenter to George Perkins, July 5, [1914]; George Perkins to Alice Carpenter, telegram, July 21, 1914; Alice Carpenter to Theodore Roosevelt, telegram, [July 27, 1914], Progressive Party Papers, Roosevelt Collection, Houghton.

43. George Perkins to Alice Carpenter, July 29, 1914, Progressive Party Papers, Roosevelt Collection, Houghton.

44. Alice Carpenter to George Perkins, August 3, 1914, Progressive Party Papers, Roosevelt Collection, Houghton.

45. George Perkins to Alice Carpenter, August 7, 1914, Progressive Party Papers, Roosevelt Collection, Houghton.

46. Alice Carpenter to George Perkins, August 10, 1914, September 16, 1914; George Perkins to Alice Carpenter, September 17, 1914, Progressive Party Papers, Roosevelt Collection, Houghton.

47. See, for example, the Frances Kellor correspondence in Progressive Party Papers, Roosevelt Collection, Houghton.

48. See 1914 entries in "Black Notebook," Gifford Pinchot Papers, LC; "Kansas Women Organize," *Progressive Bulletin,* December 28, 1912, 8; "Minutes of the Executive Committee of the National Committee of the Progressive Party," January 10, 1913, Progressive Party Papers, Roosevelt Collection, Houghton; "To the Women Voters . . . ," Johnson Papers, Schlesinger Library; "Progressive Party, List of Chairmen," *Jane Addams Papers,* microfilm.

49. *Progressive Bulletin,* April 1913, 4.

50. Eleanor Garrison to Mother, 1913, Garrison Family Papers, SSC.

51. "First Quarterly Report, Progressive National Service," March 31, 1913, Amos Pinchot Papers, LC.

52. "Minutes of the Women's Committee of the Progressive party, Chicago," December 12, 1912, *Jane Addams Papers,* microfilm; Pinchot, *History of the Progressive Party.*

53. A report in mid-December 1915 shows that the Volunteers Department had raised $33,005 between October 1913 and November 1915. John M. Parker to E. H. Hooker, December 13, 1915, Progressive Party Papers, Roosevelt Collection, Houghton.

54. Fitzpatrick, *Endless Crusade,* 157.

55. *New York Times,* February 13, 1914.

56. *New York Times,* January 26, 1913.

57. Ray, *Introduction to Political Parties and Practical Politics,* 246–47; Eckert, "Effects of Women's Suffrage on the Political Situation in the City of Chicago"; *New York Times,* February 14, 1914, July 4 and 15, 1913.

58. Goldstein, *Effects of the Adoption of Woman Suffrage,* 133. See also Flanagan, "Gender and Urban Political Reform"; Ethington, *Public City;* and Andersen, *After Suffrage.*

59. Terborg-Penn, *African American Women in the Struggle for the Vote,* 137.

60. Hendricks, "African American Women as Political Constituents in Chicago," 57–58.

61. Ibid., 62.

62. Anne Rhodes to Lillian Wald, August 22 and September 2, 1914, Wald Papers, New

York Public Library; *New York Times,* July 23, 1915. For other examples, see Andersen, *After Suffrage;* and Cott, *Grounding of Modern Feminism.*

63. Perry, *Belle Moskowitz,* 112; *New York Times,* August 5, 1914.

64. In Kansas, for example, the new voters crossed party lines to "formulate a nonpartisan declaration of principles to be placed before the various political party organizations of the State as an expression of what the women voters want included in the platforms in the next campaign." *New York Times,* November 30, 1913.

65. Terborg-Penn, *African American Women in the Struggle for the Vote,* 27.

66. Leonard, comp., *Woman's Who's Who of America.*

67. Cresap, *Party Politics in the Golden State,* 116; Woods, "Penchant for Probity," 99–113; MacRae, *Rise of the Progressive Movement in the State of California.*

68. The third-party challenger in California was the Socialist party. For women's roles in the party, see Katz, "Dual Commitments."

69. Porter and Gries, *Our Folks and Your Folks,* 229. I am grateful to Wendy Lombard Bossie of the Caribou Public Library for locating this information for me. Other information on Porter's background comes from her column "From a Woman's View-Point: A Page for Women Readers" and news reports in the *California Outlook* from 1912 to 1914. See also *New York Herald,* June 18, 1912.

70. *Temperance Tribune,* February 15, 1894.

71. At this time, the *Los Angeles Herald* was a Republican paper; it would later become a Democratic paper. See Deverell, "Neglected Twins," 72–98.

72. For background information on California women's public and political activism, see Gullett, "Feminism, Politics, and Voluntary Groups"; and Gullett, *Becoming Citizens.*

73. Porter, "From a Woman's View-Point," June 1 and July 27, 1912. The Woman's Progressive League was the southern half of the suffrage forces. It eventually changed its name to the Southern California Civic League to avoid the assumption that it was a party organization. Northerners transformed the College Equal Suffrage League into the California Civic League, whose "object shall be the study of civic problems, the education of public opinion toward a better citizenship, the promotion of legislation, and the enforcement of law. The organization shall be nonpartisan in its relation to all political parties." Minutes of the California Civic League, November 27, 1911, Huntington. In 1921, the California Civic League became the California branch of the National League of Women Voters.

74. *Woman's Bulletin,* June 1912. The *Woman's Bulletin* was edited by Harriet H. Barry, and it expressed the principles of the Woman's Progressive League of California. See also *California Outlook,* July 27, 1912; *Los Angeles Times,* October 11, October 13, and November 6, 1911.

75. Eliza Tupper Wilkes, "Why Am I a Democrat?" *Woman's Bulletin,* July–August 1914.

76. This was also a concern for other women's organizations, including the Ebell Club and the Women's Legislative Council, which was run by San Francisco women. See Lyons, ed., *Who's Who among the Women of California,* 116. The actual political issues that women and their organizations focused on are explored in Braitman, "California Stateswoman"; Gullett, "Women Progressives and the Politics of Americanization in California," 71–94; and Katz, "Socialist Women and Progressive Reform."

77. *Woman's Bulletin,* September 1912.

78. *California Outlook,* February 24, 1912.

79. Minutes of the California Civic League, October 10, 1914–September 17, 1920, Huntington.

80. According to Terborg-Penn, Charlotta Spears Bass and Joseph Bass, the editors of the *California Eagle,* the only black newspaper in the state, supported Williams. Terborg-Penn identifies Williams as "the white Democratic party candidate." Charlotta Spears Bass was active in Republican party politics until she switched to the Progressive party in 1940. In 1952 she was the vice-presidential candidate of the Progressive party. Terborg-Penn, *African American Women in the Struggle for the Vote,* 140–41.

81. *California Outlook,* June 27 and July 4, 1914. See also *San Francisco Chronicle* May 20 and November 3, 1914; Hennings, *James D. Phelan and the Wilson Progressives of California;* and Van Ingen, "Campaigning for Equal Representation."

82. *California Outlook,* July 4, 1914. Williams's candidacy resulted in her election to the Republican State Central Committee. *Woman's Bulletin,* September 1914. Meyer Lissner argued that Williams was put forward by Harrison Gray Otis of the *Los Angeles Times* to dilute or "divert" the vote of newly enfranchised women. *California Outlook,* May 23 and May 30, 1914. Williams's candidacy was supported by the California Woman's Republican Club. Just before the election, Florence Richmond, presiding over a "rally night" for the club, stated that the club was not a temporary election vehicle, but "its work would go on until it saw California women elected to high offices." *San Francisco Chronicle,* November 3, 1914. See also Brady, "Progressives' About-Face."

83. Cable, "Woman and Politics." In another refrain along the same lines, the *Woman's Bulletin* declared in early 1913: "No right minded person today talks seriously of anyone's deserving an office, as though public office were a gift for the benefit of the incumbent instead of a trust to be discharged for the benefit of the public." The *Bulletin* further argued, "It is not a question of certain women deserving political recognition because of their services to this or that cause." *Woman's Bulletin,* January 1913.

84. Meyer Lissner to Hiram Johnson, January 6, July 2, and November 13, 1912, January 21, 1914, all in Johnson Papers, Bancroft. Lissner and Johnson also took factors besides a gender balance into consideration; religion was an important concern. Meyer Lissner to Hiram Johnson, November 26, 1913, Johnson Papers, Bancroft. For more information on the views of California men, see Brady, "Progressives' About-Face."

85. Hiram Johnson to Ben Lindsay, October 27, 1911, and Hiram Johnson to Meyer Lissner, November 6, 1911 (Johnson wrote "The more I think of the situation with regard to woman's suffrage, the more I think you gentlemen in the South have given us something that will ultimately destroy us"); Hiram Johnson to Mary Gibson, September 12, 1913, Johnson Papers, Bancroft. Johnson had reluctantly supported suffrage for California women in 1910. Not until 1916 would he support a federal woman suffrage amendment.

86. Hiram Johnson to Mrs. Dana Coolidge, April 11, 1916, Johnson Papers, Bancroft.

87. For the concern of Democrats, see Grace Caukin to James Phelan, November 17, December 15, and December 26, 1913, Phelan Papers, Bancroft; *Woman's Bulletin,* April 1913 and December 1913.

88. Meyer Lissner to Hiram Johnson, December 11, 1916, Johnson Papers, Bancroft.

89. Meyer Lissner to Hiram Johnson, December 2 and December 11, 1916, Johnson Papers, Bancroft.

90. DuBois, *Harriot Stanton Blatch and the Winning of Woman Suffrage*, 103–13.

91. The NWP was created out of the Congressional Union for Woman Suffrage, which was organized in 1913 when members of the NAWSA's Congressional Committee split off from the parent organization. It took the name National Woman's Party in 1915, but I am using this identification throughout for narrative consistency. On the influence of British suffragists, see Pankhurst, *Suffragettes;* and Gluck, ed., *From Parlor to Prison.*

92. "National Woman's Party, 'Our Hat's in the Ring,'" flyer [1916], SSC.

93. I am indebted to Marjorie Spruill Wheeler for the information on the southern concern. Wheeler also points out that many southern suffragists, such as Kate Gordon, were probably correctly convinced that the NWP women were secretly Republican. After 1916 their militant tactics were denounced by many suffragists as harmful to the movement and to women's public presence overall. See also Ford, *Iron-Jawed Angels.*

94. *New York Times*, January 25, 1914. See also Alice Paul to Blanche Ames, August 14, 1914, Ames Papers, Schlesinger Library; Beard, "Woman Suffrage and Strategy," 329–31.

95. *New York Times*, August 1, 1914.

96. *New York Times*, June 8, 1915, February 25, 1916; "Concerning Non-Partisanship," NAWSA "Headquarter News Letter," July 20, 1916.

97. For information on Democratic women's responses to the NWP, see Gustafson, "Partisan Women," 337–41.

98. Progressive Party National Committee Records, Progressive Party Papers, Roosevelt Collection, Houghton.

99. Gable, *Bull Moose Years,* 223–24.

100. Ibid., chaps. 8 and 9.

101. *Springfield (Mass.) Union,* April 8, 1916, Scrapbook of Cartoons, Perkins Papers, Columbia.

102. The committee included Carpenter, Mrs. Leonard Hand, Mrs. Joseph Griswold Deane, Mary Simkhovitch, Katherine Bement Davis, Maud Howe Elliott, and Mary Ingham.

103. See boxes 11 and 12 on the 1916 election, Progressive Party Papers, Roosevelt Collection, Houghton.

104. Terborg-Penn, *African American Women in the Struggle for the Vote,* 75.

105. *New York Times*, February 18, 1916.

106. *New York Times*, April 20, 1916.

107. Gable, *Bull Moose Years,* 245. George W. Ellis to George Meyer, May 27, 1916, Progressive Party Papers, Roosevelt Collection, Houghton.

108. Theodore Roosevelt to the Conferees of the Progressive Party, June 10, 1916, in Morison, ed., *Letters of Theodore Roosevelt,* 8:1060–62; Ickes, "Who Killed the Progressive Party?"

109. Theodore Roosevelt to the Progressive National Committee, in Morison, ed., *Letters of Theodore Roosevelt,* 8:1067–74; "The Progressive Party—Its Records from January to July 1916," Progressive Party Papers, Roosevelt Collection, Houghton. On Hughes, see Perkins, *Charles Evans Hughes and American Democratic Statesmanship;* Danelski and Tulchin, eds., *Autobiographical Notes of Charles Evans Hughes.*

110. *New York Times*, June 11, 1916.

111. A "National Party" was formed in Chicago in the Spring of 1917. Florence Slown

Hyde of the National Executive Committee wrote that it was "the result of a profound conviction on the part of a goodly number of women and men from various existing parties and nonpartisan groups. . . . for the sane working out of social and economic readjustments out of which the new social order is to emerge." Boyd, *Woman Citizen,* 220.

112. Hofstadter, *Age of Reform,* 17.

113. "The Problem of the Progressive Voter," *New Republic,* July 22, 1916, 290–91.

114. See Morison, ed., *Letters of Theodore Roosevelt,* 8:1082.

115. Theodore Roosevelt to Alice Carpenter, June 29, 1916, ibid., 8:1081–82.

116. Anne Martin to Cornelia Pinchot, July 10, 1916, and Cornelia Bryce Pinchot to Charles Evans Hughes, July 26, 1916, Cornelia Pinchot Papers, LC.

117. There seem to have been three groups of women suffragists at the Democratic and Republican conventions in 1916. The NAWSA women, the NWP women, and women from the National Council of Women Voters. *The Vanguard* 1:1 (June 1, 1916).

118. The "women's menace" was identified by the *Times* as the "Woman's Party of Western Women Voters," organized by Alice Paul, in reference to the NWP's organizing efforts among western women voters. *New York Times,* June 17, 1916.

119. Hays, *Memoirs of Will H. Hays,* 142.

120. *New York Times,* March 17 and August 5, 1916.

121. Mrs. J. Clarke Thomas to Cornelia Pinchot, Cornelia Pinchot Papers, LC; Wood, "Mapping a National Campaign Strategy."

122. "Constitution and By-Laws of the National Hughes Alliance, Women's Committee," Cornelia Pinchot Papers, LC. Kellor's work with the Progressive Volunteers made her believe that individuals were more likely to contribute to local parties and candidates. This may have influenced her decision to make the Hughes Alliance a national-only organization.

123. *New York Times,* November 6, 1916.

124. Alice Carpenter to Cornelia Pinchot, September 6, 1916, Cornelia Pinchot Papers, LC.

125. *New York Times,* November 4, 1916.

126. Ford, *Iron-Jawed Angels,* 69–76.

127. *New York Times,* September 7 and September 9, 1916.

128. *New York Times,* August 17, 1916.

129. Degen, *History of the Woman's Peace Party;* Alonso, *Peace as a Women's Issue.*

130. Braitman, "Katherine Philips Edson," 280.

131. *New York Times,* July 8, 1916; Women's Committee, *Women in National Politics.*

132. Bertha Sapints to Cornelia Pinchot, September 5, 1916, Cornelia Pinchot Papers, LC. Kellor was chair of the Women's Committee. Alice Carpenter was chair of the Women's New York City Committee of the Hughes Alliance, on which Doris Stevens worked.

133. Women's Committee, *Women in National Politics,* 5.

134. All quotes are from the report. Although Kellor is not listed on the title page, she is the author of the report.

135. The *New York Times* reported that there was also a Women's National Republican Club with Mrs. John R. Speel of Washington as chair. The club had organizations in Minnesota, Illinois, Utah, Pennsylvania, and Washington, D.C., with three thousand members. It may in fact have been the WNRA, as no other information exists on its history. *New York Times,* August 5, 1916. Letterhead for the Women's New York City Committee

of the Hughes Alliance notes that it was formerly the Women's Roosevelt League. Elizabeth Crosby to Cornelia Pinchot, Cornelia Pinchot Papers, LC.

136. Women's Committee, *Women in National Politics,* 6.

137. Frances Kellor to Mrs. Frank [Narcissa Cox] Vanderlip, August 16, 1916, Cornelia Pinchot Papers, LC.

138. Women's Committee, *Women in National Politics,* 14. In 1913 the Progressive Service had a budget of thirty thousand dollars and spent $41,416.97. After June 1914, expenses were kept below one thousand dollars a month. Gable, *Bull Moose Years,* 164, 187.

139. Women's Committee, *Women in National Politics,* 13.

140. Ibid., 14; Bates and Schwartz, "Golden Special Campaign Train."

141. *New York Times,* September 17, 1916.

142. Women's Committee, *Women in National Politics,* 15–18. Other speakers included Kellor, Mary Antin, Maud Howe Elliott, and Edith Ellicott Smith.

143. *New York Herald,* October 2, 1916.

144. Frances Kellor to Mrs. Frank Vanderlip, August 16, 1916, Cornelia Pinchot Papers, LC.

145. Women's Committee, *Women in National Politics,* 16–17. The Women's Committee was supported by some influential and wealthy women, including Mrs. Willard Straight, Mrs. Cornelius Vanderbilt, Mrs. Mary Harriman Rumsey, Mrs. William Curtis Demorest, Ruth Morgan, Mrs. Harry Payne Whitney, and Mrs. Otto Kahn. "Officers and Executive Committee of the National Hughes Alliance Women's Committee," Cornelia Pinchot Papers, LC.

146. Alice Carpenter to Cornelia Pinchot, September 6, 1916, Cornelia Pinchot Papers, LC; *New York Times,* October 1, 1916.

147. *New York Times,* April 24, 1916. For negative publicity, see Bates and Schwartz, "Golden Special Campaign Train."

148. Women's Committee, *Women in National Politics,* 17.

149. Price and Spillane, "Stalking for Nine Million Voters," 663.

150. Women's Committee, *Women in National Politics,* 17.

151. *New York Times,* October 12, 1916.

152. Women's Committee, *Women in National Politics,* 18.

153. Ibid., 25–27.

154. Ibid.

155. Ibid.

156. *New York Times,* November 5, 1916.

157. On continuing divisions, see, for example, Hiram Johnson to Edwin Van Valkenburg, September 5, November 15, 1916; January 21, 1917, Progressive Party Papers, Roosevelt Collection, Houghton; and Olin, "Hiram Johnson, the California Progressives, and the Hughes Campaign of 1916."

158. Link, *Woodrow Wilson and the Progressive Era,* 249; *New York Times,* November 12, 1916.

159. Clipping from *New York Tribune,* November 13, 1916, in Carrie Chapman Catt, Personal Scrapbook, 1916–1919, Catt Papers, New York Public Library.

160. Letter signed by Katherine P. Edson, November 6, 1916, cited in Braitman, "Katherine Philips Edson," 284–85. Hughes Train women gave speeches for Rankin even though they were pledged to stay out of local and state politics.

161. NAWSA "Headquarter News Letter," November 25, 1916, 7.

162. *NAW: The Modern Period*, 566–68; Hoff-Wilson, "'Peace Is a Woman's Job.'"

Chapter 7: Claiming Victory, 1918–24

1. Theodore Roosevelt to Millicent Garrett Fawcett, November 19, 1912, in Morison, ed., *Letters of Theodore Roosevelt*, 7:651.

2. Victoria Woodhull was thirty-four years old when she ran for president in 1872, so age made her ineligible. Belva Lockwood was fifty and fifty-four when she ran in 1884 and 1888.

3. Rebecca Latimer, a Democrat from Georgia, was the first woman to serve in the U.S. Senate after she was appointed to office; she served for only two days in 1922. Hattie Wyatt Caraway of Arkansas, also a Democrat, was appointed in 1931 to fill a vacancy caused by the death of her husband. The next year she became the first woman elected to the U.S. Senate; she served from 1931 to 1945. Chamberlin, *Minority of Members.*

4. *DAB*, 16:20–21; *NAW*, 3:177–78; James, "Alice Mary Robertson, Anti-Feminist Congresswoman."

5. *NAW*, 2:231–32.

6. Qtd. in Witt, Paget, and Matthews, *Running as a Woman*, 32.

7. Forman and Shuler, *Woman Voter's Manual*, xv.

8. "Mothers of Men as Legislators of States," *National Suffrage News*, April 1917, NAWSA Papers, LC.

9. "New York Tribune Institute," newspaper clipping, June 15, 1919, Burdette Collection, Huntington.

10. *New York Times*, February 15, 1920.

11. Helen Varick Boswell argued that the Republicans should claim to have established the first woman's division because the WNRA had a campaign headquarters since 1892. Boswell, "Political Episodes" (March 1935).

12. *New York Times*, January 23, February 28, March 6, and September 28, 1918; May 30, 1919; January 14, 1920; Bass, "Political History Made for Women in 1920," 15; Clement, "Women at Past National Conventions," 28–29; Bass, "Advance of Democratic Women," 17, 39.

13. Muncy, "'Women Demand Recognition,'" 46; Braitman, "Legislated Parity," 176.

14. *New York Times*, January 23, 1918; "Proceedings of the Meeting of the Republican National Committee, February 12, 1918," *Papers of the Republican Party*, microfilm.

15. *New York Times*, June 5, 1919; *HWS*, 5:644; NAWSA, *Victory*, 133. The RNC today gives different numbers. See "History of GOP," available at <http://www.rnc.org>.

16. Cornelia Pinchot to Will Hays, March 14, 1918, Cornelia Pinchot Papers, LC.

17. Ibid.

18. *NAW: The Modern Period*, 545–47; Furlow, "Cornelia Bryce Pinchot."

19. Cornelia Pinchot to Will Hays, March 14, 1918, Cornelia Pinchot Papers, LC.

20. Ibid. According to Kristi Andersen, "New York women Republicans endorsed a fifty-fifty plan for all party committees" in the summer of 1919. Andersen, *After Suffrage*, 91. See also Harvey, *Votes without Leverage*, 88. Yawger is listed as a member of the Women's Republican Club of New York City as well as reform organizations in Leonard, comp.,

Woman's Who's Who of America, 910. On Yawger's appointment, see *New York Times,* November 15, 1917.

21. Cornelia Pinchot to Will Hays, March 14, 1918, Cornelia Pinchot Papers, LC.

22. Qtd. in Andersen, *After Suffrage,* 79.

23. Cornelia Pinchot to Will Hays, March 14, 1918, Cornelia Pinchot Papers, LC.

24. Ibid.

25. Newspaper clipping [April–May 1918], enclosed with Esther Lape to Cornelia Pinchot, [1918], Cornelia Pinchot Papers, LC.

26. Harvey, *Votes without Leverage,* 165.

27. "Report of the Republican Women's National Executive Committee, Acting with the Republican National Committee," September 3, 1918–June 8, 1920, in Burdette Collection, Huntington; Miller, *Ruth Hanna McCormick,* 120–22.

28. Miller, *Ruth Hanna McCormick,* 9–31.

29. *New York Times,* May 17, 1919. She did stay, and by the end of the decade she had come to agree with others that there was also a need for good women in office. In 1928 she was elected to the U.S. Congress.

30. Miller, *Ruth Hanna McCormick; New York Times,* November 11, 1919.

31. Porter was on the California Republican State Central Committee. See Mary Smith to Clara Burdette, February 6 and February 20, 1920, Burdette Collection, Huntington.

32. Perry, "Defying the Party Whip," 99.

33. *Woman Citizen,* October 9, 1920. *Woman Republican* identifies Boswell as the associate director of the Women's Speakers Bureau of the RNC and as a member of the Republican Women's State Executive Committee and vice chair of the New York County Committee. *Woman Republican,* November 1923; January 12, 1924. In 1931 Boswell was threatening a revolt of women in the party because men were ignoring the women leaders. Harvey, *Votes without Leverage,* 189.

34. Miller, *Ruth Hanna McCormick,* 120–21.

35. Corinne Roosevelt Robinson, "Woman as a Political Worker," [1920], clipping, Corinne Roosevelt Robinson Papers, Roosevelt Collection, Houghton.

36. Miller, *Ruth Hanna McCormick,* 120–21.

37. "Report of the Republican Women's National Executive Committee," Burdette Collection, Huntington; *New York Times,* May 24, 1919.

38. "Report of the Republican Women's National Executive Committee," Burdette Collection, Huntington.

39. *New York Times,* May 23, 1919.

40. *New York Times,* May 24, 1919.

41. *New York Times,* May 23, 1919.

42. "Report of the Republican Women's National Executive Committee," Burdette Collection, Huntington.

43. Ruth McCormick to Mary H. Loines, March 13, 1919, Women's Rights Collection, Schlesinger Library. Christine Bradley South (1879–1957) was from Frankfort, Kentucky, and the daughter of William O'Connell Bradley, an RNC member from 1890 to 1896, the governor of Kentucky from 1895 to 1899, and a U.S. Senator from 1909 until his death in 1914. She was a delegate at the 1920 and 1932 Republican National Conventions.

44. "Proceedings of the Meeting of the Republican National Committee, December 10,

1919," *Papers of the Republican Party,* microfilm. McCormick continued her efforts for the party. See Miller, *Ruth Hanna McCormick,* chap. 5; Harvey, *Votes without Leverage,* 117.

45. *NAW,* 3:501–2.

46. Harvey, *Votes without Leverage,* 219.

47. "Proceedings of the Meeting of the Republican National Committee, December 10, 1919, Washington, D.C.," *Papers of the Republican Party,* microfilm; *New York Times,* December 18, 1919.

48. *New York Times,* June 9 and 10, 1920. For the fifty-fifty rule today, see "The Rules of the Republican Party," available at <http://www.rnc.org>.

49. Braitman, "Legislated Parity," 175–76. For example, Marian Brown, the executive secretary of the Women's Division of the Maine Republican State Committee, believed that "Maine does not consider this a matter for legislation. . . . As early as February 1920, the Republican State Committee made plans for equal representation of women on committees and began the appointment of the Women's Division of sixteen members." Marian Brown to Cornelia Bryce Pinchot, January 28, 1921, Gifford Pinchot Papers, LC.

50. "Five Years under Mrs. Livermore's Leadership," *Woman Republican,* July 7, 1923.

51. *New York Times,* January 11, 1920. Her obituary also lists her as vice chair of the Westchester County Republican Committee, an organizer of the Women's Republican Club of Westchester, a member of the RNEC, and in "charge of the organization of Republican women in the Eastern states in the campaigns to elect Presidents Harding, Coolidge and Hoover." *New York Times,* October 16, 1933.

52. "Five Years under Mrs. Livermore's Leadership," *Woman Republican,* July 7, 1923.

53. Good, *Republican Womanpower,* 15.

54. The WNRC claimed 1,118 members in thirty-one states in 1923. *Woman Republican,* January 13, 1923. It claimed three thousand members in thirty-seven states by 1927, but, according to Rymph, most members were from New York and the surrounding area. Rymph, "Forward and Right," 77–78. Robinson saw the roots of the WNRC in the Women's Municipal League. See Corinne Roosevelt Robinson, "Organizations I Belong to and Why I Belong to Them," clipping [1922], Corinne Roosevelt Robinson Papers, Roosevelt Collection, Houghton.

55. "A Brief History," Women's National Republican Club, New York, available at <http://www.wnrc.org/history.html>.

56. Miller, *Ruth Hanna McCormick,* 122.

57. Chafe, *American Woman,* 39. The public and private writings of Republican women in the 1920s are filled with discussions of the tension between men and women in the party, men's opposition to women's organizing efforts, and outright misogyny. For discussions by historians, see Miller, *Ruth Hanna McCormick;* Harvey, *Votes without Leverage;* and Andersen, *After Suffrage.* As Harriet Taylor Upton wrote Corinne Roosevelt Robinson, "It seems awful that the political men are so opposed but we are going on with our own work." Harriet Taylor Upton to Corinne Roosevelt Robinson, June 16, 1921, Corinne Roosevelt Robinson Papers, Roosevelt Collection, Houghton.

58. Mary Gibson wrote to Clara Burdette, "Mr. Dickinson anxious for letter to leading women of state using a general list and urging Republicans to organize Hoover clubs at once." On the back of the telegram Burdette wrote, "Women's Republican Clubs are needed not only for the women but to [arouse?] the men." Mary Gibson to Clara Bur-

dette, with notation by Burdette, February 23, 1920, Burdette Collection, Huntington. Burdette was appointed to the Federal Food Administration and worked with Hoover in 1917. In 1928 and 1932 Burdette managed Hoover's campaigns in California.

59. *New York Times,* January 11, 1920. For Democratic women's clubs, see Blair, "Advance of Democratic Women," 15.

60. "A Brief History of the NFRW," available at <http://www.nfrw.org/aboutnfrw/nfrw_history.htm>. This history can be found on the websites of many state federations. A pamphlet issued in 1987 by the NFRW does not mention the significance of the name change. See National Federation of Republican Women, *NFRW.* See also "The Rules of the Republican Party," available at <http://www.rnc.org>; Rymph, "Forward and Right," 190; Williams, *History of the Founding and Development of the National Federation of Republican Women.*

61. "Republican Women's Ranks Rent by Effort to Oust Miss Hay from Leadership," newspaper clipping [1920], Dreier Papers, SSC.

62. "Oppose Wadsworth!" flyer, Dreier Papers, SSC. See also *New York Times,* July 24, 1920. Wadsworth's wife was the head of the National Association Opposed to Woman Suffrage. There was also a campaign against the Republican senator Frank Brandegee in Connecticut, which also failed. Cott, *Grounding of Modern Feminism,* 106.

63. "Proceedings of the Fiftieth Annual Convention of the NAWSA, March 25, 1919," League of Women Voters Papers, LC; Harvey, *Votes without Leverage,* 92–93.

64. Harvey, *Votes without Leverage,* 92.

65. *Chicago Tribune,* June 5, 1920.

66. It also probably did not help that she presented the NAWSA memorial to the Republican convention "in the form of a protest" for the party's failure to convince more Republican legislatures to ratify the woman suffrage amendment. NAWSA, *Handbook of the NAWSA,* 14–15.

67. See, for example, Catt, "Political Parties and Women Voters."

68. *New York Times,* February 13, 1920.

69. *New York Times,* February 15, 1920.

70. *New York Times,* February 15, 1920. See also Cott, *Grounding of Modern Feminism,* 86–87.

71. *New York Times,* February 14, 1920.

72. *New York Times,* February 14, 1920.

73. "California State League of Women Voters," clipping from *The Clubwoman,* [1919], Burdette Collection, Huntington.

74. *New York Times,* February 15, 1920; Catt, "Political Parties and Women Voters"; Catt and Shuler, *Woman Suffrage and Politics,* 380–81.

75. League of Women Voters, *Forty Years of a Great Idea;* Lemons, *Woman Citizen;* Black, *Social Feminism;* Gordon, *After Winning.*

76. Ruth McCormick to Mary Loines, March 13, 1919, Women's Rights Collection, Schlesinger Library. Loines disagreed and stated that the purpose of the league was not "to outwit the government but to be thoroughly nonpartisan and vote for the best man." "Reveals Party Aims of Women," clipping [April 1919], Loines Papers, Schlesinger Library.

77. Frances Kellor, "Cloisters in American Politics," n.d., Dreier Papers, SSC.

78. Corinne R. Robinson, "Women in Politics," n.d., clipping, Corinne Roosevelt Robinson Papers, Roosevelt Collection, Houghton.

79. Lucy Miller to Cornelia Bryce Pinchot, November 25, 1919, Cornelia Pinchot Papers, LC. Miller was the chair of the Pennsylvania League of Women Citizens, which grew out of the Pennsylvania Woman Suffrage Association.

80. Cornelia Bryce Pinchot to Mrs. Lucy K. Miller, November 29, 1919, Cornelia Pinchot Papers, LC.

81. Chafe, *American Woman,* 35.

82. *New York Times,* May 11 and June 7, 1920; Lemons, *Woman Citizen,* chap. 6; Ladd-Taylor, *Mother-Work,* chap. 6. Work for passage of the Sheppard-Towner Act was done not only by the NLWV but also the Women's Joint Congressional Association, organized by Maud Wood Park in 1920 as another way for women to cross party lines.

83. Forman and Shuler, *Woman Voter's Manual,* xv.

84. Harvey, *Votes without Leverage,* 233.

85. *San Francisco Examiner,* clipping, July 27, 1919, Burdette Collection, Huntington.

86. Terborg-Penn, *African American Women in the Struggle for the Vote,* 142, 148, 163.

87. *Cleveland Advocate,* April 26, 1919. By April 1920 they were called the Colored Women's Independent Republican Club, and they supported Leonard Wood's bid for the nomination. *Ohio State Monitor,* April 10, 1920. See also Terborg-Penn, *African American Women in the Struggle for the Vote,* 103 and 114.

88. *HWS,* 5:646; NAWSA, *Victory,* 133. *New York Times,* June 5, 1919, gives different numbers.

89. *Woman Citizen,* June 12, June 19, 1920; *Official Report of the Proceedings of the Seventeenth Republican National Convention.* Outside the convention hall the NWP was protesting with a banner that read "Vote Against the Republican Party as Long as it Blocks Suffrage," claiming that Republican leadership was not putting pressure on state legislatures to ratify. *New York Times,* June 12, 1920; Rymph, "Forward and Right," 28–30.

90. Republican National Committee, *Republican Campaign Text-Book, 1920,* 100; Good, *Republican Womanpower,* 12.

91. *New York Times,* June 26, 1920; Andersen, *After Suffrage,* 82. The *Republican Campaign Text-Book,* claims, "In the last National Convention there were 118 women delegates and 179 women alternates." Republican National Committee, *Republican Campaign Text-Book, 1924,* 297.

92. *New York Times,* January 6, 1942.

93. The assistant secretaries were Mrs. Jeanette Hyde of Utah, Mrs. William Morgan of Kansas, and Mrs. Guy Gannett of Maine. Gannett was also the chair of the Women's Division of the Maine Republican State Committee. Yost became the director of the RNC Women's Division in the 1930s.

94. The committee was "an aid only to the Convention and will in no sense attempt to assume or to execute the functions of the Convention Committee on Resolutions." "Republican National Committee, Advisory Committee on Policies and Platform," [1920], Burdette Collection, Huntington.

95. Republican National Committee, *Republican Campaign Text-Book, 1920,* 484. The American Association for Labor Legislation was founded in 1906. In 1913 it sponsored the first national conference on social insurance, and in 1915 it drafted the "Standard Bill" for compulsory health insurance. Andrews was a student of John Commons. See Brown and Reagan, eds., *Voluntarism, Planning, and the State.*

96. In 1928 there were eight women; in 1932, seventeen women; in 1936, twelve women; in 1940, eleven women; and in 1944, forty-three women. The numbers continue to move up after that point. Andersen, *After Suffrage,* 83.

97. *New York Times,* June 12, 1920.

98. Caroli, *Roosevelt Women,* 133–37.

99. Good, *Republican Womanpower,* 17.

100. Anna Harvey writes that the move also provided "a justification for similarly imbalanced RNC subcommittee appointments." Harvey, *Votes without Leverage,* 219.

101. See ibid., 219–37, for a discussion of these changes.

102. Ibid. 16–17.

103. "For Immediate Release," June 8, 1920, Burdette Collection, Huntington. These were five of the fifteen planks of the "Woman's Platform" presented by the NLWV. The Democrats adopted twelve. Cook, *Eleanor Roosevelt,* 275.

104. *Official Report of the Proceedings of the Seventeenth Republican National Convention.*

105. On the status of legislatures in session or soon meeting, see *New York Times,* June 5, 1919.

106. Governor Carey to Carrie Chapman Catt, June 6, 1919, Catt Papers, New York Public Library.

107. Carrie Chapman Catt to Governor Carey, June 9, 1919, Catt Papers, New York Public Library.

108. Flexner, *Century of Struggle,* 328.

109. Governor Carey to Carrie Chapman Catt, June 12, 1919, Catt Papers, New York Public Library.

110. Carrie Chapman Catt to Mrs. Andreas Ueland, July 19, 1919, Catt Papers, New York Public Library.

111. Carrie Chapman Catt to Mrs. W. R. Pattangall, September 18, 1919, Catt Papers, New York Public Library.

112. Carrie Chapman Catt to Governor Carey, June 17, 1919, Catt Papers, New York Public Library.

113. Carrie Chapman Catt to Grace Raymond Hebard, June 5, 1919, Catt Papers, New York Public Library.

114. NAWSA, *Handbook of the NAWSA* (1921), 19.

115. Andersen, *After Suffrage,* 88–89, 97–98.

116. Women working at the state level supplemented this effort. Clara Burdette wrote Will Hays that as a member of the California State Central Committee she was "sending out 100,000 cards . . . that the nonpartisan voters, mostly women, may be spurred to line up with the Republican party at the State primaries May 4th." Clara Burdette to Will Hays, March 4, 1920, Burdette Collection, Huntington.

117. Qtd. in Harvey, *Votes without Leverage,* 117–18.

118. Qtd. in Good, *Republican Womanpower,* 17.

119. Harvey, *Votes without Leverage,* 118.

120. Harriet Taylor Upton to Corinne Roosevelt Robinson, March 6, 1921, Corinne Roosevelt Robinson Papers, Roosevelt Collection, Houghton.

121. Harvey, *Votes without Leverage,* 115–16. For cooperation between white and black women, see Goodstein, "Rare Alliance."

122. Rosalyn Terborg-Penn argues that their involvement in the party declined after 1924. Terborg-Penn, *African American Women in the Struggle for the Vote*, 145, 157. Evelyn Brooks Higginbotham puts the date closer to 1932. Higginbotham, "In Politics to Stay," 211.

123. *Cleveland Advocate*, September 11, 1920.

124. Terborg-Penn, *African American Women in the Struggle for the Vote*, 143.

125. Brown, comp., *Homespun Heroines and Other Women of Distinction*, 238–40. Also influential in the party was Daisy Lampkin, who was elected president of the National Negro Republican Convention in Atlantic City in July 1924. In 1926 she was elected delegate-at-large to the Republican National Convention. *BWA*, 1:690–93.

126. Terborg-Penn, *African American Women in the Struggle for the Vote*, 145.

127. *BWA*, 1:176–78.

128. "Minutes of the National League of Republican Colored Women, 1924," Burroughs Papers, LC.

129. Higginbotham, "In Politics to Stay," 206; Andersen, *After Suffrage*, 84.

130. Higginbotham, "In Politics to Stay," 208–12.

131. Rymph, "Forward and Right," 60–61.

132. Matthews, "'There Is No Sex in Citizenship.'"

133. Carrie Chapman Catt to Lucy Anthony, November 8, 1928, Catt Papers, LC. See also Carrie Chapman Catt, "Who Won Suffrage?" undated speech, Catt Papers, LC.

134. For claims to victory just after the passage of the amendment, see Republican National Committee, *Republican Campaign Text-Book, 1924*, 292–93; Democratic National Committee, *Democratic Campaign Book, 1924*, 273–80. See also Good, *Republican Womanpower*; Blair, "Women in the Political Parties." For Republican claims today, see the RNC website under "History of the Republican Party," available at <http://www.rnc.org>.

135. Carrie Chapman Catt to Lucy Anthony, November 8, 1928, Catt Papers, LC.

136. Harvey, *Votes without Leverage*, 1.

137. Carrie Chapman Catt, "What Have Women Done with Suffrage?" n.d., Catt Papers, LC; Catt, "What Women Have Done with the Vote."

138. Carrie Chapman Catt, "What Have Women Done with Suffrage?" n.d., Catt Papers, LC.

139. Carrie Chapman Catt to Grace Raymond Hebard, November 18, 1920, Hebard Collection, University of Wyoming, American Heritage Center.

140. Carrie Chapman Catt to Miss London, October 18, 1928, Catt Papers, New York Public Library. There was an enormous public questioning of the impact of woman suffrage in the 1920s, much of it centering on the question of declining voter turnout. See Cott, *Grounding of Modern Feminism*, 99–114; Kleppner, "Were Women to Blame?"; and Andersen, *After Suffrage*, chap. 4.

Bibliography

Manuscript Collections

Bancroft Library, University of California at Berkeley
    Hiram Johnson Papers
    James Phelan Papers
Chicago Historical Society
    Irene McCoy Gaines Papers
Columbia University Library, Columbia University, New York, N.Y.
    George Perkins Papers
Houghton Library of the Harvard College Library, Harvard University, Cambridge, Mass.
    Theodore Roosevelt Collection
        Corinne Roosevelt Robinson Papers
        Progressive Party Papers
Huntington Library, San Marino, Calif.
    Alice Park Collection
    Clara Burdette Collection
    Elizabeth Harbert Collection
    Ida Husted Harper Collection
    Louise Ward Watkins Collection
    Minutes of the California Civic League
    Susan B. Anthony Memorial Collection
Library of Congress, Washington, D.C.
    Amos Pinchot Papers
    Anna Dickinson Papers
    Benjamin Harrison Papers
    Blackwell Family Papers
    Carrie Chapman Catt Papers
    Cornelia Pinchot Papers

Donald R. Richberg Papers
Douglas A. Tompkins Papers
Gifford Pinchot Papers
James Clarkson Papers
James G. Blaine Papers
League of Women Voters Papers
Mary Church Terrell Papers
Nannie Helen Burroughs Papers
National American Woman Suffrage Association Papers
Theodore Roosevelt Papers
William McKinley Papers
Massachusetts Historical Society, Boston
Caroline Wells Healey Dall Papers
New York Public Library, Manuscripts and Archives Division, Astor, Lenox, and Tilden Foundations, New York, N.Y.
Carrie Chapman Catt Papers
Joel E. Spingarn Papers
Lillian D. Wald Papers
Schlesinger Library, Radcliffe Institute for Advanced Study, Harvard University, Cambridge, Mass.
Alma Lutz's Records of the National Woman's Party
Blanche Ames Ames Correspondence
Grace Allen Johnson Papers (Women's Rights Collection)
History of Women Microfilm Collection
Mary Hillard Loines Papers (Women's Rights Collection)
Sophia Smith Collection, Smith College, Northampton, Mass.
Nonpartisan National Woman's Christian Temperance Union Records Collection
Ethel Dreier Papers
Garrison Family Papers
State Historical Society of Iowa, Des Moines
Letters of Judith Ellen Foster
Harriet Beecher Stowe Center, Hartford, Conn.
Isabella Beecher Hooker Collection
University of Wyoming, American Heritage Center, Laramie
Grace Raymond Hebard Collection
Private Collection
Florence Jaffray Harriman Scrapbook (private property of Mrs. Phyllis Darling)

Microfilm Editions

Jane Addams Papers, 1860–1960. Ed. Mary Lynn McCree Bryan. Ann Arbor, Mich.: University Microfilms International, 1984.
Papers of the Republican Party. Ed. Paul Kesaris. Frederick, Md.: University Publications of America, 1986.
Papers of the Women's Trade Union League and Its Principal Leaders. Ed. Edward T. James. Woodbridge, Conn.: Research Publications, 1981.

Selected Papers of Elizabeth Cady Stanton and Susan B. Anthony. Ed. Patricia G. Holland and Ann D. Gordon. Wilmington, Del.: Scholarly Resources, 1991.

Temperance and Prohibition Papers: A Joint Microfilm Publication of the Ohio Historical Society, Michigan Historical Collections, and Woman's Christian Temperance Union. Ed. Francis X. Blouin Jr. Columbus: Ohio Historical Society, 1977.

Published Sources

Abbott, Edith. "Grace Abbott and Hull House, 1908–1921." *Social Service Review* 24 (December 1950): 502.

———. "Julia Lathrop." *Social Service Review* 6 (September 1932): 336.

Abbott, Ernest. "The Chicago Convention and the Birth of a New Party." *Outlook,* June 29, 1912.

———. "The Progressive Convention." *Outlook,* August 17, 1912.

Adams, Elmer, and Warren Foster. *Heroines of Modern Progress.* New York: Macmillan, 1926.

Addams, Jane. "The College Woman and the Family Claim." *The Commons,* September 1898.

———. "The Communion of the Ballot." *Woman's Journal,* December 14, 1912.

———. *Democracy and Social Ethics.* New York: Macmillan, 1916.

———. "Domestic Service and the Family Claim." In *World's Congress of Representative Women.* Ed. May Wright Sewell. Chicago: Rand McNally, 1894. 626–31.

———. "Ethical Survivals in Municipal Corruption." *International Journal of Ethics* 8 (April 1898): 372–91.

———. *The Excellent Becomes the Permanent.* New York: Macmillan, 1932.

———. "If Men Were Seeking the Franchise." *Ladies' Home Journal,* June 1913.

———. "Indirect Influence." *Woman's Journal,* November 23, 1912.

———. "Larger Aspects of the Women's Movement." *Annals of the American Academy of Political and Social Science* 56 (November 1914): 1–8.

———. "Lessons of the Election." *City Club [of Chicago] Bulletin,* November 27, 1912.

———. "My Experiences as a Progressive Delegate." *McClure's,* November 1912.

———. *My Friend, Julia Lathrop.* New York: Macmillan, 1935.

———. *A New Conscience and an Ancient Evil.* New York: Macmillan, 1911.

———. "Objective Necessity for Social Settlements." In *Philanthropy and Social Progress: Seven Essays.* Ed. Jane Addams et al. Freeport, N.Y.: Books for Libraries, 1969. 27–40.

———. "Politics and Philanthropy." *Ladies' Home Journal,* January 1913.

———. "Pragmatism in Politics." *Survey,* October 5, 1912.

———. "The Progressive Party and the Negro." *Crisis,* November 1912.

———. "The Progressive's Dilemma—The New Party." *American Magazine,* November 1912.

———. *Second Twenty Years at Hull House.* New York: Macmillan, 1935.

———. "Social Justice through National Action." Address at the Second Annual Lincoln Day Dinner of the Progressive Party. Hotel Astor, New York. February 12, 1914. In *Nationalism,* pamphlet issued by the Progressive Party National Committee, 1914.

———. "Subjective Necessity for Social Settlements." In *Philanthropy and Social Progress: Seven Essays.* Ed. Jane Addams et al. Freeport, N.Y.: Books for Libraries, 1969. 1–26.

————. *Twenty Years at Hull House.* New York: Macmillan, 1910.

————. "What the Progressive Party Means to Women." *Progressive Bulletin,* October 21, 1912.

————. "Why I Seconded Roosevelt's Nomination." *Woman's Journal,* August 17, 1912.

————. "Why I Went into Politics." *Ladies' Home Journal,* January 1913.

————. "Why Women Should Vote." *Ladies' Home Journal,* January 1910.

Addams, Jane, et al., eds. *Philanthropy and Social Progress: Seven Essays.* Freeport, N.Y.: Books for Libraries, 1969.

Alexander, Thomas G. "An Experiment in Progressive Legislation: The Granting of Woman Suffrage in Utah in 1870." *Utah Historical Quarterly* 38 (Winter 1970): 20–30.

Alonso, Harriet Hyman. *Peace as a Women's Issue: A History of the U.S. Movement for World Peace and Women's Rights.* Syracuse, N.Y.: Syracuse University Press, 1993.

Altschuler, Glenn C., and Stuart M. Blumin. "Limits of Political Engagement in Antebellum America: A New Look at the Golden Age of Participatory Democracy." *Journal of American History* 84 (December 1997): 855–85.

————. "'Where Is the Real America? Politics and Popular Consciousness in the Antebellum Era." *American Quarterly* 49 (June 1997): 225–67.

Andersen, Kristi. *After Suffrage: Women in Partisan and Electoral Politics before the New Deal.* Chicago: University of Chicago Press, 1996.

Anderson, Kathryn. "Evolution of a Partisan: Emily Newell Blair and the Democratic Party, 1920–1932." In *We Have Come to Stay: American Women and Political Parties, 1880–1960.* Ed. Melanie Gustafson, Kristie Miller, and Elisabeth I. Perry. Albuquerque: University of New Mexico Press, 1999. 109–19.

Anthony, Katherine. *Susan B. Anthony: Her Personal History and Her Era.* New York: Russell and Russell, 1954.

Antler, Joyce. "'After College, What?' New Graduates and the Family Claim." *American Quarterly* 32 (Fall 1980): 409–34.

Argersinger, Peter. "The Value of the Vote: Political Representation in the Gilded Age." *Journal of American History* 76 (June 1989): 59–90.

Aron, Cindy. *Ladies and Gentlemen of the Civil Service: Middle-Class Workers in Victorian America.* New York: Oxford University Press, 1987.

Ashworth, John. *"Agrarians" and "Aristocrats": Party Political Ideology in the United States, 1837–1846.* New York: Cambridge University Press, 1987.

Avery, Rachel Foster, ed. *Transactions of the National Council of Women of the United States, Assembled in Washington, D.C., February 22 to 25, 1891.* Philadelphia: J. B. Lippincott Co., 1891.

Babcock, Barbara Allen. "Clara Shortridge Foltz: 'First Woman.'" *Valparaiso University Law Review* 28 (Summer 1994): 1231–85.

Bader, Robert Smith. *Prohibition in Kansas: A History.* Lawrence: University of Kansas Press, 1986.

Bacon, Margaret Hope. "By Moral Force Alone: The Antislavery Women and Nonresistance." In *The Abolitionist Sisterhood: Women's Political Culture in Antebellum America.* Ed. Jean Fagan Yellin and John C. Van Horne. Ithaca, N.Y.: Cornell University Press, 1994. 275–97.

————. *Valiant Friend: The Life of Lucretia Mott.* New York: Walker, 1980.

Bain, Richard C., and Judith H. Parris. *Convention Decisions and Voting Records.* Washington, D.C.: Brookings Institution, 1973.

Baker, Jean. *Affairs of Party: The Political Culture of Northern Democrats in the Mid-Nineteenth Century.* Ithaca, N.Y.: Cornell University Press, 1983.

———. "Mary (Ann) Todd Lincoln." In *American First Ladies: Their Lives and Their Legacies.* Ed. Lewis L. Gould. New York: Garland, 1996. 174–90.

Baker, Paula. "The Domestication of Politics: Women and American Political Society, 1780–1920." *American Historical Review* 89 (June 1984): 620–47.

———. *The Moral Frameworks of Public Life: Gender, Politics, and the State in Rural New York, 1870–1930.* New York: Oxford University Press, 1991.

Baker, Ray S. "Hull House and the Ward Boss." *Outlook,* March 28, 1898.

Balderston, William. "Woman Suffrage in Idaho." In *Souvenir of Western Women.* Ed. Mary Osborn Douthit. Portland, Ore.: Anderson and Duniway, Co., 1905. 117–18.

Barney, William L. *The Passage of the Republic.* Lexington, Mass.: D.C. Heath, 1987.

Barry, Kathleen. *Susan B. Anthony: A Biography.* New York: New York University Press, 1988.

Basler, Roy P., ed. *The Collected Works of Abraham Lincoln.* 9 vols. New Brunswick, N.J.: Rutgers University Press, 1953.

Bass, Elizabeth. "Advance of Democratic Women." *Democratic Digest,* February 1940.

———. "Political History Made for Women in 1920." *Democratic Digest,* July 1936.

Bates, J. Leonard, and Vanette M. Schwartz. "Golden Special Campaign Train." *Montana: The Magazine for Western History* 37 (Summer 1987): 26–35.

Baym, Nina. "Women and the Republic: Emma Willard's Rhetoric of History." *American Quarterly* 43 (March 1991): 1–23.

Beach, Cora M., comp. *Women of Wyoming.* 2 vols. Casper, Wyo.: S. E. Boyer and Co., 1927.

Beard, Charles. "Woman Suffrage and Strategy." *New Republic,* December 14, 1914.

Beard, Mary Ritter. *Woman's Work in Municipalities.* 1915. Reprint, New York: Arno Reprint, 1972.

Beatty, Bess. "Perspectives on American Women: The View from Black Newspapers, 1865–1900." *Maryland Historian* 9 (Fall 1978): 39–50.

Beeton, Beverly. *Women Vote in the West: The Woman Suffrage Movement, 1869–1896.* New York: Garland, 1986.

Belden, Thomas G., and Marva R. Belden. *So Fell the Angels.* Boston: Little, Brown, 1956.

Belmont, Eleanor. *Fabric of Memory.* New York: Farrar, Straus, and Cudahy, 1957.

Bennett, Helen. *American Women in Civic Work.* New York: Dodd Mead and Company, 1915.

Berkeley, Kathleen. "Partisan Politics Makes for Strange Bedfellows: The Political Career of Anna Elizabeth Dickinson, 1842–1932." Paper presented at the Southern Historical Association Annual Meeting, November 1995.

Berman, David R. "Political Culture, Issues, and the Electorate: Evidence from the Progressive Era." *Western Political Quarterly* 41 (March 1988): 169–80.

Black, Naomi. *Social Feminism.* Ithaca, N.Y.: Cornell University Press, 1989.

Blair, Emily Newell. "Advance of Democratic Women." *Democratic Digest,* April 1940.

———. "Women at the Conventions." *Current History,* October 1920, 26–28.

———. "Women in the Political Parties." *Annals of the American Academy of Political and Social Science* 143 (May 1929): 217–29.

Blatch, Harriot Stanton, and Alma Lutz. *Challenging Years: The Memoirs of Harriot Stanton Blatch.* New York: G. P. Putnam's Sons, 1940.

Blum, John Morton. *The Republican Roosevelt.* Cambridge, Mass.: Harvard University Press, 1980.

Bogin, Ruth, and Jean Fagan Yellin. "Introduction." In *The Abolitionist Sisterhood: Women's Political Culture in Antebellum America.* Ed. Jean Fagan Yellin and John C. Van Horne. Ithaca, N.Y.: Cornell University Press, 1994. 1–19.

Booraem, Hendrick. *The Formation of the Republican Party in New York: Politics and Conscience in the Antebellum North.* New York: New York University Press, 1983.

Bordin, Ruth. *Frances Willard: A Biography.* Chapel Hill: University of North Carolina Press, 1986.

———. *Woman and Temperance: The Quest for Power and Liberty, 1873–1900.* Philadelphia: Temple University Press, 1981.

Bostwick, Kate. "Women's Political Clubs." *Monthly Illustrator,* December 1896.

Boswell, Helen V. "Promoting Americanization." *Annals of the American Academy of Political and Social Science* 64 (March 1916): 204–9.

———. "Political Episodes." *The Woman Republican* 12 (March, April, May, June, and December 1935).

Boyd, Mary Sumner. *The Woman Citizen: A General Handbook of Civics, with Special Consideration of Women's Citizenship.* New York: Frederick A. Stokes, 1918.

Boyd, Melba. *Discarded Legacy: Politics and Poetics in the Life of Frances E. W. Harper, 1825–1911.* Detroit: Wayne State University Press, 1994.

Boyer, Paul. *Urban Masses and Moral Order in America, 1820–1920.* Cambridge, Mass.: Harvard University Press, 1978.

Boylan, Anne M. "Women in Groups: An Analysis of the Women's Benevolent Organizations in New York and Boston, 1797–1840." *Journal of American History* 71 (December 1984): 497–523.

Brady, Mark D. "The Progressives' About-Face: The Rhetoric of Maternalism in Post–Woman Suffrage Political Campaigns in California, 1912–1916." Paper presented at the American Historical Association Pacific Coast Branch Annual Meeting, August 1996.

Braitman, Jacqueline R. "A California Stateswoman: The Public Career of Katherine Philips Edson." *California History* 65 (June 1986): 82–95.

———. "Katherine Philips Edson: A Progressive-Feminist in California's Era of Reform." Ph.D. dissertation, University of California at Los Angeles, 1988.

———. "Legislated Parity: Mandating Integration of Women into California Political Parties, 1930s-1950s." In *We Have Come to Stay: American Women and Political Parties, 1880–1960.* Ed. Melanie Gustafson, Kristie Miller, and Elisabeth I. Perry. Albuquerque: University of New Mexico Press, 1999. 175–86.

Braude, Ann. *Radical Spirits: Spiritualism and Women's Rights in Nineteenth-Century America.* Boston: Beacon Press, 1989.

Breckenridge, Sophonisba P. *Women in the Twentieth Century: A Study of their Political, Social, and Economic Activities.* New York: McGraw-Hill, 1933.

Bridges, Amy. "Creating Cultures of Reform." *Studies in American Political Development* 8 (Spring 1994): 1–23.

Brooks, Robert C. *Corruption in American Politics and Life.* New York: Dodd, Mead, 1910.

Brown, Elsa Barkley. "Negotiating and Transforming the Public Sphere: African American Political Life in the Transition from Slavery to Freedom." *Public Culture* 7 (Fall 1994): 108–24.

———. "To Catch a Vision of Freedom: Reconstructing Southern Black Women's Political History, 1865–1880." In *African American Women and the Vote, 1837–1965.* Ed. Ann D. Gordon. Amherst: University of Massachusetts Press, 1997. 66–99.

———. "Uncle Ned's Children: Negotiating Community and Freedom in Postemancipation Richmond, Virginia." Ph.D. dissertation, Kent State University, 1994.

———. "Womanist Consciousness: Maggie Lena Walker and the Independent Order of Saint Luke." *Signs* 14.3 (Spring 1989): 610–33.

Brown, Hallie Q., comp. *Homespun Heroines and Other Women of Distinction.* 1926. Reprint, New York: Oxford University Press, 1988.

Brown, Jerold E., and Patrick D. Reagan, eds. *Voluntarism, Planning, and the State: The American Planning Experience, 1914–1946.* Westport, Conn.: Greenwood Press, 1988.

Brown, Joseph G. *History of Equal Suffrage in Colorado, 1868–1898.* Denver: New Jobs, 1898.

Buechler, Steven M. "Elizabeth Boynton Harbert and the Woman Suffrage Movement, 1870–1896." *Signs* 13.1 (Autumn 1987): 78–97.

———. *The Transformation of the Woman Suffrage Movement: The Case of Illinois, 1850–1920.* New Brunswick, N.J.: Rutgers University Press, 1986.

Buenker, John D. "The Urban Political Machine and Woman Suffrage: A Study in Political Adaptability." *The Historian* 33 (February 1971): 264–79.

Buhle, Mari Jo. *Women and American Socialism.* Urbana: University of Illinois Press, 1981.

Buhle, Mari Jo, and Paul Buhle, eds. *The Concise History of Woman Suffrage: Selections from the Classic Work of Stanton, Anthony, Gage, and Harper.* Urbana: University of Illinois Press, 1978.

Burns, James MacGregor. *The Power to Lead: The Crisis of the American Presidency.* New York: Simon and Schuster, 1984.

Cable, Mrs. Herbert A. "Woman and Politics: Why She Is Logically a Progressive." *Woman's Bulletin,* July/August 1914.

Campbell, Barbara Kuhn. "Prominent Women in the Progressive Era: A Study of Life Histories." Ph.D. dissertation, University of Illinois at Chicago, 1976.

Caroli, Betty Boyd. *The Roosevelt Women.* New York: Basic Books, 1998.

Casdorph, Paul D. *Republicans, Negroes, and Progressives in the South, 1912–1916.* Tuscaloosa: University of Alabama Press, 1981.

Catt, Carrie Chapman. "What Women Have Done with the Vote." *Independent,* October 17, 1925.

Catt, Carrie Chapman, and Nettie R. Shuler. *Woman Suffrage and Politics.* New York: Scribner's, 1923.

Chafe, William. *The American Woman.* New York: Oxford University Press, 1972.

———. *The Paradox of Change: American Women in the 20th Century.* New York: Oxford University Press, 1991.

Chamberlin, Hope. *A Minority of Members: Women in the U.S. Congress.* New York: Praeger, 1973.

Chambers, Clarke A. *Paul U. Kellogg and the Survey: Voices for Social Welfare and Social Justice.* Minneapolis: University of Minnesota Press, 1971.

———. "Toward a Redefinition of Welfare History." *Journal of American History* 73 (September 1986): 407–33.

Chandler, William. "Permanent Republican Clubs." *North American Review* 376 (March 1888): 240–60.

Chatham, Marie. "The Role of the National Party Chairman." Ph.D. dissertation, University of Maryland, 1953.

Chenery, W. L. "Great Public Servant." *Survey,* September 1, 1921.

Cherny, Robert W. *American Politics in the Gilded Age, 1868–1900.* Wheeling, Ill.: Harlan Davidson, 1997.

Cherrington, Ernest H. *The Evolution of Prohibition in the United States of America: A Chronological History.* Westerville, Ohio: American Issue Press, 1920.

———, ed. *Standard Encyclopedia of the Alcohol Problem.* 6 vols. Westerville, Ohio: American Issue Press, 1925–30.

Chester, Giraud. *Embattled Maiden: The Life of Anna Dickinson.* New York: G. P. Putnam's Sons, 1951.

Church, Charles A. *History of the Republican Party in Illinois, 1854–1912.* Rockford, Ill.: Wilson Brothers, 1912.

Clapp, Elizabeth J. "The Personal Touch? Ben Lindsey and the Denver Juvenile Court." *Mid-America* 75 (April-July 1993): 197–221.

Clemens, Elisabeth S. *The People's Lobby: Organizational Innovation and the Rise of Interest Group Politics in the United States, 1890–1925.* Chicago: University of Chicago Press, 1997.

Clement, E. M. "Women at Past National Conventions." *Democratic Digest,* July 1936.

Cohen, Philip N. "Nationalism and Suffrage: Gender Struggle in Nation-Building America." *Signs* 21.3 (1996): 707–27.

Collier-Thomas, Bettye. "Frances Ellen Watkins Harper: Abolitionist and Feminist Reformer, 1825–1911." In *African American Women and the Vote.* Ed. Ann D. Gordon. Amherst: University of Massachusetts Press, 1997. 41–65.

Collin, Richard H., ed. *Theodore Roosevelt and Reform Politics.* Lexington, Mass.: D. C. Heath, 1972.

Cook, Blanche Wiesen. *Eleanor Roosevelt.* Vol. 1, *1884–1933.* New York: Viking, 1992.

Cooper, John Milton, Jr. *Pivotal Decades: The United States, 1900–1920.* New York: W. W. Norton, 1990.

———. *The Warrior and the Priest: Woodrow Wilson and Theodore Roosevelt.* Cambridge, Mass.: Harvard University Press, 1983.

Cornwell, Elmer, Jr. *Presidential Leadership of Public Opinion.* Bloomington: Indiana University Press, 1965.

Coss, Clare. *Lillian D. Wald, Progressive Activist.* New York: The Feminist Press, 1989.

Costain, Anne N., and Douglas W. Costain. "Movements and Gatekeepers: Congressional Response to Women's Movement Issues, 1900–1982." *Congress and the Presidency* 12 (Spring 1985): 21–42.

Cott, Nancy. "Across the Great Divide: Women in Politics before and after 1920." In *Women, Politics, and Change.* Ed. Louise A. Tilly and Patricia Gurin. New York: Russell Sage Foundation, 1990. 153–76.

———. *The Bonds of Womanhood: 'Woman's Sphere' in New England, 1780–1835.* New Haven, Conn.: Yale University Press, 1977.

———. *The Grounding of Modern Feminism*. New Haven, Conn.: Yale University Press, 1987.

———. "What's in a Name? The Limits of 'Social Feminism'; or, Expanding the Vocabulary of Women's History." *Journal of American History* 76 (December 1989): 809–29.

———. "Women's Rights: Unspeakable Issues in the Constitution." *Yale Review* 77 (June 1988): 382–96.

Coultrap-McQuin, Susan, ed. *Gail Hamilton: Selected Writings*. New Brunswick, N.J.: Rutgers University Press, 1992.

Cox, Elizabeth M. "The Three Who Came First." *State Legislatures* 20 (November 1994): 12–19.

———. *Women State and Territorial Legislators, 1895–1995*. Jefferson, N.C.: McFarland and Co., 1996.

Cresap, Dean R. *Party Politics in the Golden State*. Los Angeles: The Haynes Foundation, 1954.

Croly, Herbert. *Marcus Alonzo Hanna: His Life and Work*. New York: Macmillan, 1912.

———. *The Promise of American Life*. New York: Macmillan, 1909.

Crunden, Robert M. *Ministers of Reform: The Progressives' Achievement in American Civilization, 1889–1920*. New York: Basic Books, 1982.

Curtis, Francis. *The History of the Republican Party: A History of Its Fifty Years' Existence and a Record of Its Measures and Leaders, 1854–1904*. 2 vols. New York: G. P. Putnam's Sons, 1904.

Danelski, David J., and Joseph S. Tulchin, eds. *The Autobiographical Notes of Charles Evans Hughes*. Cambridge, Mass.: Harvard University Press, 1973.

Daniels, Doris Groshen. *Always a Sister: The Feminism of Lillian D. Wald*. New York: The Feminist Press, 1989.

Davis, Allen F. *American Heroine: The Life and Legend of Jane Addams*. New York: Oxford University Press, 1973.

———. "The Campaign for the Industrial Relations Commission, 1911–1913." *MidAmerica* 45 (October 1963): 211–28.

———. "Social Workers and the Progressive Party, 1912–1916." *American Historical Review* 69 (April 1964): 671–88.

———. *Spearheads for Reform: Social Settlements and the Progressive Movement, 1890–1914*. New York: Oxford University Press, 1967.

Davis, Oscar King. *Released for Publication*. Boston: Houghton Mifflin, 1925.

Davis, Reda. *The Life of Marietta Stow, Cooperator*. Los Angeles: Point Pinos Editions, 1969.

Davis, Richard Harding. "The Men at Armageddon." *Collier's*, August 24, 1912.

Dawley, Alan. *Struggles for Justice: Social Responsibility and the Liberal State*. Cambridge, Mass.: Harvard University Press, 1991.

Degan, Marie. *The History of the Woman's Peace Party*. Baltimore: Johns Hopkins University Press, 1939.

Democratic Congressional Wives Forum. *History of Democratic Women*. Washington, D.C.: Democratic Congressional Wives Forum, 1960.

Democratic National Committee. *Democratic Campaign Book, 1924*. New York: Isaac Goldmann, 1924.

———. *Democratic Text-Book, 1912*. New York: Isaac Goldmann, 1912.

Deverell, William. "The Neglected Twins: California Democrats and the Progressive Bandwagon." In *California Progressivism Revisited.* Ed. William Deverell and Tom Sitton. Berkeley: University of California Press, 1994. 1–11.

Deverell, William, and Tom Sitton, eds. *California Progressivism Revisited.* Berkeley: University of California Press, 1994.

Deutsch, Sarah. "Learning to Talk More Like a Man: Boston Women's Class-Bridging Organizations, 1870–1940." *American Historical Review* 97 (April 1992): 397–404.

Dewey, John. *Characters and Events.* Vol. 1. Ed. Joseph Ratner. New York: Henry Holt, 1929.

Dietz, Mary. "Context Is All: Feminism and Theories of Citizenship." *Daedalus* 116 (Fall 1987): 1–24.

Diggs, Irene. "Du Bois and Women: A Short Story of Black Women, 1910–1934." *A Current Bibliography of African Affairs* 7 (Summer 1974): 260–303.

Dill, Bonnie Thornton. "Race, Class, and Gender: Prospects for an All-Inclusive Sisterhood." *Feminist Studies* 9 (Spring 1983): 131–50.

Diner, Steven. *A City and Its Universities: Public Policy in Chicago, 1892–1919.* Chapel Hill: University of North Carolina Press, 1980.

Dinkins, Robert J. *Before Equal Suffrage: Women in Partisan Politics from Colonial Times to 1920.* Westport, Conn.: Greenwood Press, 1995.

Dittmer, John. *Black Georgia in the Progressive Era, 1900–1920.* Urbana: University of Illinois Press, 1977.

Donovan, Josephine. *Feminist Theory: The Intellectual Traditions of American Feminism.* New York: Frederick Ungar, 1985.

DuBois, Ellen Carol. *Feminism and Suffrage: The Emergence of an Independent Women's Movement in America, 1848–1869.* Ithaca, N.Y.: Cornell University Press, 1978.

———. *Harriot Stanton Blatch and the Winning of Woman Suffrage.* New Haven, Conn.: Yale University Press, 1997.

———. "Outgrowing the Compact of the Fathers: Equal Rights, Woman Suffrage, and the United States Constitution, 1820–1878." In *Woman Suffrage and Women's Rights.* New York: New York University Press, 1998. 81–113.

———. *Woman Suffrage and Women's Rights.* New York: New York University Press, 1998.

———. "Working Women, Class Relations, and Suffrage Militancy: Harriot Stanton Blatch and the New York Woman Suffrage Movement, 1894–1909." In *Woman Suffrage and Women's Rights.* New York: New York University Press, 1998. 176–209.

———, ed. *Elizabeth Cady Stanton–Susan B. Anthony: Correspondence, Writings, Speeches.* New York: Schocken, 1981.

DuBois, Ellen Carol, et al. "Politics and Culture in Women's History: A Symposium." *Feminist Studies* 6 (Spring 1980): 26–64.

Du Bois, W. E. B. "Along the Color Line." *Crisis,* August 1912.

Dye, Nancy Schrom. *As Equals and as Sisters: Feminism, the Labor Movement, and the Women's Trade Union League of New York.* Columbia: University of Missouri Press, 1980.

Eckert, Fred. "Effects of Women's Suffrage on the Political Situation in the City of Chicago." *Political Science Quarterly* 31 (March 1916): 105–21.

Edwards, Rebecca. *Angels in the Machinery: Gender in American Party Politics from the Civil War to the Progressive Era.* New York: Oxford University Press, 1997.

———. "Gender, Class, and the Transformation of Electoral Campaigns in the Gilded Age." In *We Have Come to Stay: American Women and Political Parties, 1880–1960.* Ed.

Melanie Gustafson, Kristie Miller, and Elisabeth I. Perry. Albuquerque: University of New Mexico Press, 1999. 13–22.

Engelbarts, Rudolf. *Women in the United States Congress, 1917–1972, Their Accomplishments with Bibliographies.* Littleton, Colo.: Libraries Unlimited, 1974.

Epperson, John. *The Changing Legal Status of Political Parties in the United States.* New York: Garland, 1986.

Epstein, Barbara L. *Politics of Domesticity: Women, Evangelism, and Temperance in Nineteenth Century America.* Middletown, Conn.: Wesleyan University Press, 1981.

Epstein, Leon. *Political Parties in the American Mold.* Madison: University of Wisconsin Press, 1986.

Errett, Russell. "The Republican Nominating Conventions of 1856 and 1860." *Magazine of Western History* 10 (July 1889): 260–61.

Ethington, Philip J. *The Public City: The Political Construction of Urban Life in San Francisco, 1850–1900.* New York: Cambridge University Press, 1994.

Farmer, Lydia Hoyt, ed. *What America Owes to Women: The National Exposition Souvenier.* Buffalo, N.Y.: Charles Wells Moulton, 1893.

Farrell, John. *Beloved Lady: A History of Jane Addams' Ideas on Reform and Peace.* Baltimore: Johns Hopkins University Press, 1967.

Fahs, Alice. "The Feminized Civil War: Gender, Northern Popular Literature, and the Memory of War, 1861–1900." *Journal of American History* 85 (March 1999): 1461–94.

Fischer, Roger A. *Tippecanoe and Trinkets Too: The Material Culture of American Presidential Campaigns, 1828–1984.* Urbana: University of Illinois Press, 1988.

Fitzpatrick, Ellen. *Endless Crusade: Women Social Scientists and the Progressive Era.* New York: Oxford University Press, 1990.

Flamming, Douglas. "African Americans and the Politics of Race in Progressive-Era Los Angeles." In *California Progressivism Revisited.* Ed. William Deverell and Tom Sitton. Berkeley: University of California Press, 1994. 203–88.

Flanagan, Maureen. *Charter Reform in Chicago.* Carbondale: Southern Illinois University Press, 1987.

———. "Gender and Urban Political Reform: The City Club and the Woman's City Club of Chicago in the Progressive Era." *American Historical Review* 95 (October 1990): 1032–50.

Flexner, Eleanor. *Century of Struggle: The Woman's Rights Movement in the United States.* 2d ed. Cambridge, Mass.: Harvard University Press, 1975.

Foner, Eric. *Free Soil, Free Labor, Free Men: The Ideology of the Republican Party before the Civil War.* New York: Oxford University Press, 1970.

Ford, Linda. *Iron-Jawed Angels: The Suffrage Militancy of the National Woman's Party, 1912–1920.* Lanham, N.Y.: University Press of America, 1991.

Forman, S. E., and Marjorie Shuler. *The Woman Voter's Manual.* New York: Century Co., 1918.

Formisano, Ronald P. "The 'Party Period' Revisited." *Journal of American History* 86 (June 1999): 93–120.

———. *The Transformation of Political Culture: Massachusetts Parties, 1790s–1840s.* New York: Oxford University Press, 1983.

Foster, Judith Ellen. "Constitutional Amendment Catechism: For Bands of Hope, Woman's Unions, and Other Temperance Workers for Constitutional Prohibition Principles among the Young." New York: National Temperance Society and Publishing House, 1882.

———. "Constitutional Amendment Manual, Containing Argument, Appeal, Petitions, Forms of Constitution, Catechism and General Directions for Organized Work for Constitutional Prohibition." New York: National Temperance Society and Publishing House, 1882.

———. *The Crime against Ireland.* Boston: D. Lothrop and Co., 1888.

———. "For God and Home, and Native Land: The Truth in the Case, Concerning Partisanship and Non-Partisanship in the W.C.T.U." Clinton, Iowa.: n.p., 1889.

———. "The Influence of Women in American Politics." In *What America Owes to Women: The National Exposition Souvenier.* Ed. Lydia Hoyt Farmer. Buffalo, N.Y.: Charles Wells Moulton, 1893.

———. "The Republican Party and Temperance. Speech Delivered at Roseland Park, Woodstock, Connecticut, September 1888." N.p., n.d. [1888].

———. *The Saloon Must Go.* New York: Edward O. Jenkins' Sons, 1889.

———. "Woman's Political Evolution." *North American Review* 65 (1897): 600–609.

Fox, Stephen R. *The Guardian of Boston: William Monroe Trotter.* New York: Atheneum, 1970.

Frank, Henriette, and Amalie Jerome, comps. *Annals of the Chicago Woman's Club.* Chicago: Chicago Woman's Club, 1916.

Frankel, Noralee, and Nancy S. Dye, eds. *Gender, Class, Race and Reform in the Progressive Era.* Lexington: University Press of Kentucky, 1991.

Freedman, Estelle. "Separatism as Strategy: Female Institution Building and American Feminism, 1870–1930." *Feminist Studies* 5 (Fall 1979): 512–29.

Freeman, Jo. *A Room at a Time: How Women Entered Party Politics.* Lanham, N.Y.: Rowman and Littlefield, 2000.

Frisken, Amanda. "Sex in Politics: Victoria Woodhull as an American Public Woman, 1870–1876." *Journal of Women's History* 12 (Spring 2000): 89–110.

Furlow, John W. "Cornelia Bryce Pinchot: Feminism in the Post-Suffrage Era." *Pennsylvania History* 43 (October 1976): 329–46.

Gable, John. *Bull Moose Years: Theodore Roosevelt and the Progressive Party.* Port Washington, N.Y.: Kennikat Press, 1978.

Gallaher, Ruth A. *Legal and Political Status of Women In Iowa: An Historical Account of the Rights of Women in Iowa from 1838 to 1918.* Iowa City: State Historical Society of Iowa, 1918.

Gambone, Joseph G. "The Forgotten Feminist of Kansas: The Papers of Clarina H. Nichols, 1854–1885." *Kansas Historical Quarterly* 39 (1973): 12–57, 220–61, 392–444, 551–63.

Garraty, John. *Right-Hand Man: The Life of George Perkins.* New York: Harper, 1960.

Gatewood, Willard B., Jr. *Aristocrats of Color: The Black Elite, 1880–1920.* Bloomington: Indiana University Press, 1990.

———. *Theodore Roosevelt and the Art of Controversy.* Baton Rouge: Louisiana State University Press, 1970.

Geer, Emily Apt. *First Lady: The Life of Lucy Webb Hayes.* Fremont, Ohio: Kent State University Press, 1984.

Gerstle, Gary. "Theodore Roosevelt and the Divided Character of American Nationalism." *Journal of American History* 86 (December 1999): 1280–1307.

Giddings, Paula. *When and Where I Enter: The Impact of Black Women on Race and Sex in America.* New York: Bantam Books, 1984.

Gienapp, William E. *The Origins of the Republican Party, 1852–1856.* New York: Oxford University Press, 1987.

———. "'Politics Seem to Enter into Everything': Political Culture in the North, 1840–1860." In *Essays in American Antebellum Politics, 1840–1860.* Ed. Stephen Maizlish and John J. Kushma. College Station: University of Texas Press, 1982.

Gilmore, Glenda. *Gender and Jim Crow: Women and the Politics of White Supremacy in North Carolina, 1896–1920.* Chapel Hill: University of North Carolina Press, 1996.

Ginzberg, Lori. "'Moral Suasion Is Moral Balderdash': Women, Politics and Social Activism in the 1850s." *Journal of American History* 73 (December 1986): 601–22.

———. *Women and the Work of Benevolence: Morality, Politics, and Class in the Nineteenth Century United States.* New Haven, Conn.: Yale University Press, 1990.

Gluck, Sherna, ed. *From Parlor to Prison: Five American Suffragists Talk about Their Lives.* New York: Random House, 1976.

Goldberg, Michael L. *An Army of Women: Gender and Politics in Gilded Age Kansas.* Baltimore: Johns Hopkins University Press, 1997.

Goldmark, Josephine. *Impatient Crusader: Florence Kelley's Life Story.* Urbana: University of Illinois Press, 1953.

Goldsmith, Barbara. *Other Powers: The Age of Suffrage, Spiritualism, and the Scandalous Victoria Woodhull.* New York: Alfred A. Knopf, 1998.

Goldstein, Joel. *The Effects of the Adoption of Woman Suffrage: Sex Difference in Voting Behavior, Illinois, 1912–1921.* New York: Praeger, 1984.

Good, Josephine L. *Republican Womanpower: The History of Women in Republican National Conventions and Women in the Republican National Committee.* Washington, D.C.: Women's Division, Republican National Committee, 1963.

Goodstein, Anita Shafer. "A Rare Alliance: African American and White Women in the Tennessee Elections of 1919 and 1920." *Journal of Southern History* 64 (May 1998): 219–46.

Goodwyn, Lawrence. *Democratic Promise: The Populist Movement in America.* New York: Oxford University Press, 1976.

Gordon, Ann D., ed. *Against an Aristocracy of Sex, 1866–1873.* Vol. 2 of *The Selected Papers of Elizabeth Cady Stanton and Susan B. Anthony.* New Brunswick, N.J.: Rutgers University Press, 2000.

———. *In The School of Anti-Slavery, 1840 to 1866.* Vol. 1 of *The Selected Papers of Elizabeth Cady Stanton and Susan B. Anthony.* New Brunswick, N.J.: Rutgers University Press, 1997.

Gordon, Felice D. *After Winning: The Legacy of the New Jersey Suffragists, 1920–1947.* New Brunswick, N.J.: Rutgers University Press, 1986.

Gordon, Linda. *Heroes of Their Own Lives: The Politics and History of Family Violence.* New York: Viking, 1988.

Gosnell, Harold F. *Negro Politicians.* Chicago: University of Chicago Press, 1935.

Gould, Lewis L. *Progressives and Prohibitionists.* Austin: University of Texas Press, 1973.

———. "Theodore Roosevelt, William Howard Taft, and the Disputed Delegates of 1912: Texas as a Test Case." *Southwestern Historical Quarterly* 80 (July 1976): 33–56.

——, ed. *American First Ladies: Their Lives and Their Legacies.* New York: Garland, 1996.

Grantham, Dewey W., Jr. "The Progressive Movement and the Negro." *South Atlantic Quarterly* 54 (October 1955): 461–77.

Greeley, Horace, and John F. Cleveland, comps. *A Political Text-Book for 1860.* New York: Tribune Association, 1860.

Green, G. N. "Republicans, Bull Moose, and Negroes in Florida, 1912." *Florida Historical Quarterly* 43.2 (1964): 153–64.

Green, Paul M., and Melvin G. Holli, eds. *The Mayors: The Chicago Political Tradition.* Carbondale: Southern Illinois University Press, 1987.

Greenstone, J. David. "Political Culture and American Political Development." *Studies in American Political Development* 1 (1986): 1–49.

Griffith, Elisabeth. *In Her Own Right: The Life of Elizabeth Cady Stanton.* New York: Oxford University Press, 1984.

Grimke, Sarah. *Letters on the Equality of the Sexes and the Condition of Woman: Addressed to Mary S. Parker.* Boston: Isaac Knapp, 1837.

Gruberg, Martin. *Women in American Politics: An Assessment and Sourcebook.* Oshkosh, Wis.: Academia Press, 1968.

Gullett, Gayle Ann. *Becoming Citizens: The Emergence and Development of the California Women's Movement, 1880–1911.* Urbana: University of Illinois Press, 1999.

——. "Feminism, Politics, and Voluntary Groups: Organized Womanhood in California, 1886–1896." Ph.D. dissertation, University of California at Riverside, 1983.

——. "Women Progressives and the Politics of Americanization in California, 1915–1920." *Pacific Historical Review* 64 (February 1995): 71–94.

Gurin, Patricia, et al. *Hope and Independence: Blacks' Responses to Electoral and Party Politics.* New York: Russell Sage Foundation, 1989.

Gustafson, Melanie. "Florence Collins Porter and the Concept of the Principled Partisan Woman." *Frontiers: A Journal of Women's Studies* 18.1 (Summer 1997): 62–79.

——. "Partisan and Nonpartisan: The Political Career of Judith Ellen Foster, 1881–1910." In *We Have Come to Stay: American Women and Political Parties, 1880–1960.* Ed. Melanie Gustafson, Kristie Miller, and Elisabeth I. Perry. Albuquerque: University of New Mexico Press, 1999. 1–12.

——. "Partisan Women: Gender, Politics, and the Progressive Party of 1912." Ph.D. dissertation, New York University, 1993.

——. "Partisan Women in the Progressive Era: The Struggle for Inclusion in American Political Parties." *Journal of Women's History* 9 (Summer 1997): 7–30.

Gustafson, Melanie, Kristie Miller, and Elisabeth I. Perry, eds. *We Have Come to Stay: American Women and Political Parties, 1880–1960.* Albuquerque: University of New Mexico Press, 1999.

Hackett, C. I. "Lady Who Made Lobbying Respectable." *Woman Citizen,* April 19, 1924.

Hafen, LeRoy R. *Colorado and Its People: A Narrative and Topical History of the Centennial State.* 4 vols. New York: Lewis Historical Publishing, Co., 1948.

Hagadorn, Hermann, ed. *The National Edition of the Works of Theodore Roosevelt.* 20 vols. New York: Charles Scribner's Sons, 1926.

Hanaford, Phebe A. *Daughters of America; Or, Women of the Century.* Augusta, Maine: True and Company, 1883.

Harger, Charles Moreau. "The Two National Conventions." *Independent,* October 10, 1912.

Harley, Sharon, and Rosalyn Terborg-Penn, eds. *The Afro-American Woman: Struggles and Images.* Port Washington, N.Y.: Kennikat Press, 1978.

Harmon, Sandra D. "Altgeld the Suffragist." *Chicago History* 16 (Summer 1987): 14–25.

Harper, Ida Husted. *The Life and Work of Susan B. Anthony.* 2 vols. Indianapolis: Hollenbeck Press, 1898.

Harriman, Florence Jaffrey. *From Pinafores to Politics.* New York: Henry Holt and Company, 1923.

Harvey, Anna L. "Culture or Strategy? Women in New York State Parties, 1917–1930." In *We Have Come to Stay: American Women and Political Parties, 1880–1960.* Ed. Melanie Gustafson, Kristie Miller, and Elisabeth I. Perry. Albuquerque: University of New Mexico Press, 1999. 87–96.

———. *Votes without Leverage: Women in American Electoral Politics, 1920–1970.* New York: Cambridge University Press, 1998.

Hays, Samuel P. *American Political History as Social Analysis: Essays by Samuel P. Hays.* Knoxville: University of Tennessee Press, 1980.

———. "The Politics of Reform in Municipal Government in the Progressive Era." *Pacific Northwest Quarterly* 55 (1964): 157–69.

Hays, Will. *The Memoirs of Will H. Hays.* Garden City, N.Y.: Doubleday, 1955.

Hebard, Grace Raymond. *How Woman Suffrage Came to Wyoming, 1869.* New York: William Dean Embree, 1940.

Hechler, Kenneth W. *Insurgency: Personalities and Politics of the Taft Era.* New York: Russell and Russell, Inc., 1964.

Hendricks, Wanda A. "African American Women as Political Constituents in Chicago, 1913–1915." In *We Have Come to Stay: American Women and Political Parties, 1880–1960.* Ed. Melanie Gustafson, Kristie Miller, and Elisabeth I. Perry. Albuquerque: University of New Mexico Press, 1999. 55–64.

Hennings, Robert E. *James D. Phelan and the Wilson Progressives of California.* New York: Garland Press, 1985.

Herr, Pamela, and Mary Lee Spence, eds. *Letters of Jessie Benton Frémont.* Urbana: University of Illinois Press, 1993.

Hershberger, Mary. "Mobilizing Women, Anticipating Abolition: The Struggle against Indian Removal in the 1830s." *Journal of American History* 86 (June 1999): 15–40.

Hewitt, Nancy. "Beyond the Search for Sisterhood: American Women's History in the 1980s." *Social History* 10 (October 1985): 299–322.

———. *Women's Activism and Social Change: Rochester, New York, 1822–1872.* Ithaca, N.Y.: Cornell University Press, 1984.

Hicks, John D. *The Populist Revolt.* Minneapolis: University of Minnesota Press, 1931.

Higginbotham, Evelyn Brooks. "In Politics to Stay: Black Women Leaders and Party Politics in the 1920s." In *Women, Politics, and Change.* Ed. Louise A. Tilly and Patricia Gurin. New York: Russell Sage, 1990. 199–220.

Hine, Darlene Clark. *Black Women in White: Racial Conflict and Cooperation in the Nursing Profession, 1890–1950.* Bloomington: Indiana University Press, 1989.

Hine, Darlene Clark, Elsa Barkley Brown, and Rosalyn Terborg-Penn, eds. *Black Women in America: An Historical Encyclopedia.* 2 vols. Bloomington: Indiana University Press, 1994.

Hirshson, Stanley P. *Farewell to the Bloody Shirt: Northern Republicans and the Southern Negro, 1877–1893.* Bloomington: Indiana University Press, 1962.

Hoff-Wilson, Joan. "'Peace Is a Woman's Job . . .': Jeannette Rankin and American Foreign Policy: The Origins of Her Pacifism." *Montana: The Magazine for Western History* 30 (January 1980): 28–41.

———. "'Peace Is a Woman's Job . . .': Jeannette Rankin and American Foreign Policy: Her Lifework as a Pacifist." *Montana: The Magazine for Western History* 30 (April 1980): 38–53.

Hofstadter, Richard. *The Age of Reform.* New York: Vintage Books, 1955.

———. *The American Political Tradition and the Men Who Made It.* New York: Knopf, 1948.

Hollingsworth, J. Rogers. *The Whirligig of Politics.* Chicago: University of Chicago Press, 1963.

Holt, James. *Congressional Insurgents and the Party System, 1909–1916.* Cambridge, Mass.: Harvard University Press, 1967.

Hoogenboom, Ari. *Outlawing the Spoils: A History of the Civil Service Reform Movement, 1865–1883.* Urbana: University of Illinois Press, 1961.

Horowitz, Helen Lefkowitz. "Victoria Woodhull, Anthony Comstock, and Conflict over Sex in the United States in the 1870s." *Journal of American History* 87 (September 2000): 403–34.

Howe, Daniel Walker. "The Evangelical Movement and Political Culture in the North during the Second Party System." *Journal of American History* 77 (March 1991): 1216–39.

Howe, Julia Ward. "Woman and the Suffrage: The Case for Woman Suffrage." *Outlook,* April 3, 1909.

Huck, Winnifred. "What Happened to Me in Congress." *Woman's Home Companion,* July 1923.

Hundley, Norris, Jr. "Katherine Philips Edson and the Fight for the California Minimum Wage, 1912–1923." *Pacific Historical Review* 29 (August 1960): 271–86.

Huthmacher, J. Joseph. "Urban Liberalism and the Age of Reform." *Mississippi Valley Historical Review* 44 (September 1962): 231–41.

Ickes, Harold. "Who Killed the Progressive Party?" *American Historical Review* 46 (1941): 306–37.

Isely, Jeter Allen. *Horace Greeley and the Republican Party, 1853–1861.* Princeton, N.J.: Princeton University Press, 1947.

Isenberg, Nancy. *Sex and Citizenship in Antebellum America.* Chapel Hill: University of North Carolina Press, 1998.

James, Louise B. "Alice Mary Robertson, Anti-Feminist Congresswoman." *Chronicles of Oklahoma* 55 (Winter 1977–78): 454–62.

James, Edward T., Janet Wilson James, and Paul S. Boyer, eds. *Notable American Women, 1607–1950: A Biographical Dictionary.* 3 vols. Cambridge, Mass.: Belknap Press, 1971.

Jeffrey, Julie Roy. *The Great Silent Army of Abolitionism: Ordinary Women in the Antislavery Movement.* Chapel Hill: University of North Carolina Press, 1998.

Johnson, Alexander, ed. *Proceedings of the National Conference of Charities and Corrections.* Ft. Wayne, Ind.: Ft. Wayne Printing Company, 1912.

Johnson, Allen, and Dumas Malone, eds. *Dictionary of American Biography.* New York: Charles Scribner's Sons, 1931.

Johnson, Donald Bruce. *National Party Platforms.* Vol. 1, *1840–1956.* Urbana: University of Illinois Press, 1978.

Johnson, Reinhard O. "The Liberty Party in Massachusetts, 1840–1848." *Civil War History* 28 (September 1982): 237–65.

Karcher, Carolyn L. *The First Woman in the Republic: A Cultural Biography of Lydia Maria Child.* Durham, N.C.: Duke University Press, 1995.

Katz, Sherry. "Dual Commitments: Feminism, Socialism, and Women's Political Activism in California, 1890–1920." Ph.D. dissertation, University of California at Los Angeles, 1991.

———. "Redefining 'The Political': Socialist Women and Party Politics in California, 1900–1920." In *We Have Come to Stay: American Women and Political Parties, 1880–1960.* Ed. Melanie Gustafson, Kristie Miller, and Elisabeth I. Perry. Albuquerque: University of New Mexico Press, 1999. 23–32.

———. "Socialist Women and Progressive Reform." In *California Progressivism Revisited.* Ed. William Deverell and Tom Sitton. Berkeley: University of California Press, 1995. 117–43.

Keller, Morton. *Affairs of State: Public Life in Late Nineteenth Century America.* Cambridge, Mass.: Harvard University Press, 1977.

Kelley, Florence. "Twenty-five Years of the Consumers' League Movement." *Survey,* November 27, 1915.

Kellogg, Charles Flint. *NAACP: A History.* Baltimore: Johns Hopkins University Press, 1967.

Kellor, Frances. "A New Spirit in Party Organization." *North American Review,* June 1914.

———. *Out of Work.* New York: G. P. Putnam's Sons, 1904.

———. "The Protection of Immigrant Women." *Atlantic,* February 1908.

———. "What Women Can Do." *Progressive Bulletin,* September 1912.

———. "Women in the Campaign." *Yale Review* 6 (January 1917): 233–43.

Kelly, Frank K. *The Fight for the White House: The Story of 1912.* New York: Thomas Crowell and Co., 1961.

Kerber, Linda. "The Meanings of Citizenship." *Journal of American History* 84 (December 1997): 833–54.

———. *No Constitutional Right to Be Ladies: Women and the Obligation of Citizenship.* New York: Hill and Wang, 1998.

———. "'Ourselves and Our Daughters Forever': Women and the Constitution, 1787–1876." In *One Woman, One Vote: Rediscovering the Woman Suffrage Movement.* Ed. Marjorie Spruill Wheeler. Troutdale, Ore.: NewSage Press, 1995. 21–36.

———. "Separate Spheres, Female Worlds, Woman's Place: The Rhetoric of Women's History." *Journal of American History* 75 (June 1988): 9–39.

———. *Women of the Republic: Intellect and Ideology in Revolutionary America.* Chapel Hill: University of North Carolina Press, 1980.

Kerr, Andrea Moore. "White Women's Rights, Black Men's Wrongs, Free Love, Blackmail, and the Formation of the American Woman Suffrage Association." In *One Woman, One Vote: Rediscovering the Woman Suffrage Movement.* Ed. Marjorie Spruill Wheeler. Troutdale, Ore.: NewSage Press, 1995. 61–80.

Kessler-Harris, Alice. *Out to Work: A History of Wage-Earning Women in the United States.* New York: Oxford University Press, 1982.

Kleeberg, Gordon. *The Formation of the Republican Party.* New York: Macmillan, 1911.

Kleppner, Paul. *Continuity and Change in Electoral Politics, 1893–1928.* Westport, Conn.: Greenwood Press, 1987.

———. "Were Women to Blame? Female Suffrage and Voter Turnout." *Journal of Interdisciplinary History* 12.4 (Spring 1982): 621–43.

Kloppenberg, James L. *Uncertain Victory: Social Democracy and Progressivism in European and American Thought, 1870–1920.* New York: Oxford University Press, 1986.

Kolko, Gabriel. *The Triumph of Conservatism: A Reinterpretation of American History, 1900–1916.* New York: Free Press, 1963.

Kousser, J. Morgan. *The Shaping of Southern Politics: Suffrage Restrictions and the Establishment of the One-Party South, 1880–1910.* New Haven, Conn.: Yale University Press, 1974.

Koven, Seth, and Sonya Michel. "Womanly Duties: Maternalist Politics and the Origins of Welfare States in France, Germany, Great Britian, and the United States, 1880–1920." *American Historical Review* 95 (October 1990): 1076–1108.

Kraditor, Aileen. *The Ideas of the Woman Suffrage Movement, 1890–1920.* New York: Columbia University Press, 1965.

———. *Means and Ends in American Abolitionism: Garrison and His Critics on Strategy and Tactics.* New York: Pantheon, 1969.

Kunin, Madeleine. *Living the Political Life.* New York: Knopf, 1994.

Kunzel, Regina. "The Professionalization of Benevolence: Evangelicals and Social Workers in the Florence Crittenton Homes, 1915–1945." *Journal of Social History* 22 (Fall 1988): 21–43.

Ladd-Taylor, Molly. *Mother-Work: Women, Child Welfare, and the State, 1890–1930.* Urbana: University of Illinois Press, 1994.

———. *Raising a Baby the Government Way: Mothers' Letters to the Children's Bureau, 1915–1932.* New Brunswick, N.J.: Rutgers University Press, 1986.

LaFollette, Robert M. *LaFollette's Autobiography: A Personal Narrative of Political Experiences.* Madison, Wis.: Robert M. LaFollette, 1913.

Larsen, Charles. *The Good Fight: The Life and Times of Ben B. Lindsey.* Chicago: Quadrangle Books, 1972.

Larson, T. A. *History of Wyoming.* Lincoln: University of Nebraska Press, 1978.

———. "Petticoats at the Polls: Woman Suffrage in Territorial Wyoming." *Pacific Northwest Quarterly* 44 (April 1953): 74–79.

———. "Woman Suffrage in Western America." *Utah Historical Quarterly* 38 (Winter 1970): 7–19.

———. "Wyoming's Contribution to the Regional and National Women's Rights Movement." *Annals of Wyoming* 52 (January 1980): 2–15.

Lasch, Christopher, ed. *The Social Thought of Jane Addams.* Indianapolis: Bobbs-Merrill, 1965.

Lasch-Quinn, Elisabeth. *Black Neighbors: Race and the Limits of Reform in the American Settlement House Movement, 1890–1945.* Chapel Hill: University of North Carolina Press, 1993.

Lasser, Carol, and Marlene Deahl Merrill, eds. *Friends and Sisters: Letters between Lucy Stone and Antoinette Brown Blackwell, 1846–1893.* Urbana: University of Illinois Press, 1987.

Lathrop, Julia. "Florence Kelley, 1859–1932." *Survey,* March 15, 1932.

League of Women Voters. *Forty Years of a Great Idea.* Washington, D.C.: League of Women Voters, 1959.

Lebsock, Suzanne. *The Free Women of Petersburg: Status and Culture in a Southern Town, 1784–1860.* New York: W. W. Norton, 1984.

———. "Women and American Politics, 1880–1920." In *Women, Politics, and Change.* Ed. Louise A. Tilly and Patricia Gurin. New York: Russell Sage Foundation, 1990. 35–62.

Lemons, J. Stanley. *The Woman Citizen: Social Feminism in the 1920s.* Urbana: University of Illinois Press, 1973.

Lender, Mark E., ed. *Dictionary of American Temperance Biography.* Westport, Conn.: Greenwood Press, 1984.

Leonard, John, comp. *Woman's Who's Who of America, 1914–1915.* New York: American Commonwealth Company, 1914.

Lerner, Gerda. *The Grimke Sisters from South Carolina: Rebels against Slavery.* Boston: Houghton Mifflin, 1967.

Lerner, Gerda, ed. *Black Women in White America: A Documentary History.* New York: Random House, 1972.

Levine, Daniel. *Jane Addams and the Liberal Tradition.* Madison: State Historical Society of Wisconsin, 1971.

Levine, Edward M. *The Irish and Irish Politicians.* Notre Dame, Ind.: University of Notre Dame Press, 1966.

Levine, Lawrence. *Highbrow/Lowbrow: The Emergence of Cultural Hierarchy in America.* Cambridge, Mass.: Harvard University Press, 1988.

Lewinson, Paul. *Race, Class and Party: A History of Negro Suffrage and White Politics in the South.* New York: Oxford University Press, 1932.

Lewis, David Levering. *W. E. B. Du Bois: Biography of a Race, 1868–1919.* New York: Henry Holt, 1993.

Lewis, Jan. "The Republican Wife: Virtue and Seduction in the Early Republic." *William and Mary Quarterly* 44 (October 1987): 689–721.

Lichtman, Allan J. "Critical Election Theory and the Reality of American Presidential Politics, 1916–1940." *American Historical Review* 81 (April 1976): 317–48.

Link, Arthur. "The Negro as a Factor in the Campaign of 1912." *Journal of Negro History* 32 (January 1947): 81–99.

———. "Theodore Roosevelt and the South in 1912." *North Carolina Historical Review* 23 (July 1946): 313–24.

———. *Woodrow Wilson: A Biography.* Chicago: Quadrangle Books, 1963.

———. *Woodrow Wilson and the Progressive Era, 1910–1917.* New York: Harper and Row, 1954.

Lipshultz, Sybil. "Social Feminism and Legal Discourse, 1908–1923." *Yale Journal of Law and Feminism* 2 (Fall 1989): 131–60.

Livermore, Henrietta W. "New York State Republican Women, 1919–1929." *The Republican Woman,* July 7, 1923.

Livermore, Mary. *The Story of My Life, or, the Sunshine and Shadow of Seventy Years.* Hartford, Conn.: A. D. Worthington, 1899.

Lockwood, Belva. "How I Ran for the Presidency." *National Magazine,* March 1903.

Logan, Mary S. *The Part Taken by Women in American History.* Wilmington, Del.: Perry-Nalle Publishing, 1912.

Lowry, Edward. "With the Bull Moose in Convention." *Harper's Weekly,* August 17, 1912.

Lunardini, Christine. *From Equal Suffrage to Equal Rights: Alice Paul and the National Woman's Party, 1910–1928.* New York: New York University Press, 1986.

Lutz, Alma. *Susan B. Anthony: Rebel, Crusader, Humanitarian.* Boston: Beacon Press, 1959.

Lyons, Louis S., ed. *Who's Who among the Women of California.* San Francisco: Security Publishing, 1922.

MacRae, Allan A. "The Rise of the Progressive Movement in the State of California." M.A. thesis, Occidental College, 1923.

Macy, Jesse. *Party Organization and Machinery.* New York: Century, 1904.

Malone, Dumas, ed. *Dictionary of American Biography.* New York: Charles Scribner's Sons, 1935.

Mann, Arthur. *Yankee Reformers in an Urban Age.* Cambridge, Mass.: Harvard University Press, 1954.

Marcus, Robert. *Grand Old Party: Political Structure in the Gilded Age, 1880–1896.* New York: Oxford University Press, 1971.

Margulies, Herbert. "LaFollette, Roosevelt, and the Republican Presidential Nomination of 1912." *MidAmerica* 58 (January 1976): 54–76.

Marilley, Suzanne M. *Woman Suffrage and the Origins of Liberal Feminism in the United States, 1820–1920.* Cambridge, Mass.: Harvard University Press, 1996.

Marquis, Albert N., ed. *Who's Who in New England.* Chicago, A. N. Marquis, 1916.

Martel, May. "Woman's Part in the Campaign." *New York Age,* November 7, 1912.

Martin, Ralph G. *Ballots and Bandwagons.* Chicago: Rand McNally, 1964.

Matthews, Glenna. "'There Is No Sex in Citizenship': The Career of Congresswoman Florence Prag Kahn." In *We Have Come to Stay: American Women and Political Parties, 1880–1960.* Ed. Melanie Gustafson, Kristie Miller, and Elisabeth I. Perry. Albuquerque: University of New Mexico Press, 1999. 131–40.

Mayo, Edith P. "Campaign Appeals to Women." In *American Material Culture: The Shape of Things around Us.* Ed. Edith P. Mayo. Bowling Green, Ohio: Bowling Green State University Popular Press, 1984. 128–48.

McCarthy, Charles. *The Wisconsin Idea.* New York: Macmillan, 1912.

McCormick, Richard L. "Prelude to Progressivism: The Transformation of New York State Politics, 1890–1910." In *The Party Period and Public Policy: American Politics from the Age of Jackson to the Progressive Era.* New York: Oxford University Press, 1986. 289–310.

———. *From Realignment to Reform: Political Change in New York State, 1893–1910.* Ithaca, N.Y.: Cornell University Press, 1981.

McGerr, Michael. *The Decline of Popular Politics: The American North, 1865–1928.* New York: Oxford University Press, 1986.

McPherson, James M. *Battle Cry of Freedom: The Civil War Era.* New York: Oxford University Press, 1988.

Meier, August. *Negro Thought in America.* Ann Arbor: University of Michigan Press, 1963.

Meltzer, Milton, and Patricia G. Holland, eds. *Lydia Maria Child: Selected Letters, 1817–1880.* Amherst: University of Massachusetts Press, 1982.

Merk, Lois Bannister. "The Early Career of Maud Wood Park." *Radcliffe Quarterly* 32 (May 1948): 10–17.

Miller, Dorothy Grace. "Within the Bounds of Propriety: Clara Burdette and the Women's Movement." Ph.D. dissertation, University of California at Riverside, 1984.

Miller, Kristie. "'Eager and Anxious to Work': Daisy Harriman and the Presidential Election of 1912." In *We Have Come to Stay: American Women and Political Parties, 1880–1960*. Ed. Melanie Gustafson, Kristie Miller, and Elisabeth I. Perry. Albuquerque: University of New Mexico Press, 1999. 65–75.

———. *Ruth Hanna McCormick: A Life in Politics, 1880–1944*. Albuquerque: University of New Mexico Press, 1992.

Monoson, S. Sara. "The Lady and the Tiger: Women's Electoral Activism in New York City before Suffrage." *Journal of Women's History* 2 (Fall 1990): 100–135.

Morgan, H. Wayne. *From Hayes to McKinley: National Party Politics, 1877–1896*. Syracuse, N.Y.: Syracuse University Press, 1969.

Morgan, Murray C. "Nena Jolidon Croake, Mystery Feminist of Tacoma." *Tacoma News Tribune*, August 4, 1994.

Morison, Elting, ed. *The Letters of Theodore Roosevelt*. 8 vols. Cambridge, Mass.: Harvard University Press, 1954.

Moss, Rosalind Urbach. "The 'Girls' from Syracuse: Sex Role Negotiations of Kansas Women in Politics, 1877–1890." In *The Women's West*. Ed. Susan Armitage and Elizabeth Jameson. Norman: University of Oklahoma Press, 1987. 253–64.

Mowry, George. *The California Progressives*. Berkeley: University of California Press, 1951.

———. *The Era of Theodore Roosevelt and the Rise of Modern America*. New York: Harper and Brothers, 1958.

———. "The Progressive Party, 1912 and 1924." In *History of U.S. Political Parties*. Ed. Arthur M. Schlesinger Jr. 4 vols. New York: Chelsea House, 1973.

———. "The South and the Progressive Lily-White Party of 1912," *Journal of Southern History* 6 (May 1940): 237–47.

———. *Theodore Roosevelt and the Progressive Movement*. Madison: University of Wisconsin Press, 1946.

Moynihan, Ruth. *Rebel for Rights: Abigail Scott Duniway*. New Haven, Conn.: Yale University Press, 1983.

Muncy, Robyn. *Creating a Female Dominion in American Reform, 1890–1935*. New York: Oxford University Press, 1991.

———. "'Women Demand Recognition': Women Candidates in Colorado's Election of 1912." In *We Have Come to Stay: American Women and Political Parties, 1880–1960*. Ed. Melanie Gustafson, Kristie Miller, and Elisabeth I. Perry. Albuquerque: University of New Mexico Press, 1999. 45–54.

Musslewhite, Lynn R., and Suzanne Jones Crawford. "Kate Barnard and Feminine Politics in the Progressive Era." *Mid-America* 75 (January 1993): 45–66.

Nathan, Maud. *Once upon a Time and Today*. New York: G. P. Putnam's Sons, 1933.

———. *Story of an Epoch-Making Movement*. New York: Doubleday, Page, 1926.

National American Woman Suffrage Association. *Handbook of the NAWSA: And Proceedings of the Convention Held at Cleveland, Ohio, April 13, 1921*. New York: National American Woman Suffrage Association, 1921.

———. *Victory: How Women Won It: A Centennial Symposium, 1840–1940*. New York: H. W. Wilson, Co., 1940.

National Federation of Republican Women. *NFRW: Fifty Years of Leadership, 1938–1988*. Washington, D.C.: National Federation of Republican Women, 1987.

Nelli, Humbert S. "John Powers and the Italians: Politics in a Chicago Ward, 1896–1921." *Journal of American History* 57 (June 1970): 67–84.

Newman, Louise Michele. *White Women's Rights: The Racial Origins of Feminism in the United States.* New York: Oxford University Press, 1999.

Nichols, Carole. "Votes and More for Women: Suffrage and After in Connecticut." *Women and History* 5 (Spring 1983): 1–86.

Oakley, Mary Ann B. *Elizabeth Cady Stanton.* Old Westbury, N.Y.: The Feminist Press, 1972.

Odegard, Peter. *Pressure Politics: The Story of the Anti-Saloon League.* New York: Columbia University Press, 1966.

Official Proceedings of the Eleventh Republican National Convention Held in the City of St. Louis, Missouri, June 16, 17, 18, 1896. Pittsburgh: James F. Burke, 1896.

Official Proceedings of the National Republican Conventions of 1868, 1872, 1876, and 1880. Minneapolis: Charles W. Johnson, 1903.

Official Proceedings of the Republican National Convention Held at Chicago, June 19, 20, 21, 22, 23, and 25, 1888. Minneapolis: Charles W. Johnson, 1903.

Official Proceedings of the Thirteenth Republican National Convention, Held in Chicago, June 21, 22, 23, 1904, Resulting in the Nomination of Theodore Roosevelt, of New York, for President. Minneapolis: Harrison and Smith, 1904.

Official Proceedings of the Twelfth Republican National Convention Held in the City of Philadelphia, June 19, 20, and 21, 1900. Philadelphia: Dunlap Printing, 1900.

Official Report of the Proceedings of the Eighteenth Republican National Convention Held in Cleveland, Ohio, June 10, 11, and 12, 1924. New York: Tenny Press, 1924.

Official Report of the Proceedings of the Fifteenth Republican National Convention, Held in Chicago, Illinois, June 18, 19, 20, 21, and 22, 1912. New York: Tenny Press, 1912.

Official Report of the Proceedings of the Fourteenth Republican National Convention Held in Chicago, Illinois, June 16, 17, 18 and 19, 1908. Columbus, Ohio: F. J. Herr, 1908.

Official Report of the Proceedings of the Seventeenth Republican National Convention, Held in Chicago, Illinois, June 8, 9, 10, 11, and 12, 1920. New York: Tenny Press, 1920.

Olin, Spencer, Jr. *California's Prodigal Sons: Hiram Johnson and the Progressives, 1911–1917.* Berkeley: University of California Press, 1968.

———. "Hiram Johnson, the California Progressives, and the Hughes Campaign of 1916." *Pacific Historical Review* 31 (1962): 403–12.

Olsen, Christopher J. "Respecting 'The Wise Allotment of Our Sphere': White Women and Politics in Mississippi, 1840–1860." *Journal of Women's History* 11 (Autumn 1999): 104–25.

Orcutt, William Dana. *Burrows of Michigan and the Republican Party.* New York: Longmans, Green, 1917.

Ostrogorski, M. Moisei. *Democracy and the Party System in the United States: A Study in Extra-Constitutional Government.* New York: Macmillan, 1910.

Pankhurst, Sylvia. *The Suffragettes: The History of the Women's Militant Suffrage Movement, 1905–1910.* New York: Sturges and Walton, 1912.

Park, Maud Wood. *Front Door Lobby.* Boston: Beacon Press, 1960.

Parton, James, et al., eds. *Eminent Women of the Age.* Hartford, Conn.: S. M. Betts, 1868.

Payne, Elizabeth Anne. *Reform, Labor, and Feminism: Margaret Dreier Robins and the Women's Trade Union League.* Urbana: University of Illinois Press, 1988.

Peiss, Kathy. *Cheap Amusements: Working Women and Leisure in Turn-of-the-Century New York.* Philadelphia: Temple University Press, 1986.

Perkins, Dexter. *Charles Evans Hughes and American Democratic Statesmanship.* Boston: Little, Brown, 1956.

Perkins, Frances. "My Recollections of Florence Kelley." *Social Service Review* 28 (March 1954): 12–19.

Perkins, George. "Business and Government." *Saturday Evening Post,* March 1912.

Perry, Elisabeth I. *Belle Moskowitz: Feminine Politics and the Exercise of Power in the Age of Alfred E. Smith.* New York: Oxford University Press, 1987.

———. "Defying the Party Whip: Mary Garrett Hay and the Republican Party, 1917–1920." In *We Have Come to Stay: American Women and Political Parties, 1880–1960.* Ed. Melanie Gustafson, Kristie Miller, and Elisabeth I. Perry. Albuquerque: University of New Mexico Press, 1999. 97–107.

Perry, Lewis. *Radical Abolitionism: Anarchy and the Goverment of God in Anti-Slavery Thought.* Ithaca, N.Y.: Cornell University Press, 1973.

Peskin, Allan. "Lucretia (Randolph) Garfield." In *American First Ladies: Their Lives and Their Legacies.* Ed. Lewis L. Gould. New York: Garland, 1996. 230–42.

Petrik, Paula. *No Step Backward: Women and Family on the Rocky Mountain Mining Frontier, Helena, Montana, 1865–1900.* Helena: Montana Historical Society Press, 1987.

Pinchot, Amos. *History of the Progressive Party, 1912–1916.* New York: New York University Press, 1958.

Pinchot, Gifford. *Breaking New Ground.* New York: Harcourt, Brace, 1947.

Pitman, C. Robert. "Woman as a Political Factor." *North American Review,* November 1884.

Plunkett, Horace. "The Working of Woman Suffrage in Wyoming." *Fortnightly Review,* May 1890.

Polakoff, Keith. *Political Parties in American History.* New York: Alfred A. Knopf, 1981.

Porter, Florence Collins, and Clara Wilson Gries. "From a Woman's View-Point: A Page for Women Readers." *California Outlook,* June 1, 1912; July 27, 1912.

———. *Our Folks and Your Folks: A Volume of Family History and Biographical Sketches.* Los Angeles: Fred S. Lang, 1919.

Price, T. H., and R. Spillane. "Stalking for Nine Million Voters." *World's Work,* November 1916.

Pringle, Henry F. "Theodore Roosevelt and the South." *Virginia Quarterly Review* 9 (January 1933): 14–25.

Proceedings of the Eighth Republican National Convention Held at Chicago, Illinois, June 3, 4, 5, and 6, 1884. Chicago: Rand McNally, 1884.

Proceedings of the First Three Republican National Conventions of 1856, 1860 and 1864, Including Proceedings of the Antecedent National Convention Held at Pittsburgh, in February 1856, as Reported by Horace Greeley. Minneapolis: Charles W. Johnson, 1893.

Proceedings of the Liberal Republican Convention, 1872. New York: Baker and Godwin, Printers, 1872.

Proceedings of the National Union Republican Convention Held at Chicago, May 20th and 21st, 1868. Chicago: Evening Journal Print, 1868.

Proceedings of the National Union Republican Convention, Held at Philadelphia, June 5 and 6, 1872. Washington: Gibson Brothers, 1872.

Proceedings of the Republican National Convention Held at Cincinnati, Ohio, Wednesday, Thursday, and Friday, June 14, 15, and 16, 1876. Concord, N.H.: Republican Press Association, 1876.

Proceedings of the Republican National Convention, Held at Chicago, Illinois, June 2, 3, 4, 5, 7, 8, 1880. Chicago: Jno. B. Jeffery Printing, 1881.

Proceedings of the Tenth Republican National Convention Held in the City of Minneapolis, Minnesota, June 7, 8, 9, and 10, 1892. New York: Theodore C. Rose and James F. Burke, 1892.

Pusey, Merlo J. *Charles Evans Hughes.* New York: Macmillan Company, 1951.

Pye, Lucien, and Sidney Verba. *Political Culture and Political Development.* Princeton, N.J.: Princeton University Press, 1965.

Ray, P. Orman. *An Introduction to Political Parties and Practical Politics.* New York: Charles Scribner's Sons, 1917.

Republican Campaign Edition for the Millions, Containing the Republican Platform, the Lives of Frémont and Dayton. Boston: John P. Jewett and Co., 1856.

Republican National Committee. *Republican Campaign Text-Book, 1912.* Philadelphia: Republican National Committee, Dunlap Printing, Co., 1912.

———. *Republican Campaign Text-Book, 1920.* Washington, D.C.: Republican Congressional Committee, 1920.

———. *Republican Campaign Text-Book, 1924.* Washington, D.C.: Republican Congressional Committee, 1924.

Rhodes, Jane. *Mary Ann Shadd Cary: The Black Press and Protest in the Nineteenth Century.* Bloomington: Indiana University Press, 1998.

Richards, Laura E., and Maud Howe Elliot. *Julia Ward Howe, 1819–1910.* 2 vols. Boston: Houghton Mifflin, 1916.

Richardson, Marilyn. *Maria W. Stewart: America's First Black Woman Political Writer.* Bloomington: Indiana University Press, 1987.

Richberg, Donald R. *Tents of the Mighty.* New York: Willett Clark and Colby, 1930.

Robinson, Edgar E. "Distribution of the Presidential Vote in 1912." *American Journal of Sociology* 20 (July 1912): 18–30.

Robinson, Harriet H. *Massachusetts in the Woman Suffrage Movement: A General Political, Legal, and Legislative History from 1774 to 1881.* Boston: Roberts Brothers, 1883.

Rodgers, Daniel T. *Atlantic Crossings: Social Politics in a Progressive Age.* Cambridge, Mass.: Harvard University Press, 1998.

———. "In Search of Progressivism." *Reviews in American History* 10.4 (December 1982): 113–32.

Roosevelt, Theodore. "A Fight for Clean Government and Popular Rule." *Outlook,* October 15, 1910.

———. *Progressive Principles: Selections from Addresses Made during the Presidential Campaign of 1912.* Ed. Elmer Youngman. London: Effingham Wilson, 1913.

———. "The Progressives and the Colored Man." *Outlook,* August 24, 1912.

———. *Theodore Roosevelt: An Autobiography.* New York: Charles Scribner's Sons, 1920.

———. "Two Phases of the Chicago Convention." *Outlook,* July 20, 1912.

———. "Women's Rights; and the Duties of Both Men and Women." *Outlook,* February 3, 1912.

Rosaldo, Michelle, and Louise Lamphere. *Woman, Culture, and Society.* Stanford, Calif.: Stanford University Press, 1974.

Rose, Alice. "The Rise of California Insurgency: Origins of the League of Lincoln-Roosevelt Republican Clubs, 1900–1917." Ph.D. dissertation, Stanford University, 1943.

Roseboom, Eugene H. *A History of Presidential Elections: From George Washington to Richard M. Nixon.* New York: Macmillan, 1974.

Rosen, Ruth. *The Lost Sisterhood: Prostitution in America, 1900–1918.* Baltimore: Johns Hopkins University Press, 1982.

Rothman, David. "The State as Parent." In *Doing Good: The Limits of Benevolence.* Ed. Willard Gaylin. New York: Pantheon, 1978. 67–96.

Rowell, Chester. "The Building of the Progressive Platform." *California Outlook,* August 17, 1912.

Ruhl, Arthur. "The Bull Moose Call: A New Sound in American Politics and Those Who Answered It." *Collier's,* August 24, 1912.

Rutland, Robert Allen. *The Republicans: From Lincoln to Bush.* Columbia: University of Missouri Press, 1996.

Ryan, Daniel. "Clubs in Politics." *North American Review* 375 (February 1888): 171–77.

Ryan, Mary. "The American Parade: Representations of the Nineteenth Century Social Order." In *The New Cultural History.* Ed. Lynn Hunt. Berkeley: University of California Press, 1989. 131–53.

———. *Cradle of the Middle Class: The Family in Oneida County, New York, 1790–1865.* Cambridge: Cambridge University Press, 1981.

———. *Women in Public: Between Banners and Ballots, 1825–1880.* Baltimore: Johns Hopkins University Press, 1990.

Rymph, Catherine E. "Forward and Right: The Shaping of Republican Women's Activism, 1920–1967." Ph.D. dissertation, University of Iowa, 1998.

———. "'Keeping the Political Fires Burning': Republican Women's Clubs and Female Political Culture in Small-Town Iowa, 1928–1938." *Annals of Iowa* 56 (Winter/Spring 1997): 99–127.

Sautter, R. Craig, and Edward M. Burke. *Inside the Wigwam: Chicago Presidential Conventions, 1860–1996.* Chicago: Wild Onion Books of Loyola Press, 1996.

Schlesinger, Arthur M., Jr., and Roger Bruns, eds. *Congress Investigates: A Documented History, 1792–1974.* New York: Chelsea House, 1975.

Schneider, Elizabeth. "The Dialectic of Rights and Politics: Perspectives from the Women's Movement." *New York University Law Review* 61 (October 1986): 589–652.

Schott, Matthew J. "John M. Parker of Louisiana and the Bull Moose Progressive Party in State and Nation." Ph.D. dissertation, Tulane University, 1960.

Schuele, Donna. "In Her Own Way: Marietta Stow's Crusade for Probate Law Reform within the Nineteenth-Century Women's Rights Movement." *Yale Journal of Law and Feminism* 7.2 (1995): 279–306.

Scott, Anne F. *Natural Allies: Women's Associations in American History.* Urbana: University of Illinois Press, 1991.

Scott, Anne F., and Andrew Scott. *One Half the People: The Fight for Woman Suffrage.* Philadelphia: J. B. Lippincott, 1975.

Scott, Joan. "Deconstructing Equality-versus-Difference: Or, The Uses of Poststructuralist Theory for Feminism." In *Conflicts in Feminism.* Ed. Marianne Hirsch and Evelyn Fox Kellor. New York: Routledge, 1980. 134–48.

Semple, James Alexander, comp. *Representative Women of Colorado: A Pictorial Collection of the Women of Colorado Who Have Attained Prominence in the Social, Political, Professional, Pioneer, and Club Life of the State.* Denver: James Alexander Semple, The Alexander Art Publishing, Co., 1911.

Severn, Sue. "Frances (Clara) Folsom Cleveland." In *American First Ladies: Their Lives and Their Legacies.* Ed. Lewis Gould. New York: Garland, 1996. 243–59.

Sewell, May Wright, ed. *World's Congress of Representative Women.* Chicago: Rand McNally, 1894.

Sewell, Richard H. *Ballots for Freedom: Antislavery Politics in the United States, 1837–1860.* New York: Oxford University Press, 1976.

Sherman, Richard B. *The Republican Party and Black America: From McKinley to Hoover, 1896–1933.* Charlottesville: University Press of Virginia, 1973.

Sherrick, Rebecca. "Private Visions, Public Lives: The Hull House Women in the Progressive Era." Ph.D. dissertation, Northwestern University, 1980.

Sicherman, Barbara, and Carol Hurd Green, eds. *Notable American Women: The Modern Period.* Cambridge, Mass.: Harvard University Press, 1980.

Silbey, Joel H. *The American Political Nation, 1838–1893.* Stanford, Calif.: Stanford University Press, 1991.

———. *The Partisan Imperative: The Dynamics of American Politics before the Civil War.* New York: Oxford University Press, 1985.

———. *The Transformation of American Politics.* Englewood Cliffs, N.J.: Prentice-Hall, 1967.

Silverman, Eliane L. "Reform as a Means of Social Control: Theodore Roosevelt and Woman Suffrage." *Atlantis* 2 (Fall 1976): 22–39.

———. "Theodore Roosevelt and Women: The Inner Conflict of a President and Its Impact on His Ideology." Ph.D. dissertation, University of California at Los Angeles, 1973.

Simkhovitch, Mary. *Here Is God's Plenty: Reflections on American Social Advance.* New York: Macmillan, 1949.

Sklar, Kathryn Kish. *Catharine Beecher: A Study in American Domesticity.* New Haven, Conn.: Yale University Press, 1973.

———. *Florence Kelley and the Nation's Work: The Rise of Women's Political Culture, 1830–1900.* New Haven, Conn.: Yale University Press, 1995.

———. "Hull House in the 1890s: A Community of Women Reformers." *Signs* 10.4 (Summer 1985): 658–77.

———. "Who Funded Hull House?" In *Lady Bountiful Revisited: Women Philanthropy and Power.* Ed. Kathleen McCarthy. New Brunswick, N.J.: Rutgers University Press, 1990. 94–115.

———. "'Women Who Speak for an Entire Nation': American and British Women at the World Anti-Slavery Convention, London, 1840." In *The Abolitionist Sisterhood: Women's Political Culture in Antebellum America.* Ed. Jean Fagan Yellin and John C. Van Horne. Ithaca, N.Y.: Cornell University Press, 1994. 301–33.

Skowronek, Stephen. *Building the New American State: The Expansion of National Administrative Capacities, 1887–1920.* New York: Cambridge University Press, 1982.

Smith, Henry H., comp. *All the Republican National Conventions from Philadelphia, June 17, 1856 to and Including St. Louis, June 16, 1896.* Washington, D.C.: Robert Beall, 1896.

Smith-Rosenberg, Carroll. *Disorderly Conduct: Visions of Gender in Victorian America.* New York: Alfred A. Knopf, 1985.

Stanton, Elizabeth Cady. *Eighty Years and More: Reminiscences, 1815–1897.* 1898. Reprint, Boston: Northeastern University Press, 1993.

Stanton, Elizabeth Cady, Susan B. Anthony, Matilda Joslyn Gage, and Ida Husted Harper, eds. *History of Woman Suffrage.* 6 vols. 1881–1922. Reprint, New York: Arno, 1969.

Starr, Kevin. *Inventing the American Dream: California through the Progressive Era.* New York: Oxford University Press, 1985.

Steelman, Joseph F. "Republicanism in North Carolina: John Motley Morehead's Campaign to Revive a Moribund Party, 1908–1910." *North Carolina Historical Review* 62 (April 1965): 153–68.

Stern, Clarence. "Leadership and Formation of Policy within the Republican Party, 1889–1901." Ph.D. dissertation, University of Nebraska at Lincoln, 1958.

Storms, Roger C. *Partisan Prophets: A History of the Prohibition Party.* Denver: National Prohibition Foundation, Inc., 1972.

Stueck, William. "Progressivism and the Negro: White Liberals and the Early NAACP." *Historian* 38 (November 1975): 58–78.

Sullivan, Mark. "Armageddon at Chicago." *Collier's,* August 24, 1912.

Swisshelm, Jane Grey. *Half a Century.* Chicago: Jansen, McClurg, and Co., 1880.

Tax, Meredith. *The Rising of the Women: Feminist Solidarity and Class Conflict, 1880–1917.* New York: Monthly Review Press, 1979.

Taylor, Graham. "Jane Addams' Twenty Years of Industrial Democracy." *Survey,* December 3, 1910.

Taylor, Paul C. "The Entrance of Women into Party Politics: The 1920s." Ph.D. dissertation, Harvard University, 1967.

Terborg-Penn, Rosalyn. *African American Women in the Struggle for the Vote, 1850–1920.* Bloomington: Indiana University Press, 1998.

———. "Discontented Black Feminists: Prelude and Postscript to the Passage of the Nineteenth Amendment." In *Decades of Discontent: The Women's Movement, 1920–1940.* Ed. Lois Scharf and Joan M. Jensen. Westport, Conn.: Greenwood Press, 1983. 261–78.

———. "Discrimination against Afro-American Women in the Woman's Movement, 1830–1920." In *The Afro-American Woman: Struggles and Images.* Ed. Sharon Harley and Rosalyn Terborg-Penn. Port Washington, N.Y.: Kennikat Press, 1978. 17–27.

Terrell, Mary Church. *A Colored Woman in a White World.* Washington, D.C.: Ransdell Inc. Publishers, 1940.

Testi, Arnaldo. "The Gender of Reform Politics: Theodore Roosevelt and the Culture of Masculinity." *Journal of American History* 81 (March 1995): 1509–33.

Thelen, David P. *The New Citizenship: Origins of Progressivism in Wisconsin.* Columbia: University of Missouri Press, 1972.

———. "Social Tensions and the Origins of Progressivism." *Journal of American History* 56 (September 1969): 323–41.

Thieme, Otto Charles. "'Wave High the Red Bandanna': Some Handkerchiefs of the 1888 Presidential Campaign." In *American Material Culture: The Shape of Things around Us.*

Ed. Edith P. Mayo. Bowling Green, Ohio: Bowling Green State University Popular Press, 1984. 92–111.

Thornbrough, Emma Lou. "The Brownsville Episode and the Negro Vote." *Mississippi Valley Historical Review* 44 (1957): 469–83.

Tichner, Lisa. *The Spectacle of Women: Imagery of the Suffrage Campaign, 1907–1914.* London: Chatto and Windus, 1987.

Tilly, Louise A., and Patricia Gurin, eds. *Women, Politics, and Change.* New York: Russell Sage Foundation, 1990.

Trefousse, Hans L. "The Republican Party, 1854–1864." In *History of U.S. Political Parties.* Vol. 2. Ed. Arthur M. Schlesinger, Jr. New York: Chelsea House, 1973. 1141–72.

Trolander, Judith. *Professionalism and Social Change: From the Settlement House Movement to Neighborhood Centers, 1886 to the Present.* New York: Columbia University Press, 1987.

Trowbridge, J. R. "The Political Machine." *Yale Review* 13 (November 1904): 287–95.

Troy, Gil. *See How They Ran: The Changing Role of the Presidential Candidate.* New York: Free Press, 1991.

Tuve, Jeanette E. *First Lady of the Law: Florence Ellinwood Allen.* Lanham, N.Y.: University Press of America, 1984.

Underhill, Lois Beachy. *The Woman Who Ran for President: The Many Lives of Victoria Woodhull.* New York: Penguin Books, 1995.

Van Ingen, Linda. "Campaigning for Equal Representation: Women Candidates for California State Office, 1912–1970." Paper presented at the Organization of Historians Annual Meeting, April 1999.

Van Pelt, Lori. "Estelle Reel: Wyoming's Second Superintendent of Public Instruction." Paper presented at the American Heritage Center's Seventh Annual History Symposium, September 1998.

Van Voris, Jacqueline. *Carrie Chapman Catt: A Public Life.* New York: The Feminist Press, 1987.

Van Wagenen, Lola. "Sister-Wives and Suffragists: Polygamy and the Politics of Woman Suffrage, 1870–1896." Ph.D. dissertation, New York University, 1994.

VandeCreek, Drew E. "Unseen Influence: Lucretia Blankenburg and the Rise of Philadelphia Reform Politics in 1911." In *We Have Come to Stay: American Women and Political Parties, 1880–1960.* Ed. Melanie Gustafson, Kristie Miller, and Elisabeth I. Perry. Albuquerque: University of New Mexico Press, 1999. 33–43.

VanderMeer, Philip. "Bosses, Machines, and Democratic Leadership: Party Organization and Managers in Indiana, 1880–1910." *Social Science History* 12 (Winter 1988): 395–428.

Varon, Elizabeth R. *We Mean to Be Counted: White Women and Politics in Antebellum Virginia.* Chapel Hill: University of North Carolina Press, 1998.

Villard, Oswald Garrison. *Women in the New York Municipal Campaign of 1901.* Boston: John Youngjohn, 1902.

Voss-Hubbard, Mark. "The 'Third Party Tradition' Reconsidered: Third Parties and American Public Life, 1830–1900." *Journal of American History* 86 (June 1999): 121–50.

Wagner, MaryJo. "Farms, Families, and Reform: Women in the Farmers' Alliance and the Populist Party." Ph.D. dissertation, University of Oregon, 1986.

Wald, Lillian. "Right Woman in the Right Place." *American City* 6 (June 1912): 847.

Walters, Suzanna Dunuta. *Material Girls: Making Sense of Feminist Cultural Theory.* Berkeley: University of California Press, 1995.

Walton, Hanes, Jr. *The Negro in Third Party Politics.* Philadelphia: Dorrance and Company, 1969.

Ware, Susan. *Beyond Suffrage: Women in the New Deal.* Cambridge, Mass.: Harvard University Press, 1981.

Washburn, Charles. "Roosevelt and the 1912 Campaign." *Massachusetts Historical Society Proceedings* 59 (1925): 305–9.

Watson, Harry L. *Liberty and Power: The Politics of Jacksonian America.* New York: Hill and Wang, 1990.

Weinstein, James. *The Corporate Ideal in the Liberal State, 1900–1918.* Boston: Beacon Press, 1986.

Welsh, Herbert. "Campaign Committees: Publicity as a Cure for Corruption." *Forum* 14.6 (1892): 26–38.

Wenzel, Janie. "Dr. Grace Raymond Hebard as Western Historian." M.A. thesis, University of Wyoming, 1960.

Wheeler, Denice. *The Feminine Frontier: Wyoming Women, 1850–1900.* Privately published, 1987.

Wheeler, Marjorie Spruill. *New Women of the New South: The Leaders of the Woman Suffrage Movement in the Southern States.* New York: Oxford University Press, 1993.

———, ed. *One Woman, One Vote: Rediscovering the Woman Suffrage Movement.* Troutdale, Ore.: NewSage Press, 1995.

———, ed. *Votes for Women! The Woman Suffrage Movement in Tennessee, the South, and the Nation.* Knoxville: University of Tennessee Press, 1995.

White, Deborah Grey. *Too Heavy a Load: Black Women in Defense of Themselves, 1894–1994.* New York: W. W. Norton, 1999.

Why They Suffer, Working Women and Working Men's Wives, How the Tariff Affects Them, Testimony of Women as Witnesses: The Wilson-Gorman Act Responsible for Hard Times, Protection, Not Free Silver, The True Remedy: Labor's Protest. Chicago: n.p., 1894.

Wilentz, Sean. *Chants Democratic: New York City and the Rise of the American Working Class, 1788–1850.* New York: Oxford University Press, 1984.

Wilkes, Eliza Tupper. "Why Am I a Democrat?" *Woman's Bulletin,* July–August 1914.

Willard, C. D. "Old and New Politics." *California Outlook,* February 17, 1912.

Willard, Frances. *Glimpses of Fifty Years: The Autobiography of an American Woman.* Chicago: Woman's Christian Temperance Union, 1889.

———. *Woman and Temperance, or the Work and Workers of the Woman's Christian Temperance Union.* Hartford, Conn.: Park Publishing, 1883.

Willard, Frances, and Mary Livermore, eds. *Woman of the Century.* Buffalo, N.Y.: Charles Wells Moulton, 1893.

Williams, Clare B. *The History of the Founding and Development of the National Federation of Republican Women.* Washington, D.C.: Women's Division, Republican National Committee, 1963.

Winter, Una Richardson. *Alice Park of California, Worker for Woman Suffrage and for Children's Rights.* Upland: Susan B. Anthony Memorial Committee of California, 1948.

Wiseman, John. "Racism in Democratic Politics, 1904–1912." *MidAmerica* 51.1 (1968): 38–58.

Witt, Linda, Karen M. Paget, and Glenna Matthews. *Running as a Woman: Gender and Power in American Politics.* New York: Free Press, 1994.

Wolgemuth, Kathleen Long. "Woodrow Wilson's Appointment Policy and the Negro." *Journal of Southern History* 24 (1958): 457–71.

Women's Committee, National Hughes Alliance. *Women in National Politics.* New York: National Hughes Alliance, 1916.

Wood, Molly M. "Mapping a National Campaign Strategy: Partisan Women in the Presidential Election of 1916." In *We Have Come to Stay: American Women and Political Parties, 1880–1960.* Ed. Melanie Gustafson, Kristie Miller, and Elisabeth I. Perry. Albuquerque: University of New Mexico Press, 1999. 77–86.

Woods, Gerald. "A Penchant for Probity: California Progressives and the Disreputable Pleasures." In *California Progressivism Revisited.* Ed. William Deverell and Tom Sitton. Berkeley: University of California Press, 1994. 99–113.

Woodward, C. Vann. *Origins of the New South, 1877–1913.* Baton Rouge: Louisiana State University Press, 1951.

———. *The Strange Career of Jim Crow.* New York: Oxford University Press, 1974.

Wright, James. *The Progressive Yankees: Republican Reformers in New Hampshire, 1906–1916.* Hanover, N.H.: University Press of New England for Dartmouth College, 1987.

Yellin, Jean Fagen, and John C. Van Horne, eds. *The Abolitionist Sisterhood: Women's Political Culture in Antebellum America.* Ithaca, N.Y.: Cornell University Press, 1994.

Young, James Harvey. "Anna Elizabeth Dickinson and the Civil War: For and Against Lincoln." *Mississippi Valley Historical Review* 31 (June 1944): 59–80.

Youngman, Elmer, ed. *Theodore Roosevelt: Progressive Principles, Selections from the Addresses Made during the Presidential Campaign of 1912.* London: Effingham Wilson, 1913.

Zagarri, Rosemarie. "Gender and the First Party System." In *Federalists Reconsidered.* Ed. Doron Ben-Atar and Barbara B. Oberg. Charlottesville: University Press of Virginia, 1998. 118–34.

———. "Morals, Manners, and the Republican Mother." *American Quarterly* 44 (June 1992): 192–215.

Zangrando, Robert L. *The NAACP Crusade against Lynching, 1909–1950.* Philadelphia: Temple University Press, 1980.

Zboray, Ronald, and Mary Saracino Zboray. "Whig Women, Politics and Culture in the Campaign of 1840: Three Perspectives from Massachusetts." *Journal of the Early Republic* 17 (Summer 1997): 277–315.

Index

MELANIE SUSAN GUSTAFSON is an associate professor of history at the University of Vermont, where she teaches U.S. history and women's history.

Women in American History

Women Doctors in Gilded-Age Washington: Race, Gender, and
Professionalization   *Gloria Moldow*
Friends and Sisters: Letters between Lucy Stone and Antoinette Brown Blackwell,
1846–93   *Edited by Carol Lasser and Marlene Deahl Merrill*
Reform, Labor, and Feminism: Margaret Dreier Robins and the Women's Trade Union
League   *Elizabeth Anne Payne*
Private Matters: American Attitudes toward Childbearing and Infant Nurture in the
Urban North, 1800–1860   *Sylvia D. Hoffert*
Civil Wars: Women and the Crisis of Southern Nationalism   *George C. Rable*
I Came a Stranger: The Story of a Hull-House Girl   *Hilda Satt Polacheck; edited by
Dena J. Polacheck Epstein*
Labor's Flaming Youth: Telephone Operators and Worker Militancy, 1878–1923
Stephen H. Norwood
Winter Friends: Women Growing Old in the New Republic, 1785–1835   *Terri L. Premo*
Better Than Second Best: Love and Work in the Life of Helen Magill
Glenn C. Altschuler
Dishing It Out: Waitresses and Their Unions in the Twentieth Century
Dorothy Sue Cobble
Natural Allies: Women's Associations in American History   *Anne Firor Scott*
Beyond the Typewriter: Gender, Class, and the Origins of Modern American Office
Work, 1900–1930   *Sharon Hartman Strom*
The Challenge of Feminist Biography: Writing the Lives of Modern American
Women   *Edited by Sara Alpern, Joyce Antler, Elisabeth Israels Perry, and
Ingrid Winther Scobie*
Working Women of Collar City: Gender, Class, and Community in Troy, New York,
1864–86   *Carole Turbin*
Radicals of the Worst Sort: Laboring Women in Lawrence, Massachusetts,
1860–1912   *Ardis Cameron*
Visible Women: New Essays on American Activism   *Edited by Nancy A. Hewitt and
Suzanne Lebsock*
Mother-Work: Women, Child Welfare, and the State, 1890–1930   *Molly Ladd-Taylor*
Babe: The Life and Legend of Babe Didrikson Zaharias   *Susan E. Cayleff*
Writing Out My Heart: Selections from the Journal of Frances E. Willard, 1855–96
Edited by Carolyn De Swarte Gifford
U.S. Women in Struggle: A *Feminist Studies* Anthology   *Edited by
Claire Goldberg Moses and Heidi Hartmann*
In a Generous Spirit: A First-Person Biography of Myra Page   *Christina Looper Baker*
Mining Cultures: Men, Women, and Leisure in Butte, 1914–41   *Mary Murphy*
Gendered Strife and Confusion: The Political Culture of Reconstruction
Laura F. Edwards
The Female Economy: The Millinery and Dressmaking Trades, 1860–1930
Wendy Gamber
Mistresses and Slaves: Plantation Women in South Carolina, 1830–80   *Marli F. Weiner*

The University of Illinois Press
is a founding member of the
Association of American University Presses.

Composed in 10.5/13 Minion
with Minion display
by Celia Shapland
for the University of Illinois Press
Designed by Dennis Roberts
Manufactured by Thomson-Shore, Inc.

University of Illinois Press
1325 South Oak Street
Champaign, IL 61820-6903
www.press.uillinois.edu